W9-AVG-459

# Fodor's 93 Washington, D.C.

Fodor's Travel Publications, Inc.
New York • London • Toronto • Sydney • Auckland

## Fodor's Washington, D.C.

**Editor:** Suzanne De Galan
**Contributors:** Jeanne Cooper, John F. Kelly, Marcy Pritchard
**Creative Director:** Fabrizio La Rocca
**Cartographer:** David Lindroth
**Illustrator:** Karl Tanner
**Cover Photograph:** Peter Guttman

**Design:** Vignelli Associates

## Special Sales

# Contents

## 2 Portraits of Washington 35

## 3 Exploring Washington 57

## 4 Shopping 193

## 5 Sports and Fitness 208

## 6 Dining 218

## 7 Lodging 247

### Maps

# Foreword

While every care has been taken to assure the accuracy of the information in this guide, the passage of time will always bring change, and consequently, the publisher cannot accept responsibility for errors that may occur.

All prices and opening times quoted here are based on information supplied to us at press time. Hours and admission fees may change, however, and the prudent traveler will avoid inconvenience by calling ahead.

Fodor's wants to hear about your travel experiences, both pleasant and unpleasant. When a hotel or restaurant fails to live up to its billing, let us know and we will investigate the complaint and revise our entries where the facts warrant it.

Send your letters to the editors of Fodor's Travel Publications, 201 East 50th Street, New York, NY 10022.

# Highlights'93 and Fodor's Choice

# Highlights '93

Washington always hums after an election, and this year the capital will kick off the new year with its favorite kind of party: a presidential inauguration (though whether or not it's a *re*inauguration wasn't known at press time). When the president parades up Pennsylvania Avenue he'll see a Washington that's changed significantly since the last inaugural motorcade.

Pennsylvania Avenue itself is nearing the end of an impressive face-lift. **Pennsylvania Quarter** is the name given to the mix of apartments, condominiums, restaurants, and shops arranged near the Navy Memorial. One of the neighborhood's newcomers is the **Shakespeare Theatre,** which last year left its longtime Capitol Hill home in the Folger Library for a brand new, much bigger, state-of-the-art space in the Lansburgh building, a block off Pennsylvania.

This year will see quite a few new museums join or rejoin what is already one of the best assortments in the world. The sobering **United States Holocaust Memorial Museum** opens on the Mall in April. A month later, the **Freer Gallery of Art** welcomes visitors after a five-year renovation. Meanwhile, on Capitol Hill, the glorious **Grand Hall** of the Library of Congress Jefferson Building reopens in January. It, too, underwent a renovation, and it celebrates its rebirth with an exhibition of manuscripts, rare books, and maps from the Vatican library. Six blocks north, the **National Postal Museum,** the newest Smithsonian Institution museum in Washington, opens its doors in July.

Several old favorites reopened last year: The **First Ladies' exhibit** in the National Museum of American History is back. The collection of inaugural gowns that underwent a 4½-year renovation is back and better than ever. No longer just a display of beautiful dresses, it's now an exhibit that explores the political roles and public images of our presidents' wives. Georgetown's Georgian-style **Dumbarton House,** headquarters of the National Society of the Colonial Dames of America and home to a charming collection of Early Americana, has reopened after a renovation. The National Zoo completed two ambitious projects last year: the mini ecosystem known as **Amazonia** and the **Cheetah Conservation**

**Area,** where the world's fastest cats will be bred for other zoos.

Then there are the monuments. Veterans of the **Korean War** finally get a **memorial,** due to be dedicated just south of the Lincoln Memorial in July. A **memorial** to **women veterans** of the **Vietnam War** will be dedicated near the Wall on Veterans Day.

Keep in mind that the opening dates for the new museums and monuments are as firm as anything in Washington. They should be more reliable than a campaign promise, but check ahead before making special plans.

Expected hotel construction has been put on temporary hold here, with no word when the 600-room **Fairmont Hotel** will open in the stalled Portals project in Southwest Washington. Renovations at existing establishments, however, have been numerous. Among hotels completing major makeovers in 1992 were the **ANA Hotel,** the **Mayflower,** the **Georgetown Inn,** and the **Latham** (formerly the Georgetown Marbury) **Hotel.**

In shopping news, the **Pavilion at the Old Post Office** added a new atrium with 29 specialty stores, nearly doubling the number of boutiques and shops here. The Metrorail system continues to provide easy access to several close-in suburban centers worth noting, including the upscale **Mazza Gallerie/ Chevy Chase Pavilion** complex at the Friendship Heights Station. But the city's best treasures remain in the unique gift shops of Union Station and the Smithsonian and other museums.

Maybe these new attractions will help take Washingtonians' minds off the political problems that plague the city. Mayor Sharon Pratt Kelly, seen as a fresh breeze after the disastrous tenure of Marion Barry, has been mired in problems of her own. Washington continues to make headlines as the nation's "murder capital" (though the drug-related killings rarely spill into the monumental city most tourists see). And Congress is still unsure just how to treat the District of Columbia: Should it stay a political no man's land with no real representation, or become a state?

# Fodor's Choice

No two people will agree on what makes a perfect vacation, but it's fun and helpful to know what others think. We hope you'll have a chance to experience some of Fodor's Choices yourself while visiting Washington. For detailed information about each entry, refer to the appropriate sections (given in parentheses) within this guidebook.

## Sights

The view of Washington from Arlington House in Arlington National Cemetery

The view of the Mall from the foot of Capitol Hill

The Washington skyline from the roof of the Kennedy Center for the Performing Arts

## Buildings and Monuments

The White House (Tour 3: The White House)

The East building of the National Gallery of Art (Tour 1: The Mall)

The Jefferson Memorial (Tour 2: The Monuments)

Union Station (Tour 4: Capitol Hill)

The Vietnam Veterans Memorial (Tour 2: The Monuments)

Washington Cathedral (Churches, Temples, and Mosques)

## Activities

Strolling the streets of Georgetown on a weekend morning before 10 (Tour 6: Georgetown)

Bicycling along the C & O Canal (Excursions)

Visiting the Aviary at the National Zoo (Tour 9: Cleveland Park and the National Zoo)

Taking a boat ride to Mount Vernon (Chapter 9, Excursions)

Exploring the city with Scandal Tours (Chapter 1, Essential Information)

Seeing a movie at the Air and Space Museum
(Tour 1: The Mall)

## Museums

The Phillips Collection (Tour 7: Dupont Circle)

The National Air and Space Museum (Tour 1: The Mall)

The Corcoran Gallery of Art (Tour 3: The White House)

The National Museum of African Art (Tour 1: The Mall)

The National Museum of American History
(Tour 1: The Mall)

Capital Children's Museum (Museums and Galleries)

## Parks and Gardens

Rock Creek Park

Dumbarton Oaks Garden

Lafayette Square

The National Arboretum

## Restaurants

Jean-Louis at the Watergate (French, *Very Expensive*)

Twenty-One Federal (New American, *Very Expensive*)

Obelisk (Italian, *Expensive*)

Red Sage (Southwestern/Tex-Mex, *Expensive*)

Sarinah Satay House (Indonesian, *Moderate*)

Meskerem (Ethiopian, *Inexpensive*)

## Hotels

Hay-Adams Hotel (*Very Expensive*)

The Willard Inter-Continental (*Very Expensive*)

Omni Shoreham Hotel (*Expensive*)

Morrison-Clark Inn Hotel (*Moderate*)

Kalorama Guest House (*Inexpensive*)

## Nightlife

Blues Alley

Comedy Cafe

Gross National Product

The Dubliner

# Washington, D.C. Area

# Washington, D.C.

California St.

Massachusetts Ave.

S St.

Decatur Pl.

R St.

Sheridan Circle

Florida Ave.

T St.

S St.

New Hampshire Ave.

16th St.

15th St.

14th St.

R St.

Corcoran St.

Q St.

Q St.

22nd St.

21st St.

20th St.

19th St.

Massachusetts Ave.

**DUPONT CIRCLE** Ⓜ

Dupont Circle

Church St.

P St.

Church St.

Rhode Island Ave.

R St.

Q St.

17th St.

O St.

O St.

Rock Creek

O St.

N St.

Connecticut Ave.

18th St.

Scott Circle

Thomas Circle

P St.

30th St.

29th St.

28th St.

27th St.

N St.

M St.

26th St.

M St.

M St.

19th St.

18th St.

15th St.

29

L St.

L St.

16th St.

McPHERSON SQUARE Ⓜ

25th St.

29

Washington Circle

K St.

**FARRAGUT NORTH** Ⓜ

**FOGGY BOTTOM** Ⓜ

I St.

Ⓜ **FARRAGUT WEST** Ⓜ

66

24th St.

23rd St.

22nd St.

Pennsylvania Ave.

H St.

15th St.

New York

G St.

Virginia Ave.

F St.

E St.

**The White House**

14th St.

D St.

17th St.

**The Ellipse**

**FEDER. TRIANG**

50

C St.

Constitution Ave.

**Vietnam Veterans Memorial**

**National Museum of American History**

Mad

NW

SW

**Lincoln Memorial**

*Reflecting Pool*

**Washington Monument**

**SMITHS**

Arlington Memorial Bridge

Independence Ave.

Kutz Bridge

*Potomac River*

Ohio Dr.

West

W. Basin Dr.

Potomac Park

*Tidal Basin*

Outlet Bridge

*Columbia Island*

N

**Jefferson Memorial**

395

1

NW NE

T St.
S St.
R St.
Q St.
O St.
N St.
M St.
L St.

Vermont Ave.
Rhode Island Ave.
Florida Ave.
Lincoln Rd.

S St.
R St.
Q St.
O St.

Logan
Circle

9th St.
8th St.
7th St.
6th St.
5th St.
4th St.
3rd St.
1st St.

13th St.
12th St.
11th St.
10th St.

New Jersey Ave.

New York Ave.

1st St.

Massachusetts Ave.

North Capitol St.

MT. VERNON

Mt. Vernon
Square

I St.
H St.
G St.
F St.
E St.

New Jersey Ave.

Massachusetts Ave.

2nd St.

GALLERY
PLACE

JUDICIARY
SQUARE

UNION
STATION

Columbus
Memorial
Fountain

METRO
CENTER

D St.

ARCHIVES/
NAVY
MEMORIAL

Pennsylvania Ave.

Louisiana Ave.

NE

SE

...ERAL
...NGLE

Madison Dr.
National Museum
of Natural History
Smithsonian
Institution

...THSONIAN

Independence Ave.

THE MALL

National Gallery
of Art

Jefferson Dr.

National
Air and Space
Museum

Maryland Ave.

US
Capitol

E. Capitol St.

C St.
L'ENFANT
PLAZA

Canal St.

D St.

CAPITOL
SOUTH
E St.

D St.

FEDERAL
CENTER SW

New Jersey Ave.

Southwest Fwy.

G St.

Virginia Ave.

Francis Case
Memorial Bridge

0          500 yards

0          500 meters

SW SE

## Washington, D.C. Metro System

**ED LINE**
WHEATON

Silver Spring

Takoma

M A R Y L A N D

**ORANGE LINE**
New Carrollton

Fort Totten

Brookland-CUA

Landover

U Street-Cardozo
Shaw-Howard Univ.

**EN LINE**

Rhode Island Ave

Cheverly

Mt. Vernon
Sq.-UDC

Deanwood

Union Station

Gallery Pl

Minnesota Ave

Archives/Navy Memorial

US Capitol

RFK Stadium

**BLUE LINE**
Addison Rd

Eastern Market

Stadium-Armory

Benning Rd

Capital Heights

Potomac Ave.

Capitol S.

Federal
Center
SW

Waterfront

Navy Yard

Anacostia

**GREEN LINE**

DISTRICT OF COLUMBIA
MARYLAND

N

0        4 miles

0        6 km

# World Time Zones

Numbers below vertical bands relate each zone to Greenwich Mean Time (0 hrs.).
Local times frequently differ from these general indications,
as indicated by light-face numbers on map.

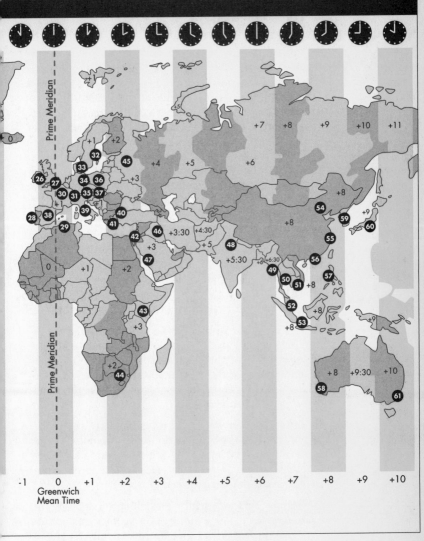

# Introduction

*By Deborah Papier*

*A native
Washingtonian,
Deborah Papier
has worked as an
editor and writer
for numerous local
newspapers and
magazines.*

To a surprising degree, Washington is a city much like any other. True, it does not have a baseball team, that sine qua non of an urban identity. But in most other respects, life in the nation's capital is not that different from life elsewhere in the nation. People are born here, grow up, get jobs—by no means invariably with the federal government—and have children who repeat the cycle. Very often, they live out their lives without ever testifying before Congress, being indicted for influence peddling, or attending a state dinner at the White House.

Which is not to say that the federal government does not cast a long shadow over the city. Among Washington's 630,000 inhabitants are an awful lot of lawyers, journalists, and people who include the word "policy" in their job titles. It's just that DC—to use the vernacular—is much more of a hometown than most tourists realize.

Just a few blocks away from the monuments and museums on the Mall are residential and business districts whose scale is very human. The houses are a crazy quilt of architectural styles, kept in linear formation by rows of lush trees. On the commercial streets, bookstores and ethnic groceries abound.

It is often said that Washington does not have any "real" neighborhoods, the way nearby Baltimore does. While it's true that Washingtonians are not given to huddling together on their front stoops, each area of the city does have a clearly defined personality.

Sometimes, this personality is a split one. Take Georgetown, for example. One of the city's most in-bred, exclusive communities—its residents successfully fought to keep out the subway—Georgetown is a magnet for the young and the restless from miles around.

On any day of the week the streets are full of teenagers with dripping ice cream cones. Friday and Saturday nights it's almost impossible to make your way through the crowds of tourists and natives. Halloween in Georgetown is as close as Washington gets to Mardi Gras, though things aren't quite as weird and wild as they were a few years ago.

Another distinctive neighborhood is Dupont Circle. Insofar as there is a bohemian Washington, it can be found here. This is where the artists and activists used to live, before the rents got too high, and where the hippies hung out, back at the dawning of the New Age. Now Dupont Circle is home to the most visible segment of Washington's gay community.

Adjacent to Dupont Circle is Adams-Morgan, long the city's most intensely ethnic neighborhood. In recent years Adams-Morgan has begun to lose some of its Hispanic flavor, as New American restaurants have begun to crowd out the Latin places. But you're still likely to hear more Spanish than English on the streets here.

As different as Georgetown, Dupont Circle, and Adams-Morgan are, they have one thing in common. They are all on the same side of the line that divides white from black Washington. With the exception of Capitol Hill, whites live west of 16th Street, while blacks—who make up the majority of the population—live to the east of it.

That's a long-standing demographic pattern, unchanged despite the supposed advent of integration. Whites and blacks now work together in the downtown offices, but they go off in different directions when they head home, and rarely encounter one another when they go out for the evening. At the Kennedy Center, for example, there are few black faces to be found.

Meanwhile, there is no comparable center for black culture. The riots of 1968 wiped out most of the black clubs and businesses, and while the area around 14th and U streets where they once flourished is finally being rebuilt, its vitality is unlikely to be re-created.

Further down on 14th Street, another aspect of Washington life is breathing its last: The 14th Street red-light district is almost gone. The city was determined to clean up the strip, and to everyone's surprise it succeeded.

**N**or is much left of the tacky commercial district around 9th and F streets. This was Washington's original downtown, which deteriorated when the city's center shifted to the west, to the "new" downtown of Connecticut Avenue and K Street. But the "old" downtown is being rejuvenated. The department stores that once drew crowds with their window displays have been renovated; there are new hotels and office buildings; and as the construction dust clears, the area is looking pretty good.

But the success or failure of an urban renewal project is probably not a matter of the utmost concern to the visitor. What many people who come here are worried about is crime. Crime is certainly a major problem here, as it is in other big cities, but Washington is not nearly as dangerous as its well-publicized homicide rate might lead you to believe. Most visitors have relatively little to fear. The drug-related shootings that have made Washington the murder capital generally take place in remote sections of the city. Unless you go seeking out the drug markets, there isn't much chance you'll get caught in the crossfire of rival drug gangs. Crimes against property are more widespread, but still far from ubiquitous. Unlike New York, Washington is not full of expert pickpockets; nor is it plagued by gold-chain snatchers.

The city's Metro is generally safe, even at night. However, if you're going to have to walk from your stop in a neighborhood that isn't well-lit and trafficked, you probably should invest in a taxi. Of course, even exercising normal prudence, it is still possible that you will have an encounter with someone who believes that what's yours ought to be his. If that happens, don't argue.

Your attachment to the contents of your wallet is certain to be tested in another way, however. Panhandlers are now a fixture of the cityscape, and there is no avoiding their importunities. How you respond to them is a matter only your conscience can advise you on. Wealth and poverty have always coexisted here, but until recently poverty kept its distance. It's now omnipresent, wearing a very human face.

# 1 Essential Information

# Before You Go

## Visitor Information

For free brochures, an up-to-date calendar of events, and other general information about the District of Columbia, contact the **Washington, D.C. Convention and Visitors Association** (1212 New York Ave. NW, Washington, DC 20005, tel. 202/789–7000).

If you're planning to visit sites in the surrounding areas of Maryland, contact the **Maryland Department of Economic and Community Development** (Office of Tourist Development, 45 Calvert St., Annapolis, MD 21401, tel. 410/269–3517). For tourist information on Virginia, contact the **Virginia Division of Tourism** (202 N. 9th St., Suite 500, Richmond, VA 23219, tel. 804/786–4484).

## Tour Groups

Joining a tour group has some advantages: Someone else worries about travel arrangements, accommodations, and baggage transfer; you are likely to save money on airfare, hotels, and ground transportation; and you will probably cover a lot of territory. The major disadvantages are that you'll have to adjust to someone else's time schedule and pacing, and you won't be as free for independent explorations. Listed below are the major companies that serve the Washington area; many of them offer packages that include trips to sites in Virginia and Maryland as well. Consult your travel agent or the Washington Convention and Visitors Association (*see* Visitor Information, *above*) for additional resources.

When considering a tour, be sure to find out (1) exactly what expenses are included—particularly tips, taxes, side trips, additional meals, and entertainment; (2) ratings of all hotels on the itinerary and the facilities they offer; (3) cancellation policies for both you and the tour operator; (4) the number of travelers in your group; and (5) if you are traveling alone, the cost of the single supplement. Most tour operators request that bookings be made through a travel agent, and in most cases there is no additional charge for doing so.

**General-interest Tours** **Maupintour** (Box 807, Lawrence, KS 66044, tel. 913/843–1211 or 800/255–4266), **Globus-Gateway/Cosmos** (95-25 Queens Blvd., Rego Park, NY 11374, tel. 718/

268–7000 or 800/221–0090), **Gadabout Tours** (700 E. Tahquitz Way, Palm Springs, CA 92262, tel. 619/325–5556 or 800/952–5068), and **Domenico Tours** (751 Broadway, Bayonne, NJ 07002, tel. 201/823–TOUR or 800/554–TOUR) offer escorted tours of Washington and its environs. **Tauck Tours** (11 Wilton Rd., Westport, CT 06881, tel. 800/468–2825 or 203/226–6911) combines Washington, D.C., with Williamsburg, Philadelphia, and the Pennyslvania Dutch Country. For a change of pace, consider touring by rail: **Amtrak** (tel. 800/USA–RAIL or 800/321–8684) offers several escorted tours as well as independent rail/hotel tours.

**Special-interest**
**Tours**
*Art/Architecture*

**National Fine Arts Associates** (tel. 202/966–3800) will custom design tours for individuals or groups. Museum-trained guides conduct general sightseeing tours and specialized itineraries highlighting museums, historic houses, gardens, and neighborhoods. Call or write in advance for detailed information.

**A Tour de Force** (tel. 703/525–2948) promises unconventional outings tailored to your interests and led by a fourth-generation Washingtonian and local historian.

*Holiday* **Maupintour** (*see* General-interest Tour Groups, *above*) has special Thanksgiving and Christmas tours.

*Music* **Dailey-Thorp** (315 W. 57th St., New York, NY 10019, tel. 212/307–1555) offers excellent programs, including the best of opera, ballet, and other performing arts, along with a walking tour of the city. Tours are scheduled around major performance events.

## Package Deals for Independent Travelers

**SuperCities** (7855 Haskell Ave., 3rd floor, Van Nuys, CA 91406, tel. 818/988–7844 or 800/333–1234) offers a package that includes hotel, a choice of tours, and entertainment. **Americantours International East** (350 5th Ave., Suite 718, New York, NY 10118, tel. 212/695–2841) has three- and six-day packages that include round-trip airport transfers, a half-day sightseeing tour and dinner at the Kennedy Center. **Amtrak** (*see* General-interest Tour Groups, *above*) offers rail/hotel packages as well as an independent sightseeing package. Also check with **American Fly AAway Vacations** (tel. 800/443–7300 or 800/321–2121), **Delta Airlines** (tel. 800/872–7786), and **United Vacations** (tel. 800/328–6877).

## Tips for British Travelers

**Tourist Information**  Contact the **United States Travel and Tourism Administration** (Box 1EN, London W1A 1EN, tel. 071/495–4466) for brochures and tourist information.

**Passports and Visas**  You will need a valid 10-year passport (cost £15). You do not need a visa if you are staying 90 days or less, have a return ticket, are flying with a major airline, and complete Visa Waiver Form I-94W, available on the plane or at the airport. There are some exceptions to this, so check with your travel agent or with the **United States Embassy** (Visa and Immigration Department, 5 Upper Grosvenor St., London W1A 2JB, tel. 071/499–3443). No vaccinations are needed for entry into the United States.

**Customs**  Visitors 21 or over can take in 200 cigarettes or 50 cigars or 2 kilograms of tobacco; 1 liter of alcohol; duty-free gifts to a value of $100. You may not take in meat or meat products, seeds, plants, or fruits. Avoid illegal drugs like the plague.

Returning to the United Kingdom, you may bring home, if you are 17 or older: (1) 200 cigarettes or 100 cigarillos or 50 cigars or 250 grams of tobacco; (2) two liters of table wine and (a) 1 liter of alcohol over 22% by volume (most spirits) or (b) 2 liters of alcohol under 22% by volume (fortified or sparkling wine) or (c) 2 more liters of table wine; (3) 60 milliliters of perfume and 250 milliliters of toilet water; and (4) other goods up to a value of £32, but not more than 50 liters of beer or 25 lighters.

**Insurance**  We recommend that you insure yourself to cover health and motoring mishaps with **Europ Assistance** (252 High St., Croydon, Surrey CR0 1NF, tel. 081/680–1234).

It is also wise to take out insurance to cover lost luggage if such loss isn't already covered in any homeowners' policies you may already have). Trip-cancellation insurance is also a good idea. **The Association of British Insurers** (51 Gresham St., London EC2V 7HQ, tel. 071/600–3333) will give you comprehensive advice on all aspects of vacation insurance.

**Tour Operators**  The on-again, off-again price battle over transatlantic fares has meant that most tour operators now offer excellent budget packages to the United States. Among those you might consider are:

**Albany Travel (Manchester) Ltd.** (Royal London House, 196 Deansgate, Manchester M3 3NF).

**British Airways Holidays** (Atlantic House, Hazelwick Ave., Three Bridges, Crawley, West Sussex RH10 1NP, tel. 0293/611611).

**Cosmos** (Ground Floor, Dale House, Tiviot Dale, Stockport, Cheshire SK1 1TB, tel. 061/480–5799).

**Key to America** (15 Feltham Rd., Ashford, Middlesex TW15 1DQ, tel. 0784/248777).

**Kuoni Travel** (Kuoni House, Dorking, Surrey RH5 4AZ, tel. 0306/76711).

**North American Vacations** (Acorn House, 172/174 Albert Rd., Jarrow, Tyne & Wear NE32 5JA, tel. 091/483–6226).

**Premier Holidays** (Premier Travel Center, Westbrook, Milton Rd., Cambridge CB4 1YQ, tel. 0223/355977).

**Airlines and Airfares**  Airlines flying to Washington, DC, include **British Airways, TWA,** and **Continental.**

**Thomas Cook Ltd** can often book you on inexpensive flights. Phone the Cook Branch nearest you and ask to be put through to the "Airfare Warehouse." Be sure to call at least 21 days in advance of when you want to travel.

Also check out the small ads in magazines such as *Time Out* in the Sunday papers, where flights are offered for especially low fares.

## When to Go

Washington has two delightful seasons: spring and autumn, each with its own best features. In spring the city's ornamental fruit trees are budding, and its many gardens are in bloom. The Cherry Blossom Festival is held every April—whether or not the pink flowers choose to grace the city with their presence. The Smithsonian Kite Flying Contest behind the Washington Monument and the White House Easter Egg Roll are other popular spring activities. By autumn most of the summer crowds have left and visitors can enjoy the museums, galleries, and timeless monuments in peace.

Summers can be uncomfortably hot and humid (local legend has it that Washington was considered a "tropical hardship post" by some European diplomats), but that doesn't stop thousands of people from converging on the Mall for the annual Smithsonian Festival of American Folklife. Winter witnesses the lighting of the National Christmas Tree and countless historic-house tours, but the winter months are often bitter, with a handful of modest snowstorms that somehow bring this "southern" city to a standstill.

Visitors interested in government will want to visit Washington when Congress is in session. When lawmakers break for recess (for Christmas, Easter, July 4, and other holiday periods), the city seems a little less vibrant.

What follows are the average daily maximum and minimum temperatures for Washington.

| Climate | Jan. | 47F | 8C | May | 76F | 24C | Sept. | 79F | 26C |
|---|---|---|---|---|---|---|---|---|---|
| | | 34 | −1 | | 58 | 14 | | 61 | 16 |
| | Feb. | 47F | 8C | June | 85F | 29C | Oct. | 70F | 21C |
| | | 31 | −1 | | 65 | 18 | | 52 | 11 |
| | Mar. | 56F | 13C | July | 88F | 31C | Nov. | 56F | 13C |
| | | 38 | 3 | | 70 | 21 | | 41 | 5 |
| | Apr. | 67F | 19C | Aug. | 86F | 30C | Dec. | 47F | 8C |
| | | 47 | 8 | | 68 | 20 | | 32 | 0 |

Current weather information for foreign and domestic cities may be obtained by calling The Weather Channel Connection at 900/WEATHER from a touch tone phone. In addition to the weather report, The Weather Channel Connection offers local time and travel tips as well as hurricane, foliage, and ski reports. The call costs 95¢ per minute. In Washington, the local weather number is 202/844–1212.

## Festivals and Seasonal Events

Washington has a lively calendar of special events; listed below are some of the most important or unusual. For further information, contact the Washington Convention and Visitors Association (*see* Visitor Information, *above*) or call the contact number noted at the end of some listings. A good place to double-check festival dates for the coming week is the "Weekend" section in Friday's *Washington Post*.

**Jan. 18: Martin Luther King's Birthday** is celebrated with speeches, dance, choral performances, and special readings throughout the area. (For more information: Martin Luther King, Jr. Memorial Library, tel. 202/727–1186; National Park Service, tel. 202/619–7222; Smithsonian, tel. 202/357–2700. For Arlington, Virginia, celebrations, tel. 703/358–5920.)
**Jan. 19: Robert E. Lee's Birthday** is marked with 19th-century music and samples of period food at Arlington

House, the Custis-Lee mansion in Arlington Cemetery. (Tel. 703/557–0613.)

**Jan. 1–10: Washington Antiques Show** at the Omni Shoreham Hotel is an established, high-quality presentation for buyers and browsers. (Tel. 202/234–0700.)

**Feb.: African-American History Month** features special events, museum exhibits, and cultural programs. (Tel. 202/357–2700 or 202/727–1186.)

**Feb. 12: Lincoln's Birthday** celebrations include a wreath-laying ceremony and a reading of the Gettysburg Address at the Lincoln Memorial. (Tel. 202/619–7222.)

**Feb. 14.: Frederick Douglass's Birthday** is celebrated with a wreath-laying ceremony at the Frederick Douglass National Historic Site in Anacostia. (Tel. 202/619–7222 or 202/426–5961.)

**Mid-Feb.: The Chinese New Year's Festival** explodes in Chinatown, amid hails of firecrackers and a dragon-led parade. (Tel. 202/638–1041 or 202/724–4091.)

**Feb. 22: George Washington's Birthday** is celebrated with a parade down Washington Street in Old Town Alexandria, a historic-homes tour, and Revolutionary War reenactments. (Tel. 703/838–4200 or 703/838–5005.)

**Mar. 5–7: The Spring Antiques Show** hosts more than 185 dealers from 20 states, Canada, and Europe, at the D.C. Armory. (Tel. 301/738–1966 or 202/547–9215 during show.)

**Mid-Mar.: St. Patrick's Day and Festival** begins with a parade down Constitution Avenue at 1 PM on March 14 (tel. 301/424–2200). The following days feature theater, folk music, and dance concerts (tel. 202/347–1450). For information on Old Town Alexandria festivities, call 703/838–4200. Arlington House in Arlington National Cemetery goes green as well (tel. 703/557–0613).

**Mar. 20–Apr. 18: The U.S. Botanic Gardens Spring Flower Show**'s theme for 1993 is the "Festival of Garden Lore." (Tel. 202/225–8333 or 202/225–7099.)

**Mid-Mar.: Annual Bach Marathon** honors Johann Sebastian's birthday. Ten organists each play the massive pipe organ at Chevy Chase Presbyterian Church (1 Chevy Chase Circle NW, tel. 202/363–2202) from 1 to 6. Boxed lunches and refreshments are available.

**Late Mar.: Smithsonian Kite Festival,** a treat for kite makers and kite flyers of all ages, is held at the Washington Monument grounds from 10–4. (Tel. 202/357–3030.)

**Mar. 28–Apr. 3: The National Cherry Blossom Festival** opens with the traditional Japanese Lantern Lighting ceremony on the 28th. Festivities continue with a marathon run, a fashion show, and a VIP-led parade on April

2. (For parade information, tel. 202/728–1137. For general information, tel. 202/737–2599 or 202/619–7222.)

**Apr.–May: The D.C. International Film Festival** is where dozens of foreign and American films premiere. Tickets are required. (Tel. 202/727–2396.)

**Apr.: Imagination Celebration,** an annual festival of the performing arts for young people, hosts some of the best national children's theater companies, at the John F. Kennedy Center for the Performing Arts. Hours and performances vary. (Tel. 202/467–4600.)

**Apr. 13:** The 250th anniversary of **Thomas Jefferson's Birthday** is marked by military drills and a wreath-laying at his memorial (tel. 202/619–7222).

**Mid-Apr.: White House Spring Garden Tours** offer walks around the Jacqueline Kennedy Rose Garden and the West Lawn; public rooms within the White House can also be visited. (Tel. 202/456–7041.)

**Mid-Apr.: Smithsonian's Washington Craft Show** presents a sales exhibition of one-of-a-kind, handcrafted objects of original design by 100 of the country's best artisans. (Tel. 202/357–2700.)

**Late Apr.–Early May: Georgetown House Tour,** now in its 66th year, affords the same opportunity to view private homes. Tours are held from noon to 5. Admission includes high tea at historic St. John's Georgetown Parish Church from 2 to 6. (Tel. 202/338–1796.)

**Apr. 12: The White House Easter Egg Roll** welcomes children ages 8 and under (accompanied by an adult) to the White House lawn. (Tel. 202/456–7041.)

**Late Apr.: "Wings & Things"** is the annual open house at the Paul E. Garber Facility, the National Air and Space Museum's storage and restoration annex in suburban Maryland. (Tel. 202/357–2700.)

**May 1: Georgetown Garden Tour** offers the opportunity to see more than a dozen private gardens in one of the city's loveliest and most historic neighborhoods 10:30–5. (Tel. 202/333–6896.)

**May 7–8: Washington National Cathedral Flower Mart** salutes a different country each year, with flower booths, crafts, and demonstrations. (Tel. 202/537–6200.)

**Mid-May: Malcolm X Day** pays tribute to the slain civil-rights leader. A week of workshops and films culminates in a commemoration on May 16, when concerts and speeches are held in Anacostia Park from noon to 7. (Tel. 202/543–8365.)

**May: The Festival of the Building Arts** at the National Building Museum is a chance for such craftspeople as bricklayers, carpenters, plasterers, and stencilers to demonstrate what they do. (Tel. 202/272–2448.)

**Late May–Mid June:** The **Shakespeare Free-for-All** brings one of the Bard's plays to the open-air Carter Barron Amphitheater for free. (Tel. 202/546–4000 or 202/619–7222.)

**May 30: The Memorial Day Weekend Concert,** performed by the National Symphony Orchestra at 8 PM on the West Lawn of the U.S. Capitol, officially welcomes the summer to Washington. Rain date, May 31. (Tel. 202/619–7222.)

**May 31: Memorial Day Jazz Festival** marks the 16th annual jazz festival in Old Town Alexandria and features big-band music performed by local bands. The festival runs from noon to 6 PM. (Tel. 703/883–4686.)

**May 31: Memorial Day** is recognized with a wreath-laying ceremony at the Vietnam Veterans Memorial and a concert by the National Symphony. (Tel. 202/619–7222.)

**Late May–Early Sept.:** The **Military Band Summer Concert Series** runs from Memorial Day to Labor Day, beginning at 8 PM. Every August the Army Band performs the 1812 Overture, complete with real cannons. (For schedules: Navy, tel. 202/433–2525; Army, tel. 703/696–3718; Marines, tel. 202/433–4011; Air Force, tel. 202/767–5658.)

**June 4–6: The Alexandria Waterfront Festival** is a family-oriented weekend designed to promote the American Red Cross and to recognize Alexandria's rich maritime heritage. Activities include visiting tall ships, arts and crafts displays, a 10K run, and the blessing of the fleet. (Tel. 703/549–8300.)

**Mid-June–Aug.: The Big Band Concert Series** offers performances at the Sylvan Theater on the Washington Monument grounds every Wednesday evening from 8 to 10. (Tel. 202/619–7222.)

**June 23–27** and **June 30–July 4: The Festival of American Folklife,** sponsored by the Smithsonian and held on the Mall, celebrates the music, arts, crafts, and foods of various cultures. (Tel. 202/357–2700.)

**July–Aug.: Washington National Cathedral's Summer Festival of Music** features everything from Renaissance choral music to contemporary instrumental fare. (Tel. 202/537–6200.)

**Early July: The Mostly Mozart Festival** is held at the John F. Kennedy Center for the Performing Arts. (Tel. 202/467–4600.)

**July 4: D.C. Free Jazz Festival** showcases the city's most accomplished and innovative musicians in free concerts (Freedom Plaza, 1300 Pennsylvania Ave., tel. 202/783–0360).

**July 4: The Independence Day Celebration** includes a grand parade that follows a route past many of the capital's historic monuments. In the evening the National Symphony Orchestra performs for free on the steps of the Capitol building (rain date is July 5); this is followed by a fireworks display over the Washington Monument. (Tel. 202/619–7222.)

**July 14–Aug. 25: The Twilight Tattoo Series** features the 3rd U.S. Infantry, the U.S. Army Band, the Drill Team, and the Old Guard Fife and Drum Corps on the Ellipse grounds, between the White House and the Washington Monument, every Wednesday evening at 7. (Tel. 703/696–3718.)

**Late July: The Virginia Scottish Games,** one of the largest Scottish festivals in the United States, features traditional Highland dance, bagpipes, a national professional heptathlon, animal events, and fiddling competitions (Episcopal High School grounds, 3901 W. Braddock Rd., Alexandria, VA, tel. 703/838–4200).

**Late July: Hispanic-American Cultural Festival** spotlights Washington's large Latino community in the Adams–Morgan and Mt. Pleasant neighborhoods (18th St. and Columbia Rd. NW, tel. 202/789–7000).

**Sept. 4: The National Frisbee Festival** is the largest noncompetitive assembly of Frisbee lovers. The disc-catching canines almost steal the show from the two-legged pros (National Mall near the Smithsonian's National Air and Space Museum, tel. 301/645–5043).

**Sept. 5: The Labor Day Weekend Concert** features the National Symphony Orchestra on the West Lawn of the U.S. Capitol, beginning at 8 PM. Rain date, Sept. 6. (Tel. 202/416–8100.)

**Sept. 12: Adams–Morgan Day** celebrates with live music, crafts, and cuisine the cultural diversity of Washington's most unique neighborhood. (Tel. 202/332–3292.)

**Sept. 12:** From noon to 6 the **John F. Kennedy Center's Open House** throws open its doors to jugglers, musicians, dancers and other performers on all five stages. Thousands throng to this free event every year. (Tel. 202/467–4600.)

**Sept. 17: The Constitution Day Commemoration** observes the anniversary of the signing of the United States Constitution. Events include a naturalization ceremony, speakers, and band concerts (National Archives, tel. 202/501–5000.)

**Sept. 25: The Washington National Cathedral Open House** is a chance to share in cathedral-related crafts, music, and activities, including a climb up the central tower. (Tel. 202/537–6200.)

**Sept. 25: Rock Creek Park Day** celebrates the park's 103rd birthday, with international and national music, children's activities, foods, and arts and crafts. The party runs from noon to dusk. (Tel. 202/426–6832.)

**Mid-Oct.: White House Fall Garden Tours** provides an opportunity to see the splendid gardens of the White House, including the famous Rose Gardens and the South Lawn. (Tel. 202/456–7041.)

**Oct. 24: Theodore Roosevelt's Birthday** is celebrated on Roosevelt Island with tours of the island, exhibits, and family activities. (Tel. 202/619–7222.)

**Late Oct.: The Washington International Horse Show** is DC's major equestrian event. (Tel. 301/840–0281.)

**Oct. 30–Nov. 28: U.S. Botanic Gardens' Chrysanthemum Show**'s theme for 1993 is "Circus, Circus, Circus." Extended hours during the show, 9–7:30. (Tel. 202/225–8333 or 202/225–7099.)

**Nov. 7: The Marine Corps Marathon** attracts thousands of world-class runners. It begins at the Iwo Jima Marine Corps Memorial in Arlington, Virginia. There is a registration fee. (Tel. 703/690–3431.)

**Nov. 11: Veteran's Day** activities include a service at Arlington National Cemetery and an 11 AM wreath-laying ceremony at the Tomb of the Unknown Soldier, led by the President or other ranking official. (Tel. 202/475–0843.)

**Dec.: Christmas** celebrations start early in the month. Major events include carol singing with the U.S. Marine Band, the Smithsonian Museum's annual display of Christmas trees, the People's Christmas Tree Lighting at the Capitol, and the Pageant of Peace and lighting of the National Christmas Tree on the Ellipse grounds.

**Early Dec.: The Washington National Cathedral's Open House** celebrates St. Nicholas Day with bagpipers, choral sing-alongs, and seasonal decorations in the Gothic-style cathedral. (Tel. 202/537–6200.)

**Dec. 4: The 23rd Annual Scottish Christmas Walk** salutes Alexandria's Scottish heritage with a parade, bagpipers, house tours, crafts, and children's events. (Tel. 703/838–4200.)

**Dec. 10–11: Old Town Christmas Candlelight Tours:** Visit historic Ramsay House, Gadsby's Tavern Museum, the Lee-Fendall House, and the Carlyle House in Old Town Alexandria. Included in the tour are music, colonial dancing, and light refreshments. (Tel. 703/838–4200.)

**Mid-Dec.: The People's Christmas Tree Lighting** on the west side of the U.S. Capitol celebrates its 30th anniversary this year. Military bands perform. (Tel. 202/224–3069.)

**Mid-Dec.–Jan. 1: The National Christmas Tree Lighting/**

**Pageant of Peace** is accompanied by seasonal music and caroling. In mid-December (usually a Thursday) the National Christmas Tree (on the Ellipse just south of the White House) is lit by the President at dusk. For the next few weeks the Ellipse grounds are the site of nightly choral performances, a Nativity scene, a burning yule log, and a display of lighted Christmas trees representing each state and territory in the United States. (Tel. 202/619–7222.)

**Dec. 18–Jan. 9, 1994: U.S. Botanic Gardens' Poinsettia Show** bursts forth with more than 3,000 of the traditional holiday red, white, and pink flowers as well as a display of Christmas wreaths and trees. (U.S. Botanic Gardens, tel. 202/225–8333 or 202/225–7099.)

**Mid–late Dec.: "Nutcracker Suite"** is performed by the Washington Ballet at Lisner Auditorium. Tickets are required. (Tel. 202/362–3606.)

**Mid-Nov.–late Dec.:** *A Christmas Carol* returns year after year to historic Ford's Theatre. Tickets are required. (Tel. 202/347–4833.)

**Dec. 23–25: The Washington National Cathedral Christmas Celebration and Services** include Christmas carols and seasonal choral performances. (Tel. 202/537–6200.)

---

## What to Pack

What you pack depends largely on where you're headed. Washington is basically informal, although many restaurants require a jacket and tie. Theaters and nightclubs in the area range from the slightly dressy (John F. Kennedy Center) to extremely casual (Wolf Trap Farm Park). For sightseeing and casual dining, jeans and sneakers are acceptable just about anywhere. Summer is usually very hot and humid, so you'll want to have shorts and light shirts. Even in August, though, you might still want to have a shawl or light jacket for air-conditioned restaurants. Good walking shoes are a must since most of the city's interesting neighborhoods and sites are best explored on foot. The only really cold months, for which you'll need a heavy coat and snow boots, are January and February.

**Carry-on Luggage** Passengers on major U.S. airlines are usually limited to two carry-on bags. For a bag you wish to store under the seat, the maximum dimensions are 9′ × 14′ × 22′. For bags that can be hung in a closet or on a luggage rack, the maximum dimensions are 4′ × 23′ × 45′. For bags you wish to store in an overhead bin, the maximum dimensions are 10′ × 14′ × 36′. Any item that exceeds the specified dimensions may be rejected as a carry-on and taken as checked baggage. Keep in mind that an airline can adapt the rules to circumstances, so on an especially crowded flight don't be surprised if you are only allowed one carry-on bag.

In addition to the two carry-ons, you may bring aboard a handbag (pocketbook or purse); an overcoat or wrap; an umbrella; a camera; a reasonable amount of reading material; an infant bag; crutches, cane, braces, or other prosthetic device; and an infant/child safety seat if a ticket has been purchased for the child or if there is space in the cabin.

Note that these regulations are for U.S. airlines only. Foreign airlines generally allow only one piece of carry-on luggage in tourist class, in addition to handbags and bags filled with duty-free goods. Passengers in first and business class are also allowed to carry on one garment bag. It is best to call your airline in advance to learn its rules regarding carry-on luggage.

**Checked Luggage**  Luggage allowances vary slightly from airline to airline. Many carriers allow three checked pieces; some allow only two. Again, it is best to check before you go. In all cases, each piece of checked luggage may not weigh more than 70 pounds or be larger than 62 inches (length + width + height).

## Cash Machines

**Withdrawals**  It's easy to use automated-teller machines (ATMs) to withdraw money from your checking account with a bank card. Just get the names of affiliated cash-machine networks before your departure. (For locations for two of the larger networks, Cirrus and Plus, call 800/4–CIRRUS or 800/THE–PLUS.) Note that you may be charged a fee for withdrawals away from your home turf. Of course, you need to get a personal identification number (PIN) if you don't have one already.

**Cash Advances**  You can also use ATMs to get cash advances on your credit card, providing you have a PIN number for your card. As with cash advances from tellers, you pay interest from the day of posting, and some banks tack on an additional service charge.

For both withdrawals and cash advances, there are usually limits on the amount you can access within given time periods. Know before you go.

## Traveling with Film

If your camera is new, shoot and develop a few rolls of film before leaving home. Pack some lens tissue and an extra battery for your built-in light meter. Invest about $10 in a skylight filter and screw it onto the front of your lens. It will protect the lens and also reduce haze.

Film doesn't like hot weather. If you're driving in summer, don't store film in your car's glove compartment or on the shelf under the rear window. Put it behind the front seat on the floor, on the side opposite the exhaust pipe.

On a plane trip, never pack unprocessed film in checked luggage; once your bags are X-rayed, your film could be ruined. Always carry undeveloped film with you through security, and ask to have it inspected by hand. (It helps to isolate your film in a plastic bag, ready for quick inspection.) Inspectors at American airports are required by law to honor requests for hand inspection; abroad, you'll have to depend on the kindness of strangers.

The old airport scanning machines—still in use in some countries—use heavy doses of radiation that can turn a family portrait into an early-morning fog. The newer models—used in all U.S. airports—are safe for anything from five to 500 scans, depending on the speed of your film. The effects are cumulative; you can put the same roll of film through several scans without worry. After five scans, though, you're asking for trouble.

If your film gets fogged and you want an explanation, send it to the National Association of Photographic Manufacturers (550 Mamaroneck Ave., Harrison, NY 10528). They will try to determine what went wrong. The service is free.

## Traveling with Children

**Getting There** On domestic flights, children under two not occupying a seat travel free. Various discounts apply to children two to 12 years of age. If you want to be sure your infant is secured in his/her own safety seat, you must buy a separate ticket and bring your own infant car seat. (Check with the airline in advance; certain seats aren't allowed. Or write for the booklet "Child/Infant Safety Seats Acceptable for Use in Aircraft," from the Federal Aviation Administration, APA–200, 800 Independence Ave. SW, Washington, DC 20591, tel. 202/267–3479.) Some airlines allow babies to travel in their own safety seats at no charge if there's a spare seat on the plane; otherwise, safety seats will be stored and the child will have to be held by a parent. If you opt to hold your baby on your lap, do so with the infant outside the seatbelt so he or she won't be crushed in case of a sudden stop.

Also inquire about special children's meals or snacks. See the February 1990 and 1992 issues of *Family Travel Times* for "TWYCH's Airline Guide," which contain a rundown of the children's services offered by 46 airlines.

**Hotels** In addition to offering family discounts and special rates for children (for example, some large hotel chains do not charge anything extra for children under 12 if they stay in their parents' room), many hotels and resorts arrange for baby-sitting services and run a variety of special children's programs. If you are going to travel with your children, be sure to check with your travel agent for more information or ask a hotel representative about children's programs when you are making reservations.

**Baby-sitting Services** Make your child-care arrangements with the hotel concierge or housekeeper.

**Publications** *Family Travel Times* is an 8- to 12-page newsletter published 10 times a year by TWYCH (Travel with Your Children, 45 W. 18th St., 7th floor Tower, New York, NY 10011, tel. 212/206–0688). The $35 subscription includes access to back issues and twice-weekly opportunities to call for specific information. Send $1 for a sample issue.

*Great Vacations with Your Kids,* by Dorothy Jordan (founder of TWYCH) and Marjorie Cohen, offers complete advice on planning a trip with children (toddlers to teens) and reports on special travel accommodations available to families (E.P. Dutton, 375 Hudson St., New York, NY 10014, tel. 212/366–2000; $12.95 paperback).

*Family Travel Guides* (Carousel Press, Box 6061, Albany, CA 94706, tel. 415/527–5849) is a catalog offering guidebooks, games, diaries, and magazine articles geared to traveling with children. To receive the catalog, send $1 for postage and handling or a business-size SASE with 45¢ postage.

*Kids and Teens in Flight* is a brochure developed by the Department of Transportation on children traveling alone. To order a free copy, tel. 202/366–2220.

*A Kid's Guide to Washington, D.C.* (Gulliver Books/ Harcourt Brace Jovanovich, 111 Fifth Ave., New York, NY 10003; $6.95) includes games, photographs, maps, and a travel diary.

*Kidding Around Washington, D.C., A Young Person's Guide to the City* by Anne Pedersen (John Muir Publications, Box 613, Santa Fe, NM 87504, tel. 505/982–4078; $9.95) highlights the sites in each neighborhood that are of most interest to children; it includes maps of each major sector of the city.

**Home Exchange** Exchanging homes is a surprisingly low-cost way to enjoy a vacation in another part of the country. **Vacation Exchange Club** (Box 820, Haleiwa, HI 96712, tel. 800/ 638–3841) specializes in domestic home exchanges. The club publishes four directories a year as well as updated, late listings. Membership ($50) includes your listing in one book, a newsletter, and copies of all publications. **Loan-a-Home** (2 Park La., 6E, Mount Vernon, NY, 10552, 914/664–7640) is popular with academics on sabbatical and businesspeople on temporary assignment. There's no annual membership fee or charge for listing your home, however one directory and a supplement costs $35.

## Hints for Disabled Travelers

**Organizations** **The Information Center for Individuals with Disabilities** (Fort Point Pl., 1st floor, 27–43 Wormwood St., Boston, MA 02210, tel. 617/727–5540) offers useful problem-solving assistance, including lists of travel agents who specialize in tours for the disabled.

**Moss Rehabilitation Hospital Travel Information Service** (1200 W. Tabor Rd., Philadelphia, PA 19141–3099, tel. 215/456–9600; TDD 215/456–9602) provides information on tourist sights, transportation, and accommodations in destinations around the world for a small fee.

**Mobility International USA** (Box 3551, Eugene, OR 97403, tel. 503/343–1284) is a membership organization with a $20 annual fee offering information on accommodations and on organized study around the world.

**The National Park Service** provides a Golden Access Passport free of charge to those who are medically blind or have a permanent disability; the passport covers the entry fee for the holder and anyone accompanying the holder in the same private, noncommercial vehicle and allows the user a 50% discount on camping, boat launching, and parking. All charges except lodging are covered. Apply for the passport in person at any national recreation facility that charges an entrance fee; proof of disability is required. For additional information, write to the National Park Service (Box 37127, Washington, DC 20013–7127).

**The Society for the Advancement of Travel for the Handicapped** (347 5th Ave., Suite 610, New York, NY 10016, tel. 212/447–7284) offers access information. Annual membership is $45, $25 for senior travelers and students. If you are not a member, send $2 and a self-addressed envelope for information on a specific country.

**Travel Industry and Disabled Exchange** (TIDE, 5435 Donna Ave., Tarzana, CA 91356, tel. 818/368–5648) is an industry-based organization with a $15-per-person annual membership fee. Members receive a quarterly newsletter and information on travel agencies and tours.

**Twin Peaks Press** (Box 129, Vancouver, WA 98666, tel. 206/694–2462 or 800/637–2256 for orders only) specializes in books for the disabled. *Travel for the Disabled* ($9.95) offers helpful hints as well as a comprehensive list of guidebooks and facilities geared to the disabled. *Directory of Travel Agencies for the Disabled* ($12.95) lists more than 350 agencies throughout the world. *Wheelchair Vagabond* ($9.95) helps independent travelers plan for extended trips in cars, vans, or campers. Twin Peaks also offers a "Traveling Nurse's Network," which provides registered nurses trained in all medical areas to accompany and assist disabled travelers.

**Transportation** **Greyhound/Trailways** (tel. 800/752–4841) will carry a disabled person and companion for the price of a single fare.

**Amtrak** (tel. 800/USA–RAIL; TDD 800/523–6590) advises requesting redcap service, special seats, or wheelchair assistance when you make reservations. Also note that not all stations are equipped to provide these services. All handicapped passengers are entitled to a 15% discount on the lowest available fare. A special children's handicapped fare is also available. For a free copy of *Access Amtrak*, a guide to special services for elderly and handicapped travelers, write to Amtrak (National Railroad Corp., 60 Massachusetts Ave. NE, Washington, DC 20002).

**Publications** *Access America: An Atlas and Guide to the National Parks for Visitors with Disabilities* (Northern Carto-

graphic, Box 133, Burlington, VT 05402, tel. 801/655–
4321) contains detailed information about access for the
37 largest and most visited national parks in the United
States. It costs $40 plus $5 shipping.

*The Itinerary* (Box 2012, Bayonne, NJ 07002, tel. 201/
858–3400) is a well-respected bimonthly travel magazine for the disabled. Call for a subscription ($10 for a
year, $20 for two); it's not available in stores.

## Hints for Older Travelers

Organizations **The American Association of Retired Persons** (AARP,
601 E St. NW, Washington, DC 20049, tel. 202/434–
2277) offers independent travelers a **Purchase Privilege
Program,** which entitles members to discounts on hotels, airfare, car rentals, and sightseeing. The AARP
also arranges group tours in conjunction with American
Express (400 Pinnacle Way, Suite 450, Norcross, GA
30071, tel. 800/927–0111). AARP members must be at
least 50 years old. Annual dues are $5 per person or per
couple.

If you're planning to use an AARP or other senior-citi-
zen identification card to obtain a reduced hotel rate,
mention it at the time you make your reservation rather
than when you check out. At participating restaurants
show your card to the maitre d' before you're seated; discounts may be limited to certain set menus, days, or
hours. Your AARP card will identify you as a retired
person but will not ensure a discount in all hotels and
restaurants. For a free list of hotels and restaurants
that offer discounts, call or write the AARP and ask for
the "Purchase Privilege" brochure or call the AARP
Travel Service. When renting a car, be sure to ask about
special promotional rates which may offer greater sav-
ings than the available discount.

**Elderhostel** (75 Federal St., 3rd floor, Boston, MA
02110–1941, tel. 617/426–7788) is an innovative, low-
cost educational program for people 60 or over (only one
member of a traveling couple has to qualify). Participants live in dormitories on some 1,600 campuses
around the world. Mornings are devoted to lectures and
seminars, afternoons to sightseeing and field trips. The
fee for a trip includes room, board, tuition (in the U.S.
and Canada), and round-trip transportation (overseas).
Special scholarships are available for those in the U.S.
and Canada who qualify financially.

**The Golden Age Passport** is a free lifetime pass to all parks, monuments, and recreation areas run by the federal government. Permanent U.S. residents over 62 may pick up a pass in person at any national park that charges admission. The passport covers the entrance fee for the holder and anyone accompanying the holder in the same private (noncommercial) vehicle. It also provides a 50% discount on camping, boat launching, and parking (lodging is not included). Proof of age is necessary.

**Mature Outlook** (6001 N. Clark St., Chicago, IL 60660, tel. 800/336–6330), a subsidiary of Sears, Roebuck, & Co., is a travel club for people over 50 years of age and offers a bimonthly newsletter and discounts at Holiday Inns. Annual membership is $9.95 per person or couple. Instant membership is available at participating Holiday Inns.

**National Council of Senior Citizens** (1331 F St. NW, Washington, D.C. 20004, tel. 202/347–8800) is a nonprofit advocacy group with some 5,000 local clubs across the country. Annual membership is $12 per person or per couple. Members receive a monthly newspaper with travel information and an ID for reduced rates on hotels and car rentals.

**Saga International Holidays** (120 Boylston St., Boston, MA 02116, tel. 800/343–0273) specializes in group travel for people over 60 and offers a variety of tour packages at various prices.

**September Days Club** (tel. 800/241–5050) is run by the moderately priced Days Inns of America. The $12 annual membership fee for individuals or couples over 50 entitles them to reduced car-rental rates and reductions of 15% to 50% at 95% of the chain's more than 350 motels.

**Vantage Travel Service** (111 Cypress St., Brookline, MA 02146, tel. 800/322–6677) offers tours geared toward senior citizens. Nonsenior adult relatives and friends are welcome.

**Transportation** **Greyhound/Trailways** (tel. 800/752–4841) offers special fares for senior citizens; these fares are subject to date and destination restrictions. Contact your local Greyhound office.

**Amtrak** (*see* Hints for Disabled Travelers, *above*).

**Publications** ***The Senior Citizens Guide to Budget Travel in the United States and Canada,*** by Paige Palmer, is available for $5.95 (includes shipping) from Pilot Books (103 Cooper St., Babylon, NY 11702, tel. 516/422–2225).

## Further Reading

Classic Washington novels include *Democracy*, by Henry Adams; *Advise and Consent*, by Allen Drury; and Gore Vidal's *Washington, D.C.*

Margaret Leach's *Reveille in Washington* re-creates the city during the Civil War. In *All the President's Men*, Bob Woodward and Carl Bernstein detail the events of Watergate.

E.J. Applewhite comments on the architecture of the city in *Washington Itself*. Louis A. Halle's *Springtime in Washington* is the definitive look at the flora and fauna of the capital. In *Ear on Washington*, gossip columnist Diana McClellan recounts some of the town's juicier stories. *Literary Washington*, by David Cutler, explores past and contemporary writers who have lived in and written about the city. Sites and stories relating to the capital's African-American history are presented in *The Guide to Black Washington*, by Sandra Fitzpatrick and Maria R. Goodwin.

Characters in Margaret Truman's mysteries have been found murdered everywhere from the Smithsonian to the Supreme Court.

# Arriving and Departing

## By Plane

**Airports** Most national and international airlines as well as many regional and commuter carriers serve one or more of Washington's three airports. **National Airport,** in Virginia, 4 miles south of downtown Washington, is popular with politicians and their staffs. It is often cramped and crowded, but it's convenient to downtown (20 minutes by subway to the Metro Center stop). Many transcontinental and international flights arrive at **Dulles International Airport,** a modern facility 26 miles west of Washington. **Baltimore-Washington International (BWI) Airport** is in Maryland, about 25 miles northeast of Washington. All three airports are served by a variety of bus and limousine companies that make scheduled trips between airports and to downtown Washington.

**Airlines**    When buying your ticket, be sure to distinguish among nonstop flights (no changes, no stops), direct flights (no changes but one or more stops), and connecting flights (two or more planes, one or more stops).

National Airport is served by **America West** (tel. 800/247–5692), **American** (tel. 800/433–7300), **Business Express** (tel. 800/345–3400), **Continental** (tel. 800/525–0280), **Delta** (tel. 800/221–1212), **Midwest** (tel. 800/452–2022), **Northwest** (tel. 800/225–2525), **TWA** (tel. 800/221–2000), **United** (tel. 800/241–6522), **USAir** (tel. 800/428–4322), and **USAir Shuttle** (tel. 800/428–4322).

Major air carriers serving Dulles include **Aeroflot** (tel. 202/429–4922), **Air France** (tel. 800/237–2747), **All Nippon Airways** (tel. 800/2FLY–ANA), **American** (tel. 800/433–7300), **British Airways** (tel. 800/247–9297), **Continental** (tel. 800/525–0280), **Delta** (tel. 800/221–1212), **Japan Air Lines** (tel. 800/525–3663), **Lufthansa** (tel. 800/645–3880), **Northwest** (tel. 800/225–2525), **Saudi Arabian** (tel. 800/4SAUDIA), **TACA** (El Salvador, tel. 800/535–8780), **Transbrazil** (tel. 800/872–3153), **TWA** (tel. 800/221–2000), **United** (tel. 800/241–6522), and **USAir** (tel. 800/428–4322).

Airlines that serve BWI include **Air Jamaica** (tel. 800/523–5585), **America West** (tel. 800/247–5692), **American** (tel. 800/433–7300), **Business Express** (tel. 800/345–3400), **Continental** (tel. 800/525–0280), **Delta** (tel. 800/221–1212), **Icelandair** (tel. 800/223–5500), **KLM Royal Dutch** (tel. 800/777–5553), **LADECO Chilean** (tel. 800/825–2332), **Midwest Express (Skyway)** (tel. 800/452–2022), **Northwest** (tel. 800/225–2525), **TWA** (tel. 800/221–2000), **United** (tel. 800/241–6522), and **USAir** (tel. 800/428–4322).

**Smoking**    Smoking is banned on all scheduled routes within the 48 contiguous states; within the states of Hawaii and Alaska; to and from the U.S. Virgin Islands and Puerto Rico; and on flights of under six hours to and from Hawaii and Alaska. The rule applies to the domestic legs of all foreign routes but does not affect international flights.

On a flight where smoking is permitted, it is best to request a no-smoking seat at the time that you book your ticket. If the airline tells you there are no seats available in the no-smoking section on the day of the flight, insist on one: Department of Transportation regulations require U.S. flag carriers to find seats for all nonsmokers, provided they meet check-in time restrictions.

**Lost Luggage** Luggage loss is usually covered as part of a comprehensive travel insurance package that includes personal accident, trip cancellation, and sometimes default and bankruptcy insurance. Several companies offer comprehensive policies:

**Access America, Inc.** (a subsidiary of Blue Cross-Blue Shield; Box 11188, Richmond, VA 23230, tel. 800/334–7525 or 800/284–8300).
**Carefree Travel Insurance** (Box 310, 120 Mineola Blvd., Mineola, NY 11501, tel. 516/294–0220 or 800/323–3149).
**Near Services** (450 Prairie Ave., Suite 101, Calumet City, IL 60409, tel. 708/868–6700 or 800/654–6700).
**Travel Guard International** (underwritten by Transamerica Occidental Life Companies; 1145 Clark St., Stevens Point, WI 54481, tel. 715/345–0505 or 800/782–5151).

**Luggage Insurance** Airlines are responsible for lost or damaged property only up to $1,250 per passenger on domestic flights; and $9.07 per pound ($20 per kilo) for checked baggage on international flights, and up to $400 per passenger for unchecked baggage on international flights. If you're carrying valuables, either take them with you on the airplane or purchase additional insurance for lost luggage. Some airlines will issue additional insurance when you check in, but many do not. One that does is American Airlines. Rates for domestic and international flights are $2 for every $100 valuation, with a maximum of $5,000 valuation per passenger. Hand luggage is not included.

Insurance for lost, damaged, or stolen luggage is available through travel agents or directly through various insurance companies. Two companies that issue luggage insurance are **Tele-Trip** (Box 31685, 3201 Farnam St., Omaha, NE 68131-0618, tel. 800/228–9792), a subsidiary of Mutual of Omaha, and **The Travelers Insurance Corporation** (Ticket and Travel Dept., 1 Tower Sq., Hartford, CT 06183–5040, tel. 203/277–0111 or 800/243–3174). Tele-Trip, which operates sales booths at airports and also issues policies through travel agents, insures checked luggage for up to 180 days; rates vary according to the length of the trip. The Travelers Insurance Corporation insures checked or hand luggage for $500 to $2,000 valuation per person, also for a maximum of 180 days. Rates for up to five days for $500 valuation are $10; for 180 days, $85. Both companies offer the same rates on domestic and international flights. Check the travel

pages of your local newspaper for the names of other
companies that insure luggage.

Before you go, itemize the contents of each bag in case
you need to file an insurance claim. Be certain to put
your home address on each piece of luggage, including
carry-on bags. If your luggage is stolen and later recovered, the airline will deliver it to your home free of
charge.

**Between the Airports and Downtown**
*By Metro* If you are coming into Washington National Airport,
don't have too much to carry, and are staying at a hotel
near a subway stop, it makes sense to take the Metro
downtown. You can walk to the station or catch the free
airport shuttle that stops at each terminal and brings
you to the National Airport station on the Blue and Yellow lines. The Metro ride downtown takes about 20 minutes and costs between $1 and $1.20, depending on the
time of day.

*By Bus* National and Dulles airports are served continuously by
the buses of **Washington Flyer** (tel. 703/685–1400). The
ride from National to downtown takes 20 minutes and
costs $7 ($12 round-trip); from Dulles the half-hour ride
costs $14 ($22 round-trip). The bus takes you to 1517 K
Street NW, where you can board a free shuttle bus that
serves downtown hotels. The shuttle bus will also bring
you here from your hotel to catch the main airport bus on
your return journey. For main and shuttle bus schedules, call the Washington Flyer (*see above*). An inter-air-
port express travels between Dulles and National. The
45-minute trip costs $14 ($22 round-trip). Washington
Flyer also provides service to various locations in the
Maryland and Virginia suburbs. Washington Flyer ac-
cepts cash only; children under age 6 ride free.

**The Airport Connection** (tel. 301/441–2345) serves BWI
airport with buses that leave every 90 minutes for downtown Washington. The 65-minute ride costs $13 ($23
round-trip).

Some hotels provide van service to and from the airports; check with your hotel when making reservations
or when you arrive.

*By Train* Free shuttle buses carry passengers between airline
terminals and the train station at BWI airport. **Amtrak**
and **MARC (Maryland Rail Commuter Service)** trains
run between BWI and Washington's Union Station from
around 6 AM to 11 PM. The cost for the 40-minute ride is
$10 on an Amtrak train, $4.25 on a MARC train (weekdays
only). For Amtrak schedule information, call 800/USA–

RAIL. For MARC schedule information, call 800/325–RAIL; BWI is on the MARC system's Penn Line.

*By Taxi* If you're traveling alone, expect to pay about $8 to get from National Airport to downtown; from Dulles or BWI, $45. Unscrupulous cabbies prey on out-of-towners so if the fare strikes you as astronomical get the driver's name and cab number and threaten to call the D.C. Taxi-cab Commission (tel. 202/767–8380). Whatever the fare, a $1 airport surcharge is added to the total.

*By Limousine* Call at least a day ahead and **Diplomat Limousine** (tel. 703/461–6800) will have a limousine waiting for you at the airport. The ride downtown from National costs $50. It costs $60 from Dulles and $90 from BWI. Sedans are about a third cheaper. **Limousines Unlimited** has a counter at BWI airport and a low limousine price from BWI to downtown ($55). Or, call ahead (tel. 301/621–9191) to have a car waiting for you at National ($60 to downtown) or Dulles ($99).

## By Car

If you are arriving by car note that I–95 skirts Washington as part of the Beltway, the six- to eight-lane highway that encircles the city. The eastern half of the Beltway is labeled both I–95 and I–495, the western half is just I–495. If coming from the south, take I–95 to I–395 and cross the 14th Street bridge to 14th Street in the District. From the north, stay on I–95 south before heading west on Route 50, the John Hanson Highway, which turns into New York Avenue.

I-66 approaches the city from the southwest, but there are weekday rush-hour restrictions. From 6:30 to 9 AM cars traveling eastbound inside the Beltway (I-495) must have at least three people in them. A similar high-occupancy vehicle (or "HOV") restriction applies westbound from 4 to 6:30 PM. If you're traveling at an off-peak hour, or have enough people in your car to satisfy the rules, you can get downtown by taking I-66 across the Theodore Roosevelt Bridge to Constitution Avenue. I-270 approaches Washington from the northwest before hitting 495. To get downtown take 495 east to Connecticut Avenue south, towards Chevy Chase.

The traffic lights in Washington sometimes stymie visitors. Most of the lights don't hang down over the middle of the streets but stand at the sides of intersections. Also keep in mind that radar detectors are illegal in Virginia and the District. Some final advice: A good map is invaluable for driving in Washington.

## Car Rentals

Ample public transportation and shuttle service from the airports to downtown make it relatively easy to get by in Washington without renting a car. Traffic is bad, and traffic rules can be confusing even to natives. If a rental car figures in your plans, however, there are plenty of companies to choose from. Most of the major car rental companies—including **Avis** (tel. 800/331–1212), **Budget** (tel. 800/527–0700), **Dollar** (tel. 800/800–4000), **Hertz** (tel. 800/654–3131), and **National** (tel. 800/227–7368)—have offices at the three airports and in the downtown hotel/business district.

## By Train

More than 50 trains a day arrive at Washington's restored **Union Station** on Capitol Hill (50 Massachusetts Ave. NE, tel. 202/484–7540 or 800/USA–RAIL). Washington is the last stop on Amtrak's Northeast Corridor line and is a major stop on most routes from the south and west. Metroliner trains travel between New York and Washington five times every weekday.

## By Bus

Washington is a major terminal for **Greyhound/ Trailways Bus Lines** (1005 1st St. NE, tel. 301/565–2662). The company also has stations in nearby Silver Spring and Laurel, Maryland, and in Springfield, Virginia. Check with your local Greyhound/Trailways ticket office for prices and schedules.

# Staying in Washington

## Important Addresses and Numbers

Because of the booming growth in Washington and its surrounding Maryland and Virginia suburbs, you must now use the area code (without first dialing 1) when calling locally between any of the three jurisdictions: 202 for Washington, 301 for Washington's Maryland suburbs, and 703 for Virginia's suburbs. The state of Maryland added a second area code—410—in 1992 for the eastern half of the state, including Annapolis and Baltimore.

**Tourist Information** The **Washington, D.C. Convention and Visitors Association** operates a tourist information center behind the Willard Hotel at 1455 Pennsylvania Avenue NW (tel. 202/789–7000; tel. 202/737–8866 for recorded announcement of upcoming events). The **International Visitor Information Service** (1623 Belmont St. NW, tel. 202/939–5566) answers foreigners' questions about Washington and has maps and brochures on area attractions in eight languages. Rangers from the National Park Service staff information-kiosks on the Mall, near the White House, next to the Vietnam Veterans Memorial, and at several other locations throughout the city. **Dial-A-Park** (tel. 202/619–PARK) is a recording of events at Park Service attractions in and around Washington. **Dial-A-Museum** (tel. 202/357–2020) is a recording of exhibits and special offerings at Smithsonian Institution museums. If you're planning on doing any sightseeing in Virginia, stop by the **Virginia Travel Center** (1629 K St. NW, tel. 202/659–5523). If Maryland figures in your travel plans, contact the state's **Office of Tourist Development** (tel. 410/333–6611 or 800/282–6632 for Baltimore information specifically).

**Emergencies** Dial 911 for assistance. The hospital closest to downtown is **George Washington University Hospital** (901 23rd St. NW, tel. 202/994–3211).

**Doctors and Dentists** **Prologue** (tel. 202/DOCTORS) is a referral service that locates doctors, dentists, and urgent-care clinics in the greater Washington area. The **DC Dental Society** (tel. 202/547–7615) operates a referral line weekdays 8 to 4.

**Late-night Pharmacies** **Peoples Drug** operates two 24-hour pharmacies in the District. One is at 14th Street and Thomas Circle NW (tel. 202/628–0720), the other at 7 Dupont Circle NW (tel. 202/785–1466).

## Opening and Closing Times

**Banks** are generally open weekdays 9 to 3. On Friday many stay open until 5 or close at 2 and open again from 4 to 6. Very few banks in the city have lobby hours on Saturday.

**Museums** are generally open daily 10 to 5:30. Many private museums are closed on Monday. The Smithsonian sets special spring and summer hours annually for some of its museums (tel. 202/357–2700 for details).

**Stores** are generally open Monday to Saturday 10 to 7 (or 8). Some have extended hours on Thursday and many—

especially those in shopping or tourist areas such as Georgetown—are open Sunday, anywhere from 10 to noon, closing at 5 or 6.

## Getting Around Washington

The city's streets are arranged, said Pierre L'Enfant, the man who designed them in 1791, "like a chessboard overlaid with a wagon wheel." Streets run north and south and east and west in a grid pattern; avenues—most named after states—run diagonally, connecting the various traffic circles scattered throughout the city. The District is divided into four sections: northwest, northeast, southwest, and southeast; the Capitol Building serves as the center of the north/south and east/west axes. North Capitol and South Capitol streets divide the city into east and west; the Mall and East Capitol Street divide the city into north and south. Streets that run north to south are numbered; those that extend east to west are lettered from A to I and K to W, the letter J having been skipped. (Note that I Street is often written as "Eye Street.") After W, two-syllable alphabetical names are used for east/west streets (Adams, Belmont, Clifton, etc.), then three-syllable names (Albemarle, Brandywine, Chesapeake). After the three-syllable names to the north have been exhausted, the streets are named for trees (Aspen, Butternut, Cedar).

Make sure you have a destination's complete address, including the quadrant designation. There are four 4th and D Street intersections in Washington: one each in NW, NE, SW, and SE. Addresses in Washington are coded to the intersections they're closest to. For example, 1785 Massachusetts Ave. NW is between 17th and 18th Streets; 600 5th St. NW is at the corner of 5th and F, the sixth letter of the alphabet.

**By Subway** The **Washington Metropolitan Area Transit Authority** (WMATA) provides bus and subway service in the District and in the Maryland and Virginia suburbs. The **Metro,** opened in 1976, is one of the country's cleanest and safest subway systems. Trains run weekdays 5:30 AM–midnight, weekends 8 AM–midnight. During the weekdays rush hours (5:30–9:30 AM and 3–7 PM) trains come along every six minutes. At other times and on weekends and holidays trains run about every 12 to 15 minutes. The base fare is $1; the actual price you pay depends on the time of day and the distance traveled. Children under five ride free when accompanied by a paying passenger, but there is a maximum of two children per paying adult.

The computerized **Farecard machines** in Metro stations can seem complicated. You'll need a pocketful of coins or crisp $1 or $5 bills to feed into the machines; machines in some stations also accept $10 and $20 bills. If the machine spits your bill back out at you, try folding and unfolding it before asking a native for help. The paper Farecard you purchase should be inserted into the turnstile to enter the platform. Make sure you hang onto the card—you'll need it to exit at your destination.

Some Washingtonians report that the Farecard's magnetic strip interferes with the strips on automatic teller and credit cards. Keep the cards separated in your pocket or wallet. You'll notice that some Farecards have advertisements on the back; others have a line with the words "Sign here" underneath. It's doubtful anyone in Washington has ever signed the back of a Farecard.

For $5 you can buy a pass that allows unlimited rail trips for one day. It's good all day on weekends and after 9:30 AM on weekdays. Passes are available at Metro Sales Outlets (including the Metro Center station) and at many hotels.

For general travel information, tel. 202/637–7000 or TTD 202/638–3780 seven days a week 6 AM to 11:30 PM; for consumer assistance, tel. 202/637–1328; for transit police, tel. 202/962–2121. A helpful brochure—"All About the Metro System"—is available by calling the travel information number or writing to: Office of Marketing, WMATA, 600 5th St. NW, Washington, DC 20001.

**By Bus** WMATA's red, white, and blue **Metrobuses** crisscross the city and nearby suburbs, with some routes running 24 hours a day. All bus rides within the District are $1.

Free transfers, good for two hours, are available on buses and in Metro stations. Bus-to-bus transfers are accepted at designated Metrobus transfer points. Rail-to-bus transfers must be picked up before boarding the train. There may be a transfer charge when boarding the bus. There are no bus-to-rail transfers.

**By Car** A car can be a drawback in Washington. Traffic is horrendous, especially at rush hours, and driving is often confusing, with many lanes and some entire streets changing direction suddenly at certain times of day. Parking is also an adventure; the police are quick to tow away or immobilize with a "boot" any vehicle parked illegally. Since the city's most popular sights are within a short walk of a Metro station anyway, it's best to leave your car at the hotel. Touring by car is a good idea only if you're considering visiting sites in suburban Maryland or Virginia.

Most of the outlying, suburban Metro stations have parking lots, though these fill quickly with city-bound commuters. If you plan to park in one of these lots, arrive early, armed with lots of quarters. Private parking lots downtown are expensive, charging as much as $4 an hour and up to $13 a day. There is free, three-hour parking around the Mall on Jefferson Drive and Madison Drive, though these spots always seem to be filled. You can park free—in some spots all day—in parking areas south of the Lincoln Memorial on Ohio Drive and West Basin Drive in West Potomac Park.

If you find you've been towed from a city street, call 202/727–5000.

**By Taxi** Taxis in the District are not metered; they operate instead on a curious zone system. Even longtime Washingtonians will ask the cabdriver ahead of time how much the fare will be. The basic single rate for traveling within one zone is $3. There is an extra $1.25 charge for each additional passenger and a $1 surcharge during the 4 to 6:30 PM rush hour. Bulky suitcases larger than three cubic feet are charged at a higher rate and a $1.50 surcharge is tacked on when you phone for a cab. Two major companies serving the District are **Capitol Cab** (tel. 202/546–2400) and **Diamond Cab** (tel. 202/387–6200). Maryland and Virginia taxis are metered but are not allowed to take passengers between points in Washington.

## Guided Tours

**Orientation Tours** Taking a narrated bus tour is a good way to get your bearings and make some decisions about what to see first. Both of the tour companies listed here allow you to get off and on as often as you like with no additional charge. If you want to conserve your energy for walking inside Washington's museums, art galleries, and other touring sights, rather than walking *between* them, a bus tour is the way to go.

**Tourmobile** (tel. 202/554–7950 or 202/554–5100). Authorized by the National Park Service, Tourmobile buses ply a route that stops at 18 historic sites between the Capitol and Arlington Cemetery; the route includes the White House and the museums on the Mall. Tickets are $8.50 for adults, $4 for children 3–11.

**Old Town Trolley Tours** (tel. 301/985–3021). Orange-and-green motorized trolleys take in the main downtown sights and also foray into Georgetown and the upper northwest, stopping at out-of-the-way attractions, such as the Washington Cathedral. Tickets are $14 for adults, $5 for children 5–12, and free for the under 5 set.

**Bus Tours** **Gray Line Tours** (tel. 301/386–8300). A four-hour motorcoach tour of Washington, Embassy Row, and Arlington National Cemetery leaves Union Station at 8:30 AM and 2:30 PM (at 2 PM December–March); tours of Mount Vernon and Alexandria depart at 8:30 AM (adults $20, children 3–11, $10). An all-day trip combining both tours leaves at 8:30 AM (adults $36, children $18). eeb

**Special-Interest Tours** Special tours of government buildings—including the Archives, the Capitol, the FBI Building, the Supreme Court, and the White House—can be arranged through your representative's or senator's office. Only limited numbers of these so-called VIP tickets are available, so it's best to contact your representative up to six months in advance of your trip. With these special passes you won't have to wait in line as long as you would in the regular lines, and your tour will often take you through rooms not open to the public.

**The Government Printing Office** (H and North Capitol Sts. NW, tel. 202/512–1995). A visit to the world's largest in-plant printing operation will help you understand why Washington is built on a foundation of paper. In addition to Federal periodicals, brochures, forms, and stationery, the Congressional Record is printed here each night, with the first copies bundled and delivered to offices on Capitol Hill by 7 AM. Craftspeople also produce colorful marbled paper here—you can take a souvenir notepad. Free tours are offered weekdays between 9 and 1. Call for reservations.

**Old Executive Office Building** (Pennsylvania Ave. and 17th St. NW, tel. 202/395–5895). Tours of this 1888 French Second Empire building, formerly the State, Navy, and War Building, are offered Saturday from 9 to noon. Inside you'll see the restored Victorian-style secretary of the navy's office (now used by the vice president), one of the building's two stained-glass rotundas, and the departmental libraries. Reservations are required.

**The Naval Observatory** (34th St. and Massachusetts Ave. NW, tel. 202/653–1543, 202/653–1541 for group reservations). Evening tours are given every Monday night, except on Federal holidays, to the first 100 people in line at the Observatory's south gate across from the British Embassy. The two-hour tour starts at 7:30 standard time, 8:30 daylight-saving time. The selection of astronomical objects shown on the tour depends on the time of year, time of month, and sky conditions.

**St. John's Parish Georgetown House Tours** (3240 O St. NW, tel. 202/338–1796). For one weekend in late April, owners of historic Georgetown houses open their doors to sightseers.

**State Department Diplomatic Reception Rooms** (23rd and C Sts. NW, tel. 202/647–3241). These opulent 18th- and early 19th-century-style rooms installed on the top floor of the State Department are patterned after great halls in Europe and rooms found in Colonial American plantations. Filled with museum-quality furnishings— including a Philadelphia Highboy, Paul Revere bowl, and the desk on which the Treaty of Paris was signed— these rooms are used 15 to 20 times a week to entertain foreign diplomats and heads of state. Tours are given weekdays at 9:30, 10:30, and 2:45. Reservations are required, and for a summer tour you may have to book up to three months in advance. (It's recommended that children be over 12.)

**Voice of America** (330 Independence Ave. SW, tel. 202/ 619–3919). The global radio network of the U.S. Information Agency, the VOA broadcasts in 43 languages. This 45-minute weekday tour takes visitors past broadcast studios and the newsroom and explains VOA's purpose. Tours are weekdays at 8:40, 9:40, and 10:40 AM and 1:40 and 2:40 PM, except federal holidays. Enter on C Street. Reservations are advised.

**Washington, D.C. Post Office** (Brentwood Rd. NE between Rhode Island and New York Aves., tel. 202/636– 1208). More than 5 million pieces of mail are processed each day at this facility, as a veritable avalanche of envelopes and packages are transferred in robot-driven bins and sorted by optical scanners and human eyes. Free tours are offered Tuesday through Friday between 9:30 and 4.

*The Washington Post* (1150 15th St. NW, tel. 202/334– 7969). Free 50-minute guided tours for ages 11 and up are run on Monday from 10 to 3. You'll take in the news room, where the reporters work; the production room, where the paper is put together; the press room, where the paper is printed; and the mail room, where finished papers are stacked and bundled for shipment. The *Post* was one of the last major papers in the country to switch to cold type, and a display contrasts this computerized method of putting the paper together with the hot-type method used until 1980. Make reservations for this tour well in advance of your trip.

**Walking Tours** **Black History National Recreation Trail.** Not a specific walking route but a group of sites within historic neighborhoods, this trail illustrates aspects of African-American history in Washington, from slavery days to the New Deal. A brochure outlining the trail is available from the National Park Service (Box 37127, Washington, DC 20013–7127, tel. 202/208–4747).

**Construction Watch and Site Seeing** (tel. 202/272–2448). The National Building Museum sponsors these architecturally oriented walking tours each spring and fall. On Construction Watch tours, architects and construction-project managers accompany visitors to buildings in various stages of completion and discuss the design and building process. Site Seeing tours are led by architectural historians and go to various Washington neighborhoods and well-known monuments, public buildings, and houses. Tickets range from $7 for Construction Watch tours to $60 for Site Seeing tours, which include bus transportation and a box lunch.

**Smithsonian Resident Associate Program** (tel. 202/357–3030). Walking and bus tours of neighborhoods in Washington and communities outside the city are routinely offered by RAP. Many tours are themed and include sites that illustrate, for example, Art Deco influences, African-American architecture, or railroad history.

**Personal Guides** **Guide Service of Washington** (tel. 202/628–2842). This company provides a licensed guide to accompany you in your car, van, or bus to show you the sights of the city, Mount Vernon, and Arlington. The cost for an English-speaking guide is $91 for a four-hour tour; $135 for an eight-hour tour. Guides are available for tours in more than 20 languages; prices are higher in a foreign language.

**Other Tours** **Goodwill Embassy Tour** (tel. 202/636–4225). Every second Saturday in May, a half dozen embassies in Washington open their doors as stops on a self-guided tour. The cost per ticket is about $25 and includes refreshments, a tour booklet, and free shuttle bus transportation between embassies.

**Scandal Tours** (tel. 202/387–2253). This outrageous tour concentrates on Washington's seamier side with a 90-minute trip past such scandalous locales as Gary Hart's Capitol Hill town house; the Tidal Basin, where Congressman Wilbur Mills and stripper Fanne Fox took an unintended dip; the Old Executive Office Building, where Fawn Hall and Ollie North shredded documents together; and, of course, the Watergate. Costumed look-alikes from the Gross National Product comedy troupe ride on the bus and act out the scandals. Tours leave the Washington Hilton and Towers on Saturday at 1 (private tours can be chartered the rest of the week). The cost is $27 per person. Reservations required. For those who want to wade through the scum at their own pace, there is **Scandal Tour In-A-Box,** a 75-minute cassette tape that promises to "bypass the monuments and take you straight into the gutter." It's available at local bookstores for $12.95, or order by calling 202/783–7212 or writing GNP (2206 Cathedral Ave. NW, Washington, DC 20008).

*The Dandy* (0 Prince St., Alexandria, VA, tel. 703/683–6076 or 703/683–6090). Moored on the waterfront in Old Town Alexandria, this enclosed boat is small enough to cruise under Washington's bridges, allowing it to venture up the Potomac past the Lincoln Memorial to the Kennedy Center and Georgetown. Lunch cruises board weekdays at 11:15 AM and weekends at 12:15 PM. Dinner cruises board Sunday–Thursday at 6:45 PM, Friday at 7:30 PM, and Sunday at 7:15 PM. Prices range from $25 to $29 for lunch, and $45 to $55 for dinner.

*Spirit of Washington* (Pier 4, 6th and Water Sts. SW, tel. 202/554–8000 or 202/554–1542). Moored at the heart of Washington's waterfront, this boat gives visitors a waterborne view of some of the area's attractions, including Old Town Alexandria, Washington National Airport, and Hains Point. Lunch cruises board Tuesday through Saturday at 11:30 AM; a Sunday brunch cruise sails at 1. Evening cruises board at 6:30 PM and include dinner and a floor show. Adult "moonlight party cruises" leave Friday and Saturday at 11:30 PM. Prices range from $19 per person for the moonlight cruise to $43.95 for dinner on a Friday or Saturday night. A sister ship, the *Potomac Spirit,* sails to Mount Vernon, George Washington's plantation home. The 4½-hour trip is offered mid-

March–mid-October, Tuesday–Sunday. During peak tourist season (mid-June–mid-October), boats embark at 9 AM and 2 PM. From mid-March through mid-June boats leave at 9 AM only. Prices are $19 adults, $17.25 senior citizens, $11.25 children 6–11, under 5 free.

# 2 Portraits of Washington

# Speaking of Washington

*Compiled by John F. Kelly*

*John F. Kelly is an editor for the* Washington Post's Weekend *section.*

**W**ashington, D.C., is a bit like the weather: Everybody likes to talk about it. Unlike the weather though, we can do something about Washington. Every few years Americans are invited to throw the bums out and usher a new crop of bums in. And there's no doubt these politicians will form some opinion of their new home.

Politicians, poets, presidents, First Ladies, humorists, foreign visitors—they've all put pen to paper in expressing their opinion of the city that literally arose from the swamp.

"That Indian swamp in the wilderness."—Thomas Jefferson, c. 1789

"A century hence, if this country keeps united, it will produce a city though not so large as London, yet of magnitude inferior to few others in Europe."—George Washington, 1789

"May the spirit which animated the great founder of this city, descend to future generations."—John Adams, 1800

"I had much rather live in the house at Philadelphia. Not one room or chamber is finished of the whole. It is habitable by fires in every part, 13 of which we are required to keep daily or sleep in wet or damp places."—Abigail Adams, 1800 (after moving into the White House)

"This boasted [Pennsylvania] Avenue is as much a wilderness as Kentucky. Some half-starved cattle browsing among the bushes present a melancholy spectacle to the stranger . . . . So very thinly is the city peopled that quails and other birds are constantly shot within a hundred yards of the Capitol."—Charles W. Jansen, 1806

"This embryo capital, where Fancy sees
Squares in morasses, obelisks in trees;
Which second-sighted seers, ev'n now, adorn
With shrines unbuilt, and heroes yet unborn.
Though nought but woods, and Jefferson they see,
Where streets should run, and sages *ought* to be."
—Thomas Moore, 1806

"Washington has certainly an air of more magnificence than any other American town. It is mean in detail, but the outline has a certain grandeur about it."—James Fenimore Cooper, 1838

"In democratic communities the imagination is compressed when men consider themselves; it expands indefinitely when they think of the state. Hence it is that the same men who live on a small scale in cramped dwellings frequently aspire to gigantic splendor in the erection of their public monuments. The Americans have traced out the circuit of an immense city on the site which they intend to make their capital, but which up to the present time is hardly more densely peopled than Pontoise, though, according to them, it will one day contain a million inhabitants. They have already rooted up trees for 10 miles around lest they should interfere with the future citizens of this imaginary metropolis. They have erected a magnificent palace for Congress in the center of the city and have given it the pompous name of the Capitol."—Alexis de Tocqueville, 1840

"This town looks like a large straggling village reared in a drained swamp."—George Combe, 1842

"It is sometimes called the City of Magnificent Distances but it might with greater propriety be termed the City of Magnificent Intentions . . . . Spacious avenues that begin in nothing and lead nowhere; streets, a mile long, that only want houses, roads, and inhabitants; public meetings that need but a public to be complete; and ornaments of great thoroughfares, which only lack great thoroughfares to ornament—are its leading features. One might fancy the season over and most of the houses gone out of town forever with their masters."—Charles Dickens, 1842

"I . . . found the capital still under the empire of King Mud . . . . Were I to say that it was intended to be typical of the condition of the government, I might be considered cynical."—Anthony Trollope, 1862

"Washington is the paradise of gamblers, and contains many handsome and elegantly-fitted-up establishments. It is said at least one hundred of these 'hells' were in full blast during the war."—Dr. John B. Ellis, 1870

"Why, when I think of those multitudes of clerks and congressmen—whole families of them—down there slaving away and keeping the country together, why then I know in my heart there is something so good and motherly about Washington, that grand old benevolent National Asylum for the Helpless."—Mark Twain, 1873

"One of these days this will be a very great city if nothing happens to it."—Henry Adams, 1877

"Wherever the American citizen may be a stranger, he is at home here."—Frederick Douglass, 1877

"Washington is no place in which to carry out inventions." — Alexander Graham Bell, 1887

"But taking it all in all and after all, Negro life in Washington is a promise rather than a fulfillment. But it is worthy of note for the really excellent things which are promised."—Paul Laurence Dunbar, 1900

"In Washington there is no life apart from government and politics: it is our daily bread; it is the thread which runs through the woof and warp of our lives; it colors everything."—A. Maurice Low, 1900

"What you want is to have a city which every one who comes from Maine, Texas, Florida, Arkansas, or Oregon can admire as being something finer and more beautiful than he had ever dreamed of before."—James Bryce, 1913

"Things get very lonely in Washington sometimes. The real voice of the great people of America sometimes sounds faint and distant in that strange city. You hear politics until you wish that both parties were smothered in their own gas."—Woodrow Wilson, 1919

"Congress has been writing my material for years and I am not ashamed of what I have had. Why should I pay some famous Author, or even myself, to sit down all day trying to dope out something funny to say on the Stage?. . . No, sir, I have found that there is nothing as funny as things that have happened . . .Nothing is so funny as something done in all seriousness . . .Each state elects the most serious man it has in the District . . .He is impressed with the fact that he is leaving Home with the idea that he is to rescue his District from Certain Destruction, and to see that it receives its just amount of Rivers and Harbors, Postoffices and Pumpkin Seeds. Naturally, you have put a pretty big load on that man . . .It's no joking matter to be grabbed up bodily from the Leading Lawyer's Office of Main Street and have the entire populace tell you what is depending on you when you get to Washington."—Will Rogers, 1924

"Washington. . . is the symbol of America. By its dignity and architectural inspiration. . . we encourage that elevation of thought and character which comes from great architecture."—Herbert Hoover, 1929

"Of my first trip to the top of the Washington Monument, which must have been made soon after it was opened in 1888, I recall only the fact that we descended by walking down the long, dark steps, and it seemed a journey without end. There was in those days a bitter debate as to whether a baseball thrown from the top of the monument could be caught by a catcher on the ground, and my father was much interested and full of mathematical proofs that it couldn't be done. Some time later it was tried, and turned out to be very easy."—H. L. Mencken, 1936

"Living in contemporary Washington, caught literally and physically in L'Enfant's dream, and encountering on every hand the brave mementos of Washington, Jefferson, Jackson, Lincoln and Roosevelt, is to live as close as possible to both the source and the climax of the major sequences of the human story."—George Sessions Perry, 1946

"Washington isn't a city, it's an abstraction."—Dylan Thomas, 1950

"There are a number of things wrong with Washington. One of them is that everyone has been too long away from home."—Dwight D. Eisenhower, 1955

"Whatever we are looking for, we come to Washington in millions to stand in silence and try to find it."—Bruce Catton, 1959

"Washington is a literal cesspool of crime and violence."—Sen. James O. Eastland, 1960

"A city of southern efficiency and northern charm."—John F. Kennedy, 1960

"Every dedicated American could be proud that a dynamic experience of democracy in his nation's capital had been made visible to the world."—Martin Luther King, Jr., 1963

"Washington is several miles square and about as tall, say, as the Washington Monument, give or take a little. It is surrounded on all four sides by reality."—Arthur Hoppe, 1975

"One of my earliest recollections of Washington is of a tragicomic speech by Michigan Congressman Fred Bradley, protesting that all the wining and dining was getting him down. 'Banquet life is a physical and mental strain on us hardly imaginable to the folks back home,' said the distraught Bradley. 'The strain is terrific.' He was dragooned into attending altogether too many parties, he complained; but his appeal for fewer invitations was greated with guffaws. Three weeks later Representative Bradley, age forty-nine, dropped dead. The official diagnosis was heart failure."—Jack Anderson, 1979

"As we quietly approached our new home, I told Rosalyn with a smile that it was a nice-looking place. She said, 'I believe we're going to be happy in the White House.' We were silent for a moment, and then I replied, I just hope that we never disappoint the people who made it possible for us to live here.' Rosalyn's prediction proved to be correct, and I did my utmost for four solid years to make my own hope come true."—Jimmy Carter, 1982, from *Keeping Faith: Memoirs of a President*

"The first thing that struck me about the White House was how cold it was. The country was still suffering from the energy crisis, and President Carter had ordered that the White House thermostats be turned down."—Nancy Reagan, 1989, from *My Turn*

# Edifice Treks

*By John F. Kelly*

**W**ashington probably produces more words than any other city in the world. Politicians orate, pundits speculate, and commentators narrate. But Washington's words have a peculiarly fleeting quality. They're copied into notebooks, transferred to computer screens, then set into type and bound into reports that are filed on shelves and forgotten. They're printed in newspapers that yellow and turn to dust. Words are spat out in sound bytes on the evening news, then released into the ether, lost forever. In the wordy war of politics, a paper trail is something best avoided.

But there is a stone trail in Washington, too: The words someone felt were important enough not just to commit to parchment, paper, or videotape, but to engrave in sandstone, marble, or granite. On the buildings of Washington are noble sentiments and self-serving ones, moving odes and contemplative ones.

A reading tour of Washington's inscriptions amounts to an aerobic classical education. The inscriptions, lofty in position and tone, are taken from the Bible, from the Greeks and Romans, from poets and playwrights, from presidents and statesmen. When viewing Washington's inscriptions, soaking up what is in most cases a perfect union of poesy and architecture, it's easy to see why the words "edifice" and "edify" spring from the same root.

Lesson one starts in Union Station, that great Beaux Arts bathhouse on Capitol Hill. Architect Daniel Burnham's 1908 train station is encrusted with carvings that do everything from romantically outline the development of the railroad to offer lessons in both humility and hospitality.

On the western end of the shining white Vermont granite structure, above the entrance to the Metro, is written (in all capital letters, as most inscriptions are):

*He that would bring home the wealth of the Indies must carry the wealth of the Indies with him. So it is in travelling. A man must carry knowledge with him if he would bring home knowledge.*

A bit heavy to digest when dashing for the *Metroliner* on a rainy Monday morning, but worth mulling over once a seat is found and you chug toward New York, briefcase at your feet, notes spread out on your lap, the words of the boss ecoing in your brain: "Sew up the Snebco account, Johnson, and there could be a vice presidency in it for you."

At the other end of the station is the perfect sentiment for the returning hero:

*Welcome the coming, speed the parting guest. Virtue alone is sweet society. It keeps the key to all heroic hearts and opens you a welcome in them all.*

These are just two of the half-dozen inscriptions on Union Station. Above allegorical statues by Louis Saint-Gaudens that stand over the main entrance are inscriptions celebrating the forces that created the railroads, including this set singing the praises of fire and electricity:

*Fire: greatest of discoveries, enabling man to live in various climates, use many foods, and compel the forces of nature to do his work. Electricity: carrier of light and power, devourer of time and space, bearer of human speech over land and sea, greatest servant of man, itself unknown. Thou has put all things under his feet.*

So inspirational were these and the other Union Station inscriptions thought to be 80 years ago that the Washington Terminal Company, operators of the station, distributed a free pamphlet imprinted with them. They probably saved more than a few sore necks.

Union Station's inscriptions were selected by Charles William Eliot, who was president of Harvard University. According to John L. Andriot's "Guide to the Inscriptions of the Nation's Capital," Eliot borrowed from such sources as the Bible, Shakespeare, Alexander Pope, and Ralph Waldo Emerson. Eliot also penned his own epigrams, a seemingly modest skill until you start to wonder what you'd come up with when confronted with a big blank wall that will bear your words forever.

Eliot wrote the two inscriptions on the City Post Office right next to the station. The inscriptions, facing Massachusetts Avenue, describe the humble letter carrier as a:

*Carrier of news and knowledge, instrument of trade and industry, promoter of mutual acquaintance of peace and of goodwill among men and nations*

. . . and a . . .

*Messenger of sympathy and love, servant of parted friends, consoler of the lonely, bond of scattered family, enlarger of the common life.*

It's said that President Woodrow Wilson edited these inscriptions, unaware that the Ivy League wordsmith Eliot had written them. Like all good editors, Wilson improved them.

Three long blocks away (right behind the Supreme Court and *Equal justice under law*) is the Folger Shakespeare Library, where the student of inscriptions can pause and contemplate Stratford-upon-Avon's favorite son. On the building's E Street side, above bas-relief panels depicting scenes from Shakespeare's plays, are three commentaries on the playwright, including this from Ben Jonson:

*Thou art a moniment without a tombe and art alive still while thy booke doth live and we have wits to read and praise to give.*

Folger architect Paul Cret obviously decided not to bury Shakespeare, but praise him.

## Rocks and Hard Places

Behind every inscription in Washington is the person who carved it, the man or woman who put chisel or pneumatic drill to stone and with a sharp eye and a steady hand made the most lasting of impressions.

Ann Hawkins is one such carver. (You can admire her chiselwork throughout the National Gallery of Art. She did the names on the Patrons' Permanent Fund in the east building, a roll call of philanthropists.)

"There are two comments I get from people who watch me carve and they make perfect symmetry," says Hawkins. "Half the people say 'Oh, that looks so tedious. You must have a lot of patience.' But I also get 'That looks *fun.*' And they wish they could do it."

Hawkins studied four years before she could carve well enough to take her first paying commission. She's been carving professionally since 1982, and in that time she's decided that stones are "living, breathing things." And each one is different. Sandstone is soft. Slates can be brittle and hard, with knots in them almost like wood. White Vermont marble feels sugary and crumbles a bit at the first stroke. Tennessee pink marble is chunky and firm.

There are a lot of things a stone carver has to take into account before striking the first blow, Hawkins says. "The nature of the stone, the light the inscription will receive, the weathering of the stone, how large the letters will be, what distance they'll be viewed from."

The most important part of carving, she says, is the layout of the inscription. The letters must be spaced correctly, not bunched too tightly together as if they were typeset, but spread comfortably and handsomely. The inscription must look as if it is *of* the stone, not *on* the stone.

Hawkins draws the letters on paper that—"after being measured from every direction" to make sure it's straight—is taped to the stone over sheets of typewriter carbon paper. She then outlines the inscription, transferring it to the stone. With a tungsten carbide-tipped chisel she starts hammering, sometimes working her way around the edges of the letter, sometimes starting in the center and working out. She turns and shifts the blade, roughing the letter in at first, then finishing it, aiming for the perfect *V*-shape indentation that is the mark of a hand-carved inscription. (Inscriptions that are machine sandblasted through a stencil have a round center.) As in everything from squash to Frisbee, it's all in the wrist.

If the inscription is outside, the sun will provide the contrast necessary for the letters to be read. As the rays rake across the inscription, the shadows will lengthen, making the words pop. If the inscription is indoors, Hawkins paints the inside of the letters with a lacquer that's mixed with pigment, deepening the color of the stone.

## Triangular Logic

If a walk around Washington's inscriptions is a classical education, a perambulation of Federal Triangle is the civics lesson. The limestone cliffs of the Triangle, stretching from their base at 15th Street down Pennsylvania and Constitution avenues, are inscribed with mottoes that immediately conjure up a nobler time.

The walls fairly sing with inscriptions, enjoining passersby to be eternally vigilant (it's *the price of liberty* says the National Archives), to *Study the past* (an understandable sentiment, appearing as it also does on the Archives), and to heed Thomas Jefferson and *Cultivate peace and commerce with all* (on the Commerce Building and an example of one of the tenets of good epigram selection: Try to work the name of the building into at least one inscription).

The Federal Triangle inscriptions also provide justification for the buildings that they decorate and government departments they praise. The inscription on the Internal Revenue Service headquarters on Constitution Avenue is not Dante's *Abandon all hope ye who enter here*, but Oliver Wendell Holmes's *Taxes are what we pay for a civilized society*. Just in case you were wondering what you were paying for every April 15.

Likewise, on the Justice Department we have:

*Justice is the great interest of man on earth. Wherever her temple stands there is a foundation for social security, general happiness and the improvement and progress of our race.*

While Justice certainly has its share of letters (including this bit of Latin: *Lege atque ordine omnia fiunt*—"By law and order all is accomplished"), the award for the most verbose structure must go to the Commerce Department building. Stretched out along 14th Street, eight stories up and spread out over hundreds of feet, is this edifying ode:

*The inspiration that guided our forefathers led them to secure above all things the unity of our country. We rest upon government by consent of the governed and the political order of the United States is the expression of a patriotic ideal which welds together all the elements of our national energy promoting the organization that fosters individual initiative. Within this edifice are established agencies that have been created to buttress the life of the people, to clarify their problems and coordinate their resources, seeking to lighten burdens without lessening the responsibility of the citizen. In serving one and all they are dedicated to the purpose of the founders and to the highest hopes of the future with their local administration given to the integrity and welfare of the nation.*

It's a mouthful. But it's also redolent of a time that seems almost hopelessly naive now, a time when we could use words like "national energy" and "purpose of the founders" without smirking. This passage and two other long ones were created especially for the building, composed, it is believed, by Royal Cortissoz, for 50 years the influential art critic of *The New York Tribune* (and author of this much pithier epigram from the Lincoln Memorial: *In this temple as in the hearts of the people for whom he saved the union the memory of Abraham Lincoln is enshrined forever.*)

You can imagine Washingtonians in the 1930s watching as the inscriptions were going up in Federal Triangle, trying to guess what would be said, as if a huge game of hangman were being played. At least one Washingtonian wasn't thrilled with what he saw. In 1934, when the giant Commerce Department Building was in its final stages of construction, one Thomas Woodward wrote a letter to a friend in the Department of Justice:

"Dear Charley, in the name of your illustrious progenitor—not the least of whose gifts was the art of epigraphy—do what you can to stop the inscriptions which are being smeared over the new Government buildings. I shiver for the English of our descendants if they are daily exposed to some of these atrocious inscriptions. Justification for my intemperance in language will be found at one glance of the inscriptions being placed upon the Department of Commerce Building."

Harrumph. It's quite clear that Mr. Woodward was not happy with the work of Mr. Cortissoz. What's interesting is to whom he addressed his complaint. The "Charley" in the letter is Charles W. Eliot II, son of the Harvard president who composed the Union Station and City Post Office epigrams. The younger Eliot forwarded the letter of complaint to Charles Moore, chairman of the Commission of Fine Arts, the body responsible— then as now—for reviewing the design of government building projects. Moore allowed as how his commission hadn't been consulted on the inscriptions. The younger Eliot followed up with a salvo of his own to Moore:

"I am very grateful to you for giving this matter your attention, but still I am regretful that the inscriptions now being carved were not previously checked by your Commission and improved as to form. They seem to be thoroughly bromidic and uninteresting—a lost opportunity."

Eliot had a point. The Commerce Department inscriptions seem lecturing rather than inspirational, long and sour rather than short and sweet. Moore must have forgotten that he once wrote: "Inscriptions are an art in themselves. They should be monumental and express in few words a great sentiment."

Still, there can be poetry in even the longest of inscriptions. Consider this moving sentiment, carved on the hemicycle of the Post Office Department building, facing 14th Street:

*The Post Office Department, in its ceaseless labors, pervades every channel of commerce and every theatre of human enterprise, and while visiting as it does kindly, every fireside, mingles with the throbbings of almost every heart in the land. In the amplitude of its beneficence, it ministers to all climes, and creeds, and pursuits, with the same eager readiness and with equal fullness of fidelity. It is the delicate ear trump through which alike nations and families and isolated individuals whisper their joys and their sorrows, their convictions and their sympathies to all who listen for their coming.*

What is it about the Post Office that inspires the most poignant inscriptions? And to whom do we talk about getting "ear trump" back into common usage?

Any classical education should include the Greeks, of course, and Washington is lucky enough to offer a textbook not far from the Triangle. The National Academy of Sciences, on Constitution Avenue between 21st and 22nd streets, has along its parapet an inscription not only from a famous Greek philosopher—Aristotle, from his *Metaphysics*—but written in that ancient tongue as well. Translated, it reads:

*The search for Truth is in one way hard and in another easy. For it is evident that no one can master it fully nor miss it wholly. But each adds a little to our knowledge of Nature, and from all the facts assembled there arises a certain grandeur.*

---

## Oops . . .

What do you do if you're a stone carver and you make a mistake? After all, the expression "carved in stone" isn't much good if fixing a typo on a chunk of marble is as easy as depressing the backspace key.

Ann Hawkins: "If I got a chip, there are epoxy resins I could apply. . . . It's very rare to make a mistake, unless you do something stupid."

On big projects, boo-boos can be lopped out entirely, the offending block of stone cut out and replaced with a "dutchman," a fresh piece that's inserted like a patch and—hopefully—carved correctly.

There's no dutchman in what is perhaps the most obvious mistake in a Washington inscription. Inscribed in three sections on the north wall of the Lincoln Memorial is Abraham Lincoln's second Inaugural address. Twenty lines down in the first block of words is a phrase that concludes: "WITH HIGH HOPES FOR THE EUTURE." The poor stone carver added an extra stroke to the *F*, transforming it into an *E*. Because the inscription is inside—away from the rays of the sun and the shadows they provide—it would be virtually unreadable if the insides of the letters weren't painted black. And so, the bottom stroke of the *E* was left unpainted, making the best of a bad situation.

## Back to the Stone Age

The capital's official buildings, monuments, and memorials urge us in various ways to remember the past or strive toward a more perfect future. None of the blank verse, mottoes, or maxims, though, are as moving as what appears on a *V*-shape set of black granite panels set into the ground near the Lincoln Memorial. The inscription isn't made up of words at all, but it's as moving as any sonnet.

Etched into the stone of the Vietnam Veterans Memorial are the names of the more than 58,000 Americans killed in that war. The names weren't carved high atop a pediment out of reach but were sandblasted delicately into the wall. Washington's other inscriptions might be meant to provide edification from a distance, but this memorial is designed to be touched, its inscriptions traced with unsteady fingers. And behind the names we see ourselves, reflected in the stone as true as any mirror.

Which leads us to the state of stone carving in Washington today. Most newer buildings in Washington aren't graced with inscriptions. While a building named after a famous American might once have warranted an inscribed quotation from that person, today we have the James Forrestal Federal Building and the William McChesney Martin, Jr. Federal Reserve Board Building with nary a peep from either gentleman.

Gone, too, is the specially commissioned aphorism meant to enlighten or fire. Inscriptions like those on the Justice and Commerce department buildings—whether you consider them quaint optimism or naive bluster—are in short supply these days.

Two new projects that would seem to cry out for inscriptions of the inspirational kind are a judicial office building going up near Union Station and an international trade and cultural center planned for Federal Triangle. But, alas, there are no plans as yet for any heroic inscriptions.

And there probably won't be. After all, the 1990s aren't like the 1930s, the period of Washington's big inscription boom. This is supposed to be the time of little, quiet government, not big, loud government. Why should government buildings assault the eyes of pedestrians and motorists with jingoistic slogans and propagandist mottoes? Shouldn't the feds just get out of our hair?

Perhaps, but somehow when we were willing to not only stand behind our words but carve them immutably into the living stone, it suggested we believed in them a little more, thought them worth remembering, no matter how self-evident or self-aggrandizing they seemed.

We don't seem to do much of that anymore. Maybe it's time to read the writing on the walls.

# The Federal Government: How Our System Works

*By Betty Ross*

*A longtime resident of the nation's capital, Betty Ross is the author of* A Museum Guide to Washington, D.C., *and* How to Beat the High Cost of Travel *and has contributed to numerous newspapers and magazines.*

**N**ew York may be the fashion capital of the United States and Los Angeles the center of entertainment, but government—and power—is the name of the game in Washington.

The federal government is a major employer, an important landlord, and a source of contracts, contacts, or conversation for Washingtonians. It is a patron of the arts and a provider for the needy. To some, pervasive government is what's wrong with Washington. To others—particularly the party in power—it's what's right.

The federal government occupies some of the choicest real estate in town, yet pays no taxes to the District of Columbia. On the other hand, although citizens of the District *do* pay taxes, they could not vote until some 20 years ago. This has changed; now they can help elect the president, but still they have only a nonvoting delegate in Congress.

In Washington, the "separation of powers" doctrine becomes more than just a phrase in the Constitution. A visit here gives you a chance to see the legislative, executive, and judicial branches of government in action, to see how the system of checks and balances works. As Boswell put it, you have an opportunity, "instead of thinking how things may be, to see them as they are."

## The Legislative Branch

In Pierre L'Enfant's 18th-century plan for the city of Washington, the U.S. Capitol and the White House were just far enough away from each other on Pennsylvania Avenue to emphasize the separation of powers between the legislative and executive branches. L'Enfant chose Jenkins Hill as the site for the Capitol; it is the focal point of an area now called Capitol Hill.

Guided tours of the Capitol leave from the Rotunda almost continuously from 9 AM to 3:30 PM daily throughout the year. The Senate side of the Capitol faces Constitution Avenue, while the House side can be approached from Independence Avenue.

Drop by the office of your senator or representative to pick up passes to the Visitors Galleries. Without a pass, you are not permitted to watch the proceedings. There are two Senate office buildings at First and Constitution Avenue NE, named, respectively, for former senators Everett Dirksen and Richard Russell. A third, honoring Senator Philip A. Hart, opened in November 1982 at Second and Constitution NE.

The House office buildings, named for former Speakers Joseph Cannon, Nicholas Longworth, and Sam Rayburn, are located in that order along Independence Avenue between First Street SE, and First Street SW. It is generally agreed by residents and visitors alike that the Rayburn Building is the least attractive and, at $75 million, one of the most expensive structures in the city.

According to the Constitution, "the Congress shall assemble at least once in every year, and such meeting shall begin at noon on the 3rd day of January, unless they shall by law appoint a different day." In the years before air-conditioning, Congress usually recessed during the summer and reconvened in the fall. Today, however, with congressional calendars more crowded and air-conditioning commonplace, sessions frequently last much longer. It is not unusual for the House and/or Senate to sit through the summer and well into the fall.

Congressional sessions usually begin at noon; committee meetings are generally held in the morning. Check the *Washington Post*'s "Today in Congress" listings to find out what is going on.

Don't be surprised to see only a handful of senators or members of Congress on the floor during a session. Much Congressional business dealing with constituent problems is done in committees or in offices. When a vote is taken during a session, bells are rung to summon absent members to the floor.

To save time, many senators and members of Congress make the brief trip between their offices and the Capitol on the congressional subway. Visitors may ride, too. The Senate restaurant in the Capitol—famed for its bean soup—is open to the public at all times. Cafeterias in the Rayburn, Longworth, and Dirksen office buildings are also open to visitors. Watch the hours, however. From 11:30 AM to 1:15 PM, only members of Congress and their staffs are admitted.

There are two senators from each state, who are elected for six-year terms at an annual salary of $101,900 each.

The 435 members of the House serve for two years and receive $125,100 per year.

## How a Bill Becomes Law

Legislation is a complicated, time-consuming process. Here, briefly, is the usual legislative procedure in the House of Representatives.

- A bill is introduced by a member, who places it in the "hopper," a box on the clerk's desk. It is numbered (H.R. . . . ), sent to the Government Printing Office, and made available the next morning in the House Document Room.
- It is referred to a committee.
- The committee reports on the bill, usually after holding a hearing, either before the full committee or before a subcommittee.
- The bill is placed on the House calendar.
- Any bill that involves the Treasury is considered by the House sitting as a Committee of the Whole. In that case, the Speaker appoints a chairman who presides and there is a period of general debate, followed by a reading for amendment, with speeches limited to five minutes.
- A bill is given a second reading and consideration in the House. (Bills considered in Committee of the Whole, however, receive a second reading in committee.) Amendments may be added after the second reading.
- It is given a third reading, which is by title only. The Speaker puts the question to a vote and it may be defeated at this stage by a negative vote.
- If it passes, however, it is sent to the Senate.
- The Senate considers the bill, usually after it has been referred to a committee and reported favorably by that committee.
- If the Senate rejects the House bill, it notifies the House. Otherwise, the bill is returned to the House from the Senate, with or without amendments.
- The House considers the Senate amendments.
- Differences between House and Senate versions of a bill are resolved by a joint House-Senate conference committee.
- The bill is printed in final form or "enrolled" on parchment paper.
- It is proofread by the enrolling clerk, who certifies its correctness.
- Once certified, the bill is signed, first by the Speaker of the House and then by the president of the Senate.

- It is sent to the president of the United States.
- The president approves or disapproves the bill, usually after referring it to the appropriate department for recommendations.
- If the president vetoes the bill, it is returned to the Congress. If it fails to pass by a two-thirds vote, no further action is taken.
- If the bill has either been approved by the president or passed over a veto, it is filed with the secretary of state and then becomes law.

Such a brief summary cannot possibly convey the intrigue, the drama, and the behind-the-scenes maneuvering by members, their staffs, and lobbyists involved in the legislative process. Often the stakes are high and the battles hard fought. If you are lucky, you may be able to watch an important debate or a newsworthy vote during your visit to Capitol Hill.

## The Executive Branch

The White House is at 1600 Pennsylvania Avenue NW, the most prestigious address in the country. However, its first occupant, Abigail Adams, was disappointed in the damp, drafty "President's Palace." She complained that it had "not a single apartment finished" and "not the least fence, yard, or other convenience without." On the other hand, Thomas Jefferson found the house "big enough for two emperors, one Pope, and the grand lama"—and still unfinished.

When Franklin Delano Roosevelt became president in 1932, the entire White House staff consisted of fewer than 50 people. Today, approximately 1,800 people work for the executive office of the president. They are crammed into offices in the east and west wings of the White House and in the ornate Executive Office Building (formerly the State, War and Navy Building), adjacent to the White House to the west on Pennsylvania Avenue.

The president's annual salary is $200,000; the vice president receives $160,600. They are elected for a four-year term. If the president dies or becomes incapacitated, the vice president is next in line of succession. He is followed, in order, by the Speaker of the House of Representatives, the president pro tempore of the Senate, the secretaries of state, treasury, and defense, the attorney general, the postmaster general, and the secretaries of the interior, agriculture, commerce, labor, health and human services, housing and urban development, transportation, energy, education, and veterans affairs.

## The Judicial Branch

Traditionally, the opening session of the Supreme Court, on the first Monday in October, marks the beginning of Washington's social season, and the quadrennial inaugural festivities add to the excitement. The inaugural week in January usually includes a star-studded gala, as well as receptions honoring the new president, vice president, and their wives.

The Supreme Court meets from October through June in a Corinthian-columned white-marble building at First Street and Maryland Avenue NE. Until 1935, the justices used various rooms in the Capitol. For a while, in the 19th century, they met in taverns, boardinghouses, and at the home of the Clerk of the Court, Elias Boudinot Caldwell, at Second and A streets SE. You can see the Old Supreme Court Chamber on the ground floor of the Capitol.

Approximately 5,000 cases are submitted for appeal each year and the justices choose about 3%—roughly 160 cases in all—those which raise constitutional questions or affect the life or liberty of citizens.

Justice Felix Frankfurter said, "The words of the Constitution are so unrestricted by their intrinsic meaning or by their history or by tradition or by prior decisions that they leave the individual Justice free, if indeed they do not compel him, to gather meaning not from reading the Constitution but from reading life."

In the courtroom, the nine black-robed justices are seated in high-backed black leather chairs in front of heavy red velvet draperies. Lawyers for each side present their oral arguments, with the justices often interjecting questions or comments. Generally, the court sits for two weeks and then recesses for two weeks to do research and write opinions.

They are on the bench Monday, Tuesday, and Wednesday from 10 AM to noon and from 1 to 3 PM from October through April and they usually hear about four cases a day. During this first part of the term, the justices meet privately every Wednesday afternoon and all day Friday to discuss the cases they have heard that week and to take a preliminary vote on decisions.

The chief justice assigns different members to write the opinions. If he is on the minority side in a particular case, however, the senior justice in the majority assigns the opinion. Any justice may write his or her own opinion, agreeing or disagreeing with the majority. During the remainder of the term, in May and June, the justices usually meet every Thursday to decide on releasing their opinions.

Monday is "Decision Day," probably the most interesting time to visit the Supreme Court. That is when the justices announce their decisions and read their opinions.

Throughout the year, in the courtroom, staff members give a brief lecture about the court Monday through Friday, every half-hour from 9:30 AM to 4:30 PM. Lectures are not given on holidays or when the justices are on the bench hearing cases. In addition to exhibits about the Supreme Court and its justices, the court boasts one of the best government cafeterias in town—second only to those at the National Gallery of Art. It is open to the public.

Supreme Court justices are appointed by the president with the advice and consent of the Senate. They serve for life or, as the Constitution says, "during good behavior."

Associate justices receive $153,600 per year; the chief justice's salary is $160,600. After ten years of service, justices may resign or retire with full pay.

Veteran court-watcher Anthony Lewis called the Supreme Court a "symbol of continuity, instrument of change," and added that "no more remarkable institution of government exists than the Supreme Court of the United States."

## Lobbyists

Virtually every special-interest group in the country, as well as a sprinkling of foreign governments, is represented by someone who "lobbies" for its cause in Washington. Lobbyists frequently conduct their business over luncheons, cocktails, and dinners, as well as on the golf courses or tennis courts of suburban country clubs. Power is the magnet that draws them to the nation's capital.

Lobbyists' backgrounds are as diverse as the causes they represent. They are usually lawyers, public relations executives, or former congressional staff members. Many were once members of Congress or high government officials from all over the U.S. who have developed "Potomac fever," that is, they do not return home but find being a Washington representative the ideal way to continue to influence public policy.

Sometimes, it appears that every group is well represented here except the average citizen. Under those circumstances, if you have a pet project, discuss it with your senator or member of Congress—he or she is your lobbyist. In doing so—like Washington's highly skilled and well-paid lobbyists—you would simply be exercising your First Amendment rights to express your beliefs and influence your government.

# 3 Exploring Washington

*By John F. Kelly* The Byzantine workings of the federal government; the nonsensical, sound-bite-ready oratory of the well-groomed politician; murky foreign policy pronouncements issued from Foggy Bottom; and $600 toilet seats ordered by the Pentagon cause many Americans to cast a skeptical eye on anything that happens "inside the Beltway." Washingtonians take it all in stride, though, reminding themselves that, after all, those responsible for political hijinks don't come *from* Washington, they come *to* Washington. Besides, such ribbing is a small price to pay for living in a city whose charms extend far beyond the bureaucratic. World-class museums and art galleries (nearly all of them free), tree-shaded and flower-filled parks and gardens, bars and restaurants that benefit from a large and creative immigrant community, and nightlife that seems to get better with every passing year are as much a part of Washington as floor debates or filibusters.

The location of the city that calls to mind politicking, back scratching, and delicate diplomacy is itself the result of a compromise. Tired of its nomadic existence after having set up shop in eight different locations, Congress voted in 1785 to establish a permanent "Federal town." Northern lawmakers wanted the capital on the Delaware River, in the north, southerners wanted it on the Potomac, in the south. A deal was struck when Virginia's Thomas Jefferson agreed to support the proposal that the federal government assume the war debts of the colonies if New York's Alexander Hamilton and other northern legislators would agree to locate the capital on the banks of the Potomac. George Washington himself selected the exact site of the capital, a diamond-shaped, 100-square-mile plot that encompassed the confluence of the Potomac and Anacostia rivers, not far from the president's estate at Mount Vernon. To give the young city a bit of a head start, Washington included the already thriving tobacco ports of Alexandria, Virginia, and Georgetown, Maryland, in the District of Columbia.

Charles Pierre L'Enfant, a young French engineer who had fought in the Revolution, offered his services in creating a capital "magnificent enough to grace a great nation." His 1791 plan owes much to Versailles, with ceremonial circles and squares, a grid pattern of streets, and broad, diagonal avenues. It was these grand streets that sparked the first debates over L'Enfant's design and its execution. The families that owned the estates and tobacco farms that would be transformed into Washington had agreed to sell the sites needed for public buildings at $66.66 an acre, with the understanding that profits could be made by selling the remaining land to those who wanted to be near the federal government. They also agreed to turn over for free the land to be used for streets and highways. When they discovered that L'Enfant's streets were 100 feet wide and that one thoroughfare—the Mall—would be 400 feet across, they were horrified. Half the land on the site would be turned over to the government for free for roads.

L'Enfant won the battle of the roads but he couldn't control his obstinate ways and fought often with the three city commissioners Washington had appointed. When the nephew of one of the commissioners started to build a manor house where L'Enfant had planned a street, the Frenchman ordered it torn down. The overzealous L'Enfant was fired and offered $2,500 and a lot near the White House in pay. He refused, thinking it poor compensation for the services he had performed. (A visionary who was a little too headstrong for his own good, L'Enfant spent his later years petitioning Congress with long, rambling missives demanding satisfaction. He died penniless in 1825.)

L'Enfant had written that his plan would "leave room for that aggrandizement and embellishment which the increase in the wealth of the nation will permit it to pursue at any period, however remote." At times it must have seemed remote indeed, for the town grew so slowly that when Charles Dickens visited Washington in 1842 what he saw were "spacious avenues that begin in nothing and lead nowhere; streets a mile long that only want houses, roads, and inhabitants; public buildings that need but a public to be complete and ornaments of great thoroughfares which need only great thoroughfares to ornament."

It took the Civil War—and every war thereafter—to energize the city, by attracting thousands of new residents and spurring building booms that extended the capital in all directions. Streets in the once-backward town were paved in the 1870s and the first streetcars ran in the 1880s. Memorials to famous Americans like Lincoln and Jefferson were built in the first decades of the 20th century, along with the massive Federal Triangle, a monument to thousands of less-famous government workers.

Despite the growth and despite the fact that blacks have always played an important role in the city's history (black mathematician Benjamin Banneker surveyed the

# Exploring Washington, D.C. *(Boxes Refer to Detail Maps)*

Tour 9

To
Tour 10

Tour 7

Tour 6

Massachusetts Ave.

Columbia Rd.

18th St.

California St.

T St.

S St.

R St.

S St.

Decatur Pl.

R St.

Florida Ave.

S St.

New Hampshire Ave.

Corcora

Sheridan
Circle

Massachusetts Ave.

Q St.

Dupont
Circle

Church St.

P St.

17th St.

32nd St.

31st St.

Wisconsin Ave.

R St.

Q St.

22nd St.

21st St.

20th St.

19th St.

Connecticut Ave.

N St.

P St.

O St.

28th St.

27th St.

29th St.

N St.

Rock Creek

O St.

M St.

30th St.

31st St.

C&O Canal

M St.

M St.

New Hampshire Ave.

M St.

M St.

Whitehurst Fwy.

26th St.

25th St.

L St.

Washington
Circle

L St.

K St.

Francis Scott Key Bridge

29

Pennsylvania Ave.

Theodore
Roosevelt
Island

24th St.

23rd St.

22nd St.

G St.

F St.

Virginia Ave.

E St.

George Washington Memorial Pkwy.

17th St.

D St.

C St.

Constitution Ave.

Tour 3

Tour 8

50

NW

SW

50

Lincoln
Memorial

Reflecting Pool

George Washington Memorial Pkwy.

Arlington Memorial
Bridge

Independence Ave.

Ohio Dr.

West

Kutz
Bridge

Memorial Dr.

Ladybird Johnson Park

Columbia
Island

W. Basin Dr.

Potomac
Park

Tidal Bas

Potomac River

ARLINGTON
NATIONAL
CEMETERY

Tour 11

V I R G I N I A

To
Tour 12

land with Pierre L'Enfant in the 18th century), Washington today remains essentially segregated. Whites— who account for about 30% of the population—reside mostly in northwest Washington. Blacks live largely east of Rock Creek Park and south of the Anacostia River.

It's a city of other unfortunate contrasts: Citizens of the capital of the free world couldn't vote in a presidential election until 1964, weren't granted limited home rule until 1974, and are represented in Congress by a single nonvoting delegate (though in 1990 residents elected two "shadow" senators, one of whom is political gadfly Jesse Jackson). Homeless people sleep on steam grates next to multimillion-dollar government buildings, and a flourishing drug trade has earned Washington the dubious distinction of murder capital of the United States. Though it's little consolation to those affected, most crime is restricted to neighborhoods far from the areas visited by tourists.

Still, there's no denying that Washington, the world's first planned capital city, is also one of its most beautiful. And though the federal government dominates the city psychologically as much as the Washington Monument dominates it physically, there are parts of the capital where you can leave politics behind. The tours that follow will take you through the monumental city, the governmental city, and the residential city. As you walk, look for evidence of L'Enfant's hand, still present despite growing pains and frequent deviations from his plan. His Washington was to be a city of vistas—pleasant views that would shift and change from block to block, a marriage of geometry and art. It remains this way today. Like its main industry, politics, Washington's design is a constantly changing kaleidoscope that invites contemplation from all angles.

Admission is free to the attractions below, except where noted.

## Tour 1: The Mall

*Numbers in the margin correspond to points of interest on the Tour 1: The Mall map.*

The Mall is the heart of nearly every visitor's trip to Washington. With nine diverse museums ringing the expanse of green, it's the closest thing the capital has to a theme park (unless you count the federal government itself, which has uncharitably been called "Disneyland on the Potomac"). As at a theme park, you may have to stand in an occasional line, but unlike the amusements at Disneyland almost everything you'll see here is free.

Don't expect to see it all in one day, though. The holdings of the museums and art galleries of the Smithsonian Institution—the largest museum complex in the world—total more than 135 million objects. Only 1% are on public display at any one time, but that's still over a million different objects vying for your attention. If you can, devote at least two days to the Mall. Do the north side one day and the south the next. Or split your sightseeing on the Mall into museums the first day, art galleries the second. Of course, the Mall is more than just a front yard for all these museums. It's a picnicking park and a jogging path, an outdoor stage for festivals and fireworks, and America's town green.

The Mall is bounded on the north and south by Constitution and Independence avenues, and on the east and west by 3rd and 14th streets. Nearly all of the Smithsonian museums lie within these boundaries. (Nearest Metro stop, Smithsonian or Archives).

The best place to start an exploration of the museums on the Mall is in front of the first one constructed, the ❶ **Smithsonian Institution Building.** British scientist and founder James Smithson had never visited America. Yet his will stipulated that, should his nephew, Henry James Hungerford, die without an heir, Smithson's entire fortune would go to the United States, "to found at Washington, under the name of the Smithsonian Institution, an establishment for the increase and diffusion of knowledge among men."

Smithson died in 1829, Hungerford in 1835, and in 1838 the United States received $515,169 worth of gold sovereigns. After eight years of congressional debate over the propriety of accepting funds from a private citizen, the Smithsonian Institution was finally established in 1846. The red sandstone, Norman-style headquarters building on Jefferson Drive was completed in 1855 and originally housed all of the Smithsonian's operations, including the science and art collections, research laboratories, and living quarters for the Institution's secretary and his family. Known as "the Castle," the building was designed by James Renwick, the architect of St. Patrick's Cathedral in New York City. The statue in front of the Castle's entrance is not of Smithson but of Joseph Henry, the scientist who served as the Institution's first secretary. Smithson's body was brought to

**Tour 1: The Mall**

Arthur M. Sackler
Gallery, **13**
Arts and Industries
Building, **2**
Bureau of Engraving
and Printing, **10**
Department of
Agriculture, **11**

Freer Gallery
of Art, **12**
Hirshhorn Museum
and Sculpture
Garden, **3**
National Air and
Space Museum, **4**
National Gallery of
Art, East Building, **6**

National Gallery of
Art, West Building, **5**
National Museum of
African Art, **14**
National Museum of
American History, **8**
National Museum of
Natural History, **7**

Smithsonian
Institution Building, **1**
United States
Holocaust Memorial
Museum, **9**

America in 1904 and is entombed in a small room to the left of the Castle's Mall entrance.

Today the Castle houses Smithsonian administrative offices and is home to the Woodrow Wilson International School for Scholars. To get your bearings or to get help deciding which Mall attractions you want to devote your time to, visit the **Smithsonian Information Center** in the Castle. An orientation film provides an overview of the various Smithsonian museums, and monitors display information on the day's events. The Information Center opens at 9 AM, an hour before the other museums open, so you can plan your day on the Mall without wasting valuable sightseeing time. *1000 Jefferson Dr. SW, tel. 202/357-2700. Open daily 9-5:30; closed Dec. 25.*

To the right of the Castle is the pagoda-like entrance to the **S. Dillon Ripley Center,** an underground collection of classrooms and offices named after a past Smithsonian secretary. Works from around the world are periodically shown in the center's International Gallery.

This tour circles the Mall counterclockwise. Start by walking east on Jefferson Drive to the **Arts and Industries Building,** the second Smithsonian museum to be constructed. In 1876 Philadelphia hosted the United States International Exposition in honor of the nation's Centennial. After the festivities, scores of exhibitors donated their displays to the federal government. In order to house the objects that had suddenly come its way, the Smithsonian commissioned this redbrick and sandstone building. Designed by Adolph Cluss, the building was originally called the United States National Museum, the name that is still engraved in stone above the doorway. It was finished in 1881, just in time to host President James Garfield's inaugural ball.

The Arts and Industries Building housed a variety of artifacts that were eventually moved to other museums as the Smithsonian grew. It was restored to its original appearance and reopened during Bicentennial celebrations in 1976. Today the museum exhibits an extensive collection of American Victoriana; many of the objects on display—which include carriages, tools, furnishings, printing presses, even a steam locomotive—are from the original Philadelphia Centennial. In 1991 the Smithsonian opened the Experimental Gallery in the south quadrant of the Arts and Industries Building. The gallery is a laboratory that allows museum curators to experiment not so much with *what* should be displayed but *how* to display it. To that end, the Experimental Gallery has hosted some unconventional exhibits. One controversial offering exploring homelessness had visitors enter the exhibit by sliding through a morgue drawer. *900 Jefferson Dr. SW, tel. 202/357–2700. Open daily 10–5:30; closed Dec. 25.*

In front of the Arts and Industries Building is a **carousel** that is popular with young and old alike. In warmer months it operates between 10 and 5:30 (75¢ a ride).

**❸** The **Hirshhorn Museum** is the next building to the east on Jefferson Drive, and you would be hard pressed to find a piece of architecture that contrasts more with the gay Victoriana of the Arts and Industries Building. Dubbed "the Doughnut on the Mall," the reinforced-concrete building designed by Gordon Bunshaft is a fitting home for contemporary art. Opened in 1974, the museum manages a collection that includes 4,000 paintings and drawings and 2,000 sculptures donated by Joseph H. Hirshhorn, a Latvian-born immigrant who made his fortune in this country running uranium mines. American artists such as Eakins, Pollock, Rothko, and Stella are represented, as are modern European and Latin masters, including Francis Bacon, Fernando Botero, Magritte, Miró, and Victor Vasarely.

The Hirshhorn's impressive sculpture collection is arranged in the open spaces between the museum's concrete piers and across Jefferson Drive in the sunken **Sculpture Garden**. The display in the Sculpture Garden includes one of the largest public American collections of works by Henry Moore, as well as works by Henri Daumier, Max Ernst, Alberto Giacometti, Pablo Picasso, and Man Ray. Auguste Rodin's *The Burghers of Calais* is a highlight. The largest piece in the Hirshhorn's collection is the 42-foot-high, 30-ton *Isis* by Mark di Suvero, which looks like a beached ship. Not surprisingly, the materials for this work were donated by the Institute of Scrap Iron and Steel, Inc. For those interested in wearable art, there is an assortment of contemporary jewelry and clothing in the museum's gift shop. *Independence Ave. at 7th St. SW, tel. 202/357–2700. Open daily 10–5:30; closed Dec. 25. Sculpture garden open daily 7:30–dusk.*

**❹** Cross 7th Street to get to the **National Air and Space Museum.** Opened in 1976, Air and Space is the most visited museum in the world, attracting 12 million people each year. (It's thought to be the single most-visited building on earth.) Twenty-three galleries tell the story of aviation, from man's earliest attempts at flight. Suspended from the ceiling like plastic models in a child's room are dozens of aircraft, including the actual "Wright Flyer" that Wilbur Wright piloted over the sands of Kitty Hawk, North Carolina; Charles Lindbergh's "Spirit of St. Louis"; the X-1 rocket plane in which Chuck Yeager broke the sound barrier; and the X-15, the fastest plane ever built.

Other highlights include a back-up model of the Skylab orbital workshop that visitors can walk through; the Voyager airplane that Dick Rutan and Jeana Yeager flew nonstop around the world; and the USS *Enterprise* model used in the "Star Trek" TV show. Visitors can also touch a piece of the moon: a 4-billion-year-old slice of rock collected by Apollo 17 astronauts. (Moon rock is one of the rarest substances on earth and, soon after the museum opened, a few zealous tourists tried to add the rock to their collections. The display is now wired with a motion alarm and watched by a uniformed guard.)

Don't let long lines deter you from seeing a show in the museum's **Langley Theater.** IMAX films shown on the five-story-high screen—including *The Dream is Alive*, *To Fly!*, and *The Blue Planet*—usually feature swooping aerial scenes that will convince you you've left the ground. Buy your tickets ($2.75 for adults; $1.75 for children, students, and senior citizens; sometimes higher for special films) as soon as you arrive, then look around the museum. (Or, if you prefer, you can buy tickets up to two weeks in advance.) Upstairs, the **Albert Einstein Planetarium** projects images of celestial bodies on a domed ceiling. *Jefferson Dr. at 6th St. SW, tel. 202/ 357-2700. Open daily 10-5:30; closed Dec. 25. Extended summer hrs determined annually. Specially priced double features are often shown in the Langley Theater after the museum has closed. For information, call 202/ 357-1686.*

---

**Time Out**  Two restaurants are located at the eastern end of the National Air and Space Museum: **The Wright Place** is a table-service restaurant that takes reservations (tel. 202/371-8777); the **Flight Line** is a self-service cafeteria. They each have a large selection of foods, but at peak times lines can be long.

---

After touring the Air and Space Museum, walk east on Jefferson Drive toward the Capitol. What has been called the last open space left for a museum on the periphery of the Mall is bounded by 3rd and 4th streets and Independence Avenue and Jefferson Drive SW. The

Smithsonian's **National Museum of the American Indian** is scheduled to open here in 1998.

To get to the museums on the north side of the Mall, walk north on 4th or 3rd Street. As you walk, look to the left for a good view of the Mall. Notice how the Castle projects slightly into the green rectangle. When it was built, in 1855, Pierre L'Enfant's plan for Washington had been all but forgotten. In this space west of the "Congress House," the Frenchman had envisioned a "Grand Avenue, 400 feet in breadth, and about a mile in length, bordered with gardens, ending in a slope from the houses on each side." In the middle of the 19th century, horticulturalist Andrew Jackson Downing took a stab at converting the Mall into a large, English-style garden, with carriageways curving through groves of trees and bushes. This was far from the "vast esplanade" L'Enfant had in mind, and by the dawn of the 20th century the Mall had become an eyesore. It was dotted with sheds and bisected by railroad tracks. There was even a railroad station at its eastern end.

In 1900 Senator James McMillan, chairman of the Committee on the District of Columbia, asked a distinguished group of architects and artists to study ways of improving Washington's park system. The McMillan Commission, which included architects Daniel Burnham and Charles McKim, landscape architect Frederick Law Olmsted, Jr., and sculptor Augustus Saint-Gaudens, didn't confine its recommendations just to parks; its 1902 report would shape the way the capital looked for decades. The Mall received much of the group's attention and is its most stunning accomplishment. L'Enfant's plan was rediscovered, the sheds, railroad tracks, and carriageways were removed, and Washington finally had the monumental core it had been denied for so long.

Cross Madison Drive to get to the two buildings of the ❺ **National Gallery of Art,** one of the world's foremost collections of paintings, sculptures, and graphics. If you want to view the museum's holdings in (more or less) chronological order, it's best to start your exploration of this magnificent gallery in the **West Building.** Opened in 1941, the domed building was a gift to the nation from financier Andrew Mellon. (The dome was one of architect John Russell Pope's favorite devices. He designed the domed Jefferson Memorial and, though it's difficult to see from outside, there's a dome on his National Archives, too.)

A wealthy banker and oilman, Andrew Mellon served as secretary of the treasury under three presidents and as ambassador to the United Kingdom. He first came to Washington in 1921, and lived for many years in a luxurious apartment near Dupont Circle, in a building that today houses the National Trust for Historic Preservation (*see* Tour 7: Dupont Circle, *below*). Mellon had long collected great works of art, acquiring them on his frequent trips to Europe. In 1931, when the Soviet government was short on cash and selling off many of its art treasures, Mellon stepped in and bought $6 million worth of Old Masters, including *The Alba Madonna* by Raphael and Botticelli's *Adoration of the Magi.* Mellon promised his collection to America in 1937, the year of his death. He also donated the funds for the construction of the huge gallery and resisted suggestions it be named after him.

The West Building's **Great Rotunda,** with its 16 marble columns surrounding a fountain topped with a statue of Mercury, sets the stage for the masterpieces on display in the more than 100 separate galleries. You'll probably want to wander the rooms at your own pace, taking in the wealth of art. A tape-recorded tour of the building's better-known holdings is available for a $3.50 rental fee ($3 for senior citizens) at the ground floor sales area. If you'd rather explore on your own, get a map at one of the two information desks; one is just inside the Mall entrance (off of Madison Drive), the other is near the Constitution Avenue entrance on the ground floor.

The National Gallery's permanent collection includes works from the 13th to the 20th century. A comprehensive survey of Italian paintings and sculpture includes *The Adoration of the Magi* by Fra Angelico and Fra Filippo Lippi and *Ginevra de'Benci*, the only painting by da Vinci outside of Europe. Flemish and Dutch works, displayed in a series of attractive panelled rooms, include *Daniel in the Lions' Den,* by Rubens, and a self-portrait by Rembrandt. The Chester Dale Collection comprises works by Impressionist painters such as Degas, Monet, Renoir, and Mary Cassatt.

**❻** To get to the **National Gallery of Art's East Building** you can take a moving walkway that travels below ground between the two buildings. But to appreciate architect I. M. Pei's impressive, angular East Building, enter it from outside rather than from underground. Exit the West Building through its eastern doors, and cross 4th Street. (As you cross, look to the north: Seeming to float above the Doric columns and pediment of the D.C. Superior Court is the green roof and redbrick pediment of the Pension Building, four blocks away.)

The East Building opened in 1978 in response to the changing needs of the National Gallery. The awkward trapezoidal shape of the building site, which had been taken up by tennis courts and rose bushes planted during Lady Bird Johnson's spruce-up campaign, prompted Pei's dramatic approach: Two interlocking spaces shaped like triangles provide room for galleries, auditoriums, and administrative offices. While the East Building's triangles contrast sharply with the symmetrical classical facade and gentle dome of the West Building, both buildings are constructed of pink marble from the same Tennessee quarries. Despite its severe angularity, Pei's building is inviting. The axe-blade-like southwest corner has been darkened and polished smooth by thousands of hands irresistibly drawn to it.

The atrium of the East Building is dominated by two massive works of art: Alexander Calder's mobile, *Untitled* (recently refurbished to make it rotate more easily), and *Woman*, a huge wall-hanging by Joan Miró. The galleries here generally display modern art, though the East Building serves as a home for major temporary exhibitions that span years and artistic styles. *Madison Dr. and 4th St. NW, tel. 202/737–4215. Open Mon.–Sat. 10–5, Sun. 11–6; closed Dec. 25. Extended summer hrs determined annually.*

---

**Time Out** Two restaurants on the concourse level between the East and West buildings of the National Gallery offer bleary-eyed and foot-sore museum goers the chance to recharge. The **buffet** serves a wide variety of soups, sandwiches, salads, hot entrees, and desserts. The **Cascade Cafe** has a smaller selection, but customers enjoy the soothing effect of the gentle waterfall that splashes against the glass-covered wall.

---

Between 7th and 9th streets is the **National Sculpture Garden and Ice Rink** (tel. 202/371–5340). In the winter skates are rented out for use on the circular rink. Ice cream and other refreshments are available at the green building during the summer.

**❼** The **National Museum of Natural History** houses the majority of the Smithsonian's collection of objects, a total of some 118 million specimens. It was constructed in 1910, and two wings were added in the '60s. It is a museum's museum, filled with bones, fossils, stuffed animals, and other natural delights. Exhibits also explore the exploits of humans, the world's most adaptive inhabitants.

The first-floor hall under the rotunda is dominated by a stuffed, eight-ton, 13-foot African bull elephant, one of the largest specimens ever found. (The tusks are fiberglass; the original ivory ones were apparently far too heavy for the stuffed elephant to support.) Off to the right is the popular **Dinosaur Hall.** Fossilized skeletons on display range from a 90-foot-long diplodocus to a tiny thesalosaurus neglectus (a small dinosaur so named because its disconnected bones sat forgotten for years in a college drawer before being reassembled).

In the west wing are displays on birds, mammals, and sea life. Many of the preserved specimens are from the collection of animals bagged by Teddy Roosevelt on his trips to Africa. Not everything in the museum is dead, though. The sea-life display features a living coral reef, complete with fish, plants, and simulated waves. The halls north of the rotunda contain tools, clothing, and other artifacts from many cultures, including those of Native America and of Asia, the Pacific, and Africa. The Discovery Room, in the northwest corner, features elephant tusks, woolly-mammoth teeth, petrified wood, and hundreds of other natural-history objects that visitors can handle and examine.

The highlight of the second floor is the **mineral and gem collection.** Objects include the largest sapphire on public display in the country (the Logan Sapphire, 423 carats), the largest uncut diamond (the Oppenheimer Diamond, 253.7 carats), and, of course, the Hope Diamond, a blue gem found in India and reputed to carry a curse (though Smithsonian guides are quick to pooh-pooh this notion). The amazing gem collection is second in value only to the crown jewels of Great Britain.

Also on the second floor is the **Insect Zoo,** which is currently closed for renovation. It's scheduled to reopen in the fall of 1993 as the O. Orkin Insect Zoo in honor of the founder of the pest-control company, which—ironic as it may seem—donated funds for the renovation. Kids also love "Uncle Beazley," a life-size fiberglass model of a triceratops (dinosaur) that sits on the Mall directly across from the museum. *Madison Dr. between 9th and 12th Sts. NW, tel. 202/357–2700. Open daily 10–5:30; closed Dec. 25. Extended summer hrs determined annually.*

**8** The **National Museum of American History**—the next building to the west, toward the Washington Monument—explores America's cultural, political, technical, and scientific past. It opened in 1964 as the National Museum of History and Technology and was renamed in 1980. The incredible diversity of artifacts here helps the Smithsonian live up to its nickname as "the Nation's attic." This is the museum that displayed Muhammed Ali's boxing gloves, the Fonz's leather jacket, and the Bunkers' living room furniture from "All in the Family." Visitors can wander for hours on the museum's three floors. The exhibits on the first floor emphasize the history of science and technology and include such items as farm machines, antique automobiles, early phonographs, and a 280-ton steam locomotive. The second floor is devoted to U.S. social and political history and features an exhibit on everyday American life just after the Revolution. After a 4½-year conservation project the gowns of the First Ladies are on display again. This new permanent exhibit, "First Ladies: Political Role and Public Image," goes beyond fashion to explore the women behind the satin, lace, and brocade. The third floor has installations on ceramics, money, graphic arts, musical instruments, photography, and news reporting. The Smithsonian's ample philately collection is scheduled to move from here to a new postal museum on Capitol Hill in the summer of 1993.

Be sure to check out Horatio Greenough's statue of the first president (by the west-wing escalators on the second floor). Commissioned by Congress in 1832, the statue was intended to grace the Capitol Rotunda. It was there for only a short while, however, since the toga-clad likeness proved shocking to legislators who grumbled that it looked as if the father of our country had just emerged from a bath. The statue was first banished to the east grounds of the Capitol, then given to the Smithsonian in 1908. *Madison Ave. between 12th and 14th Sts. NW, tel. 202/357–2700. Open daily 10–5:30; closed Dec. 25. Extended summer hrs determined annually.*

To continue the loop of the Mall, head south on 14th Street. From here you'll be able to view the length of the Mall from its western end, this time seeing the Capitol from afar. Instead of turning east on Jefferson Drive, continue south on 14th Street. On the right you'll pass a turreted, castle-like structure called the **Auditor's Building**. Built in 1879, it was the first building dedicated exclusively to the work of printing America's money. It was renovated in 1991 and is now home to the Forest Service.

**9** Next door is the **United States Holocaust Memorial Museum**, scheduled to open in April 1993. It is an atypical museum, since it doesn't celebrate the best that humanity can achieve, but instead illustrates the worst. The museum tells the story of the 11 million Jews, Gypsies, Jehovah's Witnesses, homosexuals, political prisoners, and others killed by the Nazis between 1933 and 1945. The museum's presentation is as atypical as its subject matter: Upon arrival, each visitor punches his or her sex and age into a computer and is issued an "identity card" containing biographical information on a real person from the Holocaust. As visitors move through the museum, their cards are updated. The museum recounts the Holocaust in almost cinematic fashion, with documentary films, videotaped oral histories, and a collection that includes such items as a German freight car, used to transport Jews from Warsaw to the Treblinka death camp, and the Star of David patches that Jewish prisoners were made to wear. After this sobering experience, the adjacent **Hall of Remembrance** provides a space for quiet reflection. *200 Raoul Wallenberg Pl. SW (enter from either Raoul Wallenberg Pl. or 14th St. SW), tel. 202/653–9220. Open daily 10–5:30.*

**10** In 1914 the country's money-making operation moved from the Auditor's Building to the **Bureau of Engraving and Printing.** All the paper currency in the United States, as well as stamps, military certificates, and presidential invitations, is printed in this huge building. Despite the fact that there are no free samples, the 20-minute, self-guided tour of the Bureau—which takes visitors past presses that turn out some $40 million a day—is one of the city's most popular. *14th and C Sts. SW, tel. 202/447–0193. Open weekdays 9–2; closed Dec. 25.*

**11** Return to 14th Street and turn east onto Independence Avenue. Continuing down Independence Avenue back toward the Capitol, you'll walk between the two buildings of the **Department of Agriculture.** The older building on your left was started in 1905 and was the first building to be constructed by order of the McMillan Commission on the south side of the Mall. The cornices on the north side of this white-marble building feature depictions of forests and of grains, flowers, and fruits—some of the plants the department keeps an eye on. The newer building south of Independence Avenue, to your right, covers three city blocks (an example, perhaps, of big government).

A few steps farther up Independence Avenue, across ⑫ 12th Street, is the **Freer Gallery of Art,** a gift from Detroit industrialist Charles L. Freer, who retired in 1900 and devoted the rest of his life to collecting Asian treasures. The Freer opened in 1923, four years after its benefactor's death. Its collection includes more than 26,000 works of art from the Far and Near East, including Asian porcelains, Japanese screens, Chinese paintings and bronzes, and Egyptian gold pieces. Freer's close friend James McNeill Whistler introduced him to Asian art, and the American painter is represented in the vast collection. On display in Gallery 12 is the "Peacock Room," a blue-and-gold dining room decorated with painted leather, wood, and canvas and designed by Whistler for a British shipping magnate. Freer paid $30,000 for the entire room and moved it from London to the United States in 1904. The Freer is scheduled to reopen in May 1993 after an extensive renovation that was begun in 1988. Additions include three floors of underground space, more storage space, a gift shop, and an auditorium. The spectacular Peacock Room has also received a sprucing up. *12th St. and Jefferson Dr. SW, tel. 202/357–2700. Open daily 10–5:30.*

Just beyond the Freer turn left off of Independence Avenue into the **Enid Haupt Memorial Garden.** This 4-acre Victorian-style garden is built largely on the rooftops of two Smithsonian museums, the Arthur M. Sackler Gallery and the National Museum of African Art, both of which opened in 1987 and sit underground like inverted pyramids.

When Charles Freer endowed the gallery that bears his name, he insisted on a few conditions: Objects in the collection could not be loaned out, nor could objects from outside the collections be put on display. Because of these restrictions it was necessary to build a second, complementary, Oriental art museum. The result was ⑬ the **Arthur M. Sackler Gallery.** A wealthy medical researcher and publisher who began collecting Asian art as a student, Sackler allowed Smithsonian curators to select 1,000 items from his ample collection and pledged $4 million toward the construction of the museum. The collection includes works from China, the Indian subcontinent, Persia, Thailand, and Indonesia. Articles in the permanent collection include Chinese ritual bronzes, jade ornaments from the third millenium BC,

Persian manuscripts, and Indian paintings in gold, silver, lapis lazuli, and malachite. *1050 Independence Ave. SW, tel. 202/357-2700. Open daily 10-5:30; closed Dec. 25.*

The other half of the Smithsonian's underground museum complex is the **National Museum of African Art.** Founded in 1964 as a private educational institution, the museum became part of the Smithsonian in 1979. (Before it was moved here in 1987, the collection was housed in a Capitol Hill townhouse that once belonged to ex-slave Frederick Douglass.) Dedicated to the collection, exhibition, and study of the traditional arts of sub-Saharan Africa, the museum displays artifacts representative of some 900 cultures. The permanent collection includes masks, carvings, textiles, and jewelry, all made from materials such as wood, fiber, bronze, ivory, and fired clay. Because many pieces of African art are made of organic materials, the museum also runs a conservation laboratory, where curators work to arrest the decay of the valuable collection. *950 Independence Ave. SW, tel. 202/357-2700. Open daily 10-5:30; closed Dec. 25.*

You'll find the nearest Metro station, Smithsonian, on Jefferson Drive in front of the Freer Gallery.

---

**Tour 2: The Monuments**

*Numbers in the margin correspond to points of interest on the Tour 2: The Monuments map.*

Washington is a city of monuments. In the middle of traffic circles, on tiny slivers of park, and at street corners and intersections, statues, plaques, and simple blocks of marble honor the generals, politicians, poets, and statesmen who helped shape the nation. The monuments dedicated to the most famous Americans are west of the Mall on ground reclaimed from the marshy flats of the Potomac. This is also the location of Washington's cherry trees, gifts from Japan and focus of a festival each spring.

On this tour we'll walk clockwise among the monuments and through the cherry trees. This can be a leisurely, half-day walk, depending on the speed you travel and the time you spend at each spot. If it's an extremely hot day you may want to hop a Tourmobile bus and travel between the monuments in air-conditioned comfort.

We'll start in front of the tallest of them all, the
**① Washington Monument** (nearest Metro stop, Smithsonian). Located at the western end of the Mall, the Washington Monument punctuates the capital like a huge
exclamation point. Visible from nearly everywhere in
the city, it serves as a landmark for visiting tourists and
lost motorists alike.

Congress first authorized a monument to General Washington in 1783. In his 1791 plan for the city, Pierre
L'Enfant selected a site (the point where a line drawn
west from the Capitol crossed one drawn south from the
White House), but it wasn't until 1833, after years of
quibbling in Congress, that a private National Monument Society was formed to select a designer and to
search for funds. Robert Mills's winning design called
for a 600-foot-tall decorated obelisk rising from a circular colonnaded building. The building at the base was to
be an American pantheon, adorned with statues of national heroes and a massive statue of Washington riding
in a chariot pulled by snorting horses.

Because of the marshy conditions of L'Enfant's original
site, the position of the monument was shifted to firmer
ground 100 yards southeast. (If you walk a few steps
north of the monument you can see the stone marker
that denotes L'Enfant's original axis.) The cornerstone
was laid in 1848 with the same Masonic trowel Washington himself had used to lay the Capitol's cornerstone 55
years earlier. The Monument Society continued to raise
funds after construction was begun, soliciting subscrip-
tions of one dollar from citizens across America. It also
urged states, organizations, and foreign governments
to contribute memorial stones for the construction.
Problems arose in 1854, when members of the anti-Pa-
pist "Know Nothing" party stole a block donated by
Pope Pius IX, smashed it, and dumped its shards into
the Potomac. This action, a lack of funds, and the onset
of the Civil War kept the monument at a fraction of its
final height, open at the top, and vulnerable to the rain.
A clearly visible ring about a third of the way up the obelisk testifies to this unfortunate stage of the monument's history: Although all of the marble in the obelisk
came from the same Maryland quarry, that used for the
second phase of construction came from a different stra-
tum and is of a slightly different shade.

In 1876 Congress finally appropriated $200,000 to finish
the monument, and the Army Corps of Engineers took
over construction, thankfully simplifying Mills's origi-

## Tour 2: The Monuments

Jefferson Memorial, **4**
Lincoln Memorial, **5**
Lock keeper's house, **7**
Sylvan Theater, **2**
Tidal Basin, **3**

Vietnam Veterans
Memorial and
Constitution
Gardens, **6**
Washington
Monument, **1**

nal design. Work was finally completed in December 1884, when the monument was topped with a 7½-pound piece of aluminum, then one of the most expensive metals in the world. Four years later the monument was opened to visitors, who rode to the top in a steam-operated elevator. (Only men were allowed to take the 20-minute ride; it was thought too dangerous for women, who as a result had to walk up the stairs if they wanted to see the view.)

At 555 feet 5 inches, the Washington Monument is the world's tallest masonry structure. The view from the top takes in most of the District and parts of Maryland and Virginia. Visitors are no longer permitted to climb the 898 steps leading to the top. (Incidents of vandalism and a disturbing number of heart attacks on the steps convinced the Park Service that letting people walk up on their own wasn't such a good idea.) Most Saturdays there are walk-down tours, with a volunteer guide describing the monument's construction and showing the 193 stone and metal plaques that adorn the inside.

There is usually a wait to take the minute-long elevator ride up the monument's shaft. The Park Service rangers standing at the head of the line are good at estimating how long you'll have to wait. Figure on a wait of approximately 10 to 15 minutes for each side of the monument that is lined with people. If the line goes all the way around the monument, you'll be in line anywhere from 40 minutes to an hour. *Constitution Ave. at 15th St. NW, tel. 202/426–6840. Open Apr.–Labor Day, daily 8 AM–midnight; Sept.–Mar., daily 9–5.*

After your ascent and descent, walk on the path that leads south from the monument. On your right you'll ❷ pass the open-air **Sylvan Theater,** scene of a variety of musical performances during the warmer months. Continue south and cross Independence Avenue at 15th Street. Just south of the redbrick **Auditors Building** (the first building constructed by the federal government to print money) is the **United States Holocaust Memorial Museum,** scheduled to open in the spring of 1993 (*see* Tour 1: The Mall, *above*). Beyond that is the colonnaded **Bureau of Engraving and Printing.**

Carefully cross Maine Avenue at the light and walk ❸ down to the **Tidal Basin.** This placid pond was part of the Potomac until 1882, when portions of the river were filled in to improve navigation and create additional parkland, including that upon which the Jefferson Memorial was later built. Paddleboats have been a fixture on the Tidal Basin for years. You can rent one at the boathouse on the east side of the basin, southwest of the Bureau of Engraving. *Northeast bank of Tidal Basin, tel. 202/484–0206. Paddleboat rentals $7 an hour, $1.75 each additional 15 min. Children under 16 must be accompanied by an adult. Open daily 10–6, weather permitting.*

Continue down the path that skirts the Tidal Basin and ❹ cross the Outlet Bridge to get to the **Jefferson Memorial,** the southernmost of the major monuments in the District. Congress decided that Jefferson deserved a monument positioned as prominently as those in honor of Washington and Lincoln, and this spot directly south of the White House seemed ideal. Jefferson had always admired the Pantheon in Rome—the rotundas he designed for the University of Virginia and his own Monticello were inspired by the dome of the Pantheon—so architect John Russell Pope drew from the same source when he designed this memorial to our third president. Dedicated in 1943, it houses a statue of Jefferson. Its walls are lined with inscriptions based on his writings. One of the best views of the White House can be seen from the memorial's top steps, although the view may be obstructed on your visit by the scaffolding that will surround the memorial for the next three years while it undergoes repair. *Tidal Basin, south bank, tel. 202/426–6821. Open daily 8 AM–midnight.*

After viewing the Jefferson Memorial, continue along the sidewalk that hugs the Tidal Basin. You'll see two grotesque sculpted heads on the sides of the **Inlet Bridge.** The inside walls of the bridge also sport two other interesting sculptures: bronze, human-headed fish that spout water from their mouths. The bridge was refurbished in the 1980s at the same time the chief of the park—a Mr. Jack Fish—was retiring. Sculptor Constantine Sephralis played a little joke: These fish heads are actually Fish's head.

Once you cross the bridge, you have a choice: You can walk to the left, along the Potomac, or continue along the Tidal Basin to the right. The latter route is somewhat more scenic, especially when the cherry trees are in bloom. The first batch of these trees arrived from Japan in 1909. The trees were infected with insects and fungus, however, and the Department of Agriculture ordered them destroyed. A diplomatic crisis was averted when the United States politely asked the Japanese for another batch, and in 1912 Mrs. William Howard Taft planted the first tree. The second was planted by the wife of the Japanese ambassador.

The trees are now the centerpiece of Washington's Cherry Blossom Festival, held each spring. The festivities are kicked off by the lighting of a ceremonial Japanese lantern that rests on the north shore of the Tidal Basin, not far from where the first tree was planted. The once-simple celebration has grown over the years to include concerts, fashion shows, and a parade. Park Service experts try their best to predict exactly when the buds will pop. The trees are usually in bloom for about 10 to 12 days at the beginning of April. When winter refuses to release its grip, the parade and festival are held anyway, without the presence of blossoms, no matter how inclement the weather. And when the weather complies, and the blossoms are at their peak at the time of the festivities, Washington rejoices.

**West Potomac Park,** the green expanse to the west of the Tidal Basin, is a pleasant place to sit and rest for a while, to watch the paddleboats skim the surface of the Tidal Basin, and to feed the squirrels that usually approach looking for handouts. The character of West Potomac Park will change over the next few years as the $47.2 million Franklin Delano Roosevelt Memorial is constructed. FDR asked for a simple memorial (in fact, one already sits on a wedge of grass in front of the National Archives) but boosters have for years been pushing for something more grandiose. When it's completed in 1995 the memorial will comprise a long sequence of walkways and shaded, exterior "rooms" containing sculptures and inscriptions about the 32nd president. To get to our next stop, the Lincoln Memorial, walk northwest along West Basin Drive, then cut across to Ohio Drive. Cross Independence Avenue at the light; the traffic here can be dangerous.

As you walk north along Ohio Drive you'll pass a series of playing fields. Softball has become as competitive a sport as politics in Washington, and the battle to secure a field here or elsewhere in the city starts long before the season. Further along Ohio Drive, directly south of the Lincoln Memorial, is a granite sculpture honoring **John Ericsson,** builder of the ironclad *Monitor,* which took on the Confederate *Merrimac* at Hampton Roads during the Civil War.

A memorial to veterans of the Korean War will soon be erected between Independence Avenue and the Lincoln Memorial, in a grove of trees called Ash Woods. Scheduled to be dedicated on July 27, 1993—the 40th anniversary of the Korean War armistice—**the Korean War Veterans Memorial** will consist of 19 soldiers marching toward an American flag, along with a reflecting pool and a granite wall etched with war scenes.

❺ The **Lincoln Memorial** is considered by many to be the most inspiring monument in the city. It would be hard to imagine Washington without the Lincoln and Jefferson memorials, though they were both criticized when first built. The Jefferson Memorial was dubbed "Jefferson's muffin"; critics lambasted the design as outdated and too similar to that of the Lincoln Memorial. Some also complained that the Jefferson Memorial blocked the view of the Potomac from the White House. Detractors of the Lincoln Memorial thought it inappropriate that the humble Lincoln be honored with what amounts to a modified but nonetheless rather grandiose Greek temple. The white Colorado-marble memorial was designed by Henry Bacon and completed in 1922. The 36 Doric columns represent the 36 states in the Union at the time of Lincoln's death; the names of the states appear on the frieze above the columns. Above the frieze are the names of the 48 states in the Union when the memorial was dedicated. (Alaska and Hawaii are noted by an inscription on the terrace leading up to the memorial.)

Daniel Chester French's somber statue of the seated president is in the center of the memorial and gazes out over the Reflecting Pool. While French's 19-foot-high sculpture looks as if it were cut from one huge block of stone, it actually comprises 28 interlocking pieces of Georgia marble. (The memorial's original design called for a 10-foot-high sculpture, but experiments with models revealed that a statue that size would be lost in the cavernous space.) Inscribed on the south wall is the Gettysburg Address, and on the north wall is Lincoln's second inaugural address. Above each inscription is a mural painted by Jules Guerin. On the south wall is an angel of truth freeing a slave; the unity of North and South are depicted on the opposite wall. The memorial served as a fitting backdrop for Martin Luther King's "I have a dream" speech in 1963.

Many visitors look only at the front and inside of the Lincoln Memorial, but there is much more to explore. On the lower level to the left is a display that chronicles the memorial's construction. There is also a set of windows that look onto the huge structure's foundation. Stalactites (hanging from above) and stalagmites (growing from below) have formed underneath the marble tribute to Lincoln. Some parts of the Lincoln Memorial may be off-limits when you visit. Like the Jefferson, the Lincoln is shrouded in scaffolding as it undergoes a three- to five-year program to repair the effects of acid rain, insects, jet fuel, and other destructive elements.

Although visiting the area around the Lincoln Memorial during the day allows you to take in an impressive view of the Mall to the east, the best time to see the memorial itself is at night. Spotlights illuminate the outside, while inside, light and shadows play across Lincoln's gentle face. *West end of Mall, tel. 202/426–6895. Open 24 hrs a day; staffed daily 8 AM–midnight.*

Walk down the steps of the Lincoln Memorial and to the **6** left to get to the **Vietnam Veterans Memorial** and **Constitution Gardens.** Constitution Gardens, the area south of Constitution Avenue between 17th and 23rd streets, was once home to "temporary" buildings erected by the Navy before World War I and not removed until after World War II. Many ideas were proposed to develop the 50-acre site. President Nixon is said to have favored something resembling Copenhagen's Tivoli Gardens. The final design was a little plainer, with paths winding through groves of trees and a tiny island paying tribute to the signers of the Declaration of Independence, their signatures carved into a low stone wall.

The Vietnam Veterans Memorial is another landmark that encourages introspection. The concept came from Jan Scruggs, a former infantry corporal who had served in Vietnam. The stark design of Maya Ying Lin, a 21-year-old Yale architecture student, was selected in a 1981 competition. Upon its completion in 1982, the memorial was decried by some veterans as a "black gash of shame." With the addition of Frederick Hart's statue of three soldiers and a flagpole just south of the wall, most critics were won over.

The wall is one of the most visited sites in Washington, its black granite panels reflecting the sky, the trees, and the faces of those looking for the names of friends or relatives who died in the war. The names of more than 58,000 Americans are etched on the face of the memorial in the order of their deaths. Directories at the entrance and exit to the wall list the names in alphabetical order. (It was recently discovered that because of a clerical error the names of some two dozen living vets are carved into the stone as well.) For help in finding a specific name, ask a ranger at the blue-and-white hut near the entrance. Thousands of offerings are left at the Wall each year: letters, flowers, medals, uniforms, snapshots. The National Park Service collects these and stores them in a warehouse in Lanham, Maryland, where they are fast becoming another memorial. Veterans groups often have tents set up near the wall; some provide information on soldiers who remain missing in action, others are on call to help fellow vets deal with the sometimes powerful emotions that overtake them when visiting the wall for the first time. *Constitution Gardens, 23rd St. and Constitution Ave. NW, tel. 202/634–1568. Open 24 hrs a day; staffed 8 AM–midnight.*

After years of debate over its design and necessity, the **Vietnam Womens Memorial**—in honor of the women who served in that conflict—is scheduled to be dedicated on Veterans Day, 1993. The monument—two uniformed women caring for a wounded male soldier while a third woman kneels nearby—will sit in Constitution Gardens, southeast of the Vietnam Veterans Memorial.

The FDR, Korean War, and Vietnam Womens memorials have troubled some Washingtonians, who feel the city is entering an unnecessary monument building boom in the 1990s. Each veterans and special interest group seems to want its own separate memorial and there's concern that too many grandiose designs (each group, of course, wants its to be the biggest) are clogging Washington's monumental core.

---

**Time Out**  At the circular **snack bar** just west of the Constitution Gardens lake you can get hot dogs, potato chips, candy bars, soft drinks, and beer at prices lower than those charged by most street vendors.

---

Walk north to Constitution Avenue and head east. The ❼ stone **lock keeper's house** at the corner of Constitution Avenue and 17th Street is the only remaining monument to Washington's unsuccessful experiment with a canal. L'Enfant's design called for a canal to be dug from the Tiber—a branch of the Potomac that extended from where the Lincoln Memorial is now—across the city to the Capitol and then south to the Anacostia River. (L'Enfant even envisioned the president riding in a ceremonial barge from the White House to the Capitol.) The City Canal became more nuisance than convenience, and by the Civil War it was a foul-smelling cesspool that often overran its banks. The stone building at this corner was the home of the canal's lockkeeper until the 1870s, when the waterway was covered over with B

Street, which was renamed Constitution Avenue in 1932.

The nearest Metro station is Federal Triangle, five blocks to the east on 12th Street.

---

### Tour 3: The White House

*Numbers in the margin correspond to points of interest on the Tour 3: The White House Area map.*

In a city full of immediately recognizable images, perhaps none is more familiar than the White House. This is where the buck stops and where the nation turns in times of crisis. On this tour we'll visit the White House, then strike out into the surrounding streets to explore the president's neighborhood, which includes some of the oldest houses in the city.

To reach the start of our tour, take the Metro to the McPherson Square station. We'll begin our exploration in front of 1600 Pennsylvania Avenue. Pierre L'Enfant called it the President's House; it was known formally as the Executive Mansion; and in 1902 Congress officially proclaimed it the **White House,** though, contrary to popular belief, it had been given that nickname even before its white sandstone exterior was painted to cover the fire damage it suffered during the War of 1812. Irishman James Hoban's plan, based on the Georgian design of Leinster Hall near Dublin and of other Irish country homes, was selected in a contest, in 1792. The building wasn't ready for its first occupant until 1800, so George Washington never lived here. Completed in 1829, it has undergone many structural changes since then: Thomas Jefferson, who had entered his own design in the contest under an assumed name, added terraces to the east and west wings. Andrew Jackson installed running water. James Garfield put in the first elevator. Between 1948 and 1952, Harry Truman had the entire structure gutted and restored, adding a second-story porch to the south portico. Each family that has called the White House home has left its imprint on the 132-room mansion. Most recently, George Bush installed a horseshoe pit.

Tuesday through Saturday mornings (except holidays), from 10 AM to noon, selected public rooms on the ground floor and first floor of the White House are open to visitors. Expect a long line, but the wait is worthwhile if you're interested in a firsthand look at what is perhaps the most important building in the city. Most of the year you

Tour 3: The White House Area

can simply join the line that forms along East Executive Avenue, between the White House and the Treasury Building. Between Memorial Day and Labor Day, however, you'll need tickets to tour the mansion. During the summer months there is a blue-and-green ticket booth on the **Ellipse** just south of the White House, open between 8 AM and noon, Tuesday through Saturday, dispensing tickets on a first-come, first-served basis. (Tickets are often gone by 9 AM.) Your ticket will show the approximate time of your tour. There is seating on the Ellipse for those waiting to see the White House. Volunteer marching bands, drill teams, and other musical groups usually perform here, entertaining those who are stuck in line. If you write your representative or senator's office well in advance of your trip, you can receive special VIP passes for tours between 8 and 10 AM. On selected weekends in April and October, the White House is open for garden tours. In December it's decorated for the holidays.

The **Ellipse** is bounded by Constitution Avenue, E Street, 15th Street, and 17th Street. From this vantage point you can see the Washington Monument and the Jefferson Memorial to the south and the red-tile roof of the Department of Commerce to the east, with the tower of the Old Post Office Building sticking up above it. To the north you have a good view of the back of the White House; the rounded portico and Harry Truman's second-story porch are clearly visible. The south lawn of the White House serves as a heliport for *Marine One*, the president's helicopter. Each Monday after Easter the south lawn is also the scene of the White House Easter Egg Roll. The **National Christmas Tree** grows on the northern edge of the Ellipse. Each year in mid-December it is lighted by the president during a festive ceremony that marks the beginning of the holiday season.

You'll enter the White House through the East Wing lobby on the ground floor, walking past the Jacqueline Kennedy Rose Garden. Your first stop is the large white-and-gold **East Room,** the site of presidential news conferences. In 1814 Dolley Madison saved the room's full-length portrait of George Washington from torch-carrying British soldiers by cutting it from its frame, rolling it up, and spiriting it out of the White House. (No fool she, Dolley also rescued her own portrait.) A later occupant, Teddy Roosevelt, allowed his children to ride their pet pony in the East Room.

The Federal-style **Green Room,** named for the moss-green watered silk that covers its walls, is used for informal receptions and "photo opportunities" with foreign heads of state. Notable furnishings in this room include a New England sofa that once belonged to Daniel Webster and portraits of Benjamin Franklin, John Quincy Adams, and Abigail Adams. The president and his guests are often shown on TV sitting in front of the Green Room's English Empire mantel, engaging in what are invariably described as "frank and cordial" discussions.

The elliptical **Blue Room,** the most formal space in the White House, is furnished with a gilded Empire-style settee and chairs that were ordered by James Monroe. (Monroe asked for plain wooden chairs, but the furniture manufacturer thought such unadorned furnishings too simple for the White House and took it upon himself to supply chairs more in keeping with their surroundings.) The White House Christmas tree is placed in this room each year. Another well-known elliptical room, the president's **Oval Office,** is in the semidetached West Wing of the White House, along with other executive offices.

The **Red Room** is decorated as an American Empire–style parlor of the early 19th century, with furniture by

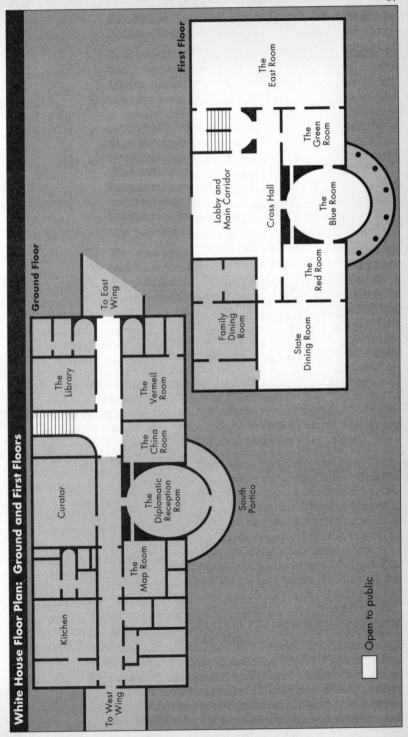

# White House Floor Plan: Ground and First Floors

## Ground Floor

To West Wing

Kitchen

The Map Room

Curator

The Diplomatic Reception Room

The China Room

The Vermeil Room

The Library

To East Wing

South Portico

## First Floor

Family Dining Room

State Dining Room

Lobby and Main Corridor

Cross Hall

The East Room

The Green Room

The Blue Room

The Red Room

■ Open to public

the New York cabinetmaker Charles-Honoré Lannuier. You'll recognize the marble mantel as the twin of the mantel in the Green Room.

The **State Dining Room,** second in size only to the East Room, can seat 140 guests. The room is dominated by G.P.A. Healy's portrait of Abraham Lincoln, painted after the president's death. The stone mantel is inscribed with a quotation from one of John Adams's letters: "I pray heaven to bestow the best of blessings on this house and all that shall hereafter inhabit it. May none but honest and wise men ever rule under this roof." In Teddy Roosevelt's day a stuffed moose head hung over the mantel. *1600 Pennsylvania Ave. NW, tel. 202/755–7798, 202/456–7041 (recording), or 202/472–3669 (Park Service). Open Tues.–Sat. 10–noon. The White House is occasionally closed without notice for official functions. Baby strollers are not allowed on the tour.*

**❸ Lafayette Square,** bordered by Pennsylvania Avenue, Madison Place, H Street, and Jackson Place, is an intimate oasis in the midst of downtown Washington. With such an important resident living across the street, National Capital Park Service gardeners lavish extra attention on the square's trees and flower beds.

When Pierre L'Enfant proposed the location for the Executive Mansion, the only building north of what is today Pennsylvania Avenue was the Pierce family farmhouse, which stood at the northeast corner of what is today Lafayette Square. An apple orchard and a family burial ground were the area's two other main features. During the construction of the White House, workers' huts and a brick kiln were set up, and soon private residences began popping up around the square (though sheep would continue to graze on it for years). L'Enfant's original plan for the city designated this area as part of "President's Park"; in essence it was the president's front yard, just as what is now the Ellipse was once his backyard. The egalitarian Thomas Jefferson, concerned that large, landscaped White House grounds would give the wrong impression in a democratic country, ordered that the area be turned into a public park. Soldiers camped in the square during the War of 1812 and the Civil War, turning it at both times into a muddy pit. Today, protesters set their placards up in Lafayette Square, jockeying for positions that face the White House. While the National Park Service can't restrict the protesters' freedom of speech, it does try to restrict the size of their signs.

Standing in the center of the park—and dominating the square—is a large **statue of Andrew Jackson.** Erected in 1853 and cast from bronze cannon that Jackson had captured during the War of 1812, this was the first equestrian statue made in America. (An exact duplicate faces St. Louis Cathedral in New Orleans' Jackson Square.)

Jackson's is the only statue of an American in the park. The other statues are of foreign-born soldiers who helped in America's fight for independence. In the southeast corner is the park's namesake, the **Marquis de Lafayette,** the young French nobleman who came to America to fight in the Revolution. When Lafayette returned to the United States in 1824 he was given a rousing welcome: He was wined and dined in the finest homes and showered with gifts of cash and land. (You can imagine how this must have made his countryman Pierre L'Enfant feel. The designer of the city Lafayette took by storm had by that time been forgotten.)

Head north on **Madison Place.** The colonnaded building across the street at the corner of Pennsylvania Avenue is an annex to the Treasury Department. The modern redbrick building at 717 Madison Place houses a variety of judicial offices. Its design—with the squared-off bay windows—is echoed in the taller building that rises behind it and is mirrored in the **New Executive Office Building** on the other side of Lafayette Square. Planners in the '20s recommended that the private homes on Lafayette Square, many built in the Federal period, be torn down and replaced with a collection of uniform neoclassical-style government buildings. A lack of funds kept the neighborhood intact, and in the early '60s John and Jacqueline Kennedy worked to save the historic town houses.

The next house down, yellow with a second-story ironwork balcony, was built in 1828 by Benjamin Ogle Tayloe. During the McKinley administration, Ohio Senator Marcus Hanna lived here, and the president's frequent visits earned it the nickname the "Little White House." Dolley Madison lived in the next-door Cutts-Madison House after her husband died. Both the Tayloe and Madison houses are now part of the Federal Judicial Center.

Continue down Madison Place. The next statue is that of **Thaddeus Kosciuszko,** the Polish general who fought alongside American colonists against the British. If you head east on H Street for half a block, you'll come to the **United States Government Bookstore** (1510 H St. NW, tel. 202/653–5075), the place to visit if you'd like to buy a few pounds of the millions of tons of paper the government churns out each year. Here is where you'll find a copy of the latest federal budget or *The Surgeon General's Report on Nutrition and Health.*

---

**Time Out** Presidential advisor Bernard Baruch used to eat his lunch in Lafayette Park, and you can, too. **Loeb's Restaurant** (around the corner at 15th and I streets NW) is a New York–style deli that serves up salads and sandwiches to eat there or to go.

---

❹ On H Street is the golden-domed **St. John's Episcopal Church,** the so-called "Church of the Presidents." Every president since Madison has visited the church, and many worshipped here on a regular basis. Built in 1816, the church was the second building on the square. Benjamin Latrobe, who worked on both the Capitol and the White House, designed it in the form of a Greek cross, with a flat dome and a lantern cupola. The church has been altered somewhat since then; later additions include the Doric portico and the cupola tower. You can best sense the intent of Latrobe's design while standing inside under the saucer-shaped dome of the original building. Not far from the center of the church is pew 54, where visiting presidents are seated. The kneelers of many of the pews are embroidered with the presidential seal and the names of several chief executives. Brochures are available inside for those who would like to take a self-guided tour. *16th and H Sts. NW, tel. 202/347–8766. Open Mon.–Sat. 8–4. Tours after 11 AM Sun. service and by appointment.*

Just east of the church is the four-story **St. John's Parish House,** built in 1836 by Matthew St. Clair Clark, clerk of the House of Representatives. The house's most famous resident was Lord Alexander Baring Ashburton, the British Minister who lived here in 1842 while negotiating a dispute over the position of the U.S.-Canadian border. The house later served as the British legation.

Across 16th Street stands the **Hay-Adams Hotel,** one of the most opulent hostelries in the city and a favorite with Washington insiders and visiting celebrities. It takes its name from a double house, owned by Lincoln biographer John Hay and historian Henry Adams, that stood on this spot. Next to it is the **Chamber of Commerce of the United States,** its neoclassical facade typical of the type of building that might have surrounded Lafayette Park had JFK not intervened. The statue at the northwest corner of Lafayette Square is of **Baron von Steuben,** the Prussian general who drilled Colonial troops during the Revolution.

**❺** The redbrick, Federal-style **Decatur House** on the corner of H Street and Jackson Place was the first private residence on President's Park (the White House doesn't really count as *private*). Designed by Benjamin Latrobe, the house was built for naval hero Stephen Decatur and his wife, Susan, in 1819. Decatur had earned the affection of the nation in battles against the British and the Barbary pirates. Planning to start a political career, he used the prize money Congress awarded him for his exploits to build this home near the White House. Tragically, only 14 months after he moved in, Decatur was killed in a duel with James Barron, a disgruntled former Navy officer who held Decatur responsible for his court-martial. Later occupants of the house included Henry Clay, Martin Van Buren, and the Beales, a prominent family from the West whose modifications of the building include a parquet floor showing the state seal of California. The house is now operated by the National Trust. The first floor is furnished as it was in Decatur's time. The second floor is furnished in the Victorian style favored by the Beale family, who owned it until 1956 (thus making Decatur House both the first and *last* private residence on Lafayette Square). The National Trust store around the corner (entrance on H Street) sells a variety of books, postcards, and gifts. *748 Jackson Pl. NW, tel. 202/842–0920. Open Tues.–Fri. 10–2, weekends noon–4. Admission: $3 adults, $1.50 senior citizens and students under 18, free to children under 6 and National Trust members. Tours on the hr and ½-hour.*

Head south on **Jackson Place.** Many of the row houses on this stretch date from the pre–Civil War or Victorian periods; even the more modern additions, though—such as those at 718 and 726—are designed in a style that blends with their more historic neighbors. **Count Rochambeau,** aide to General Lafayette, is honored with a statue at the park's southwest corner.

Directly across Pennsylvania Avenue, to the right of the **❻** White House, is the **Old Executive Office Building,** which has gone from being one of the most detested buildings in the city to one of the most beloved. It was built between 1871 and 1888 and originally housed the War, Navy, and State departments. Its architect, Alfred B. Mullett, patterned it after the Louvre, but detractors quickly criticized the busy French Empire design—with its mansard roof, tall chimneys, and 900 freestanding columns—as an inappropriate counterpoint to the Greek Revival Treasury Building that sits on the other side of the White House. Numerous plans to alter the facade foundered due to lack of money. The granite edifice may look like a wedding cake, but its high ceilings and spacious offices make it popular with occupants, who currently include the vice president, the Office of Management and Budget, the National Security Council, and other agencies of the executive branch. This building has played host to numerous historical events. It was here that Secretary of State Cordell Hull met with Japanese diplomats after the bombing of Pearl Harbor, and it was here that Oliver North and Fawn Hall shredded Iran-contra documents.

The green canopy at 1651 Pennsylvania Avenue marks the entrance to **Blair House,** the residence used by heads of state visiting Washington. Harry S. Truman lived here from 1948 to 1952, while the White House was undergoing its much-needed renovation. A plaque on the fence honors White House policeman Leslie Coffelt, who died in 1950 when Puerto Rican separatists attempted to assassinate President Truman at this site.

Head west on Pennsylvania Avenue. At the end of the block, with the motto "Dedicated to Art" engraved **❼** above the entrance, is the **Renwick Gallery.** The French Second Empire–style building was designed by Smithsonian Castle architect James Renwick in 1859 to house the art collection of Washington merchant and banker William Wilson Corcoran, founder of Riggs Bank. Corcoran was a Southern sympathizer who spent the duration of the Civil War in Europe. While he was away his unfinished building was pressed into service by the government as a Quartermaster's General post. In 1874 the Corcoran, as it was then called, opened as the first private art museum in the city. The gallery's Grand Salon at the top of the central stairway was furnished in an opulent Victorian style, with paintings hung in tiers, one atop the other. (In the background of Corcoran's portrait is the Renwick itself.) The Octagon Room, at the front of the second floor, was built to display Hiram Powers's sculpture *The Greek Slave.* The statue—a nude woman with her wrists chained—was considered so shocking that separate viewing hours were established for men and women, and children under 16 were not allowed to see it at all. Corcoran's collection quickly outgrew the building and in 1897 it was moved to a new gallery a few blocks south on 17th Street (described below). After a stint as the U.S. Court of Claims, this building was restored to its former glory, renamed after its architect, and opened as the Smithsonian's museum of American decorative arts in 1972. The collection covers a wide range of disciplines and styles; special exhibits have included such items as blown glass, Shaker furniture, and contemporary crafts. *Pennsylvania Ave. and 17th St. NW, tel. 202/357–2700. Open daily 10– 5:30; closed Dec. 25.*

Head south on 17th Street. You'll pass the **Winder Building** (604 17th St.), erected in 1848 as one of the first office blocks in the capital and used during the Civil War as the headquarters of the Union Army. Down another block on the right, at the corner of 17th Street and New York Avenue, is the **Corcoran Gallery of Art,** one of the few large museums in Washington outside the Smithsonian family. The Beaux Arts–style building, its copper roof green with age, was designed by Ernest Flagg and completed in 1897. The gallery's permanent collection numbers more than 11,000 works, including paintings by the first great American portraitists John Copley, Gilbert Stuart, and Rembrandt Peale. The Hudson River School is represented by such works as *Mount Corcoran* by Albert Bierstadt and Frederic Church's *Niagara*. There are also portraits by John Singer Sargent, Thomas Eakins, and Mary Cassatt. European artwork is included in the Walker Collection (late-19th- and early 20th-century paintings, including works by Gustave Courbet, Monet, Pissarro, and Renoir) and the Clark Collection (Dutch, Flemish, and French Romantic paintings, and the recently restored entire 18th-century Grand Salon of the Hotel d'Orsay in Paris). Also be sure to see Samuel Morse's *The Old House of Representatives* and Hiram Powers's *The Greek Slave*, which scandalized Victorian society. The adjacent Corcoran School is the only four-year art college in the Washington area. *17th St. and New York Ave. NW, tel. 202/638– 1439 (recording), 202/638–3211. Suggested donation: $3 adults, $1 students and senior citizens. Open Tues.– Sun. 10–5, Thurs. 10–9; closed Mon., Christmas, New Year's Day. Tours of the permanent collection are offered Tues.–Fri. at 12:30, weekends at 2:30.*

**Time Out** The Cafe at the Corcoran has a lunch menu that includes a selection of salads, light entrées, desserts, and a refreshing assortment of fruit and vegetable shakes. The café also serves a Continental breakfast from 10 to

11:30, an English tea, complete with scones and clotted cream, from 2:30 to 4:30, and dinner on Thursday, when the museum is open late.

---

**9** A block up New York Avenue, at the corner of 18th Street, is the **Octagon House,** built in 1801 for John Tayloe III, a wealthy Virginia plantation owner. Designed by William Thornton, the Octagon House actually has only six sides, not eight. Thornton chose the unusual shape to conform to the acute angle formed by L'Enfant's intersection of New York Avenue and 18th Street.

After the White House was burned in 1814 the Tayloes invited James and Dolley Madison to stay in the Octagon House. It was in a second-floor study that the Treaty of Ghent, ending the War of 1812, was signed. By the late 1800s the building was used as a rooming house. In this century the house served as the headquarters of the American Institute of Architects before the construction of AIA's rather unexceptional building behind it. In the '60s, Octagon House was restored to its former splendor, with detailed plaster molding around the ceilings, coal-burning stoves in the entryway, and the original 1799 Coade stone mantels (made using a now-lost method of casting crushed stone). Exhibits relating to architecture, decorative arts, and Washington history are mounted in the upstairs galies. *1799 New York Ave. NW, tel. 202/638–3105. Suggested donation: $2 adults, $1 senior citizens and children. Open Tues.–Fri. 10–4, weekends noon–4; closed Christmas and New Year's Day.*

**10** A block south on 18th Street is the **Department of the Interior** building, designed by Waddy B. Wood. At the time of its construction in 1937 it was the most modern government building in the city and the first with escalators and central air-conditioning. While the outside of the building is somewhat plain, much of the interior is decorated with paintings that reflect the Interior Department's work. Hallways feature heroic oil paintings of dam construction, panning for gold, and cattle drives. You'll pass some of these if you visit the **Department of the Interior Museum** on the first floor. (You can enter the building at its E Street or C Street doors; adults must show photo ID.) Soon after it opened in 1938, the museum became one of the most popular attractions in Washington; evening hours were maintained even during the Second World War. While some of the displays seem a bit dated—such as one that outlines "vital products derived from the range," including clock cords, emery cloth, hat sweatbands, and isinglass—this snapshot from the '30s is a welcome contrast to the high-tech, interactive video museums of today. Especially appealing are the meticulously created dioramas depicting various historical events and American locales, including a 1938 animated scene of Juneau, Alaska, complete with tiny train cars moving on a track. The Indian Craft Shop across the hall from the museum sells Native American pottery, dolls, carvings, jewelry, baskets, and books. It, too, has been part of the Department of the Interior since 1938. *C and E Sts. between 18th and 19th Sts. NW, tel. 202/208–4743. Open weekdays 8–5; closed federal holidays.*

Back on 17th Street (walk east on E Street) are the three buildings that house the headquarters of the ⑪ **American Red Cross.** The main building, a neoclassical structure of blinding white marble built in 1917, commemorates the service and devotion of the women who cared for the wounded on both sides during the Civil War. The building's Georgian-style board of governors hall features three stained-glass windows designed by Louis Tiffany. *430 17th St. NW, tel. 202/737–8300. Open weekdays 8:30–4:45.*

⑫ A block south is **Memorial Continental Hall,** headquarters of the Daughters of the American Revolution. This Beaux Arts building was the site each year of the D.A.R.'s congress until the larger Constitution Hall was built around the corner. An entrance on D Street leads to the **D.A.R. Museum.** Its 50,000-item collection includes fine examples of Colonial and Federal silver, china, porcelain, stoneware, earthenware, and glass. Thirty-three period rooms are decorated in styles representative of various U.S. states, ranging from an 1850 California adobe parlor to a New Hampshire attic filled with toys from the 18th and 19th centuries. *1776 D St. NW, tel. 202/879–3240. Open weekdays 8:30–4, Sun. 1–5. Docents available for tours weekdays 10–2:15.*

Just across C Street to the south of Continental Hall is ⑬ the **House of the Americas,** the headquarters building of the Organization of American States. The interior of this building features a cool patio adorned with a pre-Columbian–style fountain and lush tropical plants. This tiny rain forest is a good place to rest when Washington's summer heat is at its most oppressive. The upstairs Hall of Flags and Heroes contains, as the name implies, busts of generals and statesmen from the various OAS member countries as well as each country's flag. *17th St. and Constitution Ave. NW, tel. 202/458–3000. Open weekdays 9–5:30.*

**⑭** Behind the House of the Americas is the **Art Museum of the Americas,** with its entrance on 18th Street. The small gallery is in a building that formerly served as the residence for the secretary general of the OAS. It hosts changing exhibits highlighting 20th-century Latin American artists. *201 18th St. NW, tel. 202/458–6016. Open Tues.–Sat. 10–5.*

Next, head east on Constitution Avenue and take the first left, following the curving drive that encircles the Ellipse. The rather weather-beaten **gate house** at the corner of Constitution Avenue and 17th Street once stood on Capitol Hill. It was designed in 1828 by Charles Bulfinch, the first native-born American to serve as Architect of the Capitol, and was moved here in 1874 after the Capitol grounds were redesigned by Frederick Law Olmsted. A twin of the gatehouse stands at Constitution Avenue and 15th Street.

Across E Street to the northeast of the Ellipse, in a small park bounded by E Street, 15th Street, East Executive Avenue, and Alexander Hamilton Place, stands
**⑮** the massive **William Tecumseh Sherman Monument.** Just north of this memorial is the southern facade of the Treasury Building, its entrance guarded by a **statue of Alexander Hamilton,** the department's first secretary.

**⑯** Across 15th Street to the east is **Pershing Park,** a quiet, sunken garden that honors General "Blackjack" Pershing, commander of the American expeditionary force in World War I. Engravings on the stone walls recount pivotal campaigns from that war. Ice skaters glide on the square pool in the winter.

One block to the north is the venerable **Hotel Washington** (515 15th St., tel. 202/638–5900). Its lobby is narrow and unassum-ing, but the view from the rooftop Sky Top Lounge—open May to October—is one of the best in the city.

**⑰** To your left is the long side of the **Treasury Building,** the largest Greek Revival edifice in Washington. Pierre L'Enfant had intended for Pennsylvania Avenue to stretch in a straight, unbroken line from the White House to the Capitol. This plan was ruined by the construction of the Treasury Building on this site just east of the White House. Robert Mills, the architect responsible for the Washington Monument and the Patent Office (now the National Museum of American Art), designed the grand colonnade that stretches down 15th Street. Construction of the Treasury Building started in 1836 and, after several additions, was finally completed in 1869. Guided 45-minute tours are given every other Saturday and take visitors past the Andrew Johnson suite, used by Johnson as the executive office while Mrs. Lincoln moved out of the White House; the two-story marble Cash Room; and a 19th-century burglar-proof vault lining that saw duty when the Treasury once stored currency. *15th St. between Pennsylvania and New York Aves. NW, tel. 202/343–9136 or 202/535–3652 (TDD). Register at least a week ahead for the tour; visitors must provide name, date of birth, and Social Security number, and show photo I.D. at the start of the tour.*

**Time Out**   A glittering urban mall, **The Shops** (in the National Press Building, F and G Sts. between 13th and 14th Sts. NW) is home to table-service restaurants such as the **American Cafe** and the **Boston Seafood Company,** as well as faster and cheaper fare in its top-floor Food Hall.

Continue up 15th Street. The luxurious **Old Ebbitt Grill** (675 15th St. NW, tel. 202/347–4800) is a popular watering spot for journalists and television news correspondents.

The corner of 15th Street and Pennsylvania Avenue has been dubbed Washington's Wall Street. Adjacent to the imposing Treasury are brokerage firms and buildings belonging to Riggs Bank and Crestar Bank. The location is especially fitting for banks, since this stretch of 15th Street is pictured on the back of every $10 bill.

The Metro stations nearest to the end of this tour are McPherson Square, at 15th and I streets, and Metro Center, three blocks east on G Street.

## Tour 4: Capitol Hill

*Numbers in the margin correspond to points of interest on the Tour 4: Capitol Hill map.*

The people who live and work on "the Hill" do so in the shadow of the edifice that lends the neighborhood its name: the gleaming white Capitol building. More than just the center of government, however, the Hill also includes charming residential blocks lined with Victorian row houses and a fine assortment of restaurants, bars, and shops. Capitol Hill's boundaries are disputed: It's bordered to the west, north, and south by the Capitol, Union Station, and I Street respectively. Some argue that Capitol Hill extends east to the Anacostia River, others that it ends at 11th Street near Lincoln Park. The neighborhood does in fact seem to grow as members of Capitol Hill's active historic-preservation movement restore more and more 19th-century houses.

Start your exploration of the Hill inside the cavernous main hall of **Union Station,** which sits on Massachusetts Avenue north of the Capitol. In 1902 the McMillan Commission—charged with suggesting ways to improve the appearance of the city—recommended that the many train lines that sliced through the capital share one main depot. Union Station was opened in 1908 and was the first building completed under the commission's plan. Chicago architect and commission member Daniel H. Burnham patterned the station after the Roman Baths of Diocletian.

For many visitors to Washington, the capital city is first seen framed through the grand station's arched doorways. In its heyday, during World War II, more than 200,000 people swarmed through the station daily. By the '60s, however, the decline in train travel had turned the station into an expensive white-marble elephant. It was briefly, and unsuccessfully, transformed into a visitors center for the Bicentennial; but by 1981 rain was pouring in through the neglected station's roof, and passengers boarded trains at a ramshackle depot behind the station.

The Union Station you see today is the result of a restoration completed in 1988, an effort intended to be the beginning of a revival of Washington's east end. It's hoped the shops, restaurants, and nine-screen movie theater in Union Station will draw more than just train travelers to the Beaux Arts building. The jewel of the structure remains its meticulously restored main waiting room. With its 96-foot-high coffered ceiling gilded with eight pounds of gold leaf, it is one of the city's great spaces and is used for inaugural balls and other festive events. Forty-six statues of Roman legionnaires, one for each state in the Union when the station was completed, ring the grand room. The statues were the subject of controversy when the building was first opened. Pennsylvania Railroad president Alexander Cassatt (brother of artist Mary) ordered sculptor Louis Saint-Gaudens to alter the statues, convinced that the legionnaires' skimpy outfits would scandalize female passengers. The sculp-

# Tour 4: Capitol Hill

G St.

3rd St.

4th St.

Massachusetts Ave.

North Capitol St.

F St.

F St.

New Jersey Ave.

1st St.

E St.

E St.

2nd St.

M UNION STATION

Columbus Memorial Fountain

Massachusetts Ave.

D St.

C St.

Delaware Ave.

1st St.

Louisiana Ave.

C St.

Stanton Park

Maryland Ave.

Constitution Ave.

Constitution Ave.

A St.

E. Capitol St.

A St.

1st St.

Independence Ave.

Independence Ave.

Pennsylvania Ave.

New Jersey Ave.

Seward Sq.

Canal St.

C St.

N

0        400 yds

0        400 meters

Bartholdi Fountain, **9**
Capitol, **4**
City Post Office/ National Postal Museum, **2**
Folger Shakespeare Library, **11**
Frederick Douglass Townhouse, **14**

Grant Memorial, **6**
James Garfield Memorial, **7**
Library of Congress/Jefferson Building, **10**
Peace Monument, **5**
Robert A. Taft Memorial, **3**
Sewall-Belmont House, **13**

South side of East Capitol Street, **15**
Supreme Court Building, **12**
326 A Street, **16**
Union Station, **1**
United States Botanic Gardens, **8**

tor obligingly added a shield to each figure, obscuring any offending body parts.

The east hall, now filled with vendors, was once an expensive restaurant. It is decorated with Pompeiian tracery and plaster walls and columns painted to look like marble. At one time the station also featured a secure presidential waiting room, now restored. The private waiting room was by no means a frivolous addition: Twenty years before Union Station was built, President Garfield was assassinated in the public waiting room of the old Baltimore and Potomac terminal on 6th Street. Group tours available by appointment (tel. 202/289–1908).

**Time Out**   On Union Station's lower level you'll find more than 20 food stalls, offering everything from pizza to sushi. On the main level are Capitol Hill favorite the **American Cafe,** the trendy Italian restaurant **Sfuzzi,** and **America,** which offers a menu as expansive as its name: everything from Albuquerque blue corn enchiladas to New York Reuben sandwiches.

As you walk out Union Station's front doors, glance to the right. At the end of a long succession of archways is ❷ the Washington **City Post Office,** also designed by Daniel Burnham and completed in 1914. Nostalgic odes to the noble mail carrier are inscribed on the exterior of the marble building; one of them characterizes the mailman as "Messenger of sympathy and love, servant of parted friends, consoler of the lonely, bond of the scattered family, enlarger of the common life." The Post Office is currently being renovated and is scheduled to reopen in July 1993 as the home of the **National Postal Museum,** the 14th Smithsonian museum in Washington. The museum will use exhibits from rare stamps to mail-carrying airplanes to relate the development of the postal service to the growth of the United States. And while the National Museum of Natural History has the Hope Diamond, the National Postal Museum has the box used to mail the priceless gem to the Smithsonian.

Return to Union Station and walk to the plaza in front. At the center of the plaza is the **Columbus Memorial Fountain,** designed by Lorado Taft. A caped, steely-eyed Christopher Columbus stares into the distance, flanked by a hoary, bearded figure (the Old World) and an Indian brave (the New).

Head south from the fountain, away from Union Station, cross Massachusetts Avenue, and walk down Delaware Avenue. On the left you'll pass the **Russell Senate Office Building.** Note the delicate treatment below the second-story windows that resembles twisted lengths of fringed cloth. Completed in 1909, this was the first of the Senate office buildings. Beyond it are the Dirksen and Hart office buildings. To the right, sticking up

❸ above the trees, is a **memorial to Robert A. Taft,** son of the 27th president and longtime Republican senator. The monolithic carillon is rather unattractive, resembling nothing so much as a huge room deodorizer.

❹ Cross Constitution Avenue and enter the **Capitol** grounds, landscaped in the late 19th century by Frederick Law Olmsted, Sr., who, along with Calvert Vaux, created New York City's Central Park. On these 68 acres you will find both the tamest squirrels in the city and the highest concentration of television news correspondents, jockeying for a good position in front of the Capitol for their "stand-ups." A few hundred feet northeast of the Capitol are two cast-iron car shelters, left over from the days when horse-drawn trolleys served the Hill. Olmsted's six pinkish, bronze-topped lamps directly east from the Capitol are a treat, too.

When planning the city, Pierre L'Enfant described the gentle rise on which the Capitol sits, known then as Jenkins Hill, as "a pedestal waiting for a monument." The design of this monument was the result of a competition held in 1792; the winner was William Thornton, a physician and amateur architect from the West Indies. With its central rotunda and dome, Thornton's Capitol is reminiscent of Rome's Pantheon, a similarity that must have delighted the nation's founders, who felt the American government was based on the principles of the Republic of Rome.

The cornerstone was laid by George Washington in a Masonic ceremony on September 18, 1793, and in November 1800, both the Senate and the House of Representatives moved down from Philadelphia to occupy the first completed section of the Capitol: the boxlike portion between the central rotunda and today's north wing. (Subsequent efforts to find the cornerstone Washington laid have been unsuccessful, though when the east front was extended in the 1950s, workmen found a knee joint thought to be from a 500-pound ox that was roasted at the 1793 celebration.) By 1806 the House wing had been completed, just to the south of what is now the domed center, and a covered wooden walkway joined the two wings.

The Congress House grew slowly and suffered a grave setback on August 24, 1814, when British troops led by Sir George Cockburn marched on Washington and set fire to the Capitol and numerous other government buildings. (Cockburn reportedly stood on the House Speaker's chair and asked his men, "Shall this harbor of Yankee democracy be burned?" The question was rhetorical; the building was torched.) The wooden walkway was destroyed and the two wings gutted, but the walls were left standing after a violent rainstorm doused the flames. Fearful that Congress might leave Washington, residents raised money for a hastily built "Brick Capitol" that stood where the Supreme Court is today. Architect Benjamin Henry Latrobe supervised the rebuilding of the Capitol, adding such American touches as the corn-cob-and-tobacco-leaf capitals to columns in the east entrance to the Senate wing. He was followed by Boston-born Charles Bulfinch, and in 1826 the Capitol, its low wooden dome sheathed in copper, was finally finished.

North and south wings were added in the 1850s and '60s to accommodate a growing government trying to keep pace with a growing country. The elongated edifice extended farther north and south than Thornton had planned, and in 1855, to keep the scale correct, work began on a tall cast-iron dome. President Lincoln was criticized for continuing this expensive project while the country was in the throes of the bloody Civil War, but he called the construction "a sign we intend the Union shall go on." This twin-shelled dome, a marvel of 19th-century engineering, rises 285 feet above the ground and weighs 9 million pounds. It expands and contracts up to four inches a day, depending on the outside temperature. The figure on top of the dome, often mistaken for Pocahontas, is called *Freedom*. Sculptor Thomas Crawford had first planned for the 19-foot-tall bronze statue to wear the cloth liberty cap of a freed Roman slave, but southern lawmakers, led by Jefferson Davis, objected. An "American" headdress composed of a star-encircled helmet surmounted with an eagle's head and feathers was substituted.

The Capitol has continued to grow. In 1962 the east front was extended 34 feet, creating 100 additional offices. Preservationists have fought to keep the west front from being extended, since it is the last remaining

United States Capitol: Second Floor Plan

N

0        30 yards

0        30 meters

Open to public

section of the Capitol's original facade. A compromise was reached in 1983, when it was agreed that the facade's crumbling sandstone blocks would simply be replaced with stronger limestone.

Guided tours of the Capitol usually start beneath the dome in the Rotunda, but if there's a crowd you may have to wait in a line that forms at the top of the center steps on the east side. If you want to forgo the tour, which is brief but informative, you may look around on your own. Enter through one of the lower doors to the right or left of the main steps. Start your exploration under Constantino Brumidi's *Apotheosis of Washington*, the fresco in the center of the dome. Working as Michelangelo did in the Sistine Chapel, applying paint to wet plaster, Brumidi completed this fresco in 1865. The figures in the inner circle represent the 13 original states of the Union; those in the outer ring symbolize arts, sciences, and industry. The flat, sculpture-style frieze around the rim of the Rotunda depicting 400 years of American history was started by Brumidi. While painting Penn's treaty with the Indians, the 74-year-old artist slipped on the 58-foot-high scaffold and almost fell off. Brumidi managed to hang on until help arrived, but he died a few months later from shock brought on by the incident. The work was continued by another Italian, Filippo Costaggini, but the frieze wasn't finished until American Allyn Cox added the final touches in 1953.

Notice the Rotunda's eight immense oil paintings of scenes from American history. The four scenes from the Revolutionary War are by John Trumbull, who served alongside George Washington and painted the first president from life. Twenty-six people have lain in state in the Rotunda, including nine presidents, from Abraham Lincoln to Lyndon Baines Johnson. Underneath the Rotunda, above an empty crypt that was designed to hold the remains of George and Martha Washington, is an exhibit chronicling the construction of the Capitol.

South of the Rotunda is Statuary Hall, once the legislative chamber of the House of Representatives. The room has an interesting architectural feature that maddened early legislators: A slight whisper uttered on one side of the hall can be heard on the other. (Don't be disappointed if this parlor trick doesn't work when you're visiting the Capitol; sometimes the hall is just too noisy.) When the House moved out, Congress invited each state to send statues of two great deceased citizens for placement in the former chamber. Because the weight of the accumulated statues threatened to cave the floor in, some of the sculptures were dispersed to various other spots throughout the Capitol.

To the north, on the Senate side, you can visit the chamber once used by the Supreme Court as well as the splendid Old Senate Chamber, both of which have been restored. Also be sure to see the Brumidi Corridor on the ground floor of the Senate wing. Frescoes and oil paintings of birds, plants, and American inventions adorn the walls and ceilings, and an intricate, Brumidi-designed bronze stairway leads to the second floor. The Italian artist also memorialized several American heroes, painting them inside trompe l'oeil frames. Trusting that America would continue to produce heroes long after he was gone, Brumidi left some frames empty. The most recent one to be filled, in 1987, honors the crew of the space shuttle *Challenger*.

If you want to watch some of the legislative action in the **House** or **Senate chambers** while you're on the Hill you'll have to get a gallery pass from the office of your representative or senator. (To find out where those offices are, ask any Capitol police officer, or dial 202/224–3121.) In the chambers you'll notice that Democrats sit to the right of the presiding officer, Republicans to the left—the opposite, it's often noted, of their political leanings. You may be disappointed by watching from the gallery. Most of the day-to-day business is conducted in the various legislative committees, many of which meet in the Congressional office buildings. The *Washington Post*'s daily "Today in Congress" lists when and where the committees are meeting. To get to a house or Senate office building, go to the Capitol's basement and ride the miniature subway used by legislators. *East end of the Mall, tel. 202/224–3121. For guide service, tel. 202/225–6827. Open daily 9–3:45; summer hrs determined annually.*

**Time Out**    A meal at a **Capitol cafeteria** may give you a glimpse of a well-known politician or two. A public dining room on the first floor, Senate-side, is open 7:30 AM–3:30 PM (open to staff only 12:30–1). A favorite with legislators is the Senate bean soup, made and served everyday since 1901 (no one is sure exactly why, though the menu, which you can take with you, outlines a few popular theories).

When you're finished exploring the inside of the Capitol, make your way to the **west side.** In 1981, Ronald Reagan broke with tradition and moved the presidential swearing-in ceremony to this side of the Capitol, which offers a dramatic view of the Mall and monuments below and can accommodate more guests than the east side, where all previous presidents took the oath of office. Walk down the northernmost flight of steps and follow the red-and-black path that leads to Pennsylvania Avenue. The white-marble memorial in the center of the traffic

❺ circle in front of you is the **Peace Monument,** which depicts America, grief-stricken over sailors lost at sea, weeping on the shoulder of History. Cross First Street carefully and walk to the left along the **Capitol Reflect-**

❻ **ing Pool.** As you continue south you'll pass the **Grant Memorial.** At a length of 252 feet, it's the largest sculpture group in the city. The statue of Ulysses S. Grant on horseback is flanked by Union artillery and cavalry. Further south, in the intersection of First Street and

❼ Maryland Avenue SW, is the **James Garfield Memorial.** The 20th president of the United States, Garfield was assassinated in 1881 after only a few months in office.

❽ Across Maryland Avenue is the **United States Botanic Gardens,** a peaceful, plant-filled oasis between Capitol Hill and the Mall. The conservatory includes a cactus house, a fern house, and a subtropical house filled with orchids. Seasonal displays include blooming plants at Easter, chrysanthemums in the fall, and Christmas greens and poinsettias in December and January. Brochures just inside the doorway offer helpful gardening tips. *1st St. and Maryland Ave. SW, tel. 202/225–8333. Open Jun.–Aug., daily 9–9; Sept.–May, daily 9–5.*

When you exit the Botanic Gardens, walk away from the Capitol, take the first left along the pebbled sidewalk, and cross Independence Avenue. To the right is the **Hubert H. Humphrey Building,** home of the Department of Health and Human Services. The beige building gets a much-needed splash of color from *Shorepoints I*, the red abstract sculpture by James Rosati that sits in front of it.

Walk east on Independence Avenue. On the right, in a park that is part of the Botanic Garden, you'll pass the

❾ **Bartholdi Fountain.** Frédéric-Auguste Bartholdi, sculptor of the more famous—and much larger—Statue of Liberty, created this delightful fountain for the Philadelphia Centennial Exhibition of 1876. With its aquatic monsters, sea nymphs, tritons, and lighted globes (once gas, now electric), the fountain represents the elements of water and light. The U.S. government purchased the fountain after the exhibition and placed it on the grounds of the old Botanic Garden on the Mall. It was moved to its present location in 1932.

Cross 1st Street SW and continue east on Independence Avenue past the **Rayburn, Longworth,** and **Cannon House office buildings.** At Independence Avenue and 1st Street SE is the green-domed **Jefferson Building** of the **Library of Congress.** Like many buildings in Washington that seem a bit overwrought (the Old Executive Office Building is another example), the library was criticized when it was completed, in 1897. Some detractors felt its Italian-Renaissance design was a bit too florid. Congressmen were even heard to grumble that its dome competed with that of their Capitol. It is certainly decorative, with busts of Dante, Goethe, Hawthorne, and other great writers perched above its entryway. *The Court of Neptune,* Roland Hinton Perry's fountain at the base of the front steps, rivals some of Rome's best fountains.

Provisions for a library to serve members of Congress were originally made in 1800, when the government set aside $5,000 to purchase and house books that legislators might need to consult. This small collection was housed in the Capitol but was destroyed in 1814, when the British burned the city. Thomas Jefferson, then in retirement at Monticello, offered his personal library as a replacement, noting that "there is, in fact, no subject to which a Member of Congress may not have occasion to refer." Jefferson's collection of 6,487 books, for which Congress eventually paid him $23,950, laid the foundation for the great national library. (Sadly, another fire in 1851 wiped out two-thirds of Jefferson's books.) By the late 1800s it was clear the Capitol building could no longer contain the growing library, and the Jefferson Building was constructed. The **Adams Building,** on 2nd Street behind the Jefferson, was added in 1939. A third structure, the **James Madison Building,** was opened in 1980; it is just south of the Jefferson Building, between Independence Avenue and C Street.

The **Library of Congress** today holds some 90 million items, of which 30 million are books. Also part of the library is the Congressional Research Service, which, as the name implies, works on special projects for senators and representatives.

The Jefferson and Adams buildings are nearing the end of an extensive renovation and some parts may be closed on your visit. Recently reopened in the Jefferson Building, however, is the richly decorated Great Hall, adorned with mosaics, paintings, and a curving marble stairway. The grand, octagonal Main Reading Room, its central desk surrounded by mahogany readers' tables, has also reopened. Computer terminals have replaced the wooden card catalogs, but books are still retrieved and disbursed the same way: Readers (18 years or older) hand request slips to librarians and wait patiently for their materials to be delivered. Researchers aren't allowed in the stacks and only members of Congress can check books out.

But books are only part of the story. Family trees are explored in the Local History and Genealogy Reading Room. In the Folklife Reading Room, patrons can listen to LP recordings of American Indian music or hear the story of B'rer Rabbit read in the Gullah dialect of Georgia and South Carolina. Items from the library's collection—which includes a Gutenberg bible—are often on display in the Jefferson and Madison buildings. Classic films are shown for free in the 64-seat Mary Pickford Theater (tel. 202/707–5677 for information). *Jefferson Bldg., 1st St. and Independence Ave. SE, tel. 202/707–5458. Open weekdays 8:30–9:30, Sat. 8:30–5, Sun. 1–5. Tours offered on the hr weekdays 10–4, Sat. 10–3, Sun. 1–3. Groups of 10 or more should call ahead for reservations.*

**⑪** Behind the Jefferson Building stands the **Folger Shakespeare Library.** The Folger Library's collection of works by and about Shakespeare and his times is second to none. The white-marble Art Deco building, designed by architect Paul Philippe Cret, is decorated with scenes from the Bard's plays. Inside is a reproduction of an inn-yard theater, which is the setting for performances of chamber music, baroque opera, and other events appropriate to the surroundings, and a gallery, designed in the manner of an Elizabethan Great Hall, that hosts rotating exhibits from the library's collection. *201 E. Capitol St. SE, tel. 202/544–4600. Open Mon.–Sat. 10–4.*

**⑫** Walk back down East Capitol Street and turn right onto 1st Street. The stolid **Supreme Court Building** faces 1st Street here. The justices arrived in Washington in 1800 along with the rest of the government but were for years shunted around various rooms in the Capitol; for a while they even met in a tavern. It wasn't until 1935 that the court got its own building, this white-marble temple with twin rows of Corinthian columns, designed by Cass Gilbert. William Howard Taft, the only man to serve as both president and chief justice, was instrumental in getting the court a home of its own, though he died before it was completed.

The Supreme Court convenes on the first Monday in October and remains in session until it has heard all of its cases and handed down all its decisions (usually the end of July). For two weeks of each month (Monday through Wednesday), the justices hear oral arguments in the velvet-swathed court chamber. Visitors who want to listen can choose from two lines. One is a "three-to-five-minute" line, which shuttles visitors through, giving them a quick impression of the court at work. The other is for those who'd like to stay for the whole show. If you choose the latter, it's best to be in line by 8:30 AM. The main hall of the Supreme Court is lined with busts of former chief justices; the courtroom itself is decorated with allegorical friezes. Perhaps the most interesting appurtenance in the imposing building, however, is a basketball court on one of the upper floors (it's been called the highest court in the land). *1st and E. Capitol Sts. NE, tel. 202/ 479–3000. Open weekdays 9–4:30.*

One block north of the Supreme Court, at the corner of Constitution Avenue and 2nd Street, is the redbrick **⑬ Sewall-Belmont House,** built in 1800 by Robert Sewall. Part of the house dates to 1680, making it the oldest home on Capitol Hill. From 1801 to 1813 Secretary of the Treasury Albert Gallatin lived here. He finalized the details of the Louisiana Purchase in his front-parlor office. The house became the only private residence burned in Washington during the British invasion of 1814, after a resident fired on advancing British troops from an upper-story window. (It was, in fact, the only resistance the British met. The rest of the country was disgusted at Washington's inability to defend itself.) The house is now the headquarters of the National Woman's Party and features a museum that chronicles the early days of the women's movement. The museum is filled with period furniture, and portraits and busts of suffrage movement leaders, such as Lucretia Mott, Elizabeth Cady Stanton, and Alice Paul. *144 Constitution Ave. NE, tel. 202/546–3989. Open fall–spring, Tues.–Fri. 10–3, Sat. noon–4; summer, Tues.–Fri. 10–3, weekends noon–4.*

After seeing the Sewall-Belmont House, continue east on Maryland Avenue, past the headquarters of the **Veterans of Foreign Wars.** Only three blocks from the Capitol, the Hill's residential character asserts itself. At Stanton Square turn right onto 4th Street NE, walk south two blocks, and then turn right onto A Street. The gray house with the mansard roof at 316 A Street is the ⓮ **Frederick Douglass Townhouse** (not open to the public). The first Washington home of the famous abolitionist and writer, this structure housed the Museum of African Art until 1987, when the museum was moved to a new building on the Mall (*see* Tour 1, *above*).

Walk back to 4th Street and down another block to East Capitol Street, the border between the northeastern and southeastern quadrants of the city. The orange and yellow trash cans, emblazoned with the silhouette of an Indian, are reminders that East Capitol street is a main thoroughfare to RFK Stadium, home turf for the Washington Redskins. In the '50s there was a plan to construct government office buildings on both sides of East Capitol Street as far as Lincoln Park, seven blocks to the east. The neighborhood's active historic-preservation supporters successfully fought the proposal. The houses ⓯ on the **south side of East Capitol Street** are a representative sampling of homes on the Hill. The corner house, No. 329, has a striking tower with a bay window and stained-glass. Next door are two Victorian houses with iron trim below the second floor. A pre–Civil War, Greek-Revival frame house sits behind a trim garden at No. 317. The alley to the right of No. 317 also dates from the 19th century. The two parallel rows of bricks were intended for carriage wheels, while the stones in the ⓰ center were trod by horses' hooves. At **326 A St.**, in a quiet neighborhood behind the Library of Congress's Adams Building, is the stucco house that artist Constantino Brumidi lived in while he was working on the Capitol.

---

**Time Out** **Duddington's** (319 Pennsylvania Ave. SE), named for a large estate laid out on this site in the 17th century, serves up burgers, subs, and pizza made with fresh dough. The sushi-serving **Suehiro** (332 Pennsylvania Ave. SE) is a little more exotic. For dessert, sample the pastries and cookies at **Sherrill's Bakery** (233 Pennsylvania Ave. SE).

---

Turn right on Pennsylvania Avenue and head back toward the Capitol's familiar white dome. The south side of the street is lined with restaurants and bars frequented by those who live and work on the Hill.

You'll find the nearest Metro stop, Capitol South, on the corner of 1st and D streets SE.

## Tour 5: Old Downtown and Federal Triangle

*Numbers in the margin correspond to points of interest on the Tour 5: Old Downtown and Federal Triangle map.*

Just because Washington is a planned city doesn't mean the plan was executed flawlessly. Pierre L'Enfant's design has been alternately shelved and rediscovered several times in the last 200 years. Nowhere have the city's imperfections been more visible than on L'Enfant's grand thoroughfare, Pennsylvania Avenue. By the early '60s it had become a national disgrace, the dilapidated buildings that lined it home to pawn shops and cheap souvenir stores. While riding up Pennsylvania Avenue in his inaugural parade, a disgusted John F. Kennedy is said to have turned to an aide and said, "Fix it!" Washington's downtown—once within the diamond formed by Massachusetts, Louisiana, Pennsylvania, and New York avenues—had its problems, too, many as a result of the riots that rocked the capital in 1968 after the assassination of Martin Luther King, Jr. In their wake, many downtown businesses left the area and moved north of the White House.

In recent years developers have rediscovered "old downtown," and buildings are now being torn down or remodeled at an amazing pace. After several false starts Pennsylvania Avenue is shining once again. This tour explores the old downtown section of the city, then swings around to check the progress on the monumental street that links the Congress House—the Capitol—with the President's House.

**1** Start your exploration in front of the **Pension Building,** on F Street between 4th and 5th streets. (Nearest Metro stop, Judiciary Square.) The massive redbrick edifice was built between 1882 and 1887 to house workers who processed the pension claims of veterans and their survivors, an activity that intensified after the Civil War. The architect was U.S. Army Corps of Engineers General Montgomery C. Meigs, who took as his inspiration the Italian Renaissance–style Palazzo Farnese in Rome.

Before entering the building, walk down its F Street side. The terra-cotta frieze by Caspar Buberl between the first and second floors depicts soldiers marching and sailing in an endless procession around the building. Architect Meigs lost his oldest son in the Civil War, and, though the frieze depicts Union troops, he intended it as

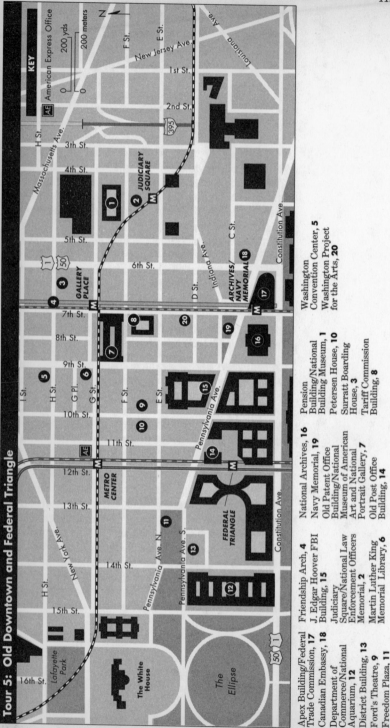

# Tour 5: Old Downtown and Federal Triangle

**KEY**

AE American Express Office

Apex Building/Federal
Trade Commission, **17**

Canadian Embassy, **18**

Department of
Commerce/National
Aquarium, **12**

District Building, **13**

Ford's Theatre, **9**

Freedom Plaza, **11**

Friendship Arch, **4**

J. Edgar Hoover FBI
Building, **15**

Judiciary
Square/National Law
Enforcement Officers
Memorial, **2**

Martin Luther King
Memorial Library, **6**

National Archives, **16**

Navy Memorial, **19**

Old Patent Office
Building/National
Museum of American
Art and National
Portrait Gallery, **7**

Old Post Office
Building, **14**

Pension
Building/National
Building Museum, **1**

Petersen House, **10**

Surratt Boarding
House, **3**

Tariff Commission
Building, **8**

Washington
Convention Center, **5**

Washington Project
for the Arts, **20**

a memorial to all who were killed in the bloody war. Meigs designed the Pension Building with workers' comfort in mind, long before anyone knew that cramped, stuffy offices could cause "sick building syndrome." Note the three "missing" bricks under each window that helped keep the building cool by allowing air to circulate.

The open interior of the building is one of the city's great spaces and has been the site of inaugural balls for more than 100 years. (The first ball was for Grover Cleveland in 1885; because the building wasn't finished at the time, a temporary wooden roof and floor were erected.) The eight central Corinthian columns are the largest in the world, rising to a height of 75 feet. Though they look like marble, each is made of 75,000 bricks, covered with plaster and painted to resemble Siena marble. Each year NBC tapes its "Christmas in Washington" TV special in the breathtaking hall.

The Pension Building now houses the **National Building Museum,** devoted to architecture and the building arts. "Washington: Symbol and City" is a permanent exhibit that outlines the capital's architectural history, from monumental core to residential neighborhoods. Recent temporary exhibits have explored the construction of the Statue of Liberty, the history of Washington's apartment buildings, and the Pension Building itself. *F St. between 4th and 5th Sts. NW, tel. 202/272–2448. Open Mon.–Sat. 10–4, Sun. noon–4; closed Thanksgiving, Christmas, New Year's Day. Tours weekdays at 12:30, weekends at 12:30 and 1:30.*

**2** Across F Street from the Pension Building is **Judiciary Square.** As the name implies, this is the District's judicial core, with both city and federal courthouses arranged around it. The **National Law Enforcement Officers Memorial** was dedicated here in October 1991. A three-foot-high wall bears the names of more than 15,000 American police officers killed in the line of duty since 1794. Given the dangerous nature of police work, it will be one of the few memorials to which names will continue to be added.

Head west on F Street. After you cross 5th Street, look back at the Pension Building. It's easier to see the interesting roof from this distance. The prison block–like structure north of the Pension Building houses the General Accounting Office.

Turn right on 6th Street and walk two blocks north. The Chinese characters on the street signs signal that you're entering Washington's compact **Chinatown,** bordered by G, E, 5th, and 8th streets. The area is somewhat down-at-the-heels—you'll find boarded-up buildings and graffiti-covered walls—but this is the place to go for Chinese food in the District. Nearly every restaurant has a roast duck hanging in the window, and the shops here sell a wide variety of Chinese goods, from paperback books to traditional medicines.

---

**Time Out**  If the smells of Chinese cooking have activated your taste buds, try the highly rated **Mr. Yung's** (740 6th St. NW). It specializes in Cantonese cuisine, and if you're lucky enough to be in the neighborhood between 11 and 3, be sure to sample the *dim sum.*

---

**❸** Turn left off 6th Street onto H Street. The **Surratt Boarding House,** where John Wilkes Booth and his co-conspirators plotted the assassination of Abraham Lincoln, is at 604 H Street NW. (It's now a Chinese restaurant called Go-Lo's.) The colorful and ornate 75-foot-**❹** wide **Friendship Arch** that spans H Street at 7th Street is a reminder of Washington's sister-city relationship with Beijing.

**❺** To the west, at 9th and H streets, is the **Washington Convention Center.** Opened in 1983, the center pumped much-needed life into this part of downtown and spurred the development of nearby hotels and office buildings. The squat black building a block down, at 9th **❻** and G streets, is the **Martin Luther King Memorial Library,** designed by Mies van der Rohe and the largest public library in the city. A mural on the first floor depicts events in the life of the Nobel Prize–winning civil rights activist. Used books are almost always on sale at bargain prices in the library's gift shop. *801 G St. NW, tel. 202/727–1111. Open Mon.–Thurs. 9–9, Fri.–Sat. 9–5:30, Sun. 1–5.*

Across the street, on the block bounded by F, G, 7th, **❼** and 9th streets, stands the **Old Patent Office Building,** which now houses two Smithsonian museums: the **National Portrait Gallery** on the south and the **National Museum of American Art** on the north. Construction on the south wing, which was designed by Washington Monument architect Robert Mills, started in 1836. When the huge Greek-Revival quadrangle was completed in 1867 it was the largest building in the country. Many of its rooms housed glass display cabinets filled with the models inventors were required to submit with their patent applications.

During the Civil War, the Patent Office, like many other buildings in the city, was turned into a hospital. Among those caring for the wounded here were Clara Barton and Walt Whitman. In the 1950s the building was threatened with demolition to make way for a parking lot, but the efforts of preservationists saved it. The Smithsonian opened it to the public in 1968.

The first floor of the National Museum of American Art holds displays of early American art and art of the West, as well as a gallery of painted miniatures. Be sure to see *The Throne of the Third Heaven of the Nations' Millennium General Assembly*, by James Hampton. Discarded materials, such as chairs, bottles, and light bulbs, are sheathed in aluminum and gold foil in this strange and moving work of religious art. On the second floor are works by the American Impressionists, including John Henry Twachtman and Childe Hassam. There are also plaster models and marble sculptures by Hiram Powers, including the plaster cast of his famous work *The Greek Slave*, the original of which is housed in the Corcoran Gallery (*see* Tour 3, *above*). Just outside the room containing Powers's work is a copy of a sculpture Augustus Saint-Gaudens created for Henry Adams. Adams's wife had committed suicide and the original of this moving, shroud-draped figure sits above her grave in Rock Creek Cemetery. Also on this floor are massive landscapes by Albert Bierstadt and Thomas Moran. The third floor is filled with modern art, including works by Leon Kroll and Edward Hopper that were commissioned during the '30s by the federal government. The Lincoln Gallery—site of the receiving line for Abraham Lincoln's 1865 inaugural ball—has been restored to its original appearance and contains modern art by Jasper Johns, Robert Rauschenberg, Milton Avery, Kenneth Noland, and others. *8th and G Sts. NW, tel. 202/357-2700. Open daily 10–5:30; closed Dec. 25.*

You can enter the National Portrait Gallery from any floor of the National Museum of American Art or walk through the courtyard between the two wings. The best place to start a circuit of the Portrait Gallery is on the restored third floor. The mezzanine level of the wonderfully busy room features a **Civil War exhibition,** with portraits, photographs, and lithographs of such wartime personalities as Julia Ward Howe, Frederick Douglass, Ulysses S. Grant, and Robert E. Lee. There are also life casts of Abraham Lincoln's hands and face. The gallery has been restored to its American Victorian Renaissance–style splendor, complete with colorful tile flooring and a stained-glass skylight. Highlights of the Portrait Gallery's second floor include the **Hall of Presidents** (featuring a portrait or sculpture of each chief executive) and the George Washington "Lansdowne" portrait. The first floor features portraits of well-known American athletes and performers. *Time* magazine gave the museum its collection of "Person of the Year" covers and many other photos and paintings that the magazine commissioned over the years. Parts of this collection are periodically on display. *8th and F Sts. NW, tel. 202/357-2700. Open daily 10–5:30; closed Dec. 25.*

---

**Time Out**     The **Patent Pending** restaurant, between the two museums, serves an ample selection of salads, sandwiches, hot entrées, and other treats. Tables and chairs in the large museum courtyard make sitting outside the thing to do when the weather is pleasant.

---

If you leave the pair of museums in the Patent Office Building by way of the National Portrait Gallery's F Street doors, you'll come upon another of Washington's beautiful views. Directly ahead, four blocks away in the Federal Triangle, is the **National Archives** building. To the east is the green barrel-roof of **Union Station,** and to the west you can see the **Treasury Department Building.** Just across the F Street pedestrian mall and to the left is **8** the **Tariff Commission Building,** designed by Robert Mills and finished in 1866. When the Capitol was burned by the British in 1814, Congress met temporarily in a hotel that stood on this site. Another earlier building on the site housed the nation's first public telegraph office, operated by Samuel F.B. Morse.

The block of F Street between 9th and 10th streets has long been a center of shopping in the District. It's dotted with cut-rate electronics stores, pawn shops, and lingerie stores, and the sidewalks are usually crowded with shoppers looking over the wares of street vendors hawking everything from sweatshirts and sunglasses to perfumes and panty hose. Many residents fear that developers' new-found interest in old downtown may threaten this lively part of the city.

Turn left off F Street onto 10th Street. Halfway down **9** the block on the left is **Ford's Theatre.** In 1861, Baltimore theater impresario John T. Ford leased the First Baptist Church building that stood on this site and turned it into a successful music hall. The building burned down late in 1862, and Ford rebuilt it. The events of April 14, 1865, would shock the nation and close the theater. On that night, during a production of *Our American Cousin*, John Wilkes Booth entered the presidential box and assassinated Abraham Lincoln. The stricken president was carried across the street to the house of tailor William Petersen. Charles Augustus Leale, a 23-year-old doctor, attended to the president, whose injuries would have left him blind had he ever regained consciousness. To let Lincoln know that someone was nearby, Leale held his hand throughout the night. Lincoln died in the

🔟 **Petersen House** (516 10th St. NW, tel. 202/426–6830; open daily 9–5) the next morning. Visitors can see the restored front and back parlors of the house, as well as the bedroom where the president died. Most of the furnishings are not original, but the pillow and bloodstained pillowcases are those used on that fateful night.

The federal government bought Ford's Theatre in 1866 for $100,000 and converted it into office space. It was remodeled as a Lincoln museum in 1932 and was restored to its 1865 appearance in 1968. The basement museum—with artifacts such as Booth's pistol and the clothes Lincoln was wearing when he was shot—reopened in 1990 after a complete renovation. The theater itself continues to present a complete schedule of plays. *A Christmas Carol is an annual holiday favorite. 511 10th St. NW, tel. 202/426–6924. Open daily 9–5. Theater closed when rehearsals or matinees are in progress (generally Thurs. and weekends); Lincoln Museum in basement remains open at these times. Closed Christmas.*

Continue south on 10th Street and turn right on E Street. These next few blocks contain some of Washington's more unimaginative office buildings, but this stretch will lead you to Freedom Plaza and the start of your walk down the hypotenuse of Federal Triangle.

**Time Out** | The **Hard Rock Cafe** (999 E St. NW, tel. 202/737–7625) opened its Washington branch in 1989, bringing hearty American food, a modest selection of beers, and lots of those famous T-shirts (the Hard Rock's gift shop opened a full year before the restaurant did). This is a popular spot for tourists, so if you're not up to waiting in line, try to arrive early for lunch or dinner.

⓫ **Freedom Plaza,** formerly Western Plaza, is bounded by 13th, 14th, and E streets and Pennsylvania Avenue. Its east end is dominated by a **statue of General Casimir Pu-**

**laski,** the Polish nobleman who led an American cavalry corps during the Revolutionary War and was mortally wounded in 1779 at the Siege of Savannah. He gazes over a plaza that is inlaid with a detail from L'Enfant's original 1791 plan for the Federal City. Bronze markers outline the President's Palace and the Congress House; the Mall is represented by a green lawn. Cut into the edges are quotations about the capital city, not all of them complimentary. To compare L'Enfant's vision with today's reality, stand in the middle of the map's Pennsylvania Avenue and look west. L'Enfant had planned an unbroken vista from the Capitol to the White House, but the Treasury Building, constructed in 1842, ruined the view. Turning to the east you'll see the U.S. Capitol sitting on Jenkins Hill like an American Taj Mahal.

There's a lot to see and explore in the blocks near Freedom Plaza. The Beaux Arts **Willard Hotel** is on the corner of 14th Street and Pennsylvania Avenue. There was a Willard Hotel on this spot long before this ornate structure was built in 1901. The original Willard was the place to stay in Washington if you were rich or influential (or wanted to give that impression). Abraham Lincoln stayed there while waiting to move into the nearby White House. Julia Ward Howe stayed there during the Civil War and wrote "The Battle Hymn of the Republic" after gazing down from her window to see Union troops drilling on Pennsylvania Avenue. It's said the term "lobbyist" was coined to describe the favor seekers who would buttonhole President Ulysses S. Grant in the hotel's public rooms. The second Willard, with its mansard roof dotted with circular windows, was designed by Henry Hardenbergh, architect of New York's Plaza Hotel. Although it was just as opulent as the hotel it replaced, it fell on hard times after the second World War. In 1968 it closed, standing empty until 1986, when it reopened, amid much fanfare, after an ambitious restoration. The Willard's rebirth is one of the most visible successes of the Pennsylvania Avenue Development Corporation, the organization charged with reversing the decay of America's Main Street.

Just north of Freedom Plaza, on F Street between 13th and 14th streets, are **The Shops,** a collection of stores in the National Press Building, itself home to dozens of domestic and foreign media organizations. **The Shops** features sit-down retaurants, such as the **American Cafe** and the **Boston Seafood Company,** as well as fast food in its upstairs Food Hall. Washington's oldest stage, the **National Theatre,** also overlooks the plaza.

To the south of Freedom Plaza is **Federal Triangle,** the mass of government buildings constructed from 1929 to 1938 between 15th Street, Pennsylvania Avenue, and Constitution Avenue. Before Federal Triangle was developed, government workers were scattered throughout the city, largely in rented offices. Looking for a place to consolidate this work force, city planners hit on the area south of Pennsylvania Avenue, then composed of a notorious collection of rooming houses, taverns, tattoo parlors, and brothels known as "Murder Bay." A uniform classical architectural style, with Italianate red-tile roofs and interior plazas reminiscent of the Louvre, was chosen for the building project.

**⑫** The base of Federal Triangle, and the first part completed, is the **Department of Commerce** building, between 14th and 15th streets. When it opened in 1932 it was the world's largest government office building. In addition to the Commerce Department, the building houses the **National Aquarium.** Established in 1873, it's the oldest public aquarium in the United States. Displays feature tropical and freshwater fish, moray eels, frogs, turtles, piranhas, even sharks. A "touch tank" allows visitors to handle sea creatures such as crabs and oysters. *14th St. and Constitution Ave., tel. 202/377–2825. Admission: $2 adults, 75¢ children 4–12 and senior citizens. Open daily 9–5; closed Dec. 25. Sharks are fed Mon., Wed., Sat. at 2; piranhas Tues., Thurs., Sun. at 2.*

Federal Triangle's planners envisioned interior courts filled with plazas and parks, but the needs of the motor car foiled any such grand plans. The park that was planned for the spot of land between 13th and 14th streets across from the Commerce Building is now an immense parking lot. A federal office building containing an international cultural and trade center is slated to **⑬** be built here. The Beaux Arts **District Building,** at the corner of 14th Street and Pennsylvania Avenue, is the seat of the city's government. It was erected in 1908, and, though it didn't fit in with the original 1929 Federal Triangle plans, it survived.

This tour continues east on Pennsylvania Avenue, against the direction taken by newly inaugurated presidents on their way to the White House. Thomas Jefferson started the parade tradition in 1805 after taking the oath of office for his second term. He was accompanied by a few friends and a handful of congressmen. Four years later James Madison made things official by instituting a proper inaugural celebration. The flag holders on the lamp posts are clues that Pennsylvania Avenue remains the city's most important parade route. With the Capitol at one end and the White House at the other, the avenue symbolizes both the distance and the connection between these two branches of government.

Such symbolism may have been lost on early inhabitants of Washington. When Pennsylvania Avenue first opened in 1796, it was an ugly and dangerous bog. Attempts by Jefferson to beautify the road by planting poplar trees were only partially successful: Many were chopped down for firewood. In the mid–19th century, crossing the rutted thoroughfare was a dangerous proposition, and rainstorms often turned the street into a river. The avenue was finally paved with wooden blocks in 1871.

The **Postal Service** stands on the southeast corner of Pennsylvania Avenue and 13th Street. Farther down, across 12th Street, is the Romanesque **Old Post Office Building.** When it was completed, in 1899, it was the largest government building in the District, the first with a clock tower, and the first with an electric power plant. Despite these innovations, it earned the sobriquet "old" after only 18 years, when a new District post office was constructed near Union Station. When urban planners in the '20s decided to impose a uniform design on Federal Triangle, the Old Post Office was slated for demolition (some critics said it stood out like an "old tooth"). First a lack of money during the Depression, then the intercession of preservationists, headed by Nancy Hanks of the National Endowment for the Arts, saved the fanciful granite building. Major renovation was begun in 1978, and in 1984 the public areas in the Old Post Office Pavilion—an assortment of shops and restaurants inside the airy central courtyard—were opened. Other shops and restaurants were added to the pavilion's three-story, glass-enclosed East Atrium in 1992, along with City Golf, an indoor miniature golf course and bar.

Park Service rangers who work at the Old Post Office consider a trip to the observation deck in the **clock tower** to be one of Washington's best-kept secrets. While not as tall as the Washington Monument it offers nearly as impressive a view. Even better, it's usually not as crowded, the windows are bigger, and—unlike the monument's windows—they're open, allowing cool breezes to waft through. On the way down be sure to look at the Congress Bells, cast at the same British foundry that made the bells in London's Westminster Abbey. The bells are rung to honor the opening and closing of Congress and on other important occasions, such as when the Redskins win the Super Bowl. *Pennsylvania Ave. and 12th St. NW, tower tel. 202/523-5691, pavilion tel. 202/289-4224. Tower open early Apr.–early Sept., daily 8 AM–11 PM; pavilion open early Sept.–early Apr., daily 10–5:45. Shops and food court open Mon.–Sat. 10–8, Sun. noon–6.*

---

**Time Out**    The waffle-cone ice-cream confections available at **Scoops Homemade Cones,** on the lower level of the Post Office Pavilion, are especially refreshing on a hot, humid day.

---

As you cross 10th Street look to your left at the delightful trompe l'oeil mural on the side of the **Lincoln Building,** two blocks up on 10th Street. It looks as if there's a hole in the building. There's also a portrait of the building's namesake. Closer to Pennsylvania Avenue on 10th Street is an example of one of Washington's most strange and popular architectural conceits: a "façadamy." The multi-arched, redbrick facade of a 1909 building has been retained—like a bug stuck in amber—on the front of a massive shop-and-office block.

Continuing down Pennsylvania Avenue, the next big building on the right is the **Department of Justice.** Like the rest of Federal Triangle, it boasts some Art Deco features, including the cylindrical aluminum torches outside the doorways, adorned with bas-relief figures of bison, dolphins, and birds.

**⓯** Across from Justice is the **J. Edgar Hoover Federal Bureau of Investigation Building.** A hulking presence on the avenue, it was decried from birth as hideous. Even Hoover himself is said to have called it the "ugliest building I've ever seen." Opened in 1974, it hangs over 9th Street like a poured-concrete Big Brother. One thing is certain, it is secure. The tour of the building remains one of the most popular tourist activities in the city. Exhibits outline famous past cases and illustrate the Bureau's fight against organized crime, terrorism, bank robbery, espionage, and extortion. The tour ends with a live-ammo firearms demonstration. *10th St. and Pennsylvania Ave. NW (tour entrance on E St. NW), tel. 202/324-3447. Tours weekdays 8:45–4:15. Closed federal* *holidays. At peak times, there may be an hour wait for the tour.*

**16** The classical **National Archives** building fills the area between 7th and 9th streets and Pennsylvania and Constitution avenues. Beside it is a small park with a modest **memorial to Franklin Roosevelt.** The desk-sized piece of marble on the sliver of grass is exactly what the president asked for (though this hasn't stopped fans of the 32nd president in their successful efforts to secure a grander memorial to FDR in West Potomac Park, due to be completed in 1995). Designed by John Russell Pope, the Archives building was erected in 1935 on the site of the old Center Market. This large block between 7th and 9th streets had been a center of commerce since the early 1800s, when barges plying the City Canal (which flowed where Constitution Avenue is now) were loaded and unloaded here. A vestige of this mercantile past lives on in the name given to the two semicircular developments across from the Archives—**Market Square.** City planners hope the residential development will enliven this stretch of Pennsylvania Avenue.

Turn right onto 9th Street and head to the Constitution Avenue side of the Archives. All the sculpture that adorns the building was carved on the site, including the two statues that flank the flight of steps facing the Mall, *Heritage* and *Guardianship*, by James Earle Fraser. Fraser also carved the scene on the pediment, which represents the transfer of historic documents to the recorder of the Archives. (Like nearly all pediment decorations in Washington, the scene is bristling with electric wires designed to thwart the advances of destructive pigeons.)

The Declaration of Independence, the Constitution, and the Bill of Rights are on display in the Rotunda of the Archives building, in a case made of bulletproof glass, illuminated with green light, and filled with helium gas (to protect the irreplaceable documents). At night and on Christmas—the only day the Archives are closed—the documents are lowered into a vault. *Constitution Ave. between 7th and 9th Sts. NW, tel. 202/501–5000. Open Apr.–Labor Day, daily 10–9; Sept.–Mar., daily 10–5:30. Behind-the-scenes tours by reservation weekdays at 10:15 and 1:15, tel. 202/501–5205 well in advance.*

**17** Continuing down Constitution Avenue you'll come to the tip of Federal Triangle. The **Apex Building,** completed in 1938, is the home of the **Federal Trade Commis-**

**sion.** The artwork that adorns this triangular building depicts various aspects of trade. Note the relief decorations representing *Agriculture* (the harvesting of grain, by Concetta Scaravaglione) and *Trade* (two men bartering over an ivory tusk, by Carl Schmitz) over the doorways on the Constitution Avenue side. Two heroic statues by Michael Lantz on either side of the rounded eastern portico, each depicting a muscular, shirtless workman wrestling with a wild horse, represent *Man Controlling Trade.* Just across 6th Street is a three-tier fountain decorated with the signs of the zodiac; it is a memorial to Andrew Mellon, who as secretary of the treasury oversaw construction of the $125 million Federal Triangle. The impressive white-stone-and-glass building across Pennsylvania Avenue from Mellon's fountain is the **Canadian Embassy,** designed by Arthur Erickson and completed in 1988. Inside, a museum periodically displays exhibits on Canadian culture and history. *501 Pennsylvania Ave. NW, tel. 202/682–1740. Open weekdays 10–5.*

Backtrack a bit by circling the rounded end of the Federal Trade Commission Building, crossing Pennsylvania Avenue, and heading west. Pioneering photographer **Mathew Brady** had his studio in the twin-towered building at 625 Pennsylvania Avenue. He's thought to have snapped some of his pictures of the city from the building's upper windows. For years after that it was better known as the home of Apex Liquors. Sears, Roebuck and Co. now owns the building, which serves as the huge retailer's Washington lobbying office.

There is a multitude of statues and monuments at this confluence of 7th Street and Pennsylvania and Indiana avenues. The **Grand Army of the Republic** memorial pays tribute to the men who won the Civil War. Less conventional is the nearby stork-surmounted **Temperance Fountain.** It was erected in the 19th century by a teetotaling physician named Cogswell who hoped the fountain, which once dispensed ice-cold water, would lure people from the evils of drink.

Across 7th Street, close by a memorial to **General Winfield Scott,** is the recently completed **Navy Memorial.** A statue of a lone sailor stares out over the largest map in the world. To the northeast, in the Market Square development, is the memorial's visitors center. It includes a movie theater, store, and the "Navy Memorial Log Room," where a computer screen continuously scrolls the names and service records of sailors entered into the log. In the summer the memorial's concert stage is the sight of military band performances. *Tel. 202/737–2300 or 800/821–8892. Visitor's center open Mon.–Sat. 10–5, Sun. noon–5.*

The redevelopment that has rejuvenated Pennsylvania Avenue hasn't been confined solely to that famous street. **Pennsylvania Quarter** is the name given to the mix of condominiums, apartments, retail spaces, and restaurants in the blocks bounded by Pennsylvania Avenue and 6th, 9th, and G streets. The area includes the Lansburgh complex, at the corner of 8th and E streets. Built around three existing buildings (including the defunct Lansburgh department store), the complex includes the Shakespeare Theatre, which in 1992 moved from its former home in the Folger Library to this state-of-the-art, 447-seat space.

**20** The **Washington Project for the Arts** shows the challenging work of contemporary artists, many of them from the Washington area. The two floors of gallery space usually include displays of avant-garde media (photography and video) as well as visual art (paintings and sculpture). *400 7th St. NW (entrance on D St.), tel. 202/347–4813. Open Tues.–Fri. 10–6, weekends 11–5.*

WPA's **Bookworks** sells an exhaustive selection of art books—both books about art and limited-edition books created by artists that are works of art themselves. *Tel. 202/347–4590. Open weekdays 11–6, weekends 11–5.*

To reach public transportation, walk up 7th Street, then turn left on F Street and right on 9th to the Gallery Place Metro station. Or you can walk back down 7th to the National Archives station.

## Tour 6: Georgetown

*Numbers in the margin correspond to points of interest on the Tour 6: Georgetown map.*

Long before the District of Columbia was formed, Georgetown, Washington's oldest neighborhood, was a separate city that boasted a harbor full of ships and warehouses filled with tobacco. Washington has filled in around Georgetown over the years, but the former tobacco port retains an air of aloofness. Its narrow streets, which refuse to conform to Pierre L'Enfant's plan for the Federal City, make up the capital's wealthiest neighborhood and are the nucleus of its nightlife.

The area that would come to be known as George (after George II), then George Towne and, finally, Georgetown, was part of Maryland when it was settled in the early 1700s by Scottish immigrants, many of whom were attracted to the region's tolerant religious climate. Georgetown's position at the farthest point up the Potomac one could reach by boat made it an ideal transit-and-inspection point for farmers who grew tobacco in Maryland's interior. In 1789 the state granted the town a charter, but two years later Georgetown—along with Alexandria, its counterpart in Virginia—was included by George Washington in the Territory of Columbia, site of the new capital.

While Washington struggled, Georgetown thrived. Wealthy traders built their mansions on the hills overlooking the river; merchants and the working class lived in more modest homes closer to the water's edge. In 1810 a third of Georgetown's population was black— both freedmen and slaves. The **Mt. Zion Church** on 29th Street is the oldest black church in the city and was a stop on the Underground Railroad. Georgetown's rich history and success instilled in citizens of both colors feelings of superiority that many feel linger today. (When Georgetowners thought the dismal capital was dragging them down, they asked to be given back to Maryland, the way Alexandria was given back to Virginia in 1845). Tobacco eventually became a less important commodity, and Georgetown became a milling center, using water power from the Potomac. When the Chesapeake & Ohio Canal was completed in 1850, the city intensified its milling operations and became the eastern end of a waterway that stretched 184 miles to the west. The canal took up some of the slack when Georgetown's harbor began to fill with silt and the port lost business to Alexandria and Baltimore, but the canal never became the success it was meant to be.

In the years that followed, Georgetown was a far cry from the fashionable spot it is today. Clustered near the water were a foundry, a fishmarket, paper and cotton mills, and a power station for the city's streetcar system, all of which made Georgetown a smelly industrial district. It still had its Georgian, Federal, and Victorian homes, though, and when the New Deal and World War II brought a flood of newcomers to Washington, Georgetown's tree-shaded streets and handsome brick houses were rediscovered. Pushed out in the process were Georgetown's blacks, most of whom rented the houses they lived in.

Today Georgetown's zoning laws are among the city's strictest, and its historic preservationists are among the most vocal. Part of what the activists want protection from is the crush of people who descend on their community every night. This is Washington's center for restaurants, bars, nightclubs, and trendy boutiques. On M Street and Wisconsin Avenue, visitors can indulge just about any taste and take home almost any up-market souvenir. Harder to find is a parking place. The lack of a Metro station in Georgetown—apocryphally attributed to residents' desires to keep out the riff-raff—means you'll have to take a bus or walk to this part of Washington. It is a leisurely stroll from either the Foggy Bottom or Dupont Circle Metro stops.

Georgetown owes some of its charm and separate growth to geography. This town-unto-itself is separated from Washington to the east by Rock Creek. On the south it's bordered by the Potomac, on the west by Georgetown University. How far north does Georgetown reach? Probably not much farther than the large estates and parks above R Street, though developers and real estate agents would be happy to take Georgetown right up to the Canadian border if it would increase the value of property along the way.

❶ Start your exploration of Georgetown in front of the **Old Stone House** (M Street between 30th and 31st streets), thought to be Washington's only surviving pre-Revolutionary building. Built in 1764 by a cabinetmaker named Christopher Layman, this fieldstone house was used both as a residence and a place of business by a succession of occupants. Five of the house's rooms are furnished with the sort of sturdy beds, spinning wheels, and simple tables associated with middle-class Colonial America. The National Park Service maintains the house and its lovely gardens in the rear, which are planted with fruit trees and seasonal blooms. Costumed guides answer questions about the house and its history. *3051 M St. NW, tel. 202/426–6851. Open Wed.–Sun. 8–4:30; closed major holidays.*

Around the corner, at 1221 31st Street, is the old Renaissance Revival–style **Customs House.** Built in 1858 to
❷ serve the port of Georgetown, it's been transformed into the Georgetown branch of the U.S. Postal Service, and there's really no reason to go inside unless you want to buy stamps or mail postcards.

Go back to M Street and cross over to Thomas Jefferson Street (between 30th and 31st streets). For most of its

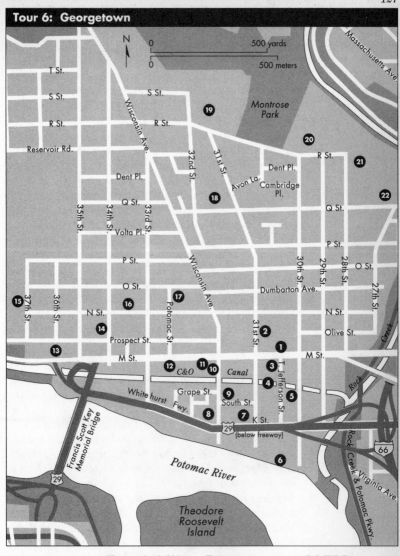

# Tour 6: Georgetown

N

0 — 500 yards
0 — 500 meters

Massachusetts Ave.

T St.
S St.
R St.
S St.
R St.
Reservoir Rd.
Wisconsin Ave.
Montrose Park
**19**
**20**
**21**
Dent Pl.
R St.
32nd St.
31st St.
Avon La.
Dent Pl.
Cambridge Pl.
**22**
Q St.
35th St.
34th St.
33rd St.
Dent Pl.
Q St.
**18**
Volta Pl.
P St.
O St.
P St.
O St.
30th St.
29th St.
28th St.
O St.
27th St.
**15**
**16**
**17**
Dumbarton Ave.
37th St.
36th St.
N St.
N St.
Olive St.
**14**
Potomac St.
**2**
**1**
Prospect St.
31st St.
**13**
M St.
M St.
**12**
C&O
**11**
**10**
Canal
**3**
T. Jefferson St.
White hurst Fwy.
Grape St.
**9**
South St.
**4**
**5**
**8**
**7**
K St.
Francis Scott Key Memorial Bridge
**29**
(below freeway)
Rock Creek
Rock Creek & Potomac Pkwy.
Virginia Ave.
**66**
**6**
**29**
Potomac River
Theodore Roosevelt Island

Chesapeake & Ohio
Canal, **4**
Cox's Row, **16**
Customs House, **2**
Dodge Warehouse, **8**
Dumbarton House, **22**
Dumbarton Oaks, **19**

Evermay, **21**
*Exorcist* steps, **13**
Foundry Mall, **5**
Georgetown Park, **11**
Georgetown
University, **15**
Grace Episcopal
Church, **9**
Halcyon House, **14**
Markethouse, **12**
Masonic lodge, **3**

Oak Hill Cemetery, **20**
Old Stone House, **1**
St. John's
Church, **17**
Suter's Tavern
plaque, **7**
Tudor Place, **18**
Vigilant Firehouse, **10**
Washington
Harbour, **6**

history, Georgetown was a working city, and the original names of its streets—Water Street, The Keys, Fishing Lane—bear witness to the importance of the harbor. The area south of M Street (originally called Bridge Street because of the bridge that spanned Rock Creek to the east) was inhabited by tradesmen, laborers, and merchants. Their homes were modest and close to Georgetown's industrial heart. The two-story brick building at 1083 **Thomas Jefferson Street** was built around 1865 as a stable for the horses and hearses of a nearby undertaker and cabinetmaker. The wide doors on the right let the horses in, while the hoist beam above the right-most window was used to lift hay and wood to the second floor. Three fine brick Federal houses stand south of the Georgetown Dutch Inn, at 1069, 1067, and 1063 Thomas Jefferson Street. The last has attractive flat lintels with keystones and a rounded keystone arch above the doorway. Across the street, at No. 1058, is a two-story brick structure built around 1810 as a ❸ **Masonic lodge.** It features interesting detailing, including a pointed facade and recessed central arch, proof of the Masons' traditional attachment to the building arts.

As you walk south on Thomas Jefferson Street, you'll ❹ pass over the **Chesapeake & Ohio Canal,** the waterway that kept Georgetown open to shipping after its harbor had filled with silt. George Washington was one of the first to advance the idea of a canal linking the Potomac with the Ohio River across the Appalachians. Work started on the C & O Canal in 1828, and when it opened in 1850, its 74 locks linked Georgetown with Cumberland, Maryland, 184 miles to the northwest (still short of its intended destination). Lumber, coal, iron, wheat, and flour moved up and down the canal, but it was never as successful as its planners had hoped it would be. Many of the bridges spanning the canal in Georgetown were too low to allow anything other than fully loaded barges to pass underneath, and competition from the Baltimore & Ohio Railroad eventually spelled an end to profitability. Today the canal is a part of the National Park system, and walkers follow the towpath once used by mules while canoers paddle the canal's calm waters. Between April and October you can go on a leisurely, mule-drawn trip aboard *The Georgetown* canal barge. ❺ Tickets are available across the canal, in the **Foundry Mall**. The mall gets its name from an old foundry that overlooked the canal at 30th Street. Around the turn of the century it was turned into a veterinary hospital that cared for mules working on the canal. Today it's a restaurant. *1055 Thomas Jefferson St., NW, tel. 202/472–4376 or 202/653–5844 for group reservations and rates. Admission: $5 adults, $3.50 senior citizens and children under 13. 90-min barge trips Apr.–Oct., daily at varied times.*

**6** Continue south, across K Street, and into **Washington Harbour,** a glittering, postmodern riverfront development designed by Arthur Cotton Moore that includes restaurants, offices, apartments, and upscale shops. The plazas around its large central fountain and gardens are dotted with the eerily realistic sculptures of J. Seward Johnson, Jr. From the edge of Washington Harbour you can see the Watergate complex and Kennedy Center to the east.

Georgetown's **K Street** is lined with the offices of architects, ad agencies, and public relations companies. In many of these offices you can hear the rumble of cars on the Whitehurst Freeway, the elevated road above K Street that leads to the Francis Scott Key Memorial Bridge. Though you'll probably have to peer through a vine-covered fence to see it, at the corner of 31st and K **7** streets is a **plaque** commemorating **Suter's Tavern.** In March 1791, in the one-story hostelry that once stood on this spot, George Washington met with the men who owned the tobacco farms and swampy marshes to the east of Georgetown and convinced them to sell their land to the government so construction of the District of Columbia could begin.

At the foot of Wisconsin Avenue is another legacy from the area's mercantile past. The last three buildings on the west side were built around 1830 by trader and merchant **Francis Dodge.** Note the heavy stone foundation **8** of the southernmost **warehouse,** its star-end braces and the broken hoist in the gable end. According to an 1838 newspaper ad, Georgetown shoppers could visit Dodge's grocery to buy such items as "Porto Rico Sugar, Marseilles soft-shelled Almonds and Havanna Segars."

Halfway up Wisconsin Avenue, on the other side of the **9** street, stands the Gothic Revival **Grace Episcopal Church.** In the mid- to late 19th century this church served the boatmen and workers from the nearby C & O Canal. At the time this was one of the poorest sections of Georgetown. (There are no "poor" sections in Georgetown anymore.)

Walking farther up Wisconsin Avenue you'll again cross the C & O Canal, this time via the only bridge that remains from the 19th century. On the north side is a simple granite obelisk honoring the men who built the waterway. A memorial of a more poignant sort can be ⑩ found at the 1840 **Vigilant Firehouse,** north of the canal at 1066 Wisconsin Avenue. A plaque set in the wall reads: "Bush, the Old Fire Dog, died of Poison, July 5th, 1869, R.I.P."

The intersection of Wisconsin Avenue and M Street is the heart of boisterous Georgetown. This spot—under the gleaming, golden dome of Riggs Bank on the northeast corner—is mobbed every weekend.

Turning left on M Street you'll come to the entrance to ⑪ **Georgetown Park** (3222 M St. NW), a multilevel shopping extravaganza that answers the question "If the Victorians had invented shopping malls, what would they look like?" Such high-ticket stores as FAO Schwarz, Liberty of London, Polo/Ralph Lauren, and Godiva Chocolates can be found within this artful, skylit mass of polished brass, tile flooring, and potted plants. If you've always looked down your nose at mall architecture, Georgetown Park might win you over.

**Time Out**    **Pizzeria Uno** (3211 M St. NW) has brought Chicago-style pizza to the heart of Georgetown. The deep-dish pies take a while to cook, but the wait is worth it. Those in a hurry may want to order the "personal-sized" pizza with soup or a salad: It's ready in five minutes and costs less than $5. Further up is **Madurai** (3318 M St. NW), a smallish, second-floor restaurant specializing in spicy vegetarian Indian cuisine.

A stroll up either M Street or Wisconsin Avenue will take you past a dizzying array of merchandise, from expensive bicycling accessories to ropes of gold, from antique jewelry and furniture to the latest fashions in clothes and records. Walking west on M Street to Poto- ⑫ mac Street you'll come to the **Markethouse,** an 1865 brick building that once housed a market filled with victual stalls. Plans are afoot to revive this once-bustling spot, which has had some variety of market here since 1795. Dean & DeLuca, the trendy Manhattan food store, plans to open a market and espresso bar here sometime in early 1993.

M Street to the west leads to the **Key Bridge** into Rosslyn, Virginia. A house owned by Francis Scott Key, author of the national anthem, was demolished in 1947 to make way for the bridge that would bear his name. A nonprofit organization has been formed to build a memorial park on the small triangle of clear ground near the bridge.

The heights of Georgetown to the north above N Street contrast with the busy jumble of the old waterfront. To reach the higher ground you can walk up M Street past the old brick streetcar barn at No. 3600 (now a block of offices), turn right, and climb the 75 **steps** that figured

⑬ prominently in the eerie climax of the movie *The Exorcist*. If you would prefer a less demanding climb, walk up 34th Street instead.

⑭ **Halcyon House,** at the corner of 34th and Prospect streets, was built in 1783 by Benjamin Stoddert, first secretary of the Navy. The object of many subsequent additions and renovations, the house is now a concatenation of architectural styles. Prospect Street gets its name from the fine views it affords of the waterfront and the river below.

The sounds of traffic diminish the farther north one walks from the bustle of M Street. To the west is

⑮ **Georgetown University,** the oldest Jesuit school in the country. It was founded in 1789 by John Carroll, first American bishop and first archbishop of Baltimore. About 12,000 students attend Georgetown, known now as much for its perennially successful basketball team as for its fine programs in law, medicine, and the liberal arts. When seen from the Potomac or from Washington's high ground, the Gothic spires of Georgetown's older buildings give the university an almost medieval look.

Architecture buffs, especially those interested in Federal and Victorian houses, enjoy wandering along the redbrick sidewalks of upper Georgetown. The average house here has two signs on it: a brass plaque notifying passersby of the building's historic interest and a window decal that warns burglars of its state-of-the-art alarm system. To get a representative taste of the houses in the area, continue north for a block on 34th Street and turn right onto N Street. The group of five Federal houses between 3339 and 3327 N Street are

⑯ known collectively as **Cox's Row,** after John Cox, a former mayor of Georgetown, who built them in 1817.

The flat-fronted, redbrick Federal house at **3307 N Street** was the home of then-Senator John F. Kennedy and his family before the White House beckoned. Turn left onto Potomac and walk a block up to O Street. O Street still has two leftovers from an earlier age: cobblestones and streetcar tracks. Residents are proud of the cobblestones, and you'll notice that even some of the concrete patches have been scored to resemble the paving stones. **St. John's Church** (3240 O St. NW, tel. 202/338–1796) was built in 1809 and is attributed to Dr. William Thornton, architect of the Capitol. Later alterations have left it looking more Victorian than Federal. At the corner of the churchyard is a memorial to Colonel Ninian Beall, the Scotsman who received the original patent for the land that would become Georgetown.

Georgetown's largest estates sit farther north, commanding fine views of Rock Creek to the east and of the old tobacco town spread out near the river below. Depending on your mood, you can walk north either on Wisconsin Avenue (the bustling commercial route) or a block east, on 31st Street (a quieter residential street). Strolling 31st Street will give you a chance to admire more of the city's finest houses.

Whichever way you go, make your way to Q Street between 31st and 32nd streets. Through the trees to the north, at the top of a sloping lawn, you'll see the neoclassical **Tudor Place,** designed by Capitol architect William Thornton and completed in 1816. The house was built for Thomas Peter, son of George-town's first mayor, and his wife Martha Custis, Martha Washington's granddaughter. It was because of this connection to the president's family that Tudor Place came to house many items from Mount Vernon. The yellow stucco house is interesting for its architecture—especially the dramatic, two-story domed portico on the south side—but its familial heritage is even more remarkable: Tudor Place stayed in the same family for 178 years, until 1983, when Armistead Peter III died. Before his death, Peter established a foundation to restore the house and open it to the public. On a house tour you'll see chairs that belonged to George Washington, Francis Scott Key's desk, and spurs of members of the Peter family who were killed in the Civil War (although the house was in Washington, the family was true to its Virginia roots and fought for Dixie). The grounds contain many specimens planted in the early 19th century. *1644 31st St. NW, tel. 202/965–0400. Suggested donation: $5. Tours Tues.–Sat. 10, 11:30, 1, and 2:30. Reservations required.*

**Dumbarton Oaks**—not to be confused with the nearby Dumbarton House—is on 32nd Street, north of R Street. Career diplomat Robert Woods Bliss and his wife, Mildred, heiress to the Fletcher's Castoria fortune, bought the property in 1920 and set about taming the sprawling grounds and removing 19th-century additions that had marred the Federal lines of the 1801 mansion. In 1940 the Blisses conveyed the estate to Harvard University, which maintains world-renowned collections of Byzantine and pre-Columbian art there. The Byzantine museum includes secular and religious items, with beautiful examples of metalwork, enameling, ivory carving, and manuscript illumination. Pre-Columbian works—artifacts and textiles from Mexico and Central and South America—are arranged in an enclosed glass pavilion designed by Philip Johnson. Events at Dumbarton Oaks have not been confined to the study of dead cultures. In 1944 representatives of the United States, Great Britain, China, and the Soviet Union met in the music room here to lay the groundwork for the United Nations.

Anyone with even a mild interest in flowers, shrubs, trees—anything that grows out of the ground—will enjoy a visit to Dumbarton Oaks' 10 acres of formal gardens, one of the loveliest spots in all of Washington (enter via R Street). Designed by noted landscape architect Beatrix Farrand, the gardens incorporate elements of traditional English, Italian, and French styles. A full-time crew of a dozen gardeners toils to maintain the stunning collection of terraces, geometric gardens, tree-shaded brick walks, fountains, arbors, and pools. Plenty of well-positioned benches make this a good place for resting weary feet, too. *Art collections: 1703 32nd St. NW, tel. 202/338–8278 (recorded information) or 202/342–3200. Suggested donation: $1. Open Tues.– Sun. 2–5. Gardens: 31st and R Sts. NW. Admission: Apr, 1–Oct. 31, $2 adults, $1 senior citizens and children, senior citizens free on Wed; Nov.1–Mar. 31, free. Open Apr. 1–Oct. 31, daily 2 –6; Nov. 1–Mar. 31, daily 2–5. Gardens and collections are closed on national holidays and Christmas eve.*

Three other sylvan retreats lie north of R Street in upper Georgetown. Originally part of the Bliss estate, **Dumbarton Oaks Park** sprawls to the north and west. **Montrose Park** lies to the east of the estate. Further ❷⓪ east is **Oak Hill Cemetery,** its funerary obelisks, crosses, and gravestones spread out like an amphitheater of the dead on a hill overlooking Rock Creek. Near the entrance is an 1850 Gothic-style chapel designed by Smithsonian Castle architect James Renwick. Across from the chapel is the resting place of actor, playwright, and diplomat John H. Payne, who is remembered today primarily for his song "Home Sweet Home." A few hundred feet to the north is the circular tomb of William Corcoran, founder of the Corcoran Gallery of Art. *30th and R Sts. NW, tel. 202/337–2835. Open Mon.–Fri. 9–4:30; closed major holidays.*

**㉑** Walking south on 28th Street you'll pass **Evermay** (1623 28th St. NW). The Georgian manor house, built around 1800 by real estate speculator Samuel Davidson, is almost hidden by its black-and-gold gates and high brick wall. Davidson wanted it that way. He sometimes took out advertisements in newspapers warning sightseers to avoid his estate "as they would a den of devils or rattlesnakes." The mansion is in private hands, but its grounds are often opened for garden tours.

**㉒** A few steps east of 28th Street on Q Street is **Dumbarton House,** the headquarters of the National Society of the Colonial Dames of America. Its symmetry and the two bow wings on the north side make Dumbarton, built around 1800, a distinctive example of Georgian architecture. The man who built the house, Joseph Nourse, was registrar of the U.S. Treasury. Other well-known Americans have spent time at the house, including Dolley Madison, who is said to have stopped here when fleeing Washington in 1814. One hundred years later, the house was moved 50 feet up the hill, when Q Street was cut through to the Dumbarton Bridge.

Eight rooms inside Dumbarton House have been restored to their Colonial splendor and are decorated with period furnishings, such as mahogany American Chippendale chairs, hallmark silver, Persian rugs, and a breakfront cabinet filled with rare books. Notable items include a 1789 Charles Willson Peale portrait of Benjamin Stoddert's children (with an early view of Georgetown harbor in the background), Martha Washington's traveling cloak, and a British redcoat's red coat. *2715 Q St. NW, tel. 202/337–2288. Open Mon.–Sat. 9–12:30. Guided tours in the afternoon by appointment. Occasionally closed weekends for private events.*

---

**Tour 7: Dupont Circle**

*Numbers in the margin correspond to points of interest on the Tour 7: Dupont Circle map.*

Three of Washington's main thoroughfares intersect at Dupont Circle: Connecticut, New Hampshire, and Massachusetts avenues. With a handsome small park and a splashing fountain in the center, Dupont Circle is more than a deserted island around which traffic flows, making it an exception among Washington circles. The activity on the circle spills over into the surrounding streets, one of the liveliest, most vibrant neighborhoods in Washington.

Development near Dupont Circle started during the post–Civil War boom of the 1870s. As the city increased in stature, the nation's wealthy and influential citizens began building their mansions near the Circle. The area underwent a different kind of transformation in the middle of this century, when the middle and upper classes deserted Washington for the suburbs, and in the '60s the Circle became the starting point for marches sponsored by various counterculture groups. Today the neighborhood is once again fashionable, and its many restaurants, off-beat shops, and specialty bookstores lend it a distinctive, cosmopolitan air.

❶ Start your exploration in **Dupont Circle** itself (Metro stop, Dupont Circle). Originally known as Pacific Circle, this hub was the westernmost circle in Pierre L'Enfant's original design for the Federal City. The name was changed in 1884, when Congress authorized construction of a bronze statue honoring Civil War hero Admiral Samuel F. Dupont. The statue fell into disrepair, and Dupont's family—who had never liked it anyway—replaced it in 1921 with the fountain you see today. The marble fountain, with its allegorical figures Sea, Stars, and Wind, was created by Daniel Chester French, the sculptor of Lincoln's statue in the Lincoln Memorial.

As you look around the circumference of the circle, you'll be able to see the special constraints within which architects in Washington must work. Since a half dozen streets converge on Dupont Circle, the buildings around it are, for the most part, wedge-shaped and set on oddly shaped plots of land like massive slices of pie.

Only two of the great houses that stood on the circle in the early 20th century remain today. The Renaissance-style house at **15 Dupont Circle,** next to P Street, was built in 1903 for Robert W. Patterson, publisher of the *Washington Times–Herald*. Patterson's daughter, Cissy, who succeeded him as publisher of the paper, was known for hosting parties that attracted such notables as William Randolph Hearst, Douglas MacArthur, and J. Edgar Hoover. In 1927, while Cissy was living in New York City and the White House was being refurbished, Calvin Coolidge and his family stayed in this Dupont

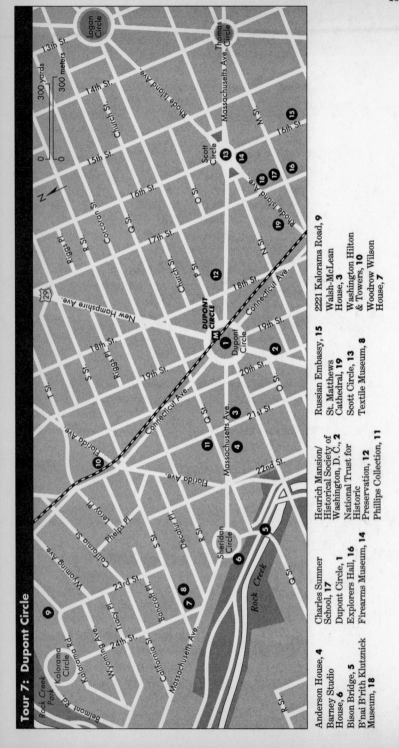

# Tour 7: Dupont Circle

Anderson House, **4**
Barney Studio House, **6**
Bison Bridge, **5**
B'nai B'rith Klutznick Museum, **18**

Charles Sumner School, **17**
Dupont Circle, **1**
Explorers Hall, **16**
Firearms Museum, **14**

Heurich Mansion/ Historical Society of Washington, D. C., **2**
National Trust for Historic Preservation, **12**
Phillips Collection, **11**

Russian Embassy, **15**
St. Matthews Cathedral, **19**
Scott Circle, **13**
Textile Museum, **8**

2221 Kalorama Road, **9**
Walsh-McLean House, **3**
Washington Hilton & Towers, **10**
Woodrow Wilson House, **7**

Circle home. The Coolidges received American flyer Charles Lindbergh here; some of the most famous photographs of Lindy were taken as he stood on the house's balcony and smiled down at the crowds below. After Patterson's death the house was bought by the Washington Club. The **Sulgrave Club,** at the corner of Massachusetts Avenue, was also once a private home and is now likewise a club. Neither is open to the public.

Cross the traffic circle carefully and head south on New Hampshire Avenue. A block down on the left is the impressive **Heurich Mansion,** whose dark sandstone walls and stolid countenance provide quite a contrast to the two gay houses on the circle. This severe Romanesque Revival mansion was the home of Christian Heurich, a German orphan who made his fortune in this country in the beer business. Heurich's brewery was located in Foggy Bottom, where the Kennedy Center stands today. Brewing was a dangerous business in the 19th century, and fires had more than once reduced Heurich's beer factory to ashes. Perhaps because of this he insisted that his home, completed in 1894, be fireproof. Although 17 fireplaces were installed—some with onyx facings, one with the bronze image of a lion staring out from the back—not a single one ever held a fire.

After Heurich's widow died, in 1955, the house was turned over to the **Historical Society of Washington, D.C.** Today it serves as the group's headquarters and houses its voluminous archives. All the furnishings in the house were owned and used by the Heurichs. The interior of the house is an eclectic Victorian treasure trove filled with plaster detailing, carved wooden doors, and painted ceilings. The downstairs breakfast room, where Heurich, his wife, and their three children ate most of their meals, is decorated like a rathskeller and is adorned with such German sayings as "A good drink makes old people young."

Heurich must have taken the German proverbs seriously. He drank his beer every day, had three wives (not all at once), and lived to be 102. (Heurich's grandson Gary recently started brewing the family beer in Pittsburgh. He ships it to Washington and vows to build someday another Heurich brewery here.) Docents who give tours of the house are adept at answering questions about other Washington landmarks, too. *1307 Connecticut Ave. NW, tel. 202/785-2068. Admission: $3 adults, $1.50 senior citizens, children through 12th grade free. Open Wed.–Sat. noon–4.*

Cross New Hampshire Avenue and turn left on O Street. The row houses on this block are a little less impressive than Heurich's castle, but they are examples of what makes Dupont Circle so attractive to Washington's young professionals: spacious brick Victorian town houses close to nightlife, offices, and public transportation.

Turn north on 21st Street and cross P Street. This area has a high concentration of restaurants and bars and is crowded and boisterous at night. It also serves as an informal crossroads for Washington's gay community. (There are several gay night spots farther up P Street.)

**Time Out** Various branches of **Pan Asian Noodles & Grill** (2020 P St. NW) have been spreading through Washington lately (they're up to three now), but luckily the quality hasn't been compromised. Reasonably priced noodle dishes from around the Orient (thus *Pan* Asian) are the specialty.

At the corner of Massachusetts Avenue and 21st Street
**3** is the opulent **Walsh-McLean House.** Tom McLean was an Irishman who made a fortune with a Colorado gold mine and came to Washington to show his wealth. Washington was the perfect place to establish a presence for America's late–19th-century nouveau riche. It was easier to enter "society" in the nation's planned capital than in New York or Philadelphia, and wealthy industrialists and lucky entrepreneurs flocked to the city on the Potomac. Walsh announced his arrival with this 60-room mansion. His daughter, Evalyn Walsh-McLean, the last private owner of the Hope diamond (now in the Smithsonian's Museum of Natural History), was one of the city's leading hostesses. Today the house is used as an embassy by the Indonesian government. The **Jockey Club** restaurant in the redbrick Ritz-Carlton Hotel across the street was a favorite lunching spot of former first lady Nancy Reagan.

Head west on Massachusetts Avenue. The palatial home at No. 2118 is a mystery even to many longtime Washingtonians, who assume it's just another embassy.
**4** **Anderson House** is not an embassy, though it does have a link to the diplomatic world. Larz Anderson was a diplomat whose career included postings to Japan and Belgium. Anderson and his heiress wife, Isabel, toured the world, picking up objects that struck their fancy. They filled their residence, which was constructed in 1905, with the booty of their travels, including choir stalls

from an Italian Renaissance church, Flemish tapestries, and a large—if spotty—collection of Asian art. All this remains in the house, for visitors to see.

In accordance with Anderson's wishes, the building also serves as the headquarters of the **Society of the Cincinnati.** The oldest patriotic organization in the country, the society was formed in 1783 by a group of officers who had served with George Washington during the Revolutionary War. The group took the name Cincinnati from Cincinnatus, a distinguished Roman who, circa 500 BC, led an army against Rome's enemies and later quelled civil disturbances in the city. After each instance he returned to the simple life on his farm. The story impressed the American officers, who saw in it a mirror of their own situation: They too would leave the battlefields behind to get on with the business of forging a new nation. (One such member went on to name the city in Ohio.) Today's members are direct descendants of those American revolutionaries.

Many of the displays in the society's museum focus on the Colonial period and the Revolutionary War. One room—painted in a marvelous trompe l'oeil style that deceives visitors into thinking the walls are covered with sculpture—is filled with military miniatures from the United States and France. (Because of the important role France played in defeating the British, French officers were invited to join the society. Pierre L'Enfant, "Artist of the Revolution" and planner of Washington, designed the society's eagle medallion.)

The house is often used by the federal government to entertain visiting dignitaries. Amid the glitz, glamour, beauty, and patriotic spectacle of the mansion are two delightful painted panels in the solarium that depict the Andersons' favorite motor-car sightseeing routes around Washington. *2118 Massachusetts Ave. NW, tel. 202/785–2040. Open Tues.–Sat. 1–4.*

Across the street at 2121 Massachusetts Avenue is the **Cosmos Club,** founded in 1878 and perhaps the most exclusive private club in the city. Neither money nor influence will get you on the membership rolls. It takes brains. Different rooms in the club celebrate members who have won Nobel prizes or appeared on postage stamps. The formerly men-only club started accepting women in 1988. Judith Martin (aka Miss Manners) was one of the first admitted.

**⑤** Head west on Q Street, past a row of expensive town houses, to the **Bison Bridge.** Tour guides at the Smithsonian's Museum of Natural History are quick to remind visitors that America never had buffalo; the big animals that roamed the plains were bison. Though many maps and guidebooks call this the Buffalo Bridge, the four bronze statues by A. Phimister Proctor are of bison. Officially called the **Dumbarton Bridge,** the structure stretches across Rock Creek Park into Georgetown. Its sides are decorated with busts of Native Americans, the work of architect Glenn Brown, who, along with his son Bedford, designed the bridge in 1914. The best way to see the busts is to walk the footpath along Rock Creek or to lean over the green railings beside the bison and peer through the trees.

Walking north on 23rd Street you'll pass between two more embassies, those of Turkey and Romania, both of which sit on **Sheridan Circle** and are topped with antennae as big as trampolines used to send messages back to the homeland.

**⑥** The Mediterranean-style **Barney Studio House** at 2306 Massachusetts Avenue was built in 1902, one of the first homes constructed on Sheridan Circle. Alice Pike Barney was a Cincinnati heiress who early on developed a love of art, artists, and the bohemian lifestyle. Having toured the capitals of Europe, she felt Washington paled in comparison. This was her assessment of Washington culture at the turn of the century: "What is capital life after all? Small talk and lots to eat, an infinite series of teas and dinners. Art? There is none." Her own home eventually became a salon, a meeting place for Washington's cultural elite. It also served as her studio (Barney was an artist as well as an art lover). The renovated home is part of the Smithsonian's National Museum of American Art and contains paintings by Barney and her friends, as well as a collection of furniture, rugs, and other antiques. *2306 Massachusetts Ave. NW, tel. 202/ 357–3111. Tours Wed. and Thurs. at 11 and 1 and 2nd and 4th Sun. of each month at 1; tour for group of 5 or more by appointment only.*

Although the entire Dupont Circle area is dotted with embassies, the stretch of Massachusetts Avenue on either side of Sheridan Circle is known as Embassy Row proper. The area is rife with delegations from foreign countries, and a stroll down the street will provide you with an opportunity to test your knowledge of the world's flags.

Continue west on Massachusetts Avenue. The **Came-
roon Embassy** is housed in the mansion at 2349 Massachusetts Avenue. This fanciful castle, with its conical
tower, bronze weathervane, and intricate detailing
around the windows and balconies, is the westernmost
of the Beaux Arts–style mansions built along Massachusetts Avenue in the late 19th and early 20th centuries.

Turn right on S Street. The statue on the left commemorates Irish patriot **Robert Emmet;** it was dedicated in
1966 to mark the 50th anniversary of Irish independence. A small reproduction can be found in the
❼ **Woodrow Wilson House,** a few hundred feet down S
Street. Wilson is the only president who stayed in Washington after leaving the White House. (He's also the
only president buried in the city, inside the Washington
Cathedral.) He and his second wife, Edith Bolling Wilson, retired in 1920 to this Georgian Revival house designed by Washington architect Waddy B. Wood. (Wood
also designed the Department of the Interior Building
on C Street.) The house had been built in 1915 for a carpet magnate, and on the first and third floors you can
still see the half-snaps that run along the edges of the
floors to hold down the long-gone wall-to-wall carpeting.

President Wilson suffered a stroke toward the end of his
second term, in 1919, and he lived out the last few years
of his life on this quiet street. Edith made sure he was
comfortable; she had a bed constructed that was the
same dimensions as the large Lincoln bed Wilson had
slept in in the White House. She also had the house's
trunk lift electrified so the partially paralyzed president could move from floor to floor. When the streetcars
stopped running in 1962 the elevator stopped working.
It had received its electricity directly from the streetcar
line.

After Edith died, in 1961, the house and its contents
were bequeathed to the National Trust for Historic Preservation. On view inside are such items as a Gobelins
tapestry, a baseball signed by King George V, and the
shell casing from the first shot fired by U.S. forces in
World War I. The house also contains memorabilia related to the history of the short-lived League of Nations, including the colorful flag Wilson hoped would be
adopted by that organization. *2340 S St. NW, tel. 202/
387–4062. Admission: $4 adults, $2.50 senior citizens*

*and students, children under 7 free. Open Tues.–Sun.
10–4; closed major holidays.*

Just next door, in a house that was also designed by
❽ Waddy Wood, is the **Textile Museum.** In the 1890s,
founder George Hewitt Myers purchased his first Oriental rug for his dorm room at Yale and subsequently collected more than 12,000 textiles and 1,500 carpets. An
heir to the Bristol-Myers fortune, Myers and his wife
lived two houses down from Wilson, at 2310 S Street, in
a home designed by John Russell Pope, architect of the
National Archives and Jefferson Memorial. Myers
bought the house next door, at No. 2320, and opened his
museum to the public in 1925. Rotating exhibits are tak-
en from a permanent collection of historic and ethno-
graphic items that include Coptic textiles, Kashmir
embroidery, Turkman tribal rugs, and pre-Columbian
textiles from Central and South America. At least one
show of modern textiles—such as quilts or fiber art—is
mounted each year. *2320 S St. NW, tel. 202/667–0441.
Suggested donation: $5. Open Mon.–Sat. 10–5, Sun.
1–5; closed major holidays. Highlight tours: Sept.–
May; Wed., Sat., and Sun. at 2.*

S Street is an informal dividing line between the Dupont
Circle area to the south and the exclusive **Kalorama**
neighborhood to the north. The name for this peaceful,
tree-filled enclave—Greek for "beautiful view"—was
contributed by politician and writer Joel Barlow, who
bought the large tract in 1807. Kalorama is filled with
embassies and luxurious homes. Walk north on 23rd
❾ Street until it dead-ends at the Tudor mansion at **2221
Kalorama Road.** This imposing house was built in 1911
for mining millionaire W.W. Lawrence, but since 1936 it
has been the residence of the French ambassador. For a
taste of the beautiful view that so captivated Barlow,
walk west on Kalorama Road, then turn right on
Kalorama Circle. At the bottom of the circle you can look
down over Rock Creek Park, the finger of green that
pokes into northwest Washington.

Walk back down 23rd Street then left down Kalorama.
The large, beige institutional building on the left near
Connecticut Avenue is the Chinese Embassy. Turn
right and walk south down Connecticut Avenue. On the
❿ left at 1919 Connecticut is the **Washington Hilton & Towers,** home of the largest ballroom on the East Coast and
site of John Hinckley's 1981 assassination attempt on
Ronald Reagan.

Turn right on R Street then left on 21st Street. Many private art galleries—selling the work of local, national, and international artists—have sprung up around here, perhaps to bask in the glow of our next stop.

Washington has many museums that are the legacy of one great patron, but the **Phillips Collection,** at 21st and Q streets, is among the most beloved. In 1918 Duncan Phillips, grandson of a founder of the Jones and Laughlin Steel Company, started to collect art for a museum that would stand as a memorial to his father and brother, who had died within 13 months of each other. Three years later what was first called the Phillips Memorial Gallery opened in two rooms of this Georgian-Revival home near Dupont Circle. It was the first permanent museum of modern art in the country.

Not interested in a painting's market value or its faddishness, Phillips searched for works that impressed him as outstanding products of a particular artist's unique vision. Holdings include works by George Braque, Paul Cézanne, Paul Klee, Henri Matisse, John Henry Twachtman, and the largest museum collection in the country of the work of Pierre Bonnard. The exhibits change regularly. The collection's best-known paintings include Renoir's *Luncheon of the Boating Party*, *Repentant Peter*s by both Goya *and* El Greco, *A Bowl of Plums* by 18thcentury artist Jean-Baptiste Siméon Chardin, Degas's *Dancers at the Bar*, Van Gogh's *Entrance to the Public Garden at Arles*, and Cézanne's self-portrait, the painting Phillips said he would save first if his gallery caught fire. During the '20s, Phillips and his wife, Marjorie, started to support American Modernists such as John Marin, Georgia O'Keeffe, and Arthur Dove.

The Phillips is a comfortable museum. Works of a favorite artist are often grouped together in "exhibition units," and unlike most other galleries (where uniformed guards appear uninterested in the masterpieces around them) the Phillips employs students of art, many of whom are artists themselves, to sit by the paintings and answer visitors' questions.

The Phillips family moved out of the house in 1930. An addition was built in 1960 and renovated and renamed the Goh Annex in 1989. It gave the Phillips 50% more exhibit space and is host to traveling exhibits and rotating selections from the museum's permanent collection. *1600–1612 21st St. NW, tel. 202/387–2151. Admission: weekends, $5 adults, $2.50 students and senior citizens;*

*suggested donation weekdays, $5 adults, $2.50 students and senior citizens. Open Tues.–Sat. 10–5, Sun. 2–7. Goh Annex closes Sun. at 5. Tours Wed. and Sat. at 2. Gallery talks 1st and 3rd Thurs. at 12:30.*

After visiting the Phillips, walk east on Q Street and turn south on Connecticut Avenue.

---

**Time Out**    Connecticut Avenue above and below Dupont Circle is chockablock with restaurants that will satisfy any craving. Two favorites are the **Chesapeake Bagel Bakery** (1636 Connecticut Ave.), a low-key lunchroom that features a wide variety of bagel sandwiches, and **Cafe Splendide** (1521 Connecticut Ave.), a cozy spot that serves soups, salads, German-style entrées, and bread and pastries baked on the premises.

---

Skirt the circle and walk east on Massachusetts Avenue. **12** The **National Trust for Historic Preservation** sits at the corner of 18th Street and Massachusetts Avenue in, naturally, a building that has been historically preserved. The building once housed some of the most luxurious apartments in the city. The Beaux Arts–style McCormick Apartments, designed by Jules H. de Sibour, were built in 1917 and contained only six apartments, one on each floor, each with 11,000 square feet of space. Some of Washington's most prominent citizens lived here, including hostess Perle Mesta and Andrew Mellon, secretary of the treasury under three presidents, whose top-floor flat contained many of the paintings that would later go to the National Gallery of Art. During World War II the building was converted to office space, and in 1977 it was bought by the National Trust. The building is closed to the public, but a quick peek at the circular lobby will give you an idea of the lavish world its one-time residents inhabited.

Continue down Massachusetts Avenue. On the left is the **Brookings Institution,** one of dozens of think tanks in Washington that offer their partisan and nonpartisan advice to whoever is in power or whoever would like to be. Farther east on the left you'll spot the **Australian Embassy,** containing a gallery that periodically shows works of art of an antipodean nature. *1601 Massachusetts Ave. NW, tel. 202/797–3255. Open weekdays 9–4:30.*

**13** **Scott Circle** is at the center of the intersections of Massachusetts and Rhode Island avenues and 16th Street. The equestrian statue of **General Winfield Scott** was cast from cannon captured in the Mexican War. On the west side of Scott Circle there is a statue of fiery orator **Daniel Webster.** If you walk to the south side of the circle and look down 16th Street you'll get a familiar view of the columns of the White House, six blocks away. Across the circle is an interesting memorial to **S.C.F. Hahnemann,** his statue sitting in a recessed wall, his head surrounded by a mosaic of colorful tiles. (Who, you ask, was S.C.F. Hahnemann? He was the founder of the homeopathic school of medicine. Washington is a city of monuments, not all of them to people whose names are household words.)

The headquarters of the National Rifle Association is also near the circle. There are dozens of guns on display **(14)** in the NRA's **Firearms Museum,** from muzzle-loading flintlocks used in the Revolutionary War to high-tech pistols used by Olympic shooting teams. Also on display are weapons that once belonged to presidents, such as Teddy Roosevelt's .32 caliber Browning pistol and a Winchester rifle used by Dwight Eisenhower. *1600 Rhode Island Ave. NW, tel. 202/828–6253. Open daily 10–4; closed major holidays.*

One block south on 16th Street stands the **Jefferson Hotel.** Designed by Jules H. de Sibour, the man responsible for the McCormick, it too started out as apartments but was converted to a hotel in the '50s. It has a reputation for luxury and discretion and is a favorite temporary home for White House cabinet members awaiting confirmation. Farther down 16th Street, the red, white, **(15)** and blue flag of Russia flies before the **Russian Embassy** (1125 16th St. NW), housed in an ornate mansion that was built for the widow of George Pullman of railroad-car fame. It first did diplomatic duty as the Imperial Russian Embassy, then became the Soviet Embassy, and now it's Russian once again. The rest of the ex-Soviet republics were left scrambling for their own embassies after the break-up of the USSR in 1991.

Turn right onto M Street. On the southwest corner of 16th and M streets sits the headquarters of the **National Geographic Society.** Founded in 1888, the society is best known for its yellow-bordered magazine, found in family rooms and attics across the country. The society has sponsored numerous expeditions throughout its 100-year history, including those of Admirals Peary and Byrd and underwater explorer Jacques Cousteau. **(16)** **Explorers Hall,** entered from 17th Street, is the magazine come to life. Recently renovated, Explorers Hall invites visitors to learn about the world in a decidedly interactive way. You can experience everything from a minitornado to video "touch-screens" that explain various geographic concepts and then quiz you on what you've learned. The most dramatic events take place in Earth Station One, a 72-seat amphitheater that sends the audience on a journey around the world. The centerpiece is a hand-painted globe, 11 feet in diameter, that floats and spins on a cushion of air, showing off different features of the planet. Less high-tech, but no less popular, is Henry, a live blue-and-gold macaw that has been a fixture in Explorers Hall since 1964. *17th and M Sts., tel. 202/857–7588 (recorded information), 202/857–7689 (group tour information). Open Mon.–Sat. and holidays 9–5, Sun. 10–5.*

**⓱** Across M Street is the **Charles Sumner School,** built in 1872 for the education of black children in the city. It takes its name from the Massachusetts senator who delivered a blistering attack against slavery in 1856 and was savagely caned as a result by a congressman from South Carolina. The building was designed by Adolph Cluss, who created the Arts and Industries Building on the Mall. It is typical of the District's Victorian-era public schools. Beautifully restored in 1986, the school serves mainly as a conference center, though it hosts changing art exhibits and houses a permanent collection of memorabilia relating to the city's public school system. *1201 17th St. NW, tel. 202/727–3419. Open Mon.–Sat. 9–5. Often closed for conferences; call ahead to arrange tours.*

Further up 17th Street, at the corner of Rhode Island
**⓲** Avenue, is the **B'nai B'rith Klutznick Museum,** devoted to the history of the Jewish people. The museum's permanent exhibits span 20 centuries and highlight Jewish festivals and the rituals employed to mark the various stages of life. A wide variety of Jewish decorative art, adorning such items as spice boxes and Torah wrappers, is on display. *1640 Rhode Island Ave. NW, tel. 202/857–6583. Open Sun.–Fri. 10–5; closed Sat. and federal and Jewish holidays.*

Half a block west on Rhode Island Avenue, across from a memorial to nuns who served as nurses during the Civil
**⓳** War, is **St. Matthews Cathedral,** the seat of Washington's Catholic archbishop. John F. Kennedy frequently worshipped in this Renaissance-style church, and in 1963 his funeral mass was held within its richly decorated walls. Set in the floor, directly in front of the main altar, is a

memorial to the slain president: "Here rested the remains of President Kennedy at the requiem mass November 25, 1963, before their removal to Arlington where they lie in expectation of a heavenly resurrection." *1725 Rhode Island Ave. NW, tel. 202/347–3215. Open weekdays and Sun. 6:30–6, Sat. 7:30–6:30. Tours Sun. 2:30–4:30.*

You are now equidistant from two Metro stations. Dupont Circle is two blocks north on Connecticut Avenue, and Farragut North is one block south.

---

### Tour 8: Foggy Bottom

*Numbers in the margin correspond to points of interest on the Tour 8: Foggy Bottom map.*

The Foggy Bottom area of Washington—roughly bordered by the Potomac and Rock Creek to the west, 20th Street to the east, Pennsylvania Avenue to the north, and Constitution Avenue to the south—has three main claims to fame: the State Department, the Kennedy Center, and George Washington University. In 1763 a German immigrant named Jacob Funk purchased this land, and a community called Funkstown sprang up on the Potomac. This nickname is only slightly less amusing than the present one, an appellation that owes its derivation to the wharves, breweries, lime kilns, and glassworks that were built near the water. Smoke from these factories combined with the swampy air of the low-lying ground to produce a permanent fog along the waterfront.

The smoke-belching factories ensured work for the hundreds of German and Irish immigrants who settled in Foggy Bottom in the 19th century. By the 1930s, however, industry was on the way out, and Foggy Bottom had become a poor, predominantly black part of Washington. The opening of the State Department headquarters in 1947 reawakened middle-class interest in the neighborhood's modest row houses. Many of them are now gone, and Foggy Bottom today suffers from a split personality, and tiny, one-room-wide row houses sit next to large, mixed-use developments.

Start your exploration near the Foggy Bottom Metro station on 23rd Street near I Street. The campus of **❶ George Washington University** covers much of Foggy Bottom south of Pennsylvania Avenue between 19th and 24th streets. George Washington had always hoped the capital would be home to a world-class university. He

**Tour 8: Foggy Bottom**

KEY

AE American Express Office

even left 50 shares of stock in the Potowmack Canal Co.
to endow it. Congress never acted upon his wishes, however, and it wasn't until 1822 that the university that
would eventually be named after the first president began to take shape. The private Columbian College in the
District of Columbia opened that year with the aim of
training students for the Baptist ministry. In 1904, the
university shed its Baptist connections and changed its
name to George Washington University. In 1912, it
moved to its present location and since that time has become the second largest landholder in the District (after
the federal government). Students have ranged from J.
Edgar Hoover to Jacqueline Kennedy Onassis. In addition to modern university buildings GWU occupies
many 19th-century houses.

Walk west from the Metro station on the I Street pedestrian mall, then turn left on New Hampshire Avenue.
Across Virginia Avenue is the **Watergate,** possibly the
world's most notorious apartment/office complex, famous for the events that took place here on June 17,
1972. As Nixon aides E. Howard Hunt, Jr., and G. Gordon Liddy sat in the Howard Johnson Motor Lodge
across the street, five men were caught trying to bug the

headquarters of the Democratic National Committee on the sixth floor of 2600 Virginia Avenue. (There's a marketing company in that space today.)

Even before the break-in, the Watergate—which first opened in 1965—was well known in the capital. Within its distinctive curving lines and behind its "toothpick" balusters have lived some of Washington's famous, including John Mitchell and Rose Mary Woods of Nixon White House fame, and such politicians as Jacob Javits, Alan Cranston, and Robert and Elizabeth Dole. The embassies of Qatar, the United Arab Emirates, Sweden, and Yemen are also in the Watergate. The suffix "-gate" is attached to any political scandal nowadays, but the Watergate itself was named after a monumental flight of steps leading down to the Potomac behind the Lincoln Memorial. The original Watergate was the sight of band concerts until airplane noise from nearby National Airport made the site impractical.

Walk south on New Hampshire Avenue, past the Saudi Arabian Embassy, to the **John F. Kennedy Center for the Performing Arts.** The opening of the Kennedy Center in 1971 established Washington as a cultural city to be reckoned with. Concerts, ballets, opera, musicals, and drama are presented in the center's five theaters, and movies are screened almost every night in the theater of the American Film Institute.

The idea for a national cultural center had been proposed by President Eisenhower in 1958. John F. Kennedy had also strongly supported the idea, and after his assassination it was decided to dedicate the center to him as a living memorial. Some critics have called the center's square design unimaginative—it's been dubbed the cake box that the more decorative Watergate came in—but no one has denied that the building is immense. The Grand Foyer, lighted by 18 one-ton Orrefors crystal chandeliers, is 630 feet long. (Even at this size it is mobbed at intermission.) Many of the center's furnishings were donated by foreign countries: The chandeliers came from Sweden, the Matisse tapestries outside the Opera House came from France, and the 3,700 tons of white Carrara marble for the interior and exterior of the building were a gift from Italy. Flags fly in the Hall of Nations and the Hall of States, and in the center of the foyer is a seven-foot-high bronze bust of Kennedy by sculptor Robert Berks.

The Library of Congress maintains a **Performing Arts Library** on the roof terrace level, mounting periodic theatrical and musical exhibits (original Mozart manuscripts were a recent offering). If you can tolerate the sound of jets screaming up the Potomac to National Airport, you can get one of the city's better views from the rooftop terrace: To the north are Georgetown and the National Cathedral; to the west Theodore Roosevelt Island and Rosslyn, Virginia; and to the south the Lincoln and Jefferson memorials. *New Hampshire Ave. and Rock Creek Pkwy. NW, tel. 202/467-4600. Open daily 10 AM–midnight. Box office open Mon.–Sat. 10–9, Sun. and holidays noon–9. Tours daily 10–1, tel. 202/416–8341 for tour information. Performing Arts Library, tel. 202/707-6245. Open Tues.–Fri. 11–8:30, Sat. 10–6.*

---

**Time Out**  There are two restaurants on the top floor of the Kennedy Center. The **Roof Terrace Restaurant** is the most expensive, with a lunch menu that offers open-faced sandwiches and salads. The **Encore Cafeteria** has soups, chili, salads, and hot entrées starting at under $5.

Walk back up New Hampshire Avenue; then turn right on G Street, right on Virginia Avenue (follow the outstretched arm of the **statue of Benito Juárez**, the famed Mexican statesman) and right on 23rd Street. The **Pan American Health Organization,** American headquarters of the World Health Organization, is at 23rd Street and Virginia Avenue, in the building that looks like a huge car air filter.

Two blocks down is the massive **Department of State building.** On the top floor are the opulent **Diplomatic Reception Rooms**, decorated in the manner of great halls of Europe and the rooms of Colonial American plantations. The museum-quality furnishings include a Philadelphia Highboy, a Paul Revere bowl, and the desk on which the Treaty of Paris was signed. The largest room boasts a specially-loomed carpet so heavy and large it had to be airlifted in by helicopter. The rooms are used 15 to 20 times a week to entertain foreign diplomats and heads of state; you can see them, too, but you need to register for a tour well in advance of your visit. *23rd and C Sts. NW, tel. 202/647–3241. Tours weekdays at 9:30, 10:30, and 3. Summer tours must be booked up to 3 months in advance.*

Across C Street is the **U.S. Naval Medical Command.** In an early sketch of Washington, Thomas Jefferson placed the Capitol atop this hill. One of the federal government's earliest scientific installations was a naval observatory built here in 1844. By the 1880s, however, Foggy

Bottom's smoke and haze forced officials to move the observatory to higher ground, in northwest Washington.

Continue down 23rd Street and turn left onto Constitution Avenue. On the south side of Constitution are the Lincoln and Vietnam Veterans memorials (*see* Tour 2:
**7** The Monuments, above). The **American Pharmaceutical Association** building is on the corner of Constitution Avenue and 23rd Street. This white-marble building was designed by John Russell Pope and completed in 1934. The APA is one of more than 3,000 trade and professional associations (as obscure as the Cast Iron Soil Pipe Institute and as well known as the National Association of Broadcasters) that have chosen Washington for their headquarters, eager to represent their members' interests before the government.

**8** One block east is the **National Academy of Sciences.** Inscribed in Greek under the cornice is a quotation from Aristotle on the value of science. Inside, there are often free art exhibits—not all of them relating to science. In front of the academy is Robert Berks's **sculpture of Albert Einstein,** done in the same lumpy, mashed-potato style as the artist's bust of JFK in the Kennedy Center. *2101 Constitution Ave. NW, tel. 202/334-2000. Open weekdays 8:30-5.*

**9** The **Federal Reserve Building** (designed by Folger Library architect Paul Cret) is on Constitution Avenue between 21st and 20th streets. The imposing marble edifice, its bronze entryway topped by a massive eagle, seems to say, "Your money's safe with us." Even so, there isn't any money here. Fort Knox and New York's Federal Reserve Bank hold most of the Federal Reserve System's gold. The stolid building is a bit more human inside, with a varied collection of artwork and several special art exhibitions every year. A 45-minute tour includes a film that attempts to explain exactly what it is that "the Fed" does. *Enter on C St., between 20th and 21st Sts., tel. 202/452-3686. Open Tues.–Fri. 11:30-2. Tours Thurs. at 2:30, tel. 202/452-2526.*

Turn left on 20th Street. The fountain one block up in
**10** **Robert Owen Park** is perfect for cooling hot and tired feet. Crossing Virginia Avenue and continuing north on 20th Street will take you back onto the campus of George Washington University. Foggy Bottom's immi-
**11** grant past is apparent in the **United Methodist Church** at 20th and G streets. Built in 1891 for blue-collar Germans in the neighborhood, the church still conducts services in German.

Walk two blocks north to Pennsylvania Avenue. To the right—near No. 1901—are the only two survivors of a string of 18th-century row houses known as the **Seven Buildings.** One of the five that have been demolished had served as President Madison's executive mansion after the British burned the White House in 1814. The two survivors are now dwarfed by the taller office block behind them.

A similar fate befell a row of residences further west on Pennsylvania Avenue between 20th and 21st streets. These Victorian houses have been hollowed out and refurbished and serve as the entryway for a modern glass office building at **2000 Pennsylvania Avenue.** The backs of the buildings are under the sloping roof of the new development, preserved as if in an urban terrarium.

---

**Time Out** Two of the transformed buildings now house good American-style restaurants that serve hearty fare such as steaks, sandwiches, oysters, and beer. **Wolensky's** and the **Devon Bar and Grill** cater to both a college crowd from nearby George Washington University and businesspeople from surrounding offices.

---

To get to the Foggy Bottom Metro station, walk three blocks west on I Street.

---

## Tour 9: Cleveland Park and the National Zoo

*Numbers in the margin correspond to points of interest on the Tour 9: Cleveland Park and the National Zoo map.*

Cleveland Park, a tree-shaded neighborhood in northwest Washington, owes its name to one-time summer resident Grover Cleveland and its development to the streetcar line that was laid along Connecticut Avenue in the 1890s. President Cleveland and his wife, Frances Folson, escaped the heat of downtown Washington in 1886 by establishing a summer White House on Newark Street between 35th and 36th streets. Many prominent Washingtonians followed suit. When the streetcar came through in 1892, construction in the area snowballed. Developer John Sherman hired local architects to design houses and provided amenities such as a fire station and a streetcar-waiting lodge to entice home buyers out of the city and into "rural" Cleveland Park. Today the neighborhood's attractive houses and suburban character are popular with Washington professionals.

Start your exploration at the Cleveland Park Metro station at Connecticut Avenue and Ordway Street NW. The colonial-style **Park and Shop** on the east side of Connecticut Avenue has the distinction of being the first shopping center with off-street parking in the city. Built in 1930, it was at the time one of only a handful of shopping centers on the East Coast to offer this convenience. Off-street parking was then a rather revolutionary notion, and business and architectural publications of the day followed the center's progress with interest. A 1930 industry magazine explained, "Customers can leave their cars here without fear of violating traffic regulations," while the *Washington Post* gushed that the development was "modern to the nth degree." The Park and Shop sat empty for several years as the very active Cleveland Park Historical Society—fearful that the building might be torn down and replaced with a high rise—lobbied to preserve it in some way. They were successful, and in 1991 the restored Park and Shop, with new green awnings and a tasteful addition, reopened with such modern-day draws as a bagel bakery and a video store.

Half a block to the south is the **Cineplex Odeon Uptown** (3426 Connecticut Ave. NW, tel. 202/966–5400), a marvelous vintage-1936 Art Deco movie house. Although many other big-screen theaters in the city have been chopped up and transformed into "multiplexes," the Uptown still has a single huge screen and an inviting balcony. The **Calliope Bookshop** next door (3424 Connecticut Ave. NW, tel. 202/364–0111) does a brisk business selling to Uptown theater patrons waiting for the next show. It has a fine selection of literary fiction, poetry, philosophy, and art.

Continue south on Connecticut Avenue. You'll cross over a finger of Rock Creek Park via a span decorated with eight Art Deco bridge lights. Beyond the bridge on the left is the city's finest Art Deco apartment house, the **Kennedy-Warren** (3133 Connecticut Ave. NW). Opened in 1931, it features such period detailing as decorative aluminum panels and a streamlined entryway, stone griffins under the pyramidal copper roof, and stylized carved eagles flanking the driveways. Perhaps in keeping with its elegant architecture, the Kennedy-Warren is one of the last apartment buildings in town to still have a doorman (not to mention weekend dancing in its Aztec art deco–style ballroom).

**Tour 9: Cleveland Park and the National Zoo**

❹ On the same side of Connecticut Avenue is the **National Zoological Park,** part of the Smithsonian Institution and one of the foremost zoos in the world. Created by an Act of Congress in 1889, the 160-acre zoo was designed by landscape architect Frederick Law Olmsted, the man who designed the U.S. Capitol grounds. (Before the zoo opened in 1890, live animals used as taxidermists' models had been kept on the Mall.) The zoo's most famous residents are Hsing-Hsing and Ling-Ling, gifts from China in 1972 and the only giant pandas in the United States. After a string of unsuccessful pregnancies, it seems unlikely the two will ever produce offspring. The zoo has had success with numerous other species, however, including red pandas, Pere David's deer, golden lion tamarins, and pygmy hippopotamuses. The only Komodo dragons in the country are at the National Zoo. Innovative compounds show many animals in naturalistic settings, including the Great Flight Cage, a walk-in aviary in which birds fly unrestricted. Giant crabs, octopuses, cuttlefish, and worms are displayed in an invertebrate exhibit. Zoolab, Herplab, and the Bird Resource Center all feature activities that teach young visitors about biology. The latest additions to the zoo are

Amazonia—an ambitious display that re-creates the ecosystem of a South American rain forest—and the Cheetah Conservation Area, where a group of the world's fastest cats live in a natural setting. *3001 Connecticut Ave. NW, tel. 202/673–4717. Admission free. Open May 1–Sept. 15, daily: grounds 8–8, animal buildings 9–6; Sept. 16–Apr. 30: grounds 8–6, animal buildings 9–4:30; closed Dec. 25. Limited paid parking is available.*

The stretch of Connecticut Avenue south of the zoo is bordered by more venerable apartment buildings. Passing Cathedral Avenue (the first cross-street south of the zoo) you enter a part of town known as **Woodley Park.** Like Cleveland Park to the north, Woodley Park grew as the streetcar advanced into this part of Washington. In 1800 Philip Barton Key, uncle of Francis Scott Key, built Woodley, a Georgian mansion on Cathedral Avenue between 29th and 31st streets. The white stucco mansion was the summer home of four presidents: Van Buren, Tyler, Buchanan, and Cleveland. It is now owned by the private Maret School.

At the corner of Connecticut Avenue and Woodley Road ❺ is the cross-shaped **Wardman Tower.** The Georgian-style tower was built by developer Harry Wardman in 1928 as a luxury apartment building to accompany a now-demolished luxury hotel he had built nearby 10 years earlier. Washingtonians called the project "Wardman's Folly," convinced no one would want to stay in a hotel so far from the city. The Wardman Tower was famous for its well-known residents, who included Dwight D. Eisenhower, Herbert Hoover, Clare Booth Luce, Dean Rusk, Earl Warren, and Caspar Weinberger. It is now part of the Sheraton Washington Hotel (*see* Upper Connecticut Avenue in Chapter 7).

Wardman's success spurred the development of the neighborhood's other large hotel, the **Omni Shoreham** (*see* Upper Connecticut Avenue in Chapter 7) on Calvert Street west of Connecticut Avenue. The Shoreham was known for the entertainers who appeared here, including Rudy Vallee, who performed at its grand opening in 1930. The Shoreham and the nearby Sheraton Washington are two of the city's main convention hotels; you'll notice that many of the people on the streets around you have plastic name badges pinned to their lapels.

The nearest Metro station is Woodley Park/Zoo, at Connecticut Avenue and Woodley Road.

## Tour 10: Adams-Morgan

To the young, the hip, the cool, and the post-modern, Washington has the reputation of being a rather staid town, more interested in bureaucracy than boogie, with all the vitality of a seersucker suit. It may have the Hope Diamond, these detractors say, but that's about the only thing that really sparkles. What these people are saying, of course, is that Washington isn't New York City. And thank goodness, say Washingtonians, who wouldn't want to give up their clean subway, comfortable standard of living, or place in the political spotlight, even if it did mean being able to get a decent corned beef sandwich or a double espresso at three in the morning. Besides, Washington does have **Adams-Morgan**. It may not be Greenwich Village, but it's close enough in spirit to satisfy all but the most hardened black-clad, shade-sporting cynics.

Adams-Morgan (roughly, the blocks north of Florida Avenue, between Connecticut Avenue and 16th Street NW) is Washington's most ethnically diverse neighborhood. And as is so often the case, that means it's one of Washington's most interesting areas, home to a veritable United Nations of cuisines, offbeat shops, and funky bars and clubs. The name itself, fashioned in the 1950s by neighborhood civic groups, serves as a symbol of the area's melting pot character: It's a conjunction of the names of two local schools, the predominantly white Adams School and the largely black Morgan School. Today Adams-Morgan is home to every shade in between, too, with large Latino and West African populations.

The neighborhood's grand 19th-century apartment buildings and row houses and its bohemian atmosphere have also attracted young urban professionals, in turn attracting the businesses that cater to them, the attendant parking and crowd problems, and the inevitable climb in real-estate values. It's all caused some longtime Adams-Morganites to wonder if their neighborhood is in danger of mutating into another Georgetown.

Adams-Morgan already has one thing in common with Georgetown: There's no Metro stop. It's a 15-minute walk from the Woodley Park/Zoo Metro station: Walk south on Connecticut, then turn left on Calvert Street, and cross over Rock Creek Park on the Duke Ellington Bridge. When you come to the crossroads of Adams Mill Road, Columbia Road, and 18th Street you're in the heart of Adams-Morgan.

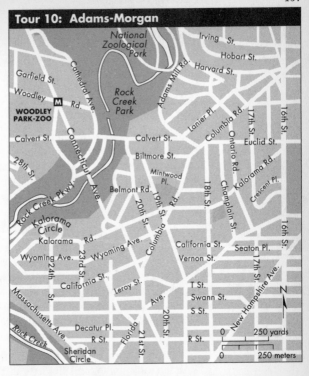

## Tour 10: Adams-Morgan

National Zoological Park

Irving St.
Hobart St.
Harvard St.

Garfield St.
Woodley

**WOODLEY PARK-ZOO**

Rd.

Cathedral Ave.

Adams Mill Rd.

Rock Creek Park

Lanier Pl.

Columbia Rd.

17th St.

16th St.

Calvert St.

Calvert St.

Euclid St.

Ontario Rd.

28th St.

Biltmore St.

Mintwood Pl.

Kalorama Rd.

Crescent Pl.

Connecticut Ave.

Belmont Rd.

19th St.

18th St.

Champlain St.

Rock Creek Pkwy.

Kalorama Circle

Kalorama

Rd.

20th St.

Columbia Rd.

16th St.

Wyoming Ave.

23rd St.

Wyoming Ave.

California St.

Seaton Pl.

Vernon St.

17th St.

24th St.

California St.

Leroy St.

T St.

Swann St.

New Hampshire Ave.

Massachusetts Ave.

Decatur Pl.

Florida

Ave.

20th St.

S St.

N

Rock Creek

R St.

21st St.

R St.

0          250 yards

Sheridan Circle

0          250 meters

What follows is more of a leisurely ramble than a tour. Visitors may want to deviate from the path described here and make their own discoveries, in a spirit in keeping with the serendipity of this fascinating area.

That Washington tolerates more than just the Democratic and Republican parties is evident in **Revolution Books** (1815 Adams Mill Rd. NW, tel. 202/265–1969). Here you will find the works of Lenin, Marx, Engels, Stalin, and Mao Tse-tung. These left-of-center books, magazines, and newspapers hail from around the world and cover the waterfront of progressive literature, philosophy, and theory. It's a comfortable store, and the friendly employees will do their best to answer your questions—and maybe even convert you.

Turn left on **Columbia Road**. At tables stretched along the street, vendors hawk watches, leather goods, knockoff perfumes, cassette tapes (blank and prerecorded), sneakers, clothes, and handmade jewelry. The store signs—Casa Lebrato, Urgente Express (the latter the name of a business that specializes in shipping to and from Central America)—are a testament to the area's Latin flavor; on these blocks you'll hear as much Spanish as English.

Cross Columbia at Ontario Road and backtrack. If you'd rather see the neighborhood on two wheels than two feet, turn left onto Champlain Street and rent a bicycle at **City Bikes** (2501 Champlain St. NW, tel. 202/265–1564; call ahead to reserve a bike on weekends).

Continue west on Columbia Road to its intersection with 18th Street. On Saturday mornings a **market** springs up on the plaza in front of the Crestar bank, at the southwest corner of 18th and Columbia, with vendors selling fruits, vegetables, flowers, and breads.

If Columbia Road east of 18th is Adams-Morgan's Latin Quarter, 18th Street south of Columbia is its restaurant corridor. In the next few blocks you'll pass—beside McDonald's—restaurants serving the cuisines of China, Mexico, India, El Salvador, Ethiopia, France, the Caribbean, Thailand, Argentina, Italy, Vietnam, and, believe it or not, America. If you can't make up your mind, there's even a palm reader who can help decide what your future has in store.

You can also feed your hunger for the outré or offbeat with the funky shops on 18th Street. Here you'll find the Mission-style furniture, Russell Wright crockery and Fiestaware, aerodynamic art deco armchairs, Bakelite telephones, massive chromium toasters, kidney-shaped Formica-topped coffee tables, skinny neckties, and tacky salt-and-pepper shakers that, through time and television reruns, have been transformed from kitsch into collectible. Among stores carrying these are **Homeworks** (2405 18th St. NW, tel. 202/483–5857), **Retrospective** (2324 18th St. NW, tel. 202/483–8112), and **Wake Up Little Suzie** (2316 18th St. NW, tel. 202/328–7577).

Once you've had your fill of Jetsons lunchboxes and gloopy lava lamps, proceed to the souklike **Bazaar Atlas** (2405 18th St. NW, no phone), located above Homeworks and specializing in ethnic goods such as geometric-patterned sweaters from Ecuador and Bolivia and leather, carved wood, rugs, and hammered metal from Morocco. Nearby is **Kobos** (2441 18th St. NW, tel. 202/332–9580), owned by a Ghanaian immigrant who sells African carvings, jewelry, and clothes fashioned from colorful kente cloth.

Down the block is **Bick's Books** (2309 18th St. NW, tel. 202/328–2356), a "serious" book store with a good selection of modern and classic fiction, poetry, philosophy, literary criticism, and literary anthologies and journals. Across the street, **Idle Time Books** (2410 18th St. NW, tel. 202/232–4774) stocks used and out-of-print titles.

The west side of 18th Street is home to a gamut of antiques shops, from the bargain-priced used furniture of **Ruff & Ready** (2220 18th St. NW, tel. 202/462–4541) to the more classic goods at **Chenonceau Antiques** (2314 18th St. NW, tel. 202/667–1651). Antiques shoppers should also keep an eye out for second-hand shops set up in alleys or warehouses here.

Nearby is the **District of Columbia Arts Center** (DCAC), a combination art gallery/performance space. DCAC exhibits the cutting-edge work of local artists and is the home of offbeat plays, including that uncategorizable category known as "performance art." *2438 18th St. NW, tel. 202/462–7833. Gallery open Thurs.–Fri. 6–10 PM, weekends 4–10 PM.*

Of course, the measure of any neighborhood is the tone it takes when the sun goes down. In the spring and summer, restaurants open their windows or set out tables on the sidewalks. Those lucky enough to have rooftop seating find diners lining up to eat under the stars. (Washington can be notoriously hot in the summer, but one of Adams-Morgan's charms has always been that its slight elevation wraps it in cooling breezes.)

Although the neighborhood's bar scene isn't as varied as its restaurant scene, there are some standouts. Tap dancers use the bar as a stage at the decidedly Gallic **Café Lautrec** (2431 18th St. NW, tel. 202/265–6436). Julia Nixon belts out jazz, R&B, and pop songs Friday and Saturday at **Mr. Henry's** (1836 Columbia Rd. NW, tel. 202/797–8882). Two nightclubs—**Ikon** (2424 18th St. NW, tel. 202/328–7194) and **Opera** (1777 Columbia Rd. NW, tel. 202/265–6600)—compete to be the closest thing the capital of the free world has to a Eurotrendy, New York–style dance club.

Remember that the last trains leave the Woodley Park Metro station at around midnight, so if you can't tear yourself away, be prepared to take a cab. For more on Adams-Morgan shops, restaurants, and nightlife, *see* Chapters 4, 6, and 8.

## Tour 11: Arlington

*Numbers in the margin correspond to points of interest on the Tour 11: Arlington map.*

The Virginia suburb of Arlington County was once part of the District of Columbia. Carved out of the Old Dominion when Washington was created, it was returned to Virginia along with the rest of the land west of the Potomac in 1845. Washington hasn't held a grudge, though, and there are three attractions in Arlington— each linked to the military—that should be a part of any complete visit to the nation's capital: Arlington National Cemetery, the U.S. Marine Corps War Memorial, and the Pentagon. All are accessible by Metro, and a trip across the Potomac makes an enjoyable half day of sightseeing.

Begin your exploration in **Arlington National Cemetery.** To get there, you can take the Metro to the Arlington Cemetery station, travel on a Tourmobile bus (*see* Staying in Washington in Chapter 1), or walk across Memorial Bridge from the District (southwest of the Lincoln Memorial). If you're driving, there's a large paid parking lot at the skylit **Visitors Center** on Memorial Drive. Stop at the center for a free brochure with a detailed map of the cemetery's 612 acres. (If you're looking for a specific grave, the staff will consult microfilm records and give you directions on how to find it. You should know the deceased's full name and, if possible, his or her branch of service and year of death.) *Tel. 703/692–0931. Open Apr.–early Sept., daily 8–7; early Sept.–Mar., daily 8–5. Parking lot open Apr.–early Sept., daily 8–8; early Sept.–Mar., daily 8–6. Parking $1/hr for first 3 hrs, $2/hr thereafter.*

Tourmobile tour buses leave from just outside the Visitors Center mid-June–early September, daily 8:30–6:30; early September–mid-June, daily 8:30–4:30. You can buy tickets here (adults $2.75, children $1.25) for the 40-minute tour of the cemetery, which includes stops at the Kennedy gravesites, the Tomb of the Unknowns, and Arlington House. Touring the cemetery on foot means a fair bit of hiking, but it will give you a closer look at some of the 200,000 graves spread over these rolling Virginia hills. If you decide to walk, head west from the Visitors Center on Roosevelt Drive and then turn right on Weeks Drive.

While you are at Arlington you will probably hear the clear, doleful sound of a trumpet playing *Taps* or the

# Tour 11: Arlington

sharp reports of a gun salute. Approximately 15 funerals are held here daily. It is projected the cemetery will be filled in 2020. While not the largest cemetery in the country, Arlington is certainly the best known, a place where visitors can trace America's history through the aftermath of its battles.

**❷** The **Kennedy graves** are located just west of the Visitors Center. John F. Kennedy is buried under an eternal flame near two of his children who died in infancy. Across from the graves is a low wall engraved with quotations from Kennedy's inaugural address. JFK's grave was opened to the public in 1967 and since that time has become the most-visited gravesite in the country. Nearby, marked by a simple white cross, is the grave of his brother Robert Kennedy.

This somber plot of land hasn't always been a cemetery. It was in Arlington that the two most famous names in Virginia history—Washington and Lee—became intertwined. George Washington Parke Custis—raised by Martha and George Washington, his grandmother and
**❸** step-grandfather—built **Arlington House** (also known as the Custis-Lee Mansion) between 1802 and 1817 on his 1,100-acre estate overlooking the Potomac. After his death, the property went to his daughter, Mary Anna Randolph Custis. In 1831, Mary Custis married Robert E. Lee, a recent graduate of West Point. For the next 30 years the Custis-Lee family lived at Arlington House.

In 1861, Lee was offered command of the Union forces. He declined, insisting that he could never take up arms against his native Virginia. The Lees left Arlington House that spring, never to return. Union troops soon occupied the estate, making it the headquarters of the officers who were charged with defending Washington. When Mrs. Lee was unable to appear in person to pay a $92.07 property tax the government had assessed, the land was confiscated and a portion set aside as a military cemetery.

Its heavy Doric columns and severe pediment make Arlington House one of the area's best examples of Greek Revival architecture. The plantation home was designed by George Hadfield, a young English architect who for a while supervised construction of the Capitol. The view of Washington from the front of the house is superb. In 1955 Arlington House was designated a memorial to Robert E. Lee. It looks much as it did in the 19th century, and a quick tour will take you past objects once owned by the Custises and the Lees. *Between Lee*

*and Sherman Drs., tel. 703/557–0613. Open Apr.–*
*Sept., daily 9:30–6; Oct.–Mar., daily 9:30–4:30; closed*
*Dec. 25 and New Year's Day.*

In front of the house, next to a flag that flies at half staff
whenever there is a funeral in the cemetery, is the flat-
topped grave of Pierre L'Enfant, designer of the Federal City. L'Enfant died in 1825, a penniless, bitter man
who felt he hadn't been recognized for his planning gen-
ius. He was originally buried in Maryland, but his body
was moved here with much ceremony in 1909.

After visiting Arlington House and the Kennedy
graves, walk south on Crook Walk past the seemingly
endless rows of simple white headstones—arranged
like soldiers on parade—and follow the signs to the
❹ **Tomb of the Unknowns.** The first burial at the Tomb of
the Unknowns was on November 11, 1921, when the Unknown soldier from World War I was interred under the
large white-marble sarcophagus. Servicemen killed in
World War II and Korea were buried in 1958. The unknown serviceman from the Vietnam War was laid to
rest on the plaza on Memorial Day 1984. Soldiers from
the Army's U.S. 3rd Infantry ("The Old Guard," por-
trayed in the movie *Gardens of Stone*) keep watch over
the tomb 24 hours a day, regardless of weather conditions. Each sentinel marches exactly 21 steps, then
faces the tomb for 21 seconds, symbolizing the 21-gun
salute, America's highest military honor. The guard is
changed with a precise ceremony during the day every
half-hour from April 1 to September 30, and every hour
the rest of the year. At night the guard is changed every
two hours. The **Memorial Amphitheater** west of the tomb
is the scene of special ceremonies on Veterans Day, Memorial Day, and Easter. Decorations awarded to the unknowns by foreign governments and U.S. and foreign
organizations are displayed in an indoor trophy room.

Across from the amphitheater are memorials to the astronauts killed in the *Challenger* shuttle explosion and
to the servicemen killed in 1980 while trying to rescue
American hostages in Iran. Rising beyond that is the
mast from the USS *Maine*, the American ship that was
sunk in Havana Harbor in 1898, killing 299 men and
sparking the Spanish-American War.

Below the Tomb of the Unknowns is **section 7A,** where
you can find the graves of many distinguished veterans,
including boxing champ Joe Louis, ABC newsman
Frank Reynolds, actor Lee Marvin, and World War II
fighter pilot Col. "Pappy" Boyington.

To reach the sites at the northern end of the cemetery and to make your way into the city of Arlington, first walk north along Roosevelt Drive to Schley Drive (you'll pass the Memorial Gate), then turn right on Custis Walk to the Ord & Weitzel Gate. On your way you'll pass **⑤ section 27,** where 3,800 former slaves are buried. They lived at Freedman's Village, established at Arlington in 1863 to provide housing, education, and employment training to ex-slaves who had traveled to the capital. The headstones are marked with their names and the words "Civilian" or "Citizen." Buried at grave 19 in the first row of section 27 is William Christman, a Union private who died of peritonitis in Washington on May 13, 1864. He was the first soldier interred at Arlington National Cemetery during the Civil War. *West end of Memorial Bridge, Arlington, VA, tel. 703/692–0931. Open Apr.–early Sept., daily 8–7; mid-Sept.–Mar., daily 8–5.*

Leaving the cemetery through the Ord & Weitzel Gate, **⑥** cross Marshall Drive carefully, and walk to **the Netherlands Carillon.** The 49-bell carillon was presented to the United States by the Dutch people in 1960 as thanks for aid received during World War II. A performance season featuring guest carillonneurs begins Easter Sunday. For one of the most inclusive views of Washington, look to the east across the Potomac. From this vantage point, the Lincoln Memorial, the Washington Monument, and the Capitol are bunched together in a side-by-side formation. *Carillon information, tel. 703/285–2598. Performances Apr., May, Sept., Sat. 2; Easter Sunday starting at 6 AM; June–Aug., Sat. 6:30 PM.*

**⑦** To the north is the **United States Marine Corps War Memorial,** honoring Marines who have given their lives since the Corps was formed in 1775. The memorial statue, sculpted by Felix W. de Weldon, is based on Joe Rosenthal's Pulitzer Prize-winning photograph of five Marines and a Navy corpsman raising a flag atop Mount Suribachi on Iwo Jima on February 19, 1945. By executive order, a real flag flies 24 hours a day from the 78-foot-high memorial. On Tuesday evenings at 7 from late May to late August there is a Marine Corps sunset parade on the grounds of the Memorial. On parade nights a free shuttle bus runs from the Arlington Cemetery visitor parking lot (for information, tel. 202/433–6060). A word of caution: It is dangerous to visit the memorial after dark.

The Arlington neighborhood of Rosslyn is north of the memorial. Like parts of downtown Washington and Crystal City further to the south, Rosslyn is almost empty at night once the thousands of people who work there have gone home. Its tall buildings do provide the preturnaturally horizontal Washington with a bit of a skyline, but this has come about not without some controversy: Some say the silvery, wing-shaped Gannett Buildings are too close to the flight path followed by jets landing at National Airport.

❽ To get to the **Pentagon,** take the Metro to the Pentagon station, which is right alongside the humongous office building. The headquarters of the Department of Defense, the Pentagon was completed in 1943 after just two years of construction. The five-sided building is an exercise in immensity: 23,000 military and civilian employees work here; it is as wide as three Washington Monuments laid end to end; inside are 17½ miles of corridors, 7,754 windows, and 691 drinking fountains. The 75-minute tour of the Pentagon takes you past only those areas that are meant to be seen by outside visitors. In other words, you won't see situation rooms, communications centers, or gigantic maps outlining U.S. and foreign troop strengths. A uniformed serviceman or -woman (who conducts the entire tour walking backwards, lest anyone slip away down a corridor) will take you past hallways lined with the portraits of past and present military leaders, scale models of Air Force planes and Navy ships, and the Hall of Heroes, where the names of all the Congressional Medal of Honor winners are inscribed. Occasionally you will catch a glimpse through an interior window of the Pentagon's 5-acre interior courtyard. In the center—at ground zero—is a hotdog stand. *Pentagon, off of I–395, Arlington, VA, tel. 703/695–1776. Tours weekdays every ½-hr 9:30–3:30. Photo I.D. required. Closed federal holidays.*

## Tour 12: Alexandria

*Numbers in the margin correspond to points of interest on the Tour 12: Alexandria map.*

Just a short Metro ride (or bike ride) away from Washington, Old Town Alexandria today attracts visitors seeking a break from the monuments and hustle-and-bustle of the District and interested in an encounter with America's Colonial heritage. Founded in 1749 by Scottish merchants eager to capitalize on the booming tobacco trade, Alexandria emerged as one of the most important ports in Colonial America. The city's history is linked to the most significant events and personages of the Colonial and Revolutionary periods. This colorful past is still alive in restored 18th- and 19th-century homes, churches, and taverns; in the cobbled streets; and on the revitalized waterfront, where clipper ships dock and artisans display their wares.

The quickest way to get to Old Town is to take the Metro to the King Street stop (about 25 minutes from Metro Center). If you're driving you can take either the George Washington Memorial Parkway or Jefferson Davis Highway (Route 1) south from Arlington.

The best place to start a tour of Old Town is at the **①** **Alexandria Convention & Visitors Bureau,** which is in **Ramsay House,** the home of the town's first postmaster and lord mayor, William Ramsay. The structure is believed to be the oldest house in Alexandria. Ramsay was a Scotsman, as a swatch of his tartan on the door proclaims. Travel counselors here provide information, brochures, and self-guided walking tours of the town. *221 King St. 22314, tel. 703/838–4200. Open daily 9–5; closed Thanksgiving, Dec. 25, and New Year's Day. Out-of-towners are given a 72-hr courtesy parking permit that allows them to park free at any 2-hr metered spot.*

Across the street, at the corner of Fairfax and King **②** streets, is the **Stabler-Leadbeater Apothecary Shop,** the second-oldest apothecary in the country. It was patronized by George Washington and the Lee family, and it was here, on October 17, 1859, that Lt. Col. Robert E. Lee received orders to move to Harper's Ferry to suppress John Brown's insurrection. The shop now houses a small museum of 18th-century apothecary memorabilia, including one of the finest collections of apothecary bottles in the country (some 800 bottles in all). *105–107 S. Fairfax St., tel. 703/836–3713. Suggested donation: $1. Open Mon.–Tues. and Thurs.–Sat. 10–4; closed Jan. 1–Presidents' Day.*

Two blocks south on Fairfax Street, just beyond Duke **③** Street, stands the **Old Presbyterian Meeting House**. Built in 1774, this was an important meeting place for Scotts patriots during the Revolution. Eulogies for George Washington were delivered here on December 29, 1799. In a corner of the churchyard you'll find the **Tomb of the Unknown Soldier of the American Revolution.** 321 S. Fairfax St., tel. 703/549–6670. Open daily 10–4:30.

Tour 12: Alexandria

Next walk back up Fairfax Street one block and turn right on Prince Street. The block between Fairfax and Lee streets is known as **Gentry Row.** One of the most noteworthy structures in the city is the **Athenaeum,** at the corner of Prince and Lee streets. The striking, reddish-brown Greek Revival edifice was built as a bank in the 1850s.

The next block of Prince Street to the east (between Lee and Union streets) is known as **Captain's Row** because this was where many of the city's sea captains built their homes. The cobblestones in the street were allegedly laid by Hessian mercenaries who fought for the British during the Revolutionary War and who were being held in Alexandria as prisoners of war.

Continuing east on Prince Street you'll come to Alexandria's lively waterfront. Two blocks to the north up Union Street (at the foot of King Street) is one of the most popular destinations in the city, the **Torpedo Factory Arts Center.** This former munitions plant (yes, naval torpedoes were actually manufactured here during World War I and World War II) has now been converted into studios and galleries for some 175 professional artists. Almost every imaginable medium is represented, from printmaking and sculpture to jewelry making, pottery, and stained glass. Visitors can view the artisans' workshops, and most of the artworks are for sale at reasonable prices. *105 N. Union St., tel. 703/838-4565. Open daily 10-5.*

The Torpedo Factory complex also houses the **Alexandria Archaeology Program,** a city-operated research facility devoted to urban archaeology and conservation. Artifacts from excavations dug in Alexandria are on display. *105 N. Union St., tel. 703/838-4399. Open Tues.-Fri. 10-3, Sat. 10-5, Sun. 1-5.*

Moving back into the town, a two-block walk up Cameron Street brings you to the grandest of the older houses in the town, **Carlyle House,** at the corner of North Fairfax Street. Patterned after a Scottish country manor house, the structure was completed in 1753 by Scottish merchant John Carlyle. This was General Braddock's headquarters and the place where he met with five Royal Governors in 1755 to plan the strategy and funding of the early campaigns of the French and Indian War. *121 N. Fairfax St., tel. 703/549-2997. Admission: $3 adults, $1 students 11-17, children under 11 free. Open Tues.-Sat. 10-4:30, Sun. noon-4:30. Tours every ½-hr.*

One block west on Royal Street is **Gadsby's Tavern Museum,** housed in the old City Tavern and Hotel, which was a center of political and social life in the late 18th century. George Washington attended birthday celebrations in the ballroom here. A tour of the facilities takes you through the taproom, game room, assembly room, ballroom, and communal bedrooms. *134-138 N. Royal St., tel. 703/838-4242. Admission: $3 adults, $1 students 11-17, children under 11 free. Open Tues.-Sat. 10-5, Sun. 1-5. Tours at quarter to and quarter after the hr.*

Continue west on Cameron Street for three blocks and turn right on Washington Street. The corner of Washington and Oronoco streets (three blocks north) is known as **Lee Corner** because at one time a Lee-owned house stood on each of the four corners. Two survive. One is the **Lee-Fendall House,** the home of several illustrious members of the Lee family, including Richard Henry Lee, signer of the Declaration of Independence, and cavalry commander "Light Horse Harry" Lee. *614 Oronoco St., tel. 703/548-1789. Admission: $3 adults, $1 students 11-17, children under 11 free. Open Tues.-*

*Sat. 10–4, Sun. noon–4. Occasionally closed weekends for private events.*

**⑪** Directly across the street is the **boyhood home of Robert E. Lee,** a fine example of a 19th-century town house. It features Federal architecture and antique furnishings and paintings. *607 Oronoco St., tel. 703/548–8454. Admission: $3 adults, $1 students 11–17, children under 11 free. Open Mon.–Sat. 10–4, Sun. 1–4; closed Dec. 15–Feb. 1 except on Sun. closest to Jan. 19 for Lee's birthday celebration. Occasionally closed weekends for private events.*

Alexandria's history isn't all Washingtons and Lees, however. The federal census of 1790 recorded 52 free blacks living in the city, and the port town was one of the largest slave exportation points in the South, with at least two bustling slave markets. The history of African Americans in Alexandria and Virginia from 1749 to the **⑫** present is recounted at the **Alexandria Black History Resource Center,** two blocks north and two blocks west of Lee's boyhood home. *638 North Alfred St., tel. 703/838–4356. Open Tues.–Sat. 10–4.*

Head back to Washington Street and move south now all the way to the corner of Queen Street. Here you'll find **⑬** the **Lloyd House,** a fine example of Georgian architecture. Built in 1797, it is now operated as part of the Alexandria Library and houses a collection of rare books and documents relating to city and state history. *220 North Washington St., tel. 703/838–4577. Open Mon.–Sat. 9–5.*

At the corner of Cameron and Washington streets, one **⑭** block south, stands **Christ Church**, where both Washington and Lee were pewholders (Washington paid 36 pounds and 10 shillings, a lot of money in those days, for Pew 60). Built in 1773, it is a fine example of an English, Georgian country-style church. The interior features a fine Palladian window, interior balcony, and a wrought-brass-and-crystal chandelier brought from England at Washington's expense. *118 N. Washington St., tel. 703/549–1450. Open Mon.–Sat. 9–4, Sun. 1–4.*

From Christ Church, walk two blocks south to the **⑮** **Lyceum** at the corner of Washington and Prince streets. Built in 1839, the structure served alternately as the Alexandria Library, a Civil War hospital, a residence, and an office building. It was restored in the '70s and now houses two art galleries, a gift shop, and a museum devoted to the area's history. A limited amount of travel information for the entire state is also available here. *201 S. Washington St., tel. 703/838–4994. Open weekdays 10–5, Sat. 10–5, Sun. 1–5; closed Thanksgiving, Dec. 25, and New Year's Day.*

Two blocks to the west on South Alfred Street is the **16** **Friendship Fire Company.** The building was recently renovated and is now outfitted like a typical 19th-century firehouse. *107 S. Alfred St. Irregular operating hours.*

**17** A little far to walk but well worth visiting is the **George Washington Masonic National Memorial** on Callahan Drive at King Street, a mile west of the center of the city. The memorial's spire dominates the surroundings, and from the entryway visitors get a spectacular view of Alexandria and Washington in the distance. Among other things, the building contains furnishings from the first Masonic lodge in Alexandria, in which George Washington was Worshipful Master at the same time he served as president. *101 Callahan Dr., tel. 703/683–2007. Open daily 9–5; closed Thanksgiving, Dec. 25, and New Year's Day. Free guided tours of the building and observation deck daily 9:15–4:10.*

## Washington for Free

Visitors will have a hard time finding attractions and events in Washington that are *not* free. There are no admission fees to any of the Smithsonian museums—including the National Zoo—and entry to many other museums and galleries is also without charge. The ride to the top of the Washington Monument used to cost a dime, but today, like admission to the rest of the memorials, that's free, too.

Concerts **Fort Dupont Summer Theater** (Minnesota Ave. and F St. SE, tel. 202/426–7723) hosts well-known jazz artists Friday and Saturday evenings at 8:30 during the summer.

**The National Building Museum's** impressive Pension Building (F St. between 4th and 5th Sts. NW, tel. 202/272–2448) is the site of lunchtime concerts the last Wednesday of each month.

**The National Symphony Orchestra** (tel. 202/416–8100) presents free concerts on the West Lawn of the Capitol on Memorial Day and Labor Day weekends and on July 4th.

**The National Gallery Orchestra** offers free classical concerts at the National Gallery of Art (6th St. and Consti-

tution Ave. NW, tel. 202/842–6941) Sunday evenings
from October to June. Admission is free, but you must
pick up a ticket to obtain a seat.

**The National Theatre** (1321 Pennsylvania Ave. NW, tel.
202/783–3372) hosts a wide-ranging free performance
series of music, dance, readings, and one-act plays most
Monday nights from October to April. "Monday Night
at the National" performances are held at 7 PM and 8:30
PM.

**The Sylvan Theater** (tel. 202/619–7222), on the grounds
of the Washington Monument, is the site of numerous
military and big-band concerts from mid-June to August.

Festivals **The Festival of American Folklife,** a celebration of home-
grown crafts, music, and food, is sponsored by the
Smithsonian and is held on the Mall each year in late
June or early July (tel. 202/ 357–2700).

**The Hispanic-American Cultural Festival** (tel. 202/789–
7000) is a day-long carnival of music, dance, and arts and
crafts that is held in late July or early August on the
Mall. Adams-Morgan heats up again in September for
**Adams-Morgan Day,** a similarly ethnic celebration (tel.
202/332–3292).

Lectures **The Library of Congress** (tel. 202/707–5394 or 202/707–
2905) sponsors periodic literary lectures and poetry
readings by well-known poets, usually on Thursday evenings.

**The Martin Luther King Memorial Library's** "Lunchtime Author Series" (901 G St. NW, tel. 202/727–1186)
features readings and discussions with local and national authors every Tuesday at noon, except during the
month of June.

**The Smithsonian Institution** (tel. 202/357–2700) offers
free lectures, demonstrations, and gallery talks by both
visiting scholars and Smithsonian fellows at many of its
museums on and off the Mall.

The "Weekend" section in Friday's *Washington Post* and
the free weekly *City Paper* are excellent sources of other
free events in and around the District.

## What to See and Do with Children

Kids who have been learning about the early days of
America or how its government works will find much to
see and enjoy in Washington. History that seems dusty
and boring in a textbook comes alive at the White
House, the Senate chamber, and the Supreme Court.

For younger children (or less politically-minded tykes) numerous museums encourage hands-on learning. For other kid-oriented fare, consult the "Carousel" listings in the Friday *Washington Post* "Weekend" section.

**Academy of Model Aeronautics.** The 150,000-member academy helps regulate model aviation activities thoughout the country. Here, in the atrium of the group's headquarters, you'll find dozens of planes on display, everything from a tiny flyable craft with a 6½-inch wingspan to a six-foot-long model of an F-104 Starfighter. Engines, radio control equipment, and club patches are also exhibited. A computer flight simulator game allows would-be pilots to test their skills. *1810 Samuel Morse Dr., Reston, VA, tel. 703/435–0750. Open weekdays 9–5, Sat. 10–3.*

**Adventure Theater** (MacArthur Blvd. and Goldsboro Rd., Glen Echo, MD, tel. 301/320–5331). Delightful plays for children ages four and up are performed year-round at the Glen Echo Park. Performances are Saturday and Sunday at 1:30 and 3:30. Reservations suggested.

**Capital Children's Museum** (*see* Museums and Galleries in Sightseeing Checklists, below). Youngsters feel at home in this museum that's designed for them. *Metro stop, Union Station.*

**Carousel** (*see* Tour 1: The Mall, above). *Metro stop, Smithsonian.*

**D.A.R. Museum** (*see* Tour 3: The White House, above). Free one-hour "Colonial Adventure" tours are usually held the first and third Sundays of the month at 2. Costumed docents lead children aged five through seven through the museum, explaining the exhibits and describing life in Colonial America. Make reservations at least 10 days in advance by calling 202/879–3239. *Metro stop, Farragut West.*

**Discovery Theater** (900 Jefferson Dr. SW, tel. 202/357–1500). Plays, puppet shows, and storytellers are featured at this theater October through June (with additional productions likely in July and August), in the west hall of the Smithsonian's Arts and Industries Building. *Metro stop, Smithsonian.*

**National Air and Space Museum, National Museum of American History, National Museum of Natural History.** (*see* Tour 1: The Mall, above). *Metro stop, Smithsonian or Federal Triangle.*

**National Aquarium** (*see* Tour 5: Old Downtown and Federal Triangle, above). *Metro stop, Federal Triangle.*

**National Geographic Explorers Hall** (*see* Tour 7: Dupont Circle, above). *Metro stop, Farragut North.*

**The National Zoo** (*see* Tour 9: Cleveland Park and the National Zoo, above). *Metro stop, Cleveland Park or Woodley Park/National Zoo.*

**"Saturday Morning at the National"** (1321 Pennsylvania Ave. NW, tel. 202/783–3372). This performance series for youngsters has featured such acts as mimes, puppet shows, dance troupes, magicians, and children's theater groups. The performances are free, on a first-come, first-seated basis, at the National Theatre, Saturday at 9:30 AM and 11 AM. *Metro stop, Metro Center.*

**Tidal Basin paddle boats** (*see* Tour 2: The Monuments, above). *Metro stop, Smithsonian.*

**Washington Dolls' House and Toy Museum of Washington** (*see* Museums and Galleries in Sightseeing Checklists, below). *Metro stop, Friendship Heights.*

**The Washington Monument** (*see* Tour 2: The Monuments, above). *Metro stops, Federal Triangle or Smithsonian.*

## Off the Beaten Track

**The Ansel Adams Collection,** a permanent exhibit of the famed photographer's most important landscapes, is on display at the Wilderness Society's headquarters. *900 17th St. NW, tel. 202/833–2300. Open weekdays 10–5; closed major holidays and day after Thanksgiving. Large groups should call ahead. Metro stops, Farragut North and Farragut West.*

**The Flying Circus Airshow** bills itself as the only remaining barnstorming show in the country. Operating out of a Virginia aerodrome about 90 minutes outside Washington, the Flying Circus features stunt flying, wing walking, and open cockpit biplane rides for the public, on Sunday from May through October. *On Rte. 17 in Bealeton, VA, between Fredericksburg and Warrenton, tel. 703/439–8661.*

**Intelsat,** the international satellite cooperative, has its headquarters in a striking glass building that looks as if it itself had come down from space. Although no tours of the building are given, twice a week a brief film about the work of the organization is shown in the high-tech

Visitors Center. Visitors see models of rockets, satellites, and control centers where satellite traffic is monitored. Space buffs will enjoy the visit. *Connecticut Ave. and Van Ness St. NW, tel. 202/944–7500. Reservations required. Metro stop, Van Ness/UDC.*

**Two outdoor murals** have become fixtures in Washington. The unmistakable face of Marilyn Monroe gazes from the side of a beauty shop in Woodley Park, on Connecticut Avenue just north of Calvert Street NW. *Metro stop, Woodley Park/Zoo.* Painted on a monolithic exhaust tower on H Street between 2nd and 3rd streets NW, just north of Massachusetts Avenue, is a trompe l'oeil "hole" through which you can see the Capitol dome. *Metro stop, Judiciary Square.*

**The Maine Avenue Seafood Market** is a reminder that Washington isn't far from the Chesapeake Bay, the Atlantic Ocean beyond that, and the bounty of both. The market bustles with activity as more than a dozen vendors sell fresh crabs, fish, shrimp, squid, clams, and other types of seafood. If you work up an appetite there are seven restaurants stretched out along Maine Avenue, including local seafood powerhouse **Phillips Flagship.** All have terraces overlooking the Washington Channel and the motorboats, houseboats, and sailboats that are moored there. *Maine Ave. SW. Metro stop, Waterfront.*

**The National Theatre** is housed in a building that was constructed in 1922, though there has been a National Theatre on this spot since 1835. After seeing her first play here at the age of six, first lady of the theater Helen Hayes vowed to become an actress. Free tours of the historic theater are offered every Monday and take in the house, stage, backstage, wardrobe room, dressing rooms, the area under the stage, the Helen Hayes Lounge, and the memorabilia-filled archives. *1321 Pennsylvania Ave. NW, tel. 202/783–3370. Make reservations at least a week ahead. Metro stop, Metro Center.*

# Sightseeing Checklists

## Historical Buildings and Sites

This list of Washington's principal buildings and sites includes both attractions that were covered in preceding tours and additional attractions that are described here for the first time.

**American Red Cross** (Tour 3: The White House) *Metro stop, Farragut West.*

**Anderson House** (Tour 7: Dupont Circle) *Metro stop, Dupont Circle.*

**Barney Studio House** (Tour 7: Dupont Circle) *Metro stop, Dupont Circle.*

**Clara Barton National Historic Site.** Home of the American Red Cross and its founder from 1897 to 1904, this 41-room building is furnished with original period artifacts, including large supply cabinets (where relief supplies were stockpiled), antique typewriters, and roll-top desks. *5801 Oxford Rd., Glen Echo, MD, tel. 301/492–6245. Open daily 10–5; last tour at 4:30. Closed Thanksgiving, Dec. 25, and New Year's Day.*

**Blair House** (Tour 3: The White House) *Metro stop, McPherson Square.*

**Cox's Row** (Tour 6: Georgetown).

**Customs House** (Tour 6: Georgetown).

**Decatur House** (Tour 3: The White House) *Metro stop, McPherson Square.*

**District (of Columbia) Building** (Tour 5: Old Downtown and Federal Triangle) *Metro stop, Federal Triangle.*

**Frederick Douglass National Historic Site.** Cedar Hill, the Anacostia home of noted abolitionist Frederick Douglass, was the first place designated by Congress as a Black National Historic Site. Douglass, an ex-slave who delivered fiery abolitionist speeches at home and abroad, was 60 when he moved here, in 1877. He lived at Cedar Hill until his death, in 1895. The house has a wonderful view of the Federal City, across the Anacostia, and contains many of Douglass's personal belongings. A short film on Douglass's life is shown at a nearby visitors center. *1411 W St. SE, tel. 202/426–5961. Open fall and winter, daily 9–4; spring and summer, daily 9–5. Tours given on the hr. Metro stop, Anacostia.*

**Dumbarton House.** (Tour 6: Georgetown).

**Dumbarton Oaks** (Tour 6: Georgetown).

**Eastern Market.** Built in 1873, Eastern Market has always been a bustling center of activity on Capitol Hill. It was designed by Adolph Cluss, the architect of the Smithsonian Arts and Industries Museum. Inside are shops, restaurants, and galleries. There is a flea market outside on weekends. *7th and C Sts. SE. Metro stop, Eastern Market.*

**Evermay** (Tour 6: Georgetown).

**Folger Shakespeare Library** (Tour 4: Capitol Hill) *Metro stop, Capitol South.*

**Ford's Theatre** (Tour 5: Old Downtown and Federal Triangle) *Metro stop, Metro Center.*

**Heurich Mansion/Historical Society of Washington, D.C.**
(Tour 7: Dupont Circle) *Metro stop, Dupont Circle.*

**House of the Americas/Organization of American States**
(Tour 3: The White House) *Metro stop, Farragut West.*

**J. Edgar Hoover FBI Building** (Tour 5: Old Downtown
and Federal Triangle) *Metro stop, Federal Triangle.*

**John F. Kennedy Center for the Performing Arts** (Tour 8:
Foggy Bottom) *Metro stop, Foggy Bottom.*

**Marine Corps Barracks.** Each Friday evening at 8:45
from May to September the Marine Corps Drum and
Bugle Corps, the Marine Band, and the Silent Drill
Team present a dress parade filled with martial music
and precision marching. *8th and I Sts. SE, tel. 202/433–
6060. Reservations required. Call 3 weeks in advance.
Metro stop, Eastern Market.*

**Martin Luther King Memorial Library** (Tour 5: Old
Downtown and Federal Triangle) *Metro stop, Gallery
Place.*

**Library of Congress, Jefferson Building** (Tour 4: Capitol
Hill) *Metro stop, Capitol South.*

**Meridian House and the White-Meyer House.** Meridian
House International, a nonprofit institution promoting
international understanding, now owns these two handsome mansions designed by John Russell Pope. The 30-
room Meridian House was built in 1920 by Irwin Boyle
Laughlin, scion of a Pittsburgh steel family and former
ambassador to Spain. The Louis XVI–style home features parquet floors, ornamental iron grillwork, handsome mouldings, period furniture, tapestries, and a
garden planted with European Linden trees. Next door
is the Georgian-style house built for Henry White (former ambassador to France) that was later the home of
the Meyer family, publishers of the *Washington Post.*
The first floors of both houses are open to the public and
are the scene of periodic art exhibits with an international flavor. *1630 and 1624 Crescent Pl. NW, tel. 202/
667–6800. Open Wed.–Sun. 2–5.*

**National Archives** (Tour 5: Old Downtown and Federal
Triangle) *Metro stop, Archives.*

**Octagon House** (Tour 3: The White House) *Metro stop,
Farragut West.*

**Old Executive Office Building** (Tour 3: The White
House) *Metro stop, Farragut West.*

**Old Post Office Building** (Tour 5: Old Downtown and
Federal Triangle) *Metro stop, Federal Triangle.*

**Old Stone House** (Tour 6: Georgetown).

**Pension Building** (Tour 5: Old Downtown and Federal
Triangle) *Metro stop, Judiciary Square.*

**Pierce Mill.** Using the water power of Rock Creek, Isaac

Pierce ground flour here from 1820 until 1897, when the mill shaft broke. The mill has been restored, and National Park Service employees grind wheat into flour that is then sold to visitors. *Rock Creek Park at Tilden St. and Beach Dr., tel. 202/426–6908. Open Wed.–Sun. 8–4:30; closed major holidays. Metro stop, Van Ness/ UDC.*

**Prospect House** (Tour 6: Georgetown).

**Sears House** (Tour 5: Old Downtown and Federal Triangle) *Metro stop, Archives.*

**Sewall-Belmont House** (Tour 4: Capitol Hill) *Metro stop, Union Station.*

**Charles Sumner School** (Tour 7: Dupont Circle) *Metro stop, Farragut North.*

**Supreme Court of the United States** (Tour 4: Capitol Hill) *Metro stop, Capitol South.*

**Treasury Building** (Tour 3: The White House) *Metro stop, McPherson Square.*

**Union Station** (Tour 4: Capitol Hill) *Metro stop, Union Station.*

**United States Capitol** (Tour 4: Capitol Hill) *Metro stop, Capitol South or Union Station.*

**Washington Navy Yard.** The yard is the Navy's oldest shore establishment, authorized in 1799 by Benjamin Stoddert, first secretary of the Navy. It was burned during the War of 1812 to prevent it from falling into the hands of British troops. Rebuilt after the war, the yard was for a time used for the construction of ships, then ordnance. The facility is now a supply and administrative center. A **Navy Museum** is housed in the former Breech Mechanism Shop of the old Naval Gun Factory. Moored nearby and on permanent display is the *Barry*, a former USN destroyer. Also on the grounds is the **Marine Corps Museum.** *9th and M Sts. SE, tel. 202/433– 2651. Open early Sept.–late May, weekdays 9–4, weekends 10–5; Memorial Day–Labor Day, daily 9–5; closed Dec. 24–25 and federal holidays. Metro stop, Eastern Market.*

**White House** (Tour 3: The White House) *Metro stop, McPherson Square.*

**Willard Hotel** (Tour 5: Old Downtown and Federal Triangle) *Metro stops, Federal Triangle and Metro Center.*

**Woodrow Wilson House** (Tour 7: Dupont Circle) *Metro stop, Dupont Circle.*

## Museums and Galleries

The Smithsonian dominates the public museum and gallery scene in Washington, but there are also many private art galleries that show and sell the work of local, national, and international artists. These galleries are concentrated near Dupont Circle, in Georgetown, and on 7th Street north of Pennsylvania Avenue. For an overview of the day's events at Smithsonian museums, call **Dial-a-Museum** (tel. 202/357–2020).

**Anacostia Neighborhood Museum.** Exhibits in this Smithsonian museum deal with African-American history and culture. Past exhibits have focused on black aviators, the Harlem Renaissance, and the development of African-American churches. *1901 Fort Pl. SE, tel. 202/287–3369. Open daily 10–5; closed Christmas.*

**Art Museum of the Americas** (Tour 3: The White House) *Metro stop, Farragut West.*

**Arts and Industries Building** (Tour 1: The Mall) *Metro stop, Smithsonian.*

**Australian Embassy** (Tour 7: Dupont Circle) *Metro stop, Dupont Circle.*

**Bethune Museum-Archives.** Born to ex-slaves in South Carolina, Mary McLeod Bethune went on to found Florida's Bethune-Cookman College, establish the National Council of Negro Women, and serve as an advisor to President Franklin D. Roosevelt. Exhibits in the museum reflect Bethune's ideals and focus on the achievements of black women. *1318 Vermont Ave. NW, tel. 202/332–1233. Open weekdays 10–4:30. Metro stop, McPherson Square.*

**B'nai B'rith Klutznick Museum** (Tour 7: Dupont Circle) *Metro stop, Farragut North.*

**Canadian Embassy** (Tour 5: Old Downtown and Federal Triangle) *Metro stop, Archives.*

**Capital Children's Museum.** In this hands-on museum children can send messages in Morse code, hoist cinder blocks with pulleys and levers, crawl through a mock sewer, climb on a fire engine, and learn about foreign countries by making traditional ethnic foods and crafts. *800 3rd St. NE, tel. 202/543–8600. Admission: $5 for ages 2–59, senior citizens $2, museum members and children under 2 free. Open daily 10–5; closed Thanksgiving, Dec. 25, New Year's Day, and Easter.*

**College Park Airport Museum.** Opened in 1909, College Park is the world's oldest operating airport and was the site of numerous aviation firsts: first mile-high flight, first machine gun to be shot from a plane, first Army aviation air school. The last received a special boost from Orville and Wilbur Wright, who tested military planes here and whose presence is evident in the museum's early aviation memorabilia. The airport's Air Fair every September features antique airplanes, hot air balloons, and a Wright Brothers lookalike contest. *6709 Cpl. Frank Scott Dr., College Park, MD, tel. 301/864–1530. Open Wed.–Fri. 11–3, Sat.–Sun. 11–5.*

**Corcoran Gallery of Art** (Tour 3: The White House) *Metro stop, Farragut West.*

**Daughters of the American Revolution Museum** (Tour 3: The White House) *Metro stop, Farragut West.*

**Department of the Interior Museum** (Tour 3: The White House) *Metro stop, Farragut West.*

**Dumbarton Oaks Collection** (Tour 6: Georgetown).

**Explorers Hall/National Geographic Society** (Tour 7: Dupont Circle) *Metro stop, Farragut North.*

**Firearms Museum/National Rifle Association** (Tour 7: Dupont Circle) *Metro stop, Farragut North.*

**Fonda Del Sol Visual Art and Media Center.** Located near Dupont Circle in a Victorian town house, this nonprofit center is devoted to the cultural heritage of the Americas. Changing exhibitions cover contemporary, pre-Columbian, and folk art. The center also offers a program of lectures, concerts, poetry readings, exhibit tours, and an annual summer festival featuring salsa and reggae music. *2112 R St. NW, tel. 202/483–2777. Open Tue.–Sat. 12:30–5. Metro stop, Dupont Circle.*

**Freer Gallery of Art** (Tour 1: The Mall) *Metro stop, Smithsonian.*

**Paul E. Garber Facility.** This collection of Smithsonian warehouses in suburban Maryland is where flight-related artifacts are stored and restored prior to their display at the National Air and Space Museum on the Mall. Among the 160 objects on view here are such historic craft as a Soviet MiG-15 from the Korean War, a Battle of Britain-era Hawker Hurricane IIC, as well as satellite models and assorted engines and propellers. A behind-the-scenes look at how the artifacts are preserved is included on the three-hour walking tour (recommended for ages 14 and up). There are no restrooms at the facility, nor heating or air-conditioning, so plan accordingly. *Old Silver Rd. at St. Barnabas Rd., Suitland, MD, tel. 202/357–1400. Tours weekdays at 10, weekends at 10 and 1. Reservations required at least 3–8 weeks in advance.*

**Goddard Space Flight Center.** Space flight is brought down to earth at this NASA museum, located on the suburban Maryland complex where scientists and technicians monitor orbiting spacecraft. Local model rocket clubs send their handiwork skyward the first and third Sundays of each month. *Baltimore-Washington Pkwy. and Greenbelt Rd., Greenbelt, MD, tel. 301/286–8981.*

*Open Wed.–Sun. 10–4. Tour Wed.–Sat. at 11:30 and 2:30.*

**Hillwood Museum.** Hillwood House, the 40-room Georgian mansion of cereal heiress Marjorie Merriweather Post, contains a large collection of 18th- and 19th-century French and Russian decorative art that includes gold and silver work, icons, lace, tapestries, china, and Fabergé eggs. Also on the estate are a dacha filled with Russian objects and an Adirondacks-style cabin that houses an assortment of Native American artifacts. The grounds are composed of lawns; formal French and Japanese gardens; and paths that wind through plantings of azaleas, laurels, and rhododendrons. *4155 Linnean Ave. NW, tel. 202/686–5807. Admission to house and grounds: $10, children under 12 not admitted on house tour. Admission to grounds only: $4. House open Mar.–Jan. by appointment only (well in advance); grounds open Tues.–Sat. 11–3. Metro stop, Van Ness/UDC.*

**Holography museums.** The nonprofit Art, Science and Technology Institute operates two Washington museums devoted to the eerie, three-dimensional, laser-produced images that seem to float in space. The permanent collection at the R Street location features 65 pieces, including the world's largest hologram—three square feet. The gallery on K Street plays host to rotating exhibits of fine art from around the world that include "holo-sculpture," "holo-painting," and "holo-photography." Gift shops allow visitors to leave with their own holograms. *2018 R St. NW, tel. 202/667–6322. Admission: $5 adults, $4 children under 12. Open Tues.–Sun. 11–6; closed major holidays. Metro stop, Dupont Circle. Techworld Plaza, 800 K St. NW, tel. 202/667–6322. Admission: $5, $4 children under 12. Open weekdays 11–6. Metro stop, Gallery Place.*

**Jewish War Veterans National Memorial Museum.** The message at this museum—opened in 1990—is that Jews in this country are first and foremost American citizens who have served in every war the nation has fought. It is primarily a military museum, with displays of weapons, uniforms, medals, recruitment posters, and other memorabilia. The few specifically religious items—a camouflage yarmulke, rabbinical supplies fashioned from shell casings and parachute silk—underscore the strange demands placed on religion during war. *1811 R St. NW, tel. 202/265–6280. Open weekdays 10–4:30; open for groups Sun. by appointment. Closed Sat. and federal and Jewish holidays. Metro Stop, Dupont Circle.*

**Joseph H. Hirshhorn Museum and Sculpture Garden** (Tour 1: The Mall) *Metro stop, Smithsonian.*

**International Monetary Fund Visitors Center.** Exhibits and films outline the origin and functions of the IMF. International photographs, paintings, and sculpture are on display. The Center also hosts cultural events—readings, recitals, and films—with an international flavor. *700 19th St. NW, tel. 202/623-6869. Open weekdays 10-6. Films usually shown between noon and 2. Closed federal holidays. Metro stop, Farragut West.*

**Marine Corps Museum.** Articles relating to the Marine Corps, from its inception in 1775 to the present day, are on display in this museum. You'll see uniforms, weapons, and a special exhibit on one of the Corps' proudest achievements: raising the flag on Iwo Jima during World War II. *Washington Navy Yard, 9th and M Sts. SE, Bldg. 58, tel. 202/433-3534. Open fall-spring, Mon.-Sat. 10-4, Sun. noon-5; summer, weekdays 10-8, Sat. 10-4, Sun. noon-5; closed Dec. 25 and New Year's Day. Metro stop, Eastern Market.*

**Mexican Cultural Institute.** This museum is in a glorious 1911 Italianate house that was once the Embassy of Mexico. Inside are highlights of 19th- and 20th-century Mexican art, including the works of Diego Rivera, José Clemente Orozco, David Alfaro, Sigueiros, and Juan O'Gorman. *2829 16th St. NW, tel. 202/728-1628. Open Thurs.-Sun. 11-6.*

**National Air and Space Museum** (Tour 1: The Mall) *Metro stop, Smithsonian.*

**National Aquarium** (Tour 5: Old Downtown and Federal Triangle) *Metro stop, Federal Triangle.*

**National Building Museum** (Tour 5: Old Downtown and Federal Triangle) *Metro stop, Judiciary Square.*

**National Capital Trolley Museum.** Trolley buffs remember with sadness the day in January 1962 when Washington's last streetcar was retired. Some of the capital's historic trolleys were rescued, restored, and are now on display at this suburban Maryland museum, along with streetcars from Europe and elsewhere in America. For a nominal fare you can go on a 2-mile ride through the country. *Bonifant Rd. between Layhill Rd. and New Hampshire Ave., Wheaton, MD, tel. 301/384-6088. Trolley-ride fare: $2 adults, $1.50 children under 18, children under 2 free. Open Jan.-Nov., weekends; Memorial Day, July 4, and Labor Day noon-5; Dec., weekends 5-9 for "Holly Trolley Illuminations"; July and Aug., Wed. noon-4.*

**National Gallery of Art** (Tour 1: The Mall) *Metro stop, Archives.*

**National Museum of African Art** (Tour 1: The Mall) *Metro stop, Smithsonian.*

**National Museum of American Art** (Tour 5: Old Downtown and Federal Triangle) *Metro stop, Gallery Place.*

**National Museum of American History** (Tour 1: The Mall) *Metro stop, Smithsonian.*

**National Museum of Health and Medicine.** Opened more than 125 years ago, the Medical Museum features exhibits that illustrate medicine's fight against injury and disease. Included are displays on the Lincoln and Garfield assassinations and one of the world's largest collection of microscopes. Since some exhibits are fairly graphic (the wax surgical models and various organs floating in alcohol, for example) the museum may not be suitable for young children or the squeamish. *Walter Reed Army Medical Center, 6825 16th St. NW, tel. 202/576-2348. Open daily 10-5:30; closed Dec. 25.*

**National Museum of Natural History** (Tour 1: The Mall) *Metro stop, Smithsonian. Open Mon.-Sat. 10-5.*

**National Museum of Women in the Arts.** Housed in a 1907 Renaissance Revival Masonic temple, this museum displays the works of prominent female artists. The permanent collection of more than 500 works ranges from the Renaissance to the present and includes paintings, drawings, sculpture, prints, and photography. Artists represented include Georgia O'Keeffe, Mary Cassatt, Vigee Le Brun, and Judy Chicago. Art from women in particular states is exhibited in the State Gallery. *1250 New York Ave. NW, tel. 202/783-5000. Suggested donation: $3 adults; $2 students, senior citizens, and children. Free to members. Open weekdays 10-5, weekends noon-5. Metro stop, Metro Center.*

**National Portrait Gallery** (Tour 5: Old Downtown and Federal Triangle) *Metro stop, Gallery Place.*

**National Postal Museum** (Tour 4: Capitol Hill) *Metro stop, Union Station.*

**National Weather Service Science and History Center.** Opened in 1990 in suburban Maryland, this museum is for people who want to do more than just talk about the weather. On display are the tools of the National Oceanic and Atmospheric Administration, including remote data collectors, weather satellites, and "TOTO," a robotlike Totable Tornado Observatory used to study twisters. There's also the actual 1891 Cairo, Ill., U.S. Weather Bureau office, complete with the original furniture, record books, and meteorological instruments. *1325 East-West Hwy., Silver Spring, MD, tel. 301/713-0622. Admission free. Open weekdays 8:30-5. Metro stop, Silver Spring.*

**Navy Museum.** The history of the U.S. Navy from the Revolution to the present is chronicled in exhibits that include the fully rigged foremast of the USS *Constitution* (better known as "Old Ironsides"), a model of America's first submarine (invented in 1776), and operating periscopes from more recent submarines. Children enjoy elevating and aiming the 40-millimeter guns and don't seem to mind much that the guns don't actually fire. *9th and M Sts. SE, tel. 202/433-2651. Open early Sept.–late May, weekdays 9–4, weekends 10–5; Memorial Day–Labor Day, daily 9–5; closed Dec. 24–25 and federal holidays. Metro stop, Eastern Market.*

**Paul VI Institute for the Arts.** Though it's part of the Catholic Archdiocese of Washington, this three-room gallery in historic Carroll Hall doesn't display what might be considered "religious" works. Instead, it's a home for art in which the "spirituality" of the artist is exposed. Past exhibits have ranged from watercolors by a Japanese Carmelite nun to lighthearted collages assembled from magazines and greeting cards. There is an Irish festival each March and works with a Christmas theme are installed during the holidays. *924 G St. NW, tel. 202/347-1450. Open Tues.–Sat. 10–5. Closed Christmas Day, Easter, and most other religious holidays. Metro stop, Gallery Place.*

**Phillips Collection** (Tour 7: Dupont Circle) *Metro stop, Dupont Circle.*

**Renwick Gallery** (Tour 3: The White House) *Metro stop, McPherson Square.*

**Sackler Gallery** (Tour 1: The Mall) *Metro stop, Smithsonian.*

**Smithsonian Institution Castle** (Tour 1: The Mall) *Metro stop, Smithsonian.*

**Tech 2000.** This hands-on museum developed by members of the Interactive Video Industry Association attempts to show how new multi-media programs that combine video and computer technologies work together to enhance communications. It's no surprise, then, to find interactive exhibits allowing visitors to do such things as browse through the collection of the National Gallery of Art using a computer tracking ball and a TV monitor, learn how to put out a fire on an F–15 jet with the help of a touch-sensitive video screen, or play with a voice-activated computer. Technophobes will be overwhelmed, the Nintendo generation enthralled. *Techworld Plaza, 800 K St. NW, tel. 202/842-0500. Admission: $5 adults, $4 students, $3 children 6–12 and senior citizens; free to children under 6. Open Wed.–Sat. 11–5. Metro stop, Gallery Place.*

**Textile Museum** (Tour 7: Dupont Circle) *Metro stop, Dupont Circle.*

**United States Holocaust Memorial Museum** (Tour 1: The Mall) *Metro stop, Smithsonian.*

**Washington Dolls' House and Toy Museum.** Founded in 1975 by a dollhouse historian, this compact museum contains a charming collection of American and imported dolls, dollhouses, toys, and games, most from the Victorian period. Highlights of the collection include a miniature Teddy Roosevelt on safari and an 1884 model of the Capitol. Miniature accessories, dollhouse kits, and antique toys and games are on sale in the museum's shops. *5236 44th St. NW, tel. 202/244–0024. Admission: $3 adults, $2 senior citizens, $1 children under 14. Open Tues.–Sat. 10–5, Sun. noon–5. Metro stop, Friendship Heights.*

**Washington Project for the Arts** (Tour 5: Old Downtown and Federal Triangle) *Metro stops, National Archives or Gallery Place.*

## Parks and Gardens

**Audubon Naturalist Society.** A self-guided nature trail winds its way through this estate and around the Audubon Society's headquarters (in a mansion known as Woodend designed in the 1920s by Jefferson Memorial architect John Russell Pope). You're never very far from the trill of birdsong here as the Audubon has turned the grounds into something of a nature preserve, forbidding the use of toxic chemicals and leaving some areas in a wild, natural state. The bookstore stocks titles on conservation, ecology, and birding, as well as birdfeeders and birdhouses. *8940 Jones Mill Rd., Chevy Chase, MD, tel. 301/652–9188. Grounds open daily sunrise–sunset. Bookstore open Mon.–Wed. and Fri. 10–5, Thurs. 10–8, Sat. 9–5.*

**The Bishop's Garden.** This traditional English-style church-garden is on the grounds of the Washington Cathedral. Boxwoods, ivy, tea roses, yew trees, and an assortment of arches, bas reliefs, and stonework from European ruins provide a restful counterpoint to the nearby cathedral's Gothic towers. *Wisconsin and Massachusetts Aves. NW. Metro stop, Woodley Park-Zoo. Grounds not lighted at night.*

**Brookside Gardens.** There's always something in bloom at this rolling 50-acre display garden in suburban Maryland. Outdoors, formal seasonal displays of bulbs, annuals, and perennials, and a sprawling azalea garden flourish. Inside, the two conservatories house—depending on the time of year—Easter lilies, tropicals, Japanese chrysanthemums, or poinsettia trees. *1500*

Glenallan Ave., Wheaton, MD, tel. 301/949–8230. Grounds open daily 9–sunset; conservatories daily 10–5; closed Dec. 25.

**Cabin John Regional Park.** Extensive playgrounds, ball fields, picnic areas, and tennis courts can be found at this suburban-Maryland park complex. Children enjoy the train ride. *7400 Tuckerman La., Rockville, MD, tel. 301/299–4555. Park open sunrise–sunset. Train operates weekends in spring, daily in summer. Cost: 95¢.*

**Constitution Gardens** (Tour 2: The Monuments) *Metro stop, Foggy Bottom.*

**Dumbarton Oaks** (Tour 6: Georgetown).

**East Potomac Park.** This 328-acre tongue of land hangs down from the Tidal Basin between the Washington Channel to the east and the Potomac River to the west. Facilities include playgrounds, picnic tables, tennis courts, swimming pools, a driving range, two 9-hole golf courses, and an 18-hole golf course. The park's miniature golf course, built during the "midget golf" craze of the '20s, is the oldest in the area; its Art Deco architecture is a welcome contrast to the artificial theme-park design of most miniature golf courses. Double-blossoming cherry trees line Ohio Drive and bloom about two weeks after the single-blossoming variety that attracts throngs to the Tidal Basin each spring. *The Awakening*, a huge, fantastical sculpture of a man emerging from the ground, sits on Hains Point, at the tip of the park. Plans are in the making to build a "Peace Garden" here that will feature plantings resembling a giant olive branch. *Approach park via Maine Ave. SW, heading west; or from Ohio Dr., heading south. Follow signs carefully. Ohio Dr. closed to traffic weekends and holidays 3 PM–6 AM. Free shuttle bus available from Park Service headquarters. Metro stops, Smithsonian or L'Enfant Plaza.*

**Fort Washington Park.** Built to protect the city from enemies sailing up the Potomac, this 1808 fort was burned by the British during the War of 1812. Rebuilt, it served as an Army post until 1945. The National Park Service maintains it now and holds historical programs there every weekend. *From the Capital Beltway (Rte. 95) take the Indian Head Hwy. exit (Rte. 210) and drive 4½ mi south; look for sign on right. Tel. 301/763–4600. Entrance fee: $3 per vehicle. Park open daily 8–sunset. Visitors center open daily 10–4:30. Fort open daily 9–5; closed Dec. 25 and New Year's Day.*

**Kahlil Gibran Memorial Garden.** Dedicated in 1991, this tiny urban park combining western and Arab symbols fosters the contemplative spirit. Limestone benches engraved with sayings from Gibran curve around a fountain and a bust of the Lebanese poet. *3100 block of Massachusetts Ave. NW.*

**Glen Echo Park.** This park was once the site of the Chautauqua Assembly, built in 1891 to promote liberal and practical education among the masses. It served a stint as an amusement park and is now run by the National Park Service, which offers space to a variety of artists who conduct classes year-round. Monthly exhibits of artists' work are shown in a stone tower left over from the Chautauqua period. An antique carousel is open in the summer, and there is big band– and square dancing in the Spanish ballroom. On weekends, Adventure Theater presents shows for children. *7300 MacArthur Blvd., Glen Echo, MD, tel. 301/492–6282. Call for information on events, tours, performances, and carousel hrs.*

**Great Falls Park.** The waters of the Potomac River cascade dramatically over a steep, jagged gorge in this 800-acre park in Virginia. Inside the park on the Virginia side are a visitors center and the ruins of George Washington's unsuccessful Potowmack Canal, designed to skirt unnavigable portions of the river. On the Maryland side, the Great Falls Tavern Visitors Center serves as a museum and headquarters for the rangers who manage the C & O Canal. You can walk over a series of bridges to Olmsted Island in the middle of the Potomac for a spectacular view of the falls. The area is ideal for hiking, picnicking, climbing, and fishing. *Virginia side: 9200 Old Dominion Dr., Great Falls, VA, tel. 703/285–2966. Open daily 8–sunset; closed Thanksgiving and Dec. 25. Maryland side: terminus of MacArthur Blvd., Potomac, MD, tel. 703/285–2966 or 301/299–2026. Admission: $3 per vehicle, $1 per person without vehicle. Open daily 8–sunset; closed Thanksgiving and Dec. 25.*

**Hillwood Museum.** The grounds of Marjorie Merriweather Post's Georgian-style Hillwood House feature a French-style *parterre*, a rose garden, a Japanese garden, paths that wind through azaleas and rhododendrons, and a greenhouse in which 5,000 orchids bloom. Tours of the Hillwood Museum are often booked up months in advance, but reservations are not needed for the garden. *4155 Linnean Ave. NW, tel. 202/686–5807. Admission: $4. Open daily 11–3. Metro stop, Van Ness/ UDC.*

**Kenilworth Aquatic Gardens.** Exotic water lilies, lotuses, hyacinths, and other water-loving plants thrive in this 12-acre sanctuary of quiet pools and marshy flats. In a pool near the visitors center bloom East Indian lotus plants grown from 350-year-old seeds recovered from a dry Manchurian lake-bed. The gardens are home to a variety of wetland animals, including turtles, frogs, muskrats, and some 40 species of birds. The best time to visit is early in the morning, when day-bloomers are just opening and night-bloomers have yet to close. Nearly everything is in bloom in July. *Kenilworth Ave. and Douglas St. NE, tel. 202/426–6905. Gardens open daily 7–4, visitors center open daily 8:30–4. Garden walks held on summer weekends at 9, 11, and 1.*

**Lafayette Square** (Tour 3: The White House) *Metro stop, McPherson Square.*

**Meridian Hill Park.** Landscape architect Horace Peaslee created this often-overlooked park after a 1917 study of the parks of Europe. It contains elements of France (a long, straight mall bordered with plants), Italy (terraces and wall fountains), and Switzerland (a lower-level reflecting pool based on one in Zurich). It's also known as Malcolm X Park. Drug activity makes it unwise to visit this park alone, even in daylight hours. Steer clear after dark. *16th and Euclid Sts. NW, tel. 202/426–6851.*

**National Arboretum.** During the azalea season, from the middle of April to the end of May, this 444-acre oasis is a blaze of color. In the summer, clematis, ferns, peonies, rhododendrons, and roses bloom. Paths and roadways make the arboretum an ideal place to visit for either a relaxing stroll or a scenic drive. Also popular are the National Bonsai Collection and National Herb Garden. *3501 New York Ave. NE, tel. 202/475–4815. Open weekdays 8–5, weekends and holidays 10–5. Bonsai Collection open daily 10–2:30; closed Dec. 25.*

**National Zoological Park** (Tour 9: Cleveland Park) *Metro stops, Cleveland Park or Woodley Park-Zoo.*

**Pershing Park** (Tour 3: The White House) *Metro stop, Federal Triangle.*

**Rock Creek Park.** The 1,800 acres of park on either side of Rock Creek have provided a cool oasis for Washington residents since Congress set them aside in 1890. There's a lot to enjoy here. Thirty picnic areas are scattered throughout the park. Bicycle routes and hiking and equestrian trails wend through the groves of dogwoods, beeches, oaks, and cedar. Rangers at the **Nature Center and Planetarium** (south of Military Rd. at 5000 Glover Rd. NW, tel. 202/426–6829; open daily 9–5, closed federal holidays and Sun. preceding a Mon. holidays) will acquaint you with the park and advise you of scheduled activities. Highlights include: **Pierce Mill,** a restored 19th-century gristmill powered by the falling water of Rock Creek (tel. 202/426–6908); **Fort Reno,** one of the original ring of forts that guarded Washington during the Civil War; and the **Rock Creek Golf Course,** an 18-hole public course. *Between 16th St. and Connecticut Ave. NW, tel. 202/426–6829 for park activities, 202/882–7332 for golf course. Park open daylight hrs only; hrs for individual sites vary.*

**Theodore Roosevelt Island.** This 88-acre island wilderness-preserve in the Potomac River is a living tribute to the conservation-minded 26th president. It features 2½ miles of nature trails through marshland, swampland, and upland forest. Cattails, arrowarum, pickerelweed, willow, ash, maple, and oak all grow on the island, providing a habitat for frogs, raccoons, birds, squirrels, and the occasional red or gray fox. There is also a 17-foot bronze statue of Roosevelt, executed by Paul Manship. *A pedestrian bridge connects the island to a parking lot on the Virginia shore and is accessible from the northbound lanes of the George Washington Memorial Pkwy. From downtown, take Constitution Ave. west across the Theodore Roosevelt Bridge to GW Memorial Pkwy. north and follow signs. Tel. 703/285–2598.*

**United States Botanic Gardens** (Tour 4: Capitol Hill) *Metro stop, Federal Center SW.*

**West Potomac Park** (Tour 2: The Monuments) *Metro stop, Smithsonian.*

---

## Churches, Temples, and Mosques

**All Souls' Unitarian Church.** The design of this church, erected in 1924, is based on that of St. Martin-in-the-Fields in London. *16th and Harvard Sts. NW, tel. 202/332–5266.*

**Franciscan Monastery and Gardens.** Not far from the Shrine of the **Immaculate Conception,** this Byzantine-style monastery contains facsimiles of such Holy-Land shrines as the Grotto of Bethlehem and the Holy Sepulcher. Underground are reproductions of the catacombs of Rome. The gardens are especially beautiful, planted with roses that bloom in the summer. *14th and Quincy Sts. NE, tel. 202/526–6800. Open daily 9–5. Tours of catacombs on the hr (except noon) Mon.–Sat. 9–4, Sun. 1–4. Metro stop, Brookland-Catholic University.*

**Grace Episcopal Church** (Tour 6: Georgetown).

**Islamic Mosque and Cultural Center.** The Moslem faithful are called to prayer five times a day from atop this mosque's 162-foot-high minaret. Each May, the Moslem Women's Association sponsors a bazaar, with crafts, clothing, and food for sale. *2551 Massachusetts Ave. NW, tel. 202/332–8343. Center open daily 10–5; mosque open for all 5 prayers, dawn–past sunset.*

**Metropolitan African Methodist Episcopal Church.** Completed in 1886, this Gothic-style church became one of the most influential black churches in the city. Abolitionist orator Frederick Douglass worshipped here. *1518 M St. NW, tel. 202/331–1426. Metro stop, Farragut North.*

**Mt. Zion United Methodist Church** (Tour 6: Georgetown).

**National Shrine of the Immaculate Conception.** This is the largest Catholic church in the United States, begun in 1920 and built with funds contributed by every parish in the country. Dedicated in 1959, the shrine is a blend of Romanesque and Byzantine styles, with a bell tower that reminds many of St. Mark's in Venice. *Michigan Ave. and 4th St. NE, tel. 202/526–8300. Open spring and summer, daily 7–7; fall and winter, daily 7–6. Sunday mass at 7:30, 9, 10:30, noon, 1:30 (in Latin), and 4:30. Metro stop, Brookland–Catholic University.*

**Old Adas Israel Synagogue.** This redbrick, Federal Revival–style building is the oldest synagogue in Washington. Dedicated in 1876, the structure originally stood at 6th and G streets NW but was moved to its present location in 1969 to make way for the construction of Metro headquarters. Exhibits in the Albert and Lillian Small Jewish Museum inside explore Jewish life in Washington. *3rd and G Sts. NW, tel. 202/789–0900. Suggested donation: $2 adult, $1 children. Open Sun.–Thurs. 11–3, Fri. by appointment. Metro stop, Judiciary Square.*

**St. John's Episcopal Church** (Tour 3: The White House) *Metro stop, McPherson Square.*

**St. Matthew's Cathedral** (Tour 7: Dupont Circle) *Metro stop, Farragut North.*

**Saint Sophia Cathedral.** This Greek Orthodox cathedral is noted for the handsome mosaic work on the interior of its dome. Saint Sophia holds a festival of Greek food and crafts each May and October. *Massachusetts Ave. and 36th St. NW, tel. 202/333–4730.*

**Scottish Rite Temple.** This dramatic Masonic shrine is patterned after the Mausoleum of Halicarnassus. Tours available weekdays on request. *1733 16th St. NW, tel. 202/232–3579.*

**Washington National Cathedral.** Construction of this stunning Gothic church—the sixth largest cathedral in the world—started in 1907 and was finished on September 30, 1990, when the cathedral was consecrated. Like its 14th-century counterparts, the National Cathedral (officially Washington's Cathedral Church of St. Peter and St. Paul) has flying buttresses, naves, transepts, and barrel vaults that were built stone by stone. It is adorned with fanciful gargoyles created by skilled stone carvers. The tomb of Woodrow Wilson, the only president buried in Washington, is on the south side of the nave. The expansive view of the city from the Pilgrim Gallery is exceptional. The cathedral is under the governance of the Episcopal church but has played host to services of many denominations. *Wisconsin and Massachusetts Aves. NW, tel. 202/537–6200. Open fall, winter, and spring, daily 10–4:30; May 1–Labor Day, weekdays 10–9, weekends 10–4:30. Sun. services at 8, 9, 10, 11; evensong at 4 PM. Tours Mon.–Sat. 10–3:15, Sun. 12:45–2. Tour information: tel. 202/537–6207.*

**Temple of the Church of Jesus Christ of Latter-Day Saints.** This striking Mormon temple in suburban Maryland—one of its white towers is topped with a golden statue of the Mormon angel and prophet, Moroni—has become a Washington landmark. It is closed to non-Mormons, but a visitors center offers a lovely view of the white-marble church and has a film about the temple and what takes place inside. Tulips, dogwoods, and azaleas bloom in the 57-acre grounds each spring. *9900 Stoneybrook Dr., Kensington, MD, tel. 301/587–0144. Visitors center open daily 10–9. Grounds open Tues.– Fri. 10–9, Sat. 10–6.*

## Statues and Monuments

Washington, perhaps more than any other city in the United States, is filled with allegorical outdoor art. Examples can be found in the middle of traffic circles and on dozens of neoclassical public buildings. *The Outdoor Sculpture of Washington, D.C.,* by architectural historian James M. Goode, provides readable histories of the well-known and little-known works to be found in the nation's capital.

***The Awakening.*** Children love this giant sculpture of a bearded man emerging from the ground near Hains Point. Adults are captivated, too. *Hains Point, East Potomac Park.*

**Bartholdi Fountain** (Tour 4: Capitol Hill) *Metro stop, Federal Center SW.*

**Boy Scouts Memorial.** Just east of the Ellipse stands this group of heroic statuary: a uniformed Boy Scout flanked by a male figure representing patriotism and a female figure who holds the light of faith. *East of Ellipse, near 15th St. NW. Metro stop, McPherson Square.*

**Columbus Memorial Fountain** (Tour 4: Capitol Hill) *Metro stop, Union Station.*

**Dumbarton Bridge** (Tour 7: Dupont Circle) *Metro stop, Dupont Circle.*

**Dupont Circle/Fountain** (Tour 7: Dupont Circle) *Metro stop, Dupont Circle.*

**Albert Einstein** (Tour 8: Foggy Bottom) *Metro stop, Foggy Bottom.*

**Freedmen's Memorial.** This bronze statue of Abraham Lincoln standing above a newly freed slave who has just broken his chains was dedicated on April 14, 1876, the 11th anniversary of the president's assassination. Money for its construction was donated by hundreds of ex-slaves. *Lincoln Park, Massachusetts Ave. between 11th and 13th Sts. NE.*

**Albert Gallatin** (Tour 4: Capitol Hill) *Metro stop, McPherson Square.*

**James Garfield Memorial** (Tour 4: Capitol Hill) *Metro stop, Capitol South.*

**Grand Army of the Republic** (Tour 5: Old Downtown and Federal Triangle) *Metro stop, Archives.*

**Grant Memorial** (Tour 4: Capitol Hill) *Metro stop, Federal Center SW.*

**Alexander Hamilton** (Tour 3: The White House) *Metro stop, Federal Triangle.*

**General Winfield Scott** (Tour 5: Old Downtown and Federal Triangle) *Metro stop, Archives.*

**Andrew Jackson** (Tour 3: The White House) *Metro stop, McPherson Square.*

**Jefferson Memorial** (Tour 2: The Monuments).

**John F. Kennedy** (Tour 8: Foggy Bottom) *Metro stop, Foggy Bottom.*

**Korean War Veterans Memorial** (Tour 2: The Monuments) *Metro stop, Smithsonian.*

**Thaddeus Kosciuszko** (Tour 3: The White House) *Metro stop, McPherson Square.*

**Marquis de Lafayette** (Tour 3: The White House) *Metro stop, McPherson Square.*

**Lincoln Memorial** (Tour 2: The Monuments).

**Marine Corps War Memorial** (Tour 11: Arlington) *Metro stop, Arlington Cemetery.*

**National Law Enforcement Officers Memorial** (Tour 5: Old Downtown and Federal Triangle). *Metro stop, Judiciary Square.*

**Navy Memorial** (Tour 5: Old Downtown and Federal Triangle) *Metro stop, Archives.*

***The Peace of God that Passeth Understanding.*** Henry Adams commissioned Augustus Saint-Gaudens to create this memorial to Adams's wife, who had committed suicide. Known by the nickname "Grief," this figure of a shroud-draped woman is thought by many to be the most moving sculpture in the city. *In Rock Creek Cemetery, Rock Creek Rd. and Webster St. NW.*

**Peace Monument** (Tour 4: Capitol Hill) *Metro stop, Union Station.*

**Comte de Rochambeau** (Tour 3: The White House) *Metro stop, McPherson Square.*

**General Casimir Pulaski** (Tour 5: Old Downtown and Federal Triangle) *Metro stop, Federal Triangle.*

**Franklin Delano Roosevelt Memorial** (Tour 5: Old Downtown and Federal Triangle) *Metro stop, Archives.*

**General Winfield Scott** (Tour 7: Dupont Circle) *Metro stop, Dupont Circle.*

**General Philip Sheridan** (Tour 7: Dupont Circle) *Metro stop, Dupont Circle.*

**General William Tecumseh Sherman Monument** (Tour 3: The White House) *Metro stop, Federal Triangle.*

**Baron von Steuben** (Tour 3: The White House) *Metro stop, McPherson Square.*

**Temperance Fountain** (Tour 5: Old Downtown and Federal Triangle) *Metro stop, Archives.*

**Vietnam Veterans Memorial** (Tour 2: The Monuments) *Metro stop, Foggy Bottom.*

**Vietnam Womens Memorial** (Tour 2: The Monuments) *Metro stop, Foggy Bottom.*

**Washington Monument** (Tour 2: The Monuments) *Metro stop, Federal Triangle or Smithsonian.*

# 4   Shopping

By Deborah Papier

*Updated by*
*Jeanne Cooper*

Not long ago, a shopping trip in the Washington area really was a trip—a long trek to one of the suburban shopping malls, which offered far more than could be found in town. It is still true that many major national retailers are bypassing the city, so that a visitor wanting to check out Bloomingdale's, Nordstrom, or Macy's has to venture to White Flint Mall in Bethesda, Maryland (the White Flint stop on Metrorail's red line), the twin megamalls in Tysons Corner, Virginia (reachable by bus but not subway), or the Fashion Centre mall at Pentagon City (on the blue and yellow Metrorail lines). In recent years, however, the city's own shopping scene has been revitalized. Washington department stores have upgraded both their facilities and their merchandise; many of the smaller one-of-a-kind shops have managed to survive urban renewal; designer boutiques are increasing; and interesting specialty shops and minimalls are popping up all over town.

For those who *prefer* suburban shopping, there are developments here as well. The newly renovated marble-trimmed Montgomery Mall in Bethesda (reachable by bus, not subway) has added Nordstrom and many smaller shops to keep up with its posh competitors. On the discount scene, several major outlet centers are within 45 minutes of the city (including Potomac Mills, the mile-long mall off I–95 that bills itself as Virginia's leading tourist attraction); closer to the District, a new all-discount mall is being developed for downtown Silver Spring, Maryland, on Metro's red line.

Store hours vary greatly, so it is safest to call ahead. In general, Georgetown stores are open late and on Sunday, while stores in the downtown district that cater to office workers close at 6 PM and may not be open at all on Saturday. Some stores extend their hours on Thursday.

Sales tax is 6% (9% for restaurant fare), and the major credit cards are accepted virtually everywhere.

## Shopping Districts

**Georgetown** remains Washington's favorite shopping area. Though it is not on a subway line, and parking is impossible, people still flock here. The attraction (aside from the lively street scene) is the profusion of specialty shops, which offer wares unavailable elsewhere in the city. Georgetown has most of the city's antiques dealers, craft shops, and high-style clothing boutiques. For books and records, it's second only to Dupont Circle.

The hub of Georgetown is the intersection of Wisconsin Avenue and M Street, with most of the stores lying to the west on M Street and to the north on Wisconsin. Near that intersection, at 3222 Wisconsin Avenue, is **Georgetown Park** (tel. 202/298–5577), a three-level mall that looks like a Victorian ice-cream parlor. Georgetown Park is anchored by Conran's (tel. 202/298–8300), which features reasonably priced, well-designed housewares, including furniture.

**Dupont Circle** has some of the same flavor as Georgetown. Here, too, there is a lively mix of shops and restaurants, with most of the action on the major artery of Connecticut Avenue. There are many book and record stores in the neighborhood, as well as stores selling coffees, stationery, and bric-a-brac.

The city's department stores can be found in the "new" downtown, which is still being built. Its fulcrum is **Metro Center,** which spans 11th and 12th streets NW along G Street. The Metro Center subway stop takes you directly into the basements of downtown's two major department stores, Woodward & Lothrop, familiarly called "Woodies," and Hecht's. Take the 11th and G streets exit to Woodies; for Hecht's, follow the signs to the 12th or 13th street exits.

Now open on weekends, **The Shops at National Place** (by Metro Center, 13th and F Sts. NW, tel. 202/783–9090), takes up three levels, one of which is devoted to food stands. The Shops is oriented primarily to younger consumers. This is a good place to drop off teenagers weary of the Smithsonian and more in the mood to buy compact discs or T-shirts. Banana Republic, Victoria's Secret, and The Sharper Image are three of the catalogue stores that have outlets here.

Although Washington doesn't have anything on the order of Boston's Faneuil Hall, it does have **The Pavilion at the Old Post Office** (12th St. NW and Pennsylvania Ave., tel. 202/289–4224), a renovated building dating from the last century. In March 1992 The Pavilion added an atrium with 29 specialty stores to its already more than 30 small shops such as Caswell & Massey (for toiletries and perfumes) and All Wound Up (selling wind-up toys). An observation deck in the building's clock tower offers an excellent view of the city.

One of the most delightful shopping enclaves in the city is **Union Station** (tel. 202/371–9441), at Massachusetts Avenue NE, near North Capitol Street on the Metrorail

Ann Taylor, **34**

Bally, **32**

Beadazzled, **11**

Betsy Fisher, **15**

Brooks Brothers, **28**

Burberrys, **23**

Camalier & Buckley, **25**

Chanel Boutique, **37**

Chapters, **35**

Charles Schwartz & Son, **4**

Cherishables, **12**

The Cheshire Cat, **6**

Church's, **31**

Crown Books, **17**

Fahrney's, **36**

The Farrell Collection, **8**

Hecht's, **38**

Hugo Boss, **21**

J. Press, **30**

John B. Adler, **9**

The Kid's Closet, **20, 29**

Kitchen Bazaar, **7**

Kramerbooks, **13**

Les Gals, **27**

Lord & Taylor, **2**

Marston Luce, **16**

Mazi Jewelry Design, **42**

Moon, Blossoms and Snow, **41**

Music Box Center, **48**

Mystery Books, **10**

Neiman Marcus, **3**

Pampillonia Jewelers, **5**

Raleighs, **26**

Rizik Bros., **33**

Saks Fifth Avenue, **1**

Second Story Books, **14**

Serenade Record Shop, **22**

Shoe Scene, **19**

The Tiny Jewel Box, **24**

Tower Records, **18**

Woodward & Lothrop, **39**

# Georgetown Shopping

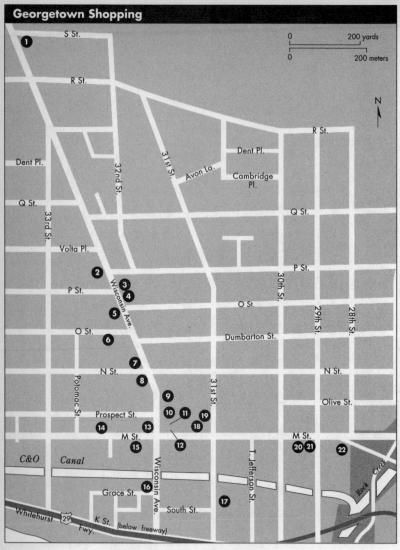

The American
Hand, **21**

Appalachian Spring, **4**

Boogie's Diner, **11**

Britches Great
Outdoors, **12**

Britches of
Georgetown, **9**

The Coach Store, **13**

Commander
Salamander, **5**

Earl Allen, **18**

F.A.O. Schwarz, **15**

Georgetown Antiques
Center, **20**

Georgetown Leather
Design, **14**

G.K.S. Bush, **22**

Indian Craft Shop, **16**

Kemp Mill Records, **8**

Little Caledonia, **3**

Martin's, **7**

Miller & Arney
Antiques, **1**

Old Print Gallery, **19**

Olsson's Books &
Records, **10**

The Phoenix, **2**

Susquehanna, **6**

Yes!, **17**

red line. Resplendent with marble floors and gilded, vaulted ceilings, it's now both a working train station and a mall with three levels of stores, including one level of food stands. The east hall, reminiscent of London's Covent Garden, is filled with vendors of expensive and ethnic wares in open stalls. Christmas is an especially pleasant time to shop here.

As the **Capitol Hill** area continues to gentrify, more unique shops and boutiques have sprung up here. Many are clustered around the 1873 building known as **Eastern Market** (7th and C Sts. SE, one block north of Metrorail's Eastern Market stop on the orange and blue lines). Inside are produce and meat counters, plus the Market Five art gallery; outside are a farmer's market (on Saturdays) and a flea market (on weekends). Across 7th Street are Mission Traders, Antiques on the Hill, and the Eastern Market Emporium, which contains antiques stores and the Harmattan Arts of Africa gallery.

The final major shopping district is on the outskirts of the city, on Wisconsin Avenue straddling the Maryland border. Here is the **Mazza Gallerie** (5300 Wisconsin Ave. NW, tel. 202/966–6114), a four-level mall anchored by the ritzy Neiman Marcus department store. Its other stores include Williams-Sonoma's kitchenware and Pierre Deux's provincial fabrics. The mall is accessible directly from the Friendship Heights station on the Metrorail red line. Three other department stores are close by: Lord & Taylor, Woodward & Lothrop, and Saks Fifth Avenue (*see* Department Stores, *below*).

Across from Mazza Gallerie is the new and growing **Chevy Chase Pavilion** (5335 Wisconsin Ave. NW, tel. 202/686–5335). Its exclusive women's clothing stores include Joan and David, Oilily, and Steilmann European Selection (which carries Karl Lagerfeld's sportier KL line). Other specialty shops of note here are David Ladd & Co. antiques and collectibles, a Pottery Barn, and Rock Creek, a two-store chain selling high-quality, fashionable men's and women's athletic clothing and shoes.

## Department Stores

**Hecht's** (12th and G Sts. NW, tel. 202/628–6661). When the Hecht company decided to abandon its store on 7th Street and build a new one, they did the job right. The new downtown Hecht's is bright and spacious, and its sensible groupings and attractive displays of merchandise make shopping relatively easy on the feet and the eyes. The clothes sold here are a mix of conservative and trendy lines, with the men's department assuming increasing importance. Cosmetics, lingerie, and housewares are also strong departments.

**Lord & Taylor** (5255 Western Ave., tel. 202/362–9600). Lord & Taylor lets other stores be all things to all people, while it focuses on nonutilitarian housewares and classic clothing by such designers as Anne Klein and Ralph Lauren. All of the clothing is American-designed and manufactured.

**Neiman Marcus** (Mazza Gallerie, tel. 202/966–9700). If you have to ask how much it costs, you probably shouldn't shop at Neiman Marcus, which caters to the customer who values quality above all. The carefully selected merchandise includes couture clothes, furs, precious jewelry, crystal, and silver.

**Saks Fifth Avenue** (5555 Wisconsin Ave., tel. 301/657–9000). Though not strictly a Washington department store, since it is located just over the Maryland line, Saks is nonetheless a Washington institution. The major draw is the wide selection of European and American couture clothes; other attractions are the shoe, jewelry, fur, and lingerie departments.

**Woodward & Lothrop** (11th and F Sts. NW, tel. 202/347–5300). The largest of the downtown stores, Woodies has eight floors of merchandise that can accommodate just about any need or whim. There are two floors of women's clothing in a variety of style and price ranges, another floor for juniors, one for men, and a large children's department. In addition, just about anything you could need for the home can be found here, including gourmet food. There is also a branch across the Maryland border at the Friendship Heights Metrorail station (Wisconsin and Western Aves., tel. 301/654–7600).

## Specialty Stores

**Adams-Morgan Shopping** In Adams-Morgan, scattered among the dozens of Latin, Ethiopian, and Caribbean restaurants in this most bohemian of Washington neighborhoods, are a score of the city's most eccentric shops. It's a mine field of quality, but great fun for the bargain hunter. A word of caution—call ahead to verify hours. Adams-Morganites are often not clockwatchers, but you can be sure a weekend afternoon stroll will find a good representation of the shops open and a great few hours of browsing.

# You've Let Your Imagination Go, Now Get Up And Follow Your Dreams.

## For The Vacation You're Dreaming Of, Call American Express® Travel Agency At 1-800-YES-AMEX*

American Express will send more than your imagination soaring. We'll fly you, sail you, drive you to any Fodor's destination and beyond. Because American Express believes the best vacations happen from Europe to the Orient, Walt Disney®World to Hawaii and everywhere in between.

For dependable service, expert advice, and value wherever your dreams take you, call on American Express. After all, the best traveling companion is a trustworthy friend.

**AMERICAN EXPRESS Travel Agency**

# It's easy to recognize a good place when you see one.

American Express Cardmembers have been doing it for years.

The secret? Instead of just relying on what they see in the window, they look at the door. If there's an American Express Blue Box on it, they know they've found an establishment that cares about high standards.

Whether it's a place to eat, to sleep, to shop, or simply meet, they know they will be warmly welcomed.

So much so, they're rarely taken in by anything else.

## Always a good sign.

**Bick's Books** (2309 18th St. NW, tel. 202/328–2356). An emphasis on literature, small presses, black studies, green politics, and philosophy characterizes this neighborhood bookstore.

**Chenonceau Antiques** (2314 18th St. NW, tel. 202/667–1651). Two floors of French and American 19th- and 20th-century pieces selected by a buyer with an exquisite eye. Beautiful 19th-century paisley scarves from India and from Scotland. French travel posters from the '30s.

**Kilimanjaro Records** (1781 California St. NW, tel. 202/483–3723). An adjunct of the popular nightclub, the shop specializes in West Indian and African popular music.

**Melinda's** (2222 18th St. NW, tel. 202/797–7484). A whimsical assortment of bric-a-brac and used furniture reflecting the proprietor's taste, which runs to the curlicue. Sets of dishes and silverplate, vases, glasses, and small furniture. Closed Monday and Tuesday.

**Nice Stuff** (2102½ 18th St. NW, no phone). An Adams-Morgan used-furniture shop with a random selection of storage and bedroom furniture from the '20s, '30s, and '40s. Odd bits of kitsch and the occasional great buy. Closed Monday–Wednesday.

**Nomad** (2407 18th St. NW, tel. 202/332–2998). Reasonably priced clothing, artifacts, and jewelry with an ethnic flair.

**Retrospective** (2324 18th St. NW, tel. 202/483–8112). A small shop crammed with high-quality furniture and accessories, mostly from the '40s and '50s. Here you can still buy the princess phone that lit up your nightstand in 1962 and the plates your mother served her meat loaf on.

**Ruff and Ready** (2220 18th St. NW, tel. 202/462–4541). It could be called Adams-Morgan's most venerable used-furniture store except that the word seems so out of place in this jumble of styles and quality. There's a great selection of estate sale furniture that moves out of the store almost as fast as it moves in—and the prices make the reason clear. Mostly 20th-century with a few 18th-century pieces, and a good assortment of bric-a-brac from the Deco period onwards.

**Skynear and Company** (1800 Wyoming Ave. NW, tel. 202/797–7160). Undoubtedly the most bizarre assortment of home accessories, gifts, and objects in Washington. The owners, an Egyptian husband and Native American wife, travel the world for the unusual, and the result is an extravagant assortment of rich materials and brilliant colors. Lighting, textiles, art, and furniture.

**Uniform** (2318 18th St. NW, tel. 202/483–4577). The best of the vintage clothing and household accessories shops in Adams-Morgan, an assortment from the '50s and '60s that makes it seem like the entire country transferred to the moon for 20 years. The mix varies, but in addition to the obligatory lava lamps you'll find three-button suits and pillbox hats, feathered mules with lucite heels, and plates, lamps, and dishes that could have been props for the Jetsons. Closed Monday.

**Wake Up Little Suzie** (2316 18th St. NW, tel. 202/328–7577). New knickknacks that look like vintage '50s, and hip modern bric-a-brac. Closed Monday.

**Antiques**   **Cherishables** (1608 20th St. NW, tel. 202/785–4087). It offers American 18th- and 19th-century furniture and decorative arts, with emphasis on the Federal period.

**Georgetown Antiques Center** (2918 M St. NW, tel. 202/338–3811). Two dealers share space in this Victorian town house: Cherub Gallery (tel. 202/337–2224) specializes in art glass and Icart etchings, and Michael Getz Antiques (tel. 202/338–3811) sells fireplace equipment and silverware.

**G.K.S. Bush** (2828 Pennsylvania Ave. NW, tel. 202/965–0653). Formal American furniture from the 18th and early 19th centuries, plus related American antiques and works of art.

**Marston Luce** (1314 21st St. NW, tel. 202/775–9460). The specialty here is American folk art, including quilts, weather vanes, and hooked rugs. There are also home and garden furnishings, primarily American, but some English and French as well.

**Miller & Arney Antiques** (1737 Wisconsin Ave. NW, tel. 202/338–2369). English, American, and European furniture and accessories from the 18th and early 19th centuries, plus Oriental porcelain.

**Old Print Gallery** (1220 31st St. NW, tel. 202/965–1818). The area's only store specializing in old prints and maps, including Washingtoniana.

**Susquehanna** (3216 O St. NW, tel. 202/333–1511). The largest antiques shop in Georgetown, specializing in American furniture and paintings.

**Books**   **Chapters** (1512 K St. NW, tel. 202/347–5495). Calling itself a "literary bookstore," Chapters eschews cartoon collections and diet guides, filling its shelves instead with the sort of books that are meant to be read—serious contemporary fiction, classics, and poetry.

**The Cheshire Cat** (5512 Connecticut Ave. NW, tel. 202/244–3956). A bookstore for children, with a selection of records, cassettes, posters, and books on parenting.

**Crown Books** (1200 New Hampshire Ave. NW, tel. 202/ 822–8331; 3131 M St. NW, tel. 202/333–4493; 2020 K St. NW, tel. 202/659–2030; 1275 K St. NW, tel. 202/289– 7170; 1155 19th St. NW, tel. 202/659–4172; 3335 Connecticut Ave. NW, tel. 202/966–7232; 4301 Connecticut Ave. NW, tel. 202/966–2576; 4400 Jennifer St. NW, tel. 202/966–8784; 1710 G St. NW, tel. 202/789–2277). This large local chain sells hardback best-sellers at significant discounts, and even lowers paperback and newsstand prices.

**Kramerbooks** (1517 Connecticut Ave., tel. 202/387– 1400). Sharing space with a café that offers late-night dining and entertainment on weekends, Kramer's is an always-bustling hangout with a small but well-selected stock.

**Mystery Books** (1715 Connecticut Ave. NW, tel. 202/ 483–1600). Washington's largest collection of detective, crime, suspense, and spy fiction, as well as mystery-related gifts, can be found here.

**Olsson's Books & Records** (1239 Wisconsin Ave., tel. 202/338–9544; 1307 19th St. NW, tel. 202/785–1133; 1200 F St. NW, tel. 202/347–3686). With its large and varied collection, this is undoubtedly the area's preeminent general bookstore. Hours vary significantly from store to store.

**Second Story Books** (2000 P St. NW, tel. 202/659–8884). Hours of browsing are possible at this used-books emporium on Dupont Circle.

**Yes!** (1035 31st St. NW, tel. 202/338–7874). A bookstore geared to self-development, Yes! has an unusual stock of volumes on spiritual growth, psychology, mythology, and travel. While the emphasis is on Asian modes of thought, the collection of Western philosophy is one of the best in town.

**Children's Clothing and Toys**

**F.A.O. Schwarz** (in Georgetown Park, 3222 M St. NW, tel. 202/342–2285). The most upscale of toy stores, carrying such items as a toy car (a Mercedes, of course) that costs almost as much as the real thing. Among the other imports are stuffed animals (many larger than life), dolls, and children's perfumes.

**The Kid's Closet** (1990 K St. NW, tel. 202/466–5589; 1226 Connecticut Ave. NW, tel. 202/429–9247). This is downtown DC's only children's clothing store. The focus is on clothes for newborns, plus other items that make suitable baby-shower gifts, but there's also a selection of clothes for older children.

**Crafts and Gifts**

**The American Hand** (2906 M St. NW, tel. 202/965–3273). One-of-a-kind functional and nonfunctional pieces from

America's foremost ceramic artists, plus limited-edition objects for home and office, such as architect-designed dinnerware.

**Appalachian Spring** (1415 Wisconsin Ave., tel. 202/337–5780, and Union Station, tel. 202/682–0505). Traditional and contemporary crafts, including quilts, jewelry, weavings, pottery, and blown glass.

**Beadazzled** (1522 Connecticut Ave. NW, tel. 202/265–2323). A truly dazzling array of ready-to-string beads and jewelry.

**Fahrney's** (1430 G St. NW, tel. 202/628–9525). Fahrney's started out as a pen bar in the Willard Hotel, a place to fill your fountain pen before embarking on the day's business. Today it offers pens in silver, gold, and lacquer by the world's leading manufacturers.

**The Farrell Collection** (2633 Connecticut Ave. NW, tel. 202/483–8334). An assortment of moderately priced American pottery, fiber, and glass.

**Indian Craft Shop** (1050 Wisconsin Ave., tel. 202/342–3918; Dept. of Interior, 1800 C St. NW, tel. 202/208–4056). Handicrafts, including jewelry, pottery, sand paintings, weavings, and baskets, from a dozen Native American tribal traditions.

**Moon, Blossoms and Snow** (225 Pennsylvania Ave. SE, tel. 202/543–8181). Wearable art is the specialty of this store, one of a growing number of shops on Capitol Hill. In addition to hand-painted, hand-woven garments, the store sells contemporary American ceramics, glass, jewelry, and wood.

**Music Box Center** (918 F St. NW, tel. 202/783–9399). Choose from more than 500 melodies played by boxes made of marble, glass, porcelain, pewter, and inlaid woods.

**The Phoenix** (1514 Wisconsin Ave., tel. 202/338–4404). Mexican crafts, including folk art, masks, silver jewelry, fabrics, and native garments.

Jewelry **Charles Schwartz & Son** (Mazza Gallerie, tel. 202/363–5432). A full-service jeweler specializing in precious stones in traditional and modern settings. Fine watches are also offered.

**Mazi Jewelry Design** (311 7th St. SE, tel. 202/547–2555). Modern jewelry is custom-made on the premises.

**Pampillonia Jewelers** (Mazza Gallerie, tel. 202/363–6305. Also at 1213 Connecticut Ave. NW, tel. 202/628–6305). Traditional designs in 18-karat gold and platinum, including many pieces for men.

**The Tiny Jewel Box** (1143 Connecticut Ave., tel. 202/393–2747). A well-chosen collection of estate jewelry.

**Kitchenware**   **Kitchen Bazaar** (4401 Connecticut Ave. NW, tel. 202/ 244–1550; Fashion Centre at Pentagon City, 1100 S. Hayes St., Arlington, VA, tel. 703/415–5545; and other suburban malls). This emporium carries just about everything one could possibly need to equip a kitchen.

**Little Caledonia** (1419 Wisconsin Ave., tel. 202/333– 4700). A "Tom Thumb department store" for the home, this old Georgetown store consists of nine rooms crammed with thousands of unusual and imported items; candles, cards, fabrics, and lamps round out the stock of decorative kitchenware.

**Martin's** (1304 Wisconsin Ave., tel. 202/338–6144). A long-established Georgetown purveyor of china, crystal, and silver, including antique silver.

**Leather Goods**   **Camalier & Buckley** (1141 Connecticut Ave., tel. 202/ 347–7700; Mazza Gallerie, tel. 202/362–8800). The city's largest collection of briefcases in a variety of skins, plus luggage, desk accessories, stationery, clocks, crystal, and porcelain.

**The Coach Store** (1214 Wisconsin Ave., tel. 202/342– 1772). The complete line of Coach's rugged, well-made handbags, briefcases, belts, and wallets.

**Georgetown Leather Design** (3265 M St. NW, tel. 202/ 333–9333; 1150 Connecticut Ave. NW, tel. 202/223– 1855). A full line of leather goods, most of them made for the store, including jackets, briefcases, wallets, gloves, and handbags.

**Men's Clothing**   **John B. Adler** (5530 Wisconsin Ave., tel. 301/652–5896). In business for almost half a century, this Washington clothier offers what used to be called the Ivy League look in suits, sportcoats, and formal and casual wear.

**Britches of Georgetown** (1247 Wisconsin Ave., tel. 202/ 338–3330; 1219 Connecticut Ave. NW, tel. 202/347– 8994). Britches carries an extensive selection of traditional but trend-conscious designs in natural fibers.

**Brooks Brothers** (1840 L St. NW, tel. 202/659–4650; 5500 Wisconsin Ave. NW, tel. 301/654–8202). The oldest men's store in America, Brooks Brothers has offered traditional formal and casual clothing since 1818. It is the largest men's specialty store in the area and has a small women's department as well.

**Hugo Boss** (1201 Connecticut Ave., tel. 202/887–5081; 1517 Wisconsin Ave. NW, tel. 202/338–0120; 5454 Wisconsin Ave. NW, tel. 301/907–7806). The Washington area has the only U.S. collection of clothes from this German designer and manufacturer, noted for his classic fabrics and unique silhouettes.

**J. Press** (1801 L St. NW, tel. 202/857–0120). Founded in

1902 as a custom shop for Yale University, J. Press is a stalwartly traditional clothier. Shetland-wool sport-coats are a specialty.

**Men's and Women's Clothing**

**Boogie's Diner** (1229 Wisconsin Ave. NW, tel. 202/298–7469). Taking the place of the old Esprit superstore in location and spirit is this combination restaurant and clothing store for the teen crowd.

**Britches Great Outdoors** (1225 Wisconsin Ave. NW, tel. 202/333–3666; 1801 M St. NW, tel. 202/775–8983). Despite its off-putting warthog mascot (or perhaps because of it), this casual version of Britches of Georgetown has filled many Washington closets with rugby shirts and other sportswear.

**Burberrys** (1155 Connecticut Ave., tel. 202/463–3000). It made its reputation with the trench coat, but this British company also manufactures traditional men's and women's apparel, a good selection of which is available here.

**Commander Salamander** (1420 Wisconsin Ave., tel. 202/333–9599). This is about as funky as Washington gets—leather, chains, silver skulls. As much entertainment as shopping, Commander Salamander is open until midnight on weekends.

**Raleighs** (1133 Connecticut Ave., tel. 202/833–0120. Also in Mazza Gallerie, tel. 202/244–6400). A specialty store catering to men and noted for its well-tailored suits, Raleighs also has a small women's department.

**Records**

**Kemp Mill Record Shops** (1260 Wisconsin Ave., tel. 202/333–1392; 1517 Connecticut Ave. NW, tel. 202/332–8247; 4304 Connecticut Ave. NW, tel. 202/362–9262; 2459 18th St. NW, tel. 202/387–1011; 1900 L St. NW, tel. 202/223–5310; 4000 Wisconsin Ave. NW, tel. 202/364–9704). This local chain store concentrates on CDs and cassettes of popular music (New Age is a particular specialty) and keeps its prices low. Also at several locations in the suburbs.

**Olsson's Books & Records** (1239 Wisconsin Ave., tel. 202/338–6712; 1307 19th St. NW, tel. 202/785–2662; 1200 F St. NW, tel. 202/393–1853). A full line of compact discs and cassettes can be found in this broad-spectrum record store.

**Serenade Record Shop** (1800 M St. NW, tel. 202/452–0075; 1710 Pennsylvania Ave. NW, with an annex at 1713 G St. NW, tel. 202/638–6648). A full-catalogue record store with a strong classical collection. The G Street annex sells classical music only.

**Tower Records** (2000 Pennsylvania Ave. NW, tel. 202/331–2400). With 16,000 square feet of selling space,

Tower offers the area's best selection of music in all categories. Open daily until midnight.

**Shoes** **Bally** (1020 Connecticut Ave. NW, tel. 202/429–0604). The Swiss manufacturer of high-quality leather goods is expanding its line of women's shoes, but the focus is still on footwear for men, primarily European-style loafers. The store also sells handbags, briefcases, and belts.

**Church's** (1742 L St. NW, tel. 202/296–3366). Church's is an English company whose handmade men's shoes are noted for their comfort and durability.

**Shoe Scene** (1330 Connecticut Ave. NW, tel. 202/659–2194). A good selection of moderately priced, fashionable shoes for women.

**Women's Clothing** **Ann Taylor** (1720 K St. NW, tel. 202/466–3544; 3222 M St. NW, tel. 202/338–5290; 5300 Wisconsin Ave. NW, tel. 202/244–1940; Union Station, tel. 202/371–8010). Sophisticated fashions for the woman who has broken out of the dress-for-success mold. Ann Taylor also has an excellent shoe department.

**Betsy Fisher** (1350 Connecticut Ave. NW, tel. 202/785–1975).Tasteful, rather than conservative, clothing appealing to women of all ages.

**Chanel Boutique** (1455 Pennsylvania Ave. NW, tel. 202/638–5055).Shoes, scarves, handbags, belts, and suits from this legendary house of fashion, at near-legendary prices.

**Earl Allen** (3109 M St. NW, tel. 202/338–1678; 1825 I St. NW, tel. 202/466–3437). Earl Allen caters to the professional woman, offering conservative but distinctive dresses and sportswear, much of it made exclusively for this shop.

**Les Gals** (1000 Vermont Ave. NW, tel. 202/371–0289). Spunky work and workout clothes appeal to the downtown work force.

**Rizik Bros.** (1100 Connecticut Ave. NW, tel. 202/223–4050). A Washington institution for more than 70 years, Rizik's combines designer clothing and accessories with expert service. The sales staff is trained to find styles and prices that meet customers' desires from the large inventory, over half of which is in the stock room. Take the elevator from the northwest corner of Connecticut and L Street to the second-story boutique.

# 5 Sports and Fitness

*Updated by*
*John F. Kelly*

When the experts at the local bar begin to discuss the nation's great sports towns, Washington is not often high on the list. The honors usually go to New York, Los Angeles, or Boston. Nevertheless, Washington is home to an impressive variety of opportunities for both spectators and participants. According to national surveys, the residents of metropolitan Washington are more active than the nation as a whole. Washingtonians jog, cycle, swim, fish, lift weights, play tennis, and sail more than the residents of any other major city in the United States. One reason may be that Washington's climate is generally mild year-round. Another reason is that there are plenty of parks, trails, and athletic facilities throughout the area to entice an active population.

Whether you're coming to Washington for a few days of sightseeing or a few days of business, don't forget to bring your sweats. There is more to the District than national monuments and boardrooms.

## Participant Sports and Fitness

**Bicycling**  Bicycling is one of the most popular activities in Washington for locals and visitors alike. The numerous trails in the District and the surrounding areas are well-maintained and clearly marked, which makes for pleasant and safe bike-touring. Most of the paths described below in the section on jogging—the Mall, the C & O Canal, the Mount Vernon Trail, and Rock Creek Park—are also well-suited for use by bikers.

**The Greater Washington Bicycle Atlas,** published by the American Youth Hostels Association, is the complete guide to tours within 100 miles of Washington. It is available for $10 at most Washington area bookstores or from the Washington Area Bicyclist Association (1819 H St. NW, Suite 640, 20006, tel. 202/872–9830).

Bicycles can be rented at the following locations:

**Bicycle Exchange** (1506-C Belleview Blvd., Alexandria, VA, tel. 703/768–3444), near the Mt. Vernon bike trail.
**Big Wheel Bikes** (1034 33rd St. NW, Georgetown, tel. 202/337–0254, near the C & O Canal Towpath; 315 7th St. SE, tel. 202/543–1600, near Capitol Hill; 2 Prince St., Alexandria, VA, tel. 703/739–2300, near the Mt. Vernon bike trail).
**City Bikes** (2501 Champlain St. NW, tel. 202/265–1564, near the Rock Creek bike path).
**Fletcher's Boat House** (C & O Canal Towpath, near Reservoir Rd. NW, tel. 202/244–0461).

**Metropolis Bike & Scooter** (709 8th St. SE, Capitol Hill, tel. 202/543–8900; also rents rollerblades).
**Proteus Bicycle Shop** (2422 18th St. NW, Adams-Morgan, tel. 202/332–6666; 7945 MacArthur Blvd. NW, tel. 202/229–5900, near the C & O Canal).
**Thompson's Boat House** (Virginia Ave. and Rock Creek Park, behind Kennedy Center, tel. 202/333–4861).
**Tow Path Cycle** (823 S. Washington St., Alexandria, VA, tel. 703/549–5368).

Cyclists interested in serious training might want to try the 3-mile loop around the golf course in East Potomac Park, Hains Point (the entryway is near the Jefferson Memorial). This is a favorite training course for dedicated local racers and would-be triathletes. A note of caution, though: Restrict your workouts to the daytime; the area is not safe after dark.

**Boating** Canoeing, sailing, and powerboating are all popular in the region. There are several places to rent boats along the Potomac River north and south of the city. The two boat houses listed here are convenient for tourists.

**Fletcher's Boat House** (tel. 202/244–0461), about 2 miles north of Georgetown on the C & O Canal, rents rowboats and canoes for use in the canal.
**Thompson's Boat House** (tel. 202/333–9543), at Virginia Avenue and Rock Creek Parkway behind the Kennedy Center, rents canoes, rowboats, rowing shells, and sailboards.
**Paddleboats** (tel. 202/484–0206) are available on the east side of the **Tidal Basin** in front of the Jefferson Memorial.

If you're interested in **sailing,** consider taking a day trip to Annapolis, Maryland (about an hour's drive from the District). Annapolis is one of the best sailing centers on the East Coast, and the Chesapeake Bay is without a doubt one of the great sailing basins of the world. The **Annapolis Sailing School** (tel. 410/267–7205) is a world-renowned school and charter company.

If you can't make time for a day on the bay, the **Washington Sailing Marina** (tel. 703/548–9027), just south of National Airport on the George Washington Parkway, and the **Belle Haven Marina** (tel. 703/768–0018), just south of Old Town Alexandria on the George Washington Parkway, rent Sunfish, Windsurfers, and larger boats to those qualified to sail.

Although it is not widely known, Washington is home to some of the best white-water **kayakers** and white-water canoeists in the country. On weekends they can be seen practicing below Great Falls in **Mather Gorge,** a canyon carved by the Potomac River just north of the city, above Chain Bridge. The water there is deceptive and dangerous, and only top-level kayakers should consider kayaking there. It is, however, safe to watch the experts at play from a post above the gorge. For information call the **ranger station** at Great Falls, Virginia (tel. 703/285–2966) or Great Falls, Maryland (tel. 301/443–0024).

**Fishing**  A 5-mile stretch of the Potomac River—running roughly from the Wilson Memorial Bridge in Alexandria south to Fort Washington National Park—is one of the best spots for largemouth bass fishing in the country. It has, in fact, become something of an East Coast mecca for anglers in search of this particular fish. But the simple act of renting a boat and going fishing is complicated by the fact that this stretch of the Potomac is divided among three jurisdictions: Virginia, Maryland, and the District of Columbia. It's not always easy to determine in whose water you're fishing or which licenses you should have. The best solution is to hire a guide. **Outdoor Life Unlimited** (tel. 301/937–0010), run by nationally known fisherman and conservationist Ken Penrod, is an umbrella group of area freshwater fishing guides. Thirty of the area's best guides are listed with Penrod, and for about $175–$250 a day a professional guide will take care of all your needs, from licenses to tackle to boats. Penrod's guides are all professionals and will teach novices or guide experts.

Other fish species found in the region include striped bass, shad, and white and yellow perch. The area around Fletcher's Boat House on the C & O Canal is one of the best spots for perch.

The two best tackle shops in the area are both in Alexandria, Virginia: **Delta Tackle** (1435 Powhatan St., tel. 703/549–5729) and **Potomac Sports Center** (6233 Richmond Hwy., tel. 703/765–2220).

**Gene Mueller,** a nationally known hunting and fishing writer, has a column three times a week (Mon., Wed., and Fri.) in the *Washington Times.* He takes readers' telephone calls Thursday mornings at 202/636–3268. Also watch for the fishing column in the *Washington Post's* Friday "Weekend" section.

**Golf**  Serious golfers must resign themselves to driving out of the District to find a worthwhile course. There are three public courses in town, but the greens and fairways are in poor shape and should be considered only for hitting practice and only if there is no alternative.

The **Hains Point course** (tel. 202/863–9007) in East Potomac Park near the Jefferson Memorial is a flat, wide, 6,303-yard, par-72 course. Its greatest claim to fame is that professional golfer and Washington resident Lee Elder got his start there. The weekend fee is $12 for 18 holes.

**Langston Golf Course** (26th St. and Benning Rd. NE, tel. 202/397–8638) is a 6,300-yard, par-72 course. The weekend fee is $12 for 18 holes.

**Rock Creek Park** (16th and Rittenhouse Sts. NW, tel. 202/882–7332) has a 4,798-yard, par-65 course with an easy front-nine and challenging back. It is not in good condition. The weekend fee is $12 for 18 holes.

There are several excellent public courses within a half hour of downtown:

**Reston South** (11875 Sunrise Valley Dr., Reston, VA, tel. 703/620–9333) is a four-star, 6,480-yard, par-71 course widely considered the best public course in the metropolitan area. Well-maintained, it is heavily wooded but not too difficult for the average player. The fee is $16 on weekdays, $21 weekends.

Also 30 minutes from town is **Northwest Park** (15701 Layhill Rd., Wheaton, MD, tel. 301/598–6100). This 6,732-yard, par-72 course is extremely long, making for slow play, but it is immaculately groomed and fair. The fee is $14.50 weekdays, $16 weekends.

If you are flying in or out of Dulles Airport and want to fit in a round of golf, try **Penderbrook** (at Rte. 50 and I–66, tel. 703/385–3700). A short but imaginative 5,927-yard, par-72 course, it is one of the best public greens in the area. The 5th, 11th, and 15th holes are exceptional. The weekday fee is $18 and the weekend fee is $22 for 18 holes. Tee times are given one day in advance.

**Health Clubs** The number of health clubs in the area has steadily risen for the past several years. All of the clubs in Washington require that you be a member—or at least a member of an affiliated club—in order to use their facilities. Some hotels, however, have made private arrangements with neighboring health clubs to enable hotel guests to use the club's facilities (in some cases guests pay a daily fee). Check with your hotel when making reservations. A number of downtown hotels are associated with the **fitness center at the ANA Hotel**. All you need to do is show your hotel room key to the center's employees and pay a $15 daily fee. One of the fanciest fitness centers in Washington, the ANA is the place where celebrities such as Cybill Sheperd, Holly Hunter, and Arnold Schwarzenegger come to sweat (ANA Hotel, 2401 M St. NW, tel. 202/457–5070).

Card-carrying members of the **International Racquet Sports Association (I.R.S.A.)** can use the facilities at one of the many member clubs in Washington for a daily fee. You must present your membership card from your home club. The I.R.S.A. "Passport" lists member clubs.

The **National Capital YMCA** (1711 Rhode Island Ave. NW, tel. 202/862–9622) offers just about everything a body could want, from basketball, weights, racquetball, squash, and swimming to exercise equipment. Some downtown hotels offer free one-day passes to the YMCA for their guests—check with your concierge. Members of out-of-town Ys must show their membership cards and pay a usage fee ranging from $5–$20 per visit depending on the time of day.

**Horseback Riding**  **Rock Creek Park Equestrian Center** (Military Rd. and Glover Rd. NW, tel. 202/362–0117) is open all year; the hours vary according to season.

**Ice Skating**  The **Sculpture Garden Outdoor Rink** (Constitution Ave. between 7th and 9th Sts. NW, tel. 202/371–5343) appears each winter with the cold weather. **Pershing Park Ice Rink** (Pennsylvania Ave. between 14th and 15th Sts. NW, tel. 202/737–6938) is also popular. Skates can be rented at both locations. **Fort Dupont Park** (37th and Ely Pl. SE, tel. 202/581–0199) has a beautiful rink; the park itself, though, is in a less-than-wonderful section of town. Equally close to the downtown area is the **Mount Vernon Ice Rink** (2017 Belle View Blvd., Alexandria, VA 22307, tel. 703/768–3222). It, too, has rentals.

**Jogging**  If you really want to know who runs Washington, go for a jog. Congressmen, senators, and Supreme Court justices can often be spotted on the Mall, running loops around the monuments. Georgetown power brokers are seen hoofing the towpaths along the C & O Canal or the meandering trails in Rock Creek Park. And at lunchtime in Arlington, the Pentagon empties out along the Mount Vernon Trail.

Whatever your reason for coming to Washington, don't leave your running shoes at home. Downtown Washington and nearby northern Virginia offer some of the most scenic running trails in the country, and running is one of the best ways to take in the vistas of the city. The most popular paths are presented below. A word of caution: Joggers unfamiliar with the city should not go out at night, and, even in daylight, it's best to run in pairs if you venture beyond the most public areas and the more heavily used sections of the trails.

For information on weekend races, check the calendar in the "Weekend" section of the Thursday *Washington Times* or the Friday *Washington Post*. For general information about running and races in the area, call the **Gatorade/Road Runners Clubs of America Hotline** (tel. 703/683–7722).

**The Mall.** The loop around the Capitol and past the Smithsonian museums, the Washington Monument, the Reflecting Pool, and the Lincoln Memorial is the most popular of all Washington running trails. At any time of day, hundreds of joggers, speed walkers, bicyclists, and tourists can be seen making their way along the gravel pathways of this 4½-mile loop. If you're looking for a longer run, you can veer south of the Mall on either side of the Tidal Basin and head for the Jefferson Memorial and East Potomac Park, the site of many races.

**The Mount Vernon Trail.** Just across the Potomac in Virginia, this trail is another favorite with Washington runners. The northern (shorter) section begins near the pedestrian causeway leading to Theodore Roosevelt Island (directly across the river from the Kennedy Center), goes past National Airport and on to Old Town Alexandria. This stretch is approximately 3½ miles one-way. You can get to the trail from the District by crossing either the Theodore Roosevelt Bridge (at the Lincoln Memorial) or the Rochambeau Memorial Bridge (also known as the 14th Street Bridge, at the Jefferson Memorial). South of National Airport, the trail runs down to the Washington Marina. The final mile of the trail's northern section meanders through protected wetlands before ending in the heart of Old Town Alexandria. The longer southern section of the trail (approximately 9 miles) takes you along the coast of the Potomac from Alexandria all the way to George Washington's home, Mount Vernon.

For more than 10 years, on Tuesday evenings year-round, the **Fairfax Running Center** (tel. 703/549–7688) in Old Town Alexandria has sponsored informal runs along the Mount Vernon Trail.

**Rock Creek Park.** A miraculously preserved bit of wilderness in the middle of Washington, Rock Creek Park has 15 miles of trails, a bicycle path, bridle path, picnic groves, playgrounds, and a boulder-strewn rolling stream from which it gets its name (the creek is not safe for swimming). Starting at P Street on the edge of Georgetown, Rock Creek Park runs all the way to Montgomery County, Maryland. The most popular run in the park is a trail along the creek extending from Georgetown to the National Zoo (about a 4-mile loop). In summer, there is considerable shade, and there are water fountains at an exercise station along the way. The roadway is closed to traffic on weekends. On Sunday mornings, the **Fleet Feet Triathlete** store in Adams-Morgan near the National Zoo, sponsors 5-mile runs in Rock Creek Park (tel. 202/387–3888).

**The C & O Canal.** Now maintained by the National Park Service, the Chesapeake and Ohio Canal National Historical Park is a favorite spot with both runners and bikers. A pancake-flat gravel trail leads from Georgetown through wooded areas along the Potomac and northward into Maryland. The most popular loop is from a point just north of Key Bridge in Georgetown to Fletcher's Boat House (approximately 4 miles roundtrip).

**Swimming** There are no beaches in the Washington area. If you want to swim during your visit, it's best to stay at a hotel that has a pool. A few years ago it was possible to gain entry to some hotel pools for a small fee, but that practice has by and large been discontinued. Health-club pools, too, are open only to members. The only alternative is public pools. The District of Columbia maintains eight indoor pools, 20 large outdoor pools, and another 25 outdoor "walk-to" pools which are smaller but still fun for children. For more information and a list of public facilities, contact the Aquatic Department of the DC Department of Recreation (1230 Taylor St. NW, 20011, tel. 202/576–6436).

**Tennis** Tennis being the sport of the rich, powerful, and famous, it's no surprise the sport is extremely popular in Washington. The District of Columbia maintains 144 outdoor courts. Some of these courts are located in rather seedy parts of town, however, so it is best to check on the neighborhood in question before heading out. Free permits, required at all public courts, are issued by the Department of Recreation. Send a self-addressed, stamped envelope for a permit and a list of all city-run courts. You can also call for information on specific courts (3149 16th St. NW, 20010, tel. 202/673–7646).

The best courts in the area are at two locations: **Hains Point** (East Potomac Park, tel. 202/554–5962) has outdoor courts as well as courts under a bubble for wintertime play. Fees run from $11 to $23 an hour depending on the time and season. The **Washington Tennis Center** (16th and Kennedy Sts. NW, tel. 202/722–5949) has clay and hard courts. Fees range from $15 to $24 an hour depending on the time. Both locations will take court reservations up to one week in advance.

## Spectator Sports

Tickets for all Capital Centre, Patriot Centre, and Baltimore Arena events can be purchased through **TicketMaster** (tel. 202/432–7328 in DC, 410/481–7328 in Baltimore, or 800/551–7328 in other areas).

**Baseball**  Because the District does not have its own professional baseball team, baseball fans from the area go to Baltimore to root for the **Orioles**, who moved to a brand-new ballpark in 1992. Oriole Park at Camden Yards (333 W. Camden St., Baltimore, MD, tel. 800/551–7328 for tickets) seats 48,000, with tickets ranging from $4.75 for general admission seats to $13 for lower box seats. You can buy tickets to O's games—and also find out about bus and train packages to the stadium in Baltimore—at the **Orioles Baseball Store** (914 17th St. NW, tel. 202/296–2473) in downtown Washington.

If you prefer Class A baseball à la Bull Durham, you might want to make a trip out of town. South of the Beltway at the County Stadium Complex in Woodbridge, Virginia, you can watch the New York Yankee–affiliated **Prince William Cannons**. Tickets range from $3 to $5.50 (tel. 703/690–3622). Or travel north up I–270 in Maryland to either the **Frederick Keys** or the **Bowie Suns** (tel. 301/662–0013). Both are Oriole farm teams. Tickets range from $2 to $6, and at Hagerstown, children under 14 wearing Little League uniforms get in free.

**Basketball**  The **Washington Bullets'** home games are held at the Capital Centre in Landover, Maryland, just outside the Beltway. Their schedule runs from September to April. For tickets, call TicketMaster (tel. 202/432–7328 or 800/551–7328), or call 301/NBA-DUNK for detailed schedule information. Tickets range from $10 to $100.

Among the Division I **college basketball** teams in the area, former NCAA national champion Georgetown University's Hoyas are the best known. Their home games are played at the Capital Centre (tel. 301/350–3400).

Other Division I schools include the University of Maryland (tel. 301/314–7070), George Mason University (tel. 703/993–3033), George Washington University (tel. 202/994–3865), American University (tel. 202/885–3267), the Naval Academy (tel. 410/268–6226), and Howard University (tel. 202/806–7198).

**Football**  Washington is a football-crazy town—never, *never* say anything bad about the **Redskins**. Unfortunately, unless you happen to be a relative of the team's owner you may as well forget about trying to get tickets to a home game. Since 1966, all Redskins games at the 55,750-seat Robert F. Kennedy Stadium on the eastern edge of Capitol Hill have been sold out to season-ticket holders. Tickets are occasionally advertised in the classified section of the *Post*, but expect to pay considerably more than face value. You might have better luck trying to get tickets to one of the Skins' preseason games in August.

The **area colleges** offer an excellent alternative for frustrated football fans. Teams from the University of Maryland (tel. 301/314–7070), the Naval Academy (tel. 410/268–6226) in Annapolis, and Howard University (tel. 202/806–7198) all play a full schedule of college football.

**Horse Racing**  Maryland has a long-standing affection for the ponies. You can watch and wager on Thoroughbreds at **Laurel Race Course** (Rte. 198 and Race Track Rd., Laurel, MD, tel. 301/725–0400) during a season that runs from January to mid-March, July through August, and October through December. On the third Saturday of May, the Preakness Stakes is run at Baltimore's **Pimlico Race Course** (Hayward and Winner Aves., Baltimore, MD, tel. 410/542–9400). The course has additional Thoroughbred racing from the end of March through June, and September to the beginning of October. Race days at both Laurel and Pimlico are Tuesday and Thursday–Sunday. You'll find harness racing just outside the Beltway at **Rosecroft Raceway** (6336 Rosecroft Dr., Fort Washington, MD, tel. 301/567–4000). Race days are usually Wednesday through Sunday from February to mid-December.

**Ice Hockey**  The **Washington Capitals'** season runs from October through April. In recent years the team has come close to greatness, but they've always choked at playoff time. Washingtonians love them nonetheless. Home games are played at the Capital Centre. Tickets range from $11 to $28. Call 301/350–3400 or TicketMaster (tel. 202/432–7328 or 800/551–7328).

# 6 Dining

*By Deborah Papier*
*Updated by*
*Jeanne Cooper*

Although particular restaurants may falter or fall, in general, Washington's restaurants are getting better and better. (And sometimes, cheaper and cheaper: The sluggish economy of the last two years has meant more reasonably priced fare and fixed-price specials in many of the city's top dining rooms.) In the past few years Italian restaurants have come to rival French establishments, which for a long time set the standard in fine dining. There has also been an explosion of the kind of cooking usually called New American. Its practitioners don't much like that label, but whatever you call the cuisine, it has brought considerable style and energy to the area's restaurant scene, as well as raising the standards of healthy eating in this health-conscious town.

Despite the dearth of ethnic neighborhoods in Washington and the corresponding lack of the kinds of restaurant districts found in many cities, you *can* find almost any type of food here, from Nepalese to Salvadoran to Ethiopian. In only one category of food is the city falling short these days, and that's Chinese. The restaurants that for years were considered preeminent in the city's minuscule **Chinatown** (centered on G and H streets between 6th and 8th) have been slipping, and no new ones have emerged to fill their place. (First-rate Thai restaurants, however, are common throughout the city.)

Aside from Chinatown, there are six areas of the city where restaurants are concentrated:

Most of the deluxe restaurants are on or near **K Street NW,** also the location of many of the city's blue-chip law firms. These are the restaurants that feed and feed off of expense-account diners and provide the most elegant atmosphere, attentive service, and often the best food. Needless to say, this restaurant row is not renowned for budget dining, although you may find more bargains here than you did in the 1980s.

In the old downtown district, existing structures are being remodeled and new office buildings are going up at a dizzying rate. All this construction has provided space for restaurants, and many of the city's best and newest are located here, particularly along redeveloped **Pennsylvania Avenue.**

The other area of town long known as a restaurant district is **Georgetown,** whose central intersection is Wisconsin Avenue and M Street. Georgetown contains some of the city's priciest houses as well as some of its cheesiest businesses, and its restaurants are similarly diverse,

# Washington Dining

with white-tablecloth dining places next door to hole-in-the-wall carryouts. Keep an eye out, also, for restaurants in the adjacent West End district. This area, roughly bounded by Rock Creek Park to the west, N Street to the north, 20th Street to the east, and K Street to the south, is increasingly bridging the gap between Georgetown and downtown restaurant zones.

A youthful culinary competitor to Georgetown is **Adams-Morgan.** Eighteenth Street NW extending south from Columbia Road is wall-to-wall restaurants, with new ones opening so fast it's almost impossible to track them. Although the area has retained some of its Hispanic identity, the new eating establishments tend to be either Italian, New American, or Afro-Caribbean. The area is not served by the subway, and parking is a problem; it's better to take a cab if you're coming here at night.

South from Adams-Morgan and north from K Street is **Dupont Circle,** around which a number of restaurants are clustered. Some of the city's best Italian places can be found here as well as a variety of cafés, most boasting outdoor seating.

**Capitol Hill** has a number of bar/eateries that cater to congressional types in need of fortification after a day spent running the country. Many of these serve good bar fare, and some of them can turn out quite a credible meal. The dining possibilities on Capitol Hill have nearly doubled in the last couple of years with the opening of the newly renovated Union Station, which contains some very good restaurants and a large food court with fast food ranging from barbecue to sushi.

Outside the city limits are some thriving restaurant districts. **Bethesda, Maryland,** offers a wealth of possibilities, from diners on up; a number of successful DC restaurants have opened branches here. Virginia has its Georgetown equivalent, in **Old Town Alexandria,** as well as some of the area's best Asian restaurants. Wilson Boulevard in **Arlington** features many popular Vietnamese establishments and branches of other DC restaurants. The Bethesda, King Street, and Clarendon Metro stations make these gourmet enclaves accessible to visitors.

Highly recommended restaurants are indicated by a star ★.

| Category | Cost* |
|---|---|
| Very Expensive | over $35 |
| Expensive | $25–$35 |
| Moderate | $15–$25 |
| Inexpensive | under $15 |

*average cost of a 3-course dinner, per person, excluding drinks, service, and (9%) sales tax*

## Adams-Morgan

**American** **Belmont Kitchen.** Dining outside on a warm spring night at this popular Adams-Morgan neighborhood spot is one of the best ways to get a flavor of the rich street life of the neighborhood. The kitchen specializes in upside-down pizzas and simple, well-prepared grilled fish and meats. *2400 18th St. NW (6 blocks from Woodley Park/Zoo Metro stop), tel. 202/667–1200. Reservations advised. Dress: casual. DC, MC, V. Moderate.*

**Caribbean** **Café Atlantico.** One of the liveliest spots in Adams-Mor-
★ gan, Café Atlantico serves Caribbean specialties in a casual atmosphere. Appetizers include conch or cod fritters, shrimp and potato croquettes, and yucca fritters, all beautifully fried. Pork loin, jerk chicken, a vegetarian plate, and lamb curry are among the main courses. Service is friendly and helpful. *1819 Columbia Rd. NW (5½ blocks from Woodley Park/Zoo Metro stop), tel. 202/575–2233. No reservations. Dress: casual. AE, MC, V. Closed lunch. Moderate.*

**Fish, Wings & Tings.** This Caribbean café (or *mini kafe*, according to the menu) is the idiosyncratic creation of a husband-and-wife team. She's from Jamaica and works in the kitchen. He's a Panamanian with dreadlocks who keeps a semblance of order in the tiny dining room, which is barely able to contain the crowds that wait for carryout or for one of the few tables. The menu includes stewed oxtail and curry goat, but most people come here for the curry-ginger chicken wings, or the jerk (barbecued) thighs. *2418 18th St. NW (6 blocks from Woodley Park/Zoo Metro stop), tel. 202/234–0322. No reservations. No no-smoking area. Dress: casual. AE. Closed Sun. Inexpensive.*

**Ethiopian** **Meskerem.** Adams-Morgan has about a dozen Ethiopian
★ restaurants in a three-block stretch of 18th Street. While all of them have virtually identical menus, Meskerem is distinctive for its bright, appealingly decorated dining room. Another attractive feature: The res-

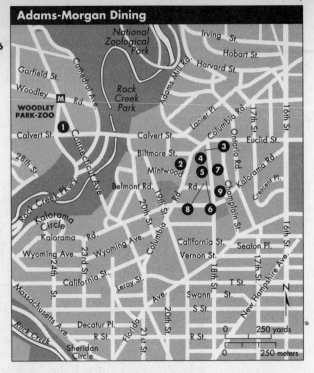

taurant has a balcony where you can eat Ethiopian-style—seated on the floor on leather cushions, with large woven baskets for tables. There is no silverware here; instead, the food is scooped up with *injera*, a spongy flat bread that also does duty as the platter on which the meal is presented. The country's main dish is the *watt*, or stew, which may be made with chicken, lamb, beef, or shrimp in either a spicy or a mild sauce. Several mild or spicy vegetarian watts are also available. *2434 18th St. NW (6 blocks from Woodley Park/Zoo Metro stop), tel. 202/462–4100. Reservations advised. Dress: casual but neat. AE, DC, MC, V. Closed lunch Mon.–Thurs. Inexpensive.*

**French** **La Fourchette.** Located on a block in Adams-Morgan where new restaurants are opening almost weekly and closing just as fast, La Fourchette has stayed in business for more than 15 years by offering good bistro food at reasonable prices. Most of the menu consists of daily specials and an early-bird fixed-price menu, but you can pretty much count on finding bouillabaisse and rabbit on the list. The most popular entrées on the regular menu are the hearty veal and lamb shanks. La Fourchette also looks the way a bistro should, with an exposed brick wall, tin ceiling, bentwood chairs, and quasi-post-Impressionist murals. *2429 18th St. NW (6 blocks from Woodley Park/Zoo Metro stop), tel. 202/332–3077. Reservations advised for groups. Dress: casual but neat. AE, DC, MC, V. Closed lunch Sat. and Sun. Moderate.*

**International** **Cities.** The owners of this trendy Adams-Morgan restaurant ask us to imagine that the concrete and chain-link decor represents a different city every four months or so as the menu changes. In the past few years this culinary odyssey has taken diners from Rio to Istanbul, from Bangkok to Mexico City. Wherever the destination, pasta, pizzas, and grilled dishes are standard fare. The crowd is young and noisy, the food and service not as consistent as one would wish, but Cities is still a good place for a light, informal meal. *2424 18th St. NW (6 blocks from Woodley Park/Zoo Metro stop), tel. 202/ 328–7194. Reservations advised. Dress: casual but neat. AE, DC, MC, V. Closed lunch Mon.–Sat. Moderate.*

**Italian** **i Matti.** Owned by chef Roberto Donna of the highly praised Galileo, i Matti is a much less formal but just as popular restaurant. The stark modern setting and the crowds of well-dressed young people somehow encapsulate Adams-Morgan trendiness. It's possible to order anything from a pizza to a multi-course meal from the large menu. The breads, including the foccacia (available at dinner) and the pizzas, are delicious. Osso buco is a good bet in winter. *2436 18th St. NW (6 blocks from Woodley Park/Zoo Metro stop), tel. 202/462–8844. Reservations advised. Dress: casual. AE, DC, MC, V. Moderate.*

**New American** **New Heights.** With its precise geometrical design softened by pastel colors, New Heights is one of Washington's most attractive restaurants. The food is New American but not radically so; in response to customer preference the restaurant is taking a more traditional approach. The menu varies seasonally but always includes a vegetarian entrée, such as asparagus strudel. Salmon, a frequent offering, might be cooked in a black-bean sauce with sprouts and bell peppers. The restaurant is a good choice for Sunday brunch. *2317 Calvert St. NW (1 block from Woodley Park/Zoo Metro stop), tel. 202/234–4110. Reservations advised. Dress: casual but neat. AE, DC, MC, V. Closed lunch. Expensive.*

**Southwestern/** **Peyote Café.** Located downstairs from Roxanne Restau-
**Tex-Mex** rant, this Southwestern pub takes cheeky liberties with its decor and food, and wins with both. Twinkling

lights, tables with bar stools, and a swinging jukebox attract a young crowd of primarily students and singles. The eclectic menu aims to please everyone: Meat eaters can choose from such dishes as *carne asada* (ribeye steak), grilled salmon, "gringo-killer" fried chicken, and "sweat hot fire" shrimp, while vegetarians look for the cactus sign on the menu that indicates meatless dishes. *2319 18th St. NW (7 blocks from Woodley Park/ Zoo Metro stop), tel. 202/462–8330. No reservations. Dress: casual. AE, MC, V. Closed weekday lunch. Inexpensive.*

## Capitol Hill

**American** **America.** A Washington outpost of owner Michael Weinstein's America in New York, Union Station's America is installed in the west front of the station, in a former men's room that has been opened up and transformed into this lively and attractive bar and restaurant. The disparate design elements—WPA-style murals, Western landscapes, aluminum outlines of states, superheroes—seem to be united only by the fact that they all somehow pertain to America, but the space itself is so impressive that they all seem to cohere. The menu is enormous, with nearly four square feet of regular offerings ranging from Kansas City steaks to Minnesota scrambled eggs, New Orleans muffalata sandwiches to New Mexico–style pasta, Jersey pork chops to San Diego fish tacos. The kitchen has its successes and failures—a good general rule is "the simpler the better." Desserts are good, and service is pleasant though chaotic. *Union Station, 50 Massachusetts Ave. NE (Union Station Metro stop), tel. 202/682–9555. Reservations advised. Dress: casual but neat. AE, DC, MC, V. 2-hr parking validated in Union Station lot. Expensive.*

**The Monocle.** The bar at The Monocle is probably the closest thing on the Hill to the smoke-filled political hangout from the movies, but in truth, nobody smokes much anymore, and drinking is on the decline, too. But The Monocle is still a hangout, probably the best place for spotting senators at lunch and dinner; management keeps members of Congress informed on when it's time to vote. The cooking, American cuisine with a Continental touch, is quite good and moderately priced considering its clientele. Seafood is a specialty; try the crab cakes, and take advantage of the fresh fish specials. The fireplaces and political portraits in this former town house add to the aura of cozy tradition. *107 D St. NE (1½* *blocks from Union Station Metro stop), tel. 202/546–4488. Reservations advised. Jacket and tie advised. AE, DC, MC, V. Closed Sat. lunch and Sun. Valet parking. Expensive.*

**French**   **La Brasserie.** La Brasserie is one of Capitol Hill's most pleasant and most satisfying restaurants. The dining rooms are on two floors of adjoining town houses, and what was once the front yard is now one of the Hill's best spots for outdoor dining. Chef Gaby Aubouin's basically French cooking changes daily to take advantage of the best market products. Fixed-price menus (two at dinner, one at lunch) are worth trying. The crème brûlée, served cold or hot with fruit, is superb. *239 Massachusetts Ave. NE (2 blocks from Union Station Metro stop), tel. 202/546–9154. Reservations advised. Dress: casual but neat. AE, DC, MC, V. Expensive.*

★  **La Colline.** For the past decade chef Robert Gréault has worked to make La Colline into one of the city's best French restaurants and the best of any type on Capitol Hill. The menu, which changes daily, strikes the perfect balance between innovation and tradition. The emphasis is on seafood, with offerings ranging from simple grilled preparations to fricassées and gratins with imaginative sauces. The nonseafood menu usually offers duck with an orange or cassis sauce and veal with chanterelles. Desserts are superb, as is the wine list. Capitol Hill power brokers also favor La Colline for breakfast. *400 N. Capitol St. (3 blocks from Union Station Metro stop), tel. 202/737–0400. Reservations advised. Jacket and tie advised. AE, DC, MC, V. Closed weekend lunch. Free parking in underground lot. Expensive.*

**Italian**   **Sfuzzi.** Since its opening in 1989, this Italian restaurant in the northeast corner of Union Station has been one of the most popular spots in town, mixing Hill politicos and staffers with Washington's young, fashionable (and noisy) set. The interior is strikingly attractive; trompe l'oeil murals create an Italian fantasy of classical ruins and crumbling frescoes. No other dining room in Washington has a better view of the Capitol dome than the upstairs here. House-baked breads here are flavorful and firm textured. Salads are interestingly conceived and carefully prepared. The best items on the menu, however, are the pizzas, which may be ordered as an appetizer to be shared or as a main course. The crust is crisp, yeasty, and flavorful, and the toppings immaculately fresh and varied. *Union Station, 50 Massachusetts Ave. NE (Union Station Metro stop), tel. 202/842–4141. Reservations advised. Dress: casual but neat.*

*AE, DC, MC, V. Parking validated in Union Station garage. Expensive.*

## Downtown

**American**  **The Palm.** Food trends come and go, but the Palm pays no attention; it offers the same hearty food it always has—gargantuan steaks and lobsters, several kinds of potatoes, New York cheesecake. The staff's been packing them in for 18 years with this kind of fare, and they're not about to let the calorie- and cholesterol-counters spoil the party. The look of the restaurant is basement basic—acoustic ceiling tiles, wooden fans—nothing to distract one from the serious business of chowing down. In addition to the beef and lobsters it is famous for, the Palm also offers a bargain lunch menu that includes shrimp, veal, and chicken salad. *1225 19th St. NW (2 blocks from Dupont Circle Metro stop), tel. 202/293–9091. Reservations advised. Dress: casual but neat. AE, DC, MC, V. Closed Sat. lunch and Sun. Very Expensive.*

**Prime Rib.** Despite its name, the Prime Rib is no longer really a steakhouse. In response to the increasing popularity of seafood, it now devotes half its menu to fish and shellfish, some of it shipped express from Florida. The most popular of the seafood dishes is the imperial crab, made only of jumbo lump-crabmeat; you can also order it stuffed in a two-pound lobster. The aged beef from Chicago includes a steak au poivre in addition to New York strip, porterhouse, filet mignon, and the restaurant's namesake. Also served are simple preparations of veal, pork, lamb, and chicken. The black walls, leather chairs, and leopardskin print rugs give this attractive restaurant a timeless sophistication. *2020 K St. NW (1 block from Farragut West Metro stop), tel. 202/466–8811. Reservations advised. Jacket and tie required. AE, DC, MC, V. Closed Sat. lunch and Sun. Very Expensive.*

**Sam and Harry's.** When Sam and Harry's opened, most observers wondered if Washington really needed another expensive steakhouse. Obviously the answer was yes. The surroundings are understated and genteel, the bar is a popular downtown gathering place, and the dining room is packed at lunch and dinner. While the miniature crab cakes are a good way to begin, the main attractions are the porterhouse steak, the prime rib, and the signature strip steak. For those who've sworn off beef, Sam and Harry's also has good pork chops and daily fish specials. Desserts are lackluster, but who needs them after all that meat. *1200 19th St. NW (2 blocks from Dupont Circle Metro stop), tel. 202/296–4333. Reservations advised. Jacket and tie advised. AE, DC, MC, V. Closed Sat. lunch and Sun. Very Expensive.*

**Duke Zeibert's.** At lunch, this 450-seat restaurant is filled with regulars who come to talk sports with Duke and eat heartily from a menu that essentially hasn't changed in 40 years—boiled beef and chicken in a pot, deli sandwiches, and specials, such as corned beef and cabbage. At dinner, only the front room is used, and the restaurant becomes a different place, with couples and families replacing the deal-makers. In the evening the signature chicken and beef in a pot are still available, but the menu leans toward broiled items, such as lamb chops and sirloin, not to mention two dishes for which the restaurant is famous—prime rib and crab cakes. *1050 Connecticut Ave. NW (on the mezzanine of the Washington Sq. Bldg. at Farragut North Metro stop), tel. 202/466–3730. Reservations required. Jacket and tie advised. AE, DC, MC, V. Closed lunch Sun. Closed Sun. in July and Aug. Validated parking at Washington Sq. lot. Expensive.*

**Gary's.** Though it is located in a claustrophobic new shopping complex, Gary's is a spacious, elegant restaurant with an old-money look. Furnished with rich wood paneling, etched glass, and Oriental carpets, the dining room is reminiscent of an English men's club, but the food is American, with some Italian accents. The regular menu is heavy on meat—rack of lamb and pork, in addition to steak and prime rib. But the daily specials emphasize fish in a variety of preparations, from blackened redfish to soft-shell crabs to linguine pesto with shrimp. *1800 M St. NW (1½ blocks from Farragut North Metro stop), tel. 202/463–6470. Reservations advised. Dress: casual but neat. AE, DC, MC, V. Closed Sat. lunch and Sun. Closed Sat. in July and Aug. Expensive.*

**The Peasant.** The Atlanta-based Peasant Corporation, which also owns the Pleasant Peasant in Mazza Gallerie at the Friendship Heights Metro stop has opened its second Washington operation in the new Market Square development. This downtown Peasant Restaurant and Bar is traditional and clubby, with dark-wood paneling and crisp white tablecloths, and its proximity to Capitol Hill has already made it a popular spot for lobbying lunches. The daily menu, which is presented on individual chalkboards, is in the new American melting pot style, and likely to include pasta selections, grilled fish, and steaks. The signature desserts are enormous and rich. Service, in the tradition of the Peasant restaurants, is almost obsessively helpful. *801 Pennsylvania Ave. NW (1½ blocks from Archives Metro stop), tel. 202/638–2140. Reservations advised. Dress: casual but neat. AE, DC, MC, V. Valet parking at dinner. Closed weekend lunch. Expensive.*

**Foggy Bottom Café.** Because of zoning restrictions, the area around the Kennedy Center is almost bereft of dining options. One possibility for a hungry theatergoer who doesn't want to eat at the center's own restaurants (which tend to be seriously overcrowded) is the Foggy Bottom Café. A small, pleasant eatery located in the River Inn, about a five-block walk from the center, the Foggy Bottom Café is a place where you can have either a snack—a hamburger, sandwich, or salad—or a full meal. Keep the Foggy Bottom Café in mind if you're looking for a place for breakfast—the sunny room and the muffins baked fresh every morning are good incentives for getting out of bed. *924 25th St. NW (2 blocks from Foggy Bottom Metro stop), tel. 202/338–8707. Reservations required. No no-smoking area. Dress: casual but neat. AE, DC, MC, V. Moderate.*

**Old Ebbitt Grill.** It doesn't have the charm of the old Old Ebbitt, which was urban-renewed out of existence, but this incarnation of Washington's longest-lived restaurant is obviously doing something right—it does more business than almost any other eating place in town. People flock here to drink at the several bars, which seem to go on for miles, and to enjoy carefully prepared bar food that includes buffalo chicken wings, hamburgers, and reuben sandwiches. But this is not just a place for casual nibbling; the Old Ebbitt offers serious diners homemade pastas and a list of daily specials, with the emphasis on fish dishes and steak. Despite the crowds, the restaurant never feels cramped, thanks to its well-spaced, comfortable booths. Service can be slow at lunch. *675 15th St. NW (2 blocks from Metro Center Metro stop), tel. 202/347–4800. Reservations advised. Dress: casual but neat. AE, MC, V. Moderate.*

**French** **Jean-Louis at the Watergate Hotel.** A showcase for the
★ cooking of Jean-Louis Palladin, who was the youngest chef in France ever to be recognized with two stars by the Michelin raters, this small restaurant is often cited as one of the best in the United States. The contemporary French fare is based on regional American ingredients—crawfish from Louisiana, wild mushrooms from Oregon, game from Texas—combined in innovative ways. There are two limited-choice fixed-price dinners:

one with five courses for $85 per person, the other with six courses (the additional course is a foie-gras dish), for $95. There is also a pre-theater menu of four courses for $43, designed for but not limited to those attending the nearby Kennedy Center. In general, the first course is a soup or terrine; corn soup with oysters and lobster quenelles is a signature offering. Next comes a shellfish preparation, perhaps a potato stuffed with lobster mousseline; then a fish course, such as snapper with braised cabbage; and last, a meat dish, perhaps rack of lamb with artichoke ragout. The wine cellar is said to be the largest on the East Coast. *2650 Virginia Ave. NW (downstairs in the Watergate Hotel, which can be entered from Virginia or New Hampshire Aves., 3 blocks from Foggy Bottom Metro stop), tel. 202/298-4488. Reservations required. Jacket and tie required. AE, DC, MC, V. Closed lunch, Sun. and Aug. Validated parking. Very Expensive.*

★ **Le Lion D'Or.** Other French restaurants may flirt with fads, but this one sticks to the classics—or at any rate the neoclassics—and does them so well that its popularity remains undiminished year after year. Aside from the owner's collection of faience and the abundant floral arrangements, the decor doesn't do much to entertain the eye. But the palate is another story. This is the sort of food that makes the French posture of cultural superiority almost defensible: lobster soufflé, crêpes with oysters and caviar, ravioli with foie gras, salmon with crayfish, and roast pigeon with mushrooms. The long list of daily specials can get rather confusing unless you take notes while the waiter recites them. But don't forget to place an order for a dessert soufflé—it will leave you breathless. *1150 Connecticut Ave. NW (at Farragut North Metro stop), tel. 202/296-7972. Reservations required. Jacket and tie required. AE, DC, MC, V. Closed Sat. lunch and Sun. Free parking in lot next door at dinner. Very Expensive.*

**Maison Blanche.** No matter whether Democrats or Republicans are in power, Maison Blanche is the restaurant elected by the city's power brokers and those who enjoy gawking at them. It owes its bipartisan popularity in large part to its location near the White House and executive office buildings, but also to its Old World elegance, the friendliness of the family that runs it, and its large repertory of classic and modern French dishes. The menu, which changes four times a year, is supplemented by a large number of daily specials, primarily fish. Maison Blanche goes to great lengths to obtain Dover sole, which it serves simply grilled in butter. This is perhaps the restaurant's most popular dish, but also exceptional are the rack of lamb and the pasta dishes, such as shrimp sautéed with tomatoes and garlic, served over angelhair pasta. The pastry chef has a proper reverence for chocolate, and the wine list is extensive, with California wines well represented. *1725 F St. NW (4 blocks from Farragut West Metro stop), tel. 202/842–0070. Reservations advised. Jacket and tie advised. AE, D, DC, MC, V. Closed Sat. lunch and Sun. Free valet parking at dinner. Very Expensive.*

★ **The Place on K.** In 1991, Jean-Michel Farret closed thepopular but pricey Jean-Pierre restaurant at this location and reopened as the more moderately priced but still elegant The Place on K. Chef Guy Gateau emphasizes country French cooking with urbane touches. Dishes are generally hearty—a lunch entrée of grilled chicken breast, for instance, might come sandwiched between savory potato pancakes. Dinner fare is even heavier—filet mignon and coq au vin—with well-chosen accompaniments, such as crisp vegetables. Desserts are exquisite, ranging from delicate pastries to housemade ice creams. The interior's soft hues encourage romantic dining. *1835 K St. NW (1½ blocks from Farragut North Metro stop), tel. 202/466–2022. Reservations advised. Jacket and tie advised. AE, DC, MC, V. Closed Sat. lunch and Sun. Expensive.*

**Indian** **The Bombay Club.** Located just a block from the White House, the Bombay Club tries to re-create for tired Executive Office bureaucrats, power lawyers, and journalists the kind of solace they might have found in a private club had they been 19th-century British colonialists in India rather than late-20th-century Washingtonians. It's a beautiful restaurant. The bar, which serves hot hors d'oeuvres at cocktail hour, is furnished with rattan chairs and paneled with dark wood. The dining room, with potted palms and a bright blue ceiling above white plaster moldings, is elegant and decorous. The menu includes unusual seafood specialties, such as lobster Malabar and a large number of vegetarian dishes, but the real standouts are the breads and the seafood appetizers. *815 Connecticut Ave. NW (1 block from Farragut West Metro stop), tel. 202/659–3727. Reservations advised. Jacket and tie advised. AE, DC, MC, V. Closed Sat. lunch and Sun. dinner. Moderate.*

**Bombay Palace.** As the number of Indo-Pakistani restaurants dwindles in Washington, this one stands out. An international operation that trains all its chefs in New York to maintain consistency throughout the chain,

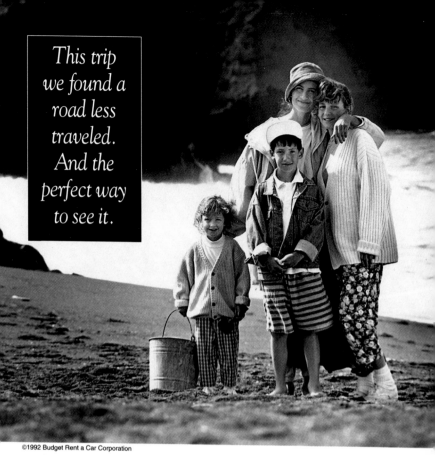

This trip we found a road less traveled. And the perfect way to see it.

*Vacation Cars. Vacation Prices.* Wherever you travel, Budget offers you a wide selection of quality cars – from economy models to roomy minivans and even convertibles. You'll find them all at competitively low rates that include unlimited mileage. At over 1500 locations in the U.S. and Canada. For information and reservations, call your travel consultant or Budget at 800-527-0700. In Canada, call 800-268-8900.

## THE SMART MONEY IS ON BUDGET.®

*We feature Lincoln-Mercury and other fine cars.*      *A system of corporate and licensee owned locations.*

# No matter what your travel style, the best trips start with **Fodor's**

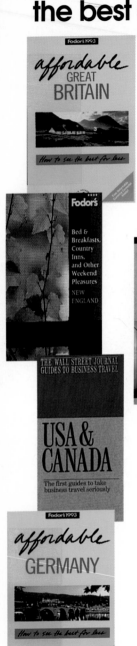

Fodor's 1993

*affordable*
GREAT
BRITAIN

*How to see the best for less*

**Fodor's**

Bed &
Breakfasts,
Country
Inns,
and Other
Weekend
Pleasures

NEW
ENGLAND

THE WALL STREET JOURNAL
GUIDES TO BUSINESS TRAVEL

USA &
CANADA

The first guides to take
business travel seriously

Fodor's 1993

*affordable*
GERMANY

*How to see the best for less*

**Fodor's**

GREAT AMERICAN
VACATIONS

50 AFFORDABLE,
HEALTH-CONSCIOUS TRIPS
TO THE COUNTRY'S BEST-LOVED
TRAVEL DESTINATIONS

"The King of Guidebooks" — *Newsweek*

**Fodor's 93**

San Francisco
*And the Best of
the Wine Country*

"The King of Guidebooks" — *Newsweek*

**Fodor's 93**

**Spain**
*Including Mallorca,
Ibiza and the
Canary Islands*

**Fodor's**

HEALTHY
ESCAPES
SPAS · FITNESS RESORTS · CRUISES

**Fodor's**

Canada's
Great
Country
Inns
*The Best in
Food and
Lodging*
by Anita
Stewart

**Fodor's**

NATIONAL PARKS
OF THE
WEST

A COMPLETE GUIDE TO THE
30 BEST-LOVED NATIONAL PARKS
AND MONUMENTS IN THE
WESTERN UNITED STATES
AND CANADA

A FODOR'S VACATION PLANNER

"The King of Guidebooks" — *Newsweek*

**Fodor's 93**

**Caribbean**
*A Complete Guide to
27 Island Destinations*

# **Fodor's**
## TRAVEL GUIDES
### The name that means smart travel
Available at bookstores everywhere.
See back pages for complete title listing.

it offers authentic Indian food in a cosmopolitan setting. The descriptive menu makes clear which dishes are hot and which are mild, though all can be adjusted to the diner's taste. Among the recommended entrées are the chicken and prawns cooked in the tandoor oven, the *gosht patiala* (a stew of meat, potatoes, and onion in a ginger sauce), and the butter chicken (tandoori chicken in a tomato sauce). At lunch, the restaurant offers "executive" specials—meals that can be prepared quickly, at discount prices. *1835 K St. NW (1½ blocks from Farragut North Metro stop), tel. 202/331–0111. Reservations advised. Dress: casual but neat. AE, DC, MC, V. Moderate.*

**International** **701 Pennsylvania Avenue.** This sleek new restaurant features an eclectic, international cuisine drawn from Italy, France, Asia, and the Americas. You might start your meal with an Indian appetizer of crab masala with tomatoes and cumin cream; progress to a Mexican fish dish of pescado pibil with chipotle chili, steamed in banana leaves; and finish with an Italian almond-and-cherry tart. The restaurant's Caviar Lounge offers choices ranging from Beluga at $55 a serving to Louisiana "Choupiquet Royale" at $8.50, smoked fish, Russian specialties, and 18 different vodkas. *701 Pennsylvania Ave. NW (at Archives Metro stop), tel. 202/393–0701. Reservations advised. Dress: casual but neat. AE, DC, MC, V. Closed Sun. Valet parking at dinner. Expensive.*

**Italian** **Bice.** Washington's Bice, like its other American locations in Chicago and Beverly Hills, owes its appearance to New York interior designer Adam Tihany, who uses elements—wood, brass, warm lighting, and art deco details—suggested by the original in Milan. The large menu, which changes twice daily, features Milanese and Northern Italian specialities, such as risotto verdi with mascarpone cheese and spinach, and a classic breaded veal cutlet alla Milanese. Pasta dishes, featuring homemade pastas, might include lobster in a fresh tomato and basil sauce or fettuccine with wild mushrooms and chives. The wine list is excellent. *601 Pennsylvania Ave. NW (1 block from Archives Metro stop), tel. 202/638–2423. Reservations advised. Jacket and tie advised. AE, DC, MC, V. Closed weekend lunch. Very Expensive.*

★ **Galileo.** Chef Roberto Donna's more formal companion to i Matti (*see above*), this spacious, popular restaurant boasts homemade everything, from breadsticks to mozzarella. And it all tastes terrific. The menu changes daily, but there is always risotto; a long list of grilled fish; a game bird, such as quail, guinea hen, or woodcock; and one or two beef or veal dishes. Preparations are generally simple. For example, the veal chop may be served with mushroom-and-rosemary sauce, the beef with black-olive sauce and polenta. *1110 21st St. NW (3 blocks from Foggy Bottom Metro stop), tel 202/293–7191. Reservations advised. Jacket and tie advised. AE, DC, MC, V. Closed weekend lunch. Valet parking at dinner (except Sun.). Very Expensive.*

★ **i Ricchi.** Priced for expense accounts, i Ricchi remains a favorite of critics and crowds for its earthy Tuscan cuisine. There are two menus, one for spring and summer, one for fall and winter. The spring list includes such offerings as rolled pork and rabbit roasted in wine and fresh herbs, and skewered shrimp; winter brings grilled goat chops, thick soups and spare ribs. But whatever the calendar says, it always feels like spring in this airy dining room, which is decorated with terra-cotta tiles, cream-colored archways, and floral frescoes. *1220 19th St. NW (2 blocks from Dupont Circle Metro stop), tel. 202/835–0459. Reservations required. Jacket and tie advised. AE, DC, MC, V. Closed Sat. lunch and Sun. Expensive.*

**Madeo.** Each month the adventurous chef here offers a different three-course fixed-price dinner ($18.95) to tempt large appetites. Recent choices have included spinach lasagna with duck confit, pistachio-crusted veal paillard with winter marmalade, and baked lobster with curried risotto and clams. Be prepared for hefty portions of desserts, such as bread pudding and cannoli. The long, narrow shape of this pretty room is mitigated by an airy atrium ceiling. *1113 23rd St. NW (3 blocks from Foggy Bottom Metro stop), tel. 202/457–0057. Reservations advised. Dress: casual but neat. AE, DC, MC, V. Parking $1.50 in lot next door. Moderate.*

**Notte Luna.** This glitzy, power-lunch spot features a dramatic black-and-neon dining room, an open kitchen with wood-burning pizza oven, and informal, ambitious cuisine. The menu offers the Italian-restaurant staples of pasta, pizza, and veal dishes, but with unexpected twists. You can order your cracker-thin pizza topped with gravlax or duck confit or your pasta with smoked salmon. All meals start with crisp bread, cheese spread, and olives. Desserts, such as berries served in a cookie-dough basket, are spectacular. *809 15th St. NW (½ block from McPherson Square Metro stop), tel. 202/408–9500. Reservations advised. Dress: casual but neat. AE, DC, MC, V. Closed weekend lunch. Valet parking at dinner (except Sun.). Moderate.*

**Primi Piatti.** A meal here is like a taxi ride in Rome at rush hour—the crowds and the noise are overwhelming, but you'll never forget the trip. What makes eating at Primi Piatti a memorable experience—aside from the manic exuberance of the dining room—is the food. The restaurant makes a point of serving dishes that are both authentically Italian, and light and healthful. There's a wood-burning grill, on which several kinds of fish are cooked each day—tuna with fresh mint sauce is one preparation—as well as lamb and veal chops. Meat is also done to a succulent turn on the rotisserie. Pastas, made in house, are outstanding, as are the pizzas. The wine list is unusually descriptive. *2013 I St. NW (2 blocks from Farragut West and Foggy Bottom Metro stops), tel. 202/223–3600; Fairfax Square, VA tel. 703/893–0300. Reservations advised. Jacket and tie advised. AE, DC, MC, V. Closed weekend lunch. Moderate.*

**Moroccan** **Marrakesh.** This is one of Washington's happy surprises: a bit of Morocco located in a part of the city better known for auto-supply shops. The menu is a fixed-price, seven-course feast shared by everyone at your table and eaten without silverware. The first course is a platter of three salads; the second, *b'stella*, the pigeon-stuffed pie (Marrakesh substitutes chicken) that is one of the glories of Moroccan cuisine. For the first main course, you choose among several chicken preparations; the second main course consists of beef or lamb. These are followed by vegetable couscous, fresh fruit, mint tea, and pastries. Belly dancers put on a nightly show, and when the moon is full you just may find yourself joining in. *617 New York Ave. NW (½ block from Mount Vernon Square Metro stop), 202/393–9393. Reservations required. Jacket and tie advised. No credit cards (checks accepted). Closed lunch. Valet parking. Moderate.*

**New American** **Twenty-One Federal.** Offering New American cuisine in
★ a sophisticated setting, Twenty-One Federal is one of the city's hottest restaurants. The menu changes seasonally but always includes a spit-roasted chicken; lamb, pheasant, and rabbit are also prepared on the rotisserie. The chef has a way with seafood, as exemplified in his grilled oysters and pancetta. But meat eaters will find much to satisfy them as well—such dishes as beef in a marrow-shallot crust, and a lamb plate that includes a rack chop, a loin stuffed with veal, and a grilled, butterflied slice of leg. A pianist plays nightly in the large dining room, which is decorated primarily in black and gray, with marble tiles and brass gridwork adding a

touch of class. *1736 L St. NW (½ block from Farragut North Metro stop), tel. 202/331–9771. Reservations advised. Jacket and tie advised. AE, DC, MC, V. Closed Sat. lunch and Sun. Free valet parking at dinner. Very Expensive.*

★ **The Willard.** An exact replica of the 1904 dining room of the historic Willard Hotel, this restaurant exudes turn-of-the-century splendor. The food, however, is strictly contemporary and might include seafood medley with wilted spinach and angelhair pasta; rack of Delaware lamb coated with mustard and fresh herbs; and veal steak with Belgian endive and basil cream sauce. The unusual wine list includes regional American varieties drawn from the vineyards of Virginia and the Pacific Northwest as well as California; an extensive selection of cognacs is presented on a rolling cart. As one might expect, such luxury does not come cheap, but this is one place where a meal really is an occasion. *1401 Pennsylvania Ave. NW (2 blocks from Metro Center Metro stop), tel. 202/637–7440. Reservations required. Jacket and tie required. AE, DC, MC, V. Free valet parking at dinner. Very Expensive.*

★ **Occidental Grill.** In the stately Willard Hotel complex, this popular restaurant used to be two separate establishments: the formal Occidental upstairs and the clubby Occidental Grill downstairs. But in keeping with the economizing sensibility of today's city, the two were merged in late 1991. Now both levels offer innovative and artful dishes, attentive service, and lots of photos of politicians and other power brokers past and present. The menu changes frequently, but you can count on chicken, fish, and steak as grilled options (the steak might be served with mustard seed, thyme, and bourbon sauce), plus salads and sandwiches. *1475 Pennsylvania Ave. NW (2 blocks from Metro Center Metro Stop), tel. 202/783–1475. Reservations advised. Dress: casual but neat. AE, DC, MC, V. Expensive.*

**Southwestern/** **Red Sage.** Within lassoing distance of the White House,
**Tex-Mex** this upscale rancher's delight has pulled in George Bush
★ and numerous others since its opening early last year. Millions were spent on the decor, which includes simulated lightning in thunderclouds, a barbed-wire-and-lizard theme, and a pseudo-adobe rabbit warren of dining rooms. Upstairs is the chili bar, where drinks are more carefully prepared than the comparatively inexpensive sandwiches and appetizers. Downstairs, chef Mark Miller's Berkeley/Santa Fe background surfaces in elaborate, artful presentations, such as pecan-cov-

ered chicken breast served with a towering heap of shoestring potatoes. The menu is heavy on meat and game dishes, with little for vegetarians or calorie watchers. That's too bad, because you'll want to save room for homey desserts, such as plum cobbler with cinnamon ice cream. *605 14th St. NW (1 block from Metro Center Metro stop), tel. 202/638-4444. Reservations advised. Dress: casual but neat. AE, DC, MC, V. Closed Sun. lunch. Expensive.*

Thai **Thai Kingdom.** At most of the restaurants on K Street an expense account is essential. At the Thai Kingdom, you need less than $20 for a fairly sumptuous meal. The authentic Thai fare is evenly divided between mild and hot dishes. Diners with incendiary inclinations should try "Anna and the King"—scallops wrapped in minced chicken and served in a basil sauce—or the crispy chili fish. Among the milder dishes, the grilled chicken and the *Pad Thai* (shrimp with noodles and bean sprouts) are outstanding. Fresh squid, served in several guises, is sweet and tender, without the rubberiness that comes from doing hard time in the freezer. *2021 K St. NW (3 blocks from Farragut West Metro stop), tel. 202/835-1700. Reservations advised. Dress: casual but neat. AE, DC, MC, V. Closed Sun. lunch. Validated parking in lot next door at dinner. Inexpensive.*

## Dupont Circle

Greek **Zorba's Cafe.** A family of four can eat heartily—and tastily—for under $25 at this popular Greek eatery. Two inside levels and outdoor seating in season accommodate fans of Zorba's grilled meat and homey vegetable dishes. The half-chicken marinated in oregano is a winner, but be sure to check out the specials. Vegetarians and light eaters will find much to choose from. Pizza, subs, and sandwiches are available for non-Greek palates. Service is from a counter, but moves quickly. The grill is open until 11 PM daily. *1612 20th St. NW (1 block from Q St. exit of Dupont Circle Metro Stop), tel. 202/387-8555. No reservations. Dress: casual. No credit cards. Inexpensive.*

Italian **Vincenzo.** Vincenzo has relaxed somewhat since its early days, when it was so determined to be authentically
★ Italian that it refused to serve butter with the bread. Butter is now available (on request), and the once exclusively seafood menu has been supplemented with a few meat dishes—game in autumn, pork in winter, lamb in spring. But it is still a restaurant for purists who appre-

ciate its commitment to finding the best fish it can and serving it as simply as possible. The fixed-price dinner ($29) includes an appetizer, first course, main dish, side dish, and dessert; lunch is à la carte. Along with its enlarged menu, Vincenzo has expanded its dining space, adding a glassed-in courtyard to an already light and airy space. *1606 20th St. NW (1 block from Q St. exit of Dupont Circle Metro stop), tel. 202/667–0047. Reservations advised. Dress: casual but neat. AE, DC, MC, V. Closed Sat. lunch and Sun. Very Expensive.*

★ **Obelisk.** One of the most exciting restaurants in Washington, Obelisk serves eclectic Italian cuisine, with a small, fixed-price menu ($30–$33) that includes both traditional dishes and the chef's imaginative innovations. The list, which changes daily, usually offers one meat, one fish, and one poultry entrée. The meat is likely to be lamb, with garlic and sage or perhaps anchovies; fish might be a pompano stuffed with bay leaves; a typical poultry selection is the hardly typical pigeon with chanterelles. In winter there is lasagna, but what lasagna—layered with wild mushrooms or with artichokes and sweetbreads. The minimally decorated dining room is tiny, with tables so closely spaced that even whispers can be overheard. But it doesn't matter, because with food like this, who needs conversation? *2029 P St. NW (3 blocks from Dupont Circle Metro stop), tel. 202/872–1180. Reservations advised. No no-smoking area. Dress: casual but neat. AE, MC. Dinner only. Closed Sun. and last 2 weeks of Aug. Expensive.*

**Odeon Café.** Odeon is a preeminent example of the slick pizza-and-pasta parlors that are the latest Italian invasion here. On the surface Odeon *seems* all surface—glossy to the point of being almost intimidating. But amid all the glass and marble and the resultant din is some very good food, served in hefty portions. Pasta and pizza dough are made in house and topped with first-class ingredients. In addition, there is a good list of grilled dishes, and specials change every two weeks. *1714 Connecticut Ave. NW (2 blocks from Q Street exit of Dupont Circle Metro stop), tel. 202/328–6228. Reservations advised weekdays, not accepted weekends. Dress: casual but neat. AE, MC, V. Closed weekend lunch. Moderate.*

**Pizzeria Paradiso.** Sharing a kitchen with elite Obelisk, this petite pizzeria sticks to crowd-pleasing basics: pizzas, *panini* (sandwiches), a few salads, and desserts. Although the standard pizza is satisfying, you can enliven things by ordering it with fresh buffalo mozzarella or unusual toppings such as potatoes, capers, and mussels.

The sandwiches are assembled with homemade focaccia; the gelato is also a house specialty. The airy, trompe l'oeil ceiling adds space and light to a simple interior. *2029 P St. NW (3 blocks from Dupont Circle Metro stop), tel. 202/223–1245. No reservations. No no-smoking area. Dress: casual. MC, V. Inexpensive.*

**Middle Eastern**  **Bacchus.** The name is somewhat misleading; Bacchus is a Middle Eastern restaurant, specifically Lebanese, that has no real competition in Washington. In the Lebanese tradition, appetizers far outnumber entrées; it is possible to put together a feast just from the list of hot and cold first courses, which include impeccable versions of such standards as hummus and baba ghannouj, as well as more exotic concoctions of ground beef, eggplant, and yogurt. Among the main courses, *ouzi* (lamb with spiced rice, mushrooms, almonds, and pine kernels), *kafta* (grilled logs of ground beef), and *shish taouk* (grilled chunks of marinated chicken) are outstanding, but you really can't go wrong with anything served here. *1827 Jefferson St. NW (2 blocks from Dupont Circle Metro stop), tel. 202/785–0734; Bethesda, MD, tel. 301/657–1722. Reservations advised. Dress: casual but neat. AE, MC, V. Closed Sat. lunch and Sun. Moderate.*

**Skewers.** As the name implies, Skewers's specialty is kebabs, served with almond-flaked rice or pasta. The lamb with eggplant and the chicken with roasted pepper are the most popular, but filet mignon and shrimp are equally tasty. The vegetable kebabs and the array of appetizers, such as hummus with *foole* (warm baked beans) make this ideal for vegetarians. For those wanting less meat—perhaps to leave room for scrumptious desserts, such as Key-lime pie or chocolate cake—minikebabs are available, served either with pita bread or in a salad. If the restaurant is too crowded, you can enjoy the lively coffeehouse style and cheap California eats downstairs at Café Luna (tel. 202/387–4005). *1633 P St. NW (2 blocks from Dupont Circle Metro stop), tel. 202/387–7400. Reservations advised weekends. Dress: casual. AE, DC, MC, V. Moderate.*

**New American**  **Tabard Inn.** With its artfully artless decor, absentminded waiters, and quasi–health-food menu, the Tabard is an idiosyncratic restaurant that has a devoted clientele of baby-boomers with '60s values and '80s incomes. The lounge looks like a garage sale waiting to happen, and the two dining rooms are likewise somewhat shabby. But the courtyard may be Washington's prettiest outdoor eatery, and the Tabard's New American cuisine, although it doesn't always quite come off, is fresh and interesting. The Tabard raises much of its produce, without pesticides, on its own farm; meat is additive-free. Most of the menu changes daily; complicated preparations of fish are a specialty. In a city where finding a good breakfast—or any breakfast at all—can be a major challenge, the Tabard is outstanding for the quantity and quality of its offerings. *1739 N St. NW (3 blocks from Dupont Circle Metro stop), tel. 202/833–2668. Reservations advised. Dress: casual. MC, V. Expensive.*

**Southwestern/** **Lauriol Plaza.** Located in upper Dupont Circle, halfway
**Tex-Mex** to Adams-Morgan, this charming corner enclave offers a menu combining sophisticated Spanish dishes with zesty Mexican favorites. In the former category, watch for seafood and duck offerings; the latter has plenty of crowd-pleasing guacamole, enchiladas, and tortilla chips. The simply-decorated dining room, with white tablecloths and white walls enlivened by gilt-framed paintings, can get noisy; the terrace is preferable in good weather. *1801 18th St. NW, tel. 202/387–0035. Reservations advised. No no-smoking area. Dress: casual but neat. AE, DC, MC, V. Moderate.*

**Thai** **Sala Thai.** This is not the sort of Thai restaurant where you go for the burn; the Sala Thai will make the food as spicy as you wish, but the chef is interested in flavor, not fire. Among the subtly seasoned offerings are *panang goong* (shrimp in curry-peanut sauce), chicken sautéed with ginger and pineapple, and flounder with a choice of four sauces. The *Pad Thai* P Street is an exceptional treatment of that signature dish, which consists of noodles with shrimp and bean sprouts in a peanut sauce. Sala Thai is decorated in the currently fashionable minimalist style, but mirrored walls and soft lights soften the ambience of this small downstairs dining room. *2016 P St. NW (3 blocks from Dupont Circle Metro stop), tel. 202/872–1144. Reservations accepted. No no-smoking area. Dress: casual but neat. AE, DC, MC, V. Closed Sun. lunch. Moderate.*

## Georgetown

**Afghani** **Bamiyan.** Although the area's best Afghani restaurants are in suburban Virginia, Bamiyan is the oldest in the area and so enjoys a loyal following, even though it does look like a motel that has seen better days. Kebabs—of chicken, beef, or lamb—are succulent. More adventurous souls should try the *quabili palow* (lamb with saffron rice, carrots, and raisins) or the *aushak* (dumplings with scallions, meat sauce, and yogurt). For a side vegetable, order the sautéed pumpkin; it will make you forget every other winter squash dish you've ever had. Vegetarians may order any of these side vegetables as main courses. *3320 M St. NW, tel. 202/338–1896. Reservations accepted. Dress: casual. AE, MC, V. Closed lunch. Moderate.*

**American**  **Morton's of Chicago.** Unless you come early, you'll have to wait up to an hour for a table at the Washington branch of this national steakhouse chain, which claims to serve the country's best beef. The claim must have merit, because the crowds patiently doing time at the bar clearly have not come for the restaurant's ambience—there are bus stations that have more class than this vinyl-boothed dining room. In the classic steakhouse tradition, Morton's emphasizes quantity as well as quality. The New York strip and porterhouse steaks, two of the most popular offerings, are well over a pound each. For diners with even larger appetites, there's a three-pound porterhouse. Morton's also includes lamb, veal, chicken, lobster, and grilled fish on its menu—which for some reason is not printed, but instead recited by a waiter who displays the raw ingredients on a cart. *3251 Prospect St., tel. 202/342–6258; Tysons Corner, VA, tel. 703/883–0800. Reservations advised. Jacket and tie advised. AE, DC, MC, V. Closed lunch and Sun. Valet parking. Very Expensive.*

**Georgetown Seafood Grill.** For years you would never have guessed that the Chesapeake Bay was in Washington's backyard, so landlocked were the kitchens in most of the city's restaurants. That's changed, but the city still has very few of the sort of restaurants you expect to find near water—unpretentious places where your oysters are shucked in front of you. The Georgetown Seafood Grill does not have unpretentious prices, but in every other respect it is the perfect seafood eatery. It has an appropriately weathered visage—old tilework and exposed brick decorated with nautical photographs—and its menu casts a wide net. There are four or five kinds of oysters at the raw bar, plus clams, spiced shrimp, and crab claws. Crab cakes are made with jumbo lump-meat and no filler, and soft-shell crabs are served in season. On weekends you can order steamed lobsters, and each night you can choose among about seven fish specials—everything from fried catfish to broiled red snapper with macadamia pesto. Sunday brunch is also popular. *3063 M St. NW, tel. 202/333–*

*7038. Reservations accepted for large parties. Dress: casual but neat. AE, DC, MC, V. Expensive.*

**American Café.** Thirteen years ago someone had the bright idea of opening a Georgetown restaurant that would serve fresh, healthy food—but not health food—at affordable prices in a casual but sophisticated environment. And so the American Café empire, which now numbers 15 restaurants in the Washington area, was born. Sandwiches, such as the namesake roast beef on a humongous croissant, are still the mainstay of the café, with salads and nibbles rounding off the regular menu. But the list of specials, which changes every two weeks, offers intriguing possibilities for those wanting a larger meal. There's always a fresh fish, a seafood pie, a chicken dish, and barbecued ribs. It's a good choice for family outings and Sunday meals downtown. Weekend brunches offer temptations such as strawberry-banana-nut waffles and stuffed French toast. *1211 Wisconsin Ave. NW (also at 227 Massachusetts Ave. NE, tel. 202/547–8500; 1331 Pennsylvania Ave. NW, tel 202/626–0770; 1701 Pennsylvania Ave. NW, tel. 202/833–3434; 529 14th St. NW, tel. 202/393–6400; Union Station, tel. 202/682–0937;1200 19th St. NW, tel. 202/223–2121; and 5252 Wisconsin Ave. NW), tel. 202/363–5400), tel. 202/944–9464. Reservations accepted only for large parties. Dress: casual. AE, DC, MC, V. Inexpensive.*

**Argentinian Las Pampas.** Fish is edging meat off the menu at most of the city's restaurants, but there's no danger of that happening at Las Pampas, an Argentinian restaurant many think serves the best steak in town. The beef, which is fresh, not aged, is cooked over a special grill that simulates charcoal heat; the result is a firm-textured steak with a crusty surface and a juicy interior. The familiar New York strip and filet mignon are available from the grill, but the preferred choice is the *churrasco*, a special Argentinian cut. Daily specials usually include swordfish; brochettes of beef, seafood, lamb, or chicken; and a pasta. The wine list includes a preponderance of Argentinian vintages. The restaurant's South American authenticity does not extend to its ambience—aside from a couple of wall hangings, Las Pampas is decorated in international nondescript. *3291 M St. NW, tel. 202/333–5151. Reservations advised. No no-smoking area. Dress: casual but neat. AE, DC, MC, V. Closed Sat. lunch. Moderate.*

**Ethiopian Zed's.** Adams-Morgan may have the city's greatest concentration of Ethiopian restaurants, but Georgetown has one of the most authentic. All of the *injera* bread here is made with *teff*, giving it a light sourdough taste that encourages you to scoop up more of the richly spiced stews. The chicken *doro wat* and yellow lentil *kik alicha* are classics; specialties include a dried cottage cheese called *ayeeb* and short ribs. Vegetarians will find lots to choose from. The honey wine (*tej*) is cooling but strong. Note: Dishes ending in *wat* are red-chili hot, while those ending in *alicha* are mild but savory. *3318 M St. NW, tel. 202/333-4710. Reservations advised. Dress: casual but neat. AE, MC, V. Moderate.*

French **Bistro Français.** A longtime fixture on M Street, this French country restaurant is a favorite among the city's chefs. What do the professionals order when they want to eat someone else's cooking? The Minute Steak Maître d'Hotel, a sirloin with herb butter, accompanied by french fries. Among amateur eaters, the big draw is the rotisserie chicken. While the bistro excels at such simple fare, it also does well with the more complicated dishes it offers on the extensive list of daily specials, such as suprême of salmon with broccoli mousse and beurre blanc. The restaurant is divided into two parts, the café side and the more formal dining room. Both have the same comfortable, lived-in look, but the café menu includes sandwiches and omelets in addition to the entrées. The bistro also offers fixed-price lunches and early and late-night dinner specials and stays open until 2:45 AM Sunday–Thursday, 3:45 AM Friday and Saturday. *3128 M St. NW, tel. 202/338-3830. Reservations advised. Dress: casual but neat. AE, DC, MC, V. Moderate.*

**La Chaumière.** A longtime favorite of Washingtonians seeking an escape from the hurly-burly of Georgetown, La Chaumière has the rustic charm of a French country inn, particularly during the winter, when its central stone fireplace warms the room. The food is country French, with an emphasis on seafood—crab meat in a crêpe, mussels, and scampi are on the regular menu, and there is usually a grilled fish special and a seafood brochette. The restaurant also has a devoted following for its meat dishes, which include such hard-to-find entrées as blood sausage and calf's brain. Many local diners plan their meals around La Chaumière's rotating specials, particularly the couscous on Wednesday and the cassoulet on Thursday. *2813. M St. NW, tel. 202/ 338-1784. Reservations required. No no-smoking area. Jacket and tie advised. AE, DC, MC, V. Closed Sat. lunch. and Sun. 2-hr validated parking at dinner at Four Seasons Hotel lot. Moderate.*

**Indian** **Aditi.** At first glance this two-story dining room seems to be too elegant for a moderately priced Indian restaurant. The dim interior features burgundy carpets and chairs and pale mint-colored walls with brass sconces. There's a small first floor, with a dramatic staircase leading to a larger room with windows that overlook the busy street. But the decor is not the only draw: Tandoor and curry dishes, although not aggressively spiced, are otherwise expertly prepared. The rice *biryani* entrées are good for lighter appetites, and $4.95 will get you a delicious bread sampler. *3299 M St. NW, tel. 202/625–6825. Dress: casual but neat. AE, DC, MC, V. Closed Mon. lunch. Moderate.*

**Tandoor.** The crucible of Indian cuisine is the *tandoor*, a charcoal-burning clay oven. Meat is cooked on skewers held upright by the coals, and bread is baked directly on the oven walls. This namesake restaurant was the first in town to install a tandoor and consequently the first to give area diners a taste of the real India. Chicken, lamb filet, and minced lamb, beef, and shrimp are available from the oven, as is a combination platter. The tandoor-cooked meats are also used in a variety of curries, with chicken tikka masala one of the best. This restaurant is not as luxurious as some of the newer Indian restaurants, but its prints of Indian dancers and orange tablecloths make it cheerful. *3316 M St. NW, tel. 202/333–3376, and 2623 Connecticut Ave. NW, tel. 202/483–1115. Reservations advised. Dress: casual but neat. AE, DC, MC, V. Moderate.*

**Madurai.** Although the dining room (just above Zed's restaurant, *see above*) is plain and worn, the extensive menu and well-prepared dishes at this all-vegetarian Indian establishment make up for the ambience. Seasonings range from mild to piquant, with hot spices largely contained in side condiments. The mushroom, eggplant, and exotic lotus root curries are specialties. Students and other cost-conscious diners stake out the restaurant's Sunday buffet (noon to 4 and 5 to 10 PM), which offers all-you-can-eat curries, basmati rice and Indian breads for $6.95. Service is pleasant but languid. *3318 M St. NW, tel. 202/333–0997. Reservations accepted. Dress: casual. AE, MC, V. Inexpensive.*

**Indonesian** **Sarinah Satay House.** All you can see of this delightful
★ restaurant from busy Wisconsin Avenue is its wooden sign above a green door. Open it, follow the stairs down and up again, and you're in a lush, enclosed garden with real trees growing through the ceiling. Carved monkeys, parrots, and puppets add to the setting, where

batik-clad waiters offer gentle, unrushed service. The food is exquisite. Potato croquettes, spring rolls, and the traditional *loempia* (crisp egg rolls) come with a tangy, chili-spiked peanut dipping sauce, while the perfectly grilled chicken *satay* is accompanied by a smoky-sweet peanut dip. One of the menu's best bargains is the combination *nasi rames:* chicken in coconut sauce, beef skewers, and spicy green beans with rice ($7.95). Vegetarians may order well-seasoned noodle, rice, and vegetable dishes. Cool your palate afterwards with an *es teler,* a shaved-ice dessert with exotic fruits. *1338 Wisconsin Ave. NW, tel. 202/337–2955. Reservations advised. Dress: casual but neat. AE, DC, MC, V. Closed Sun. lunch and Mon. Moderate.*

**Italian** **Paolo's.** This glitzy pizza-and-pasta emporium is one of Georgetown's most bustling restaurants (expect a long wait for a table). The action revolves around the central wood-burning pizza oven, out of which emerges an endless parade of new- and old-style pies. One version has four cheeses, red peppers, and smoked salmon; another has goat cheese, sun-dried tomatoes, and duck sausage. Customers can also create a "personal pie" by picking three ingredients from the cornucopia arrayed around the oven. Pastas are equally eclectic: capellini with shrimp and scallops, penne in vodka, as well as the traditional bolognese and carbonara. There's also a short list of entrées that includes grilled homemade sausage and shrimp scampi. *1303 Wisconsin Ave. NW, tel. 202/333–7353; Rockville, MD, tel. 301/984–2211. No reservations. Dress: casual but neat. AE, DC, MC, V. Moderate.*

**Japanese** **Sushi-Ko.** This was Washington's first sushi bar, and it's still the best in Georgetown. In addition to the à la carte items and assortments of sushi and sashimi, which vary according to the availability of fish that meets Sushi-Ko's stringent standards for freshness, the menu includes seafood and vegetable tempuras, fish teriyaki, and udonsuki (noodles with seafood and vegetables). Sushi novices might want to test the waters by ordering tuna or yellowtail as an appetizer, followed by one of the cooked dishes. Those looking for more exotic fare will find it on the back of the menu—printed in Japanese, but your waiter can be prevailed upon to translate. *2309 Wisconsin Ave. NW, tel. 202/333–4187. Reservations advised. Dress: casual but neat. AE, MC, V. Closed weekend lunch and Mon. Moderate.*

**New American**   **The River Club.** Until someone invents a time machine, ★ there is no better way to experience the Jazz Age than by taking a trip to The River Club, an art deco extravaganza in an out-of-the-way part of Georgetown. Decorated in ebony, silver, neon, and marble, The River Club is in fact a club, with a disc jockey who plays '30 and '40s music for the two dance floors. But this is more than just a place to feed your fantasies: Even though original chef Jeff Tunks has left, the River Club is still a real restaurant that takes its cooking very seriously. Salmon is flown in from Iceland and beef from Chicago. The inspiration for much of the food comes from the Orient—the salmon is served Thai style, with a basil sauce; lobster is smoked and comes with fried spinach with ginger and scallions. But the menu, which changes seasonally, is not limited to Asian-American creations. There might also be veal stuffed with wild mushrooms, swordfish with mint pesto, and grilled chicken stuffed with goat cheese. And of course there's always the option of nibbling on caviar while you dream the night away. *3223 K St. NW, tel. 202/333–8118. Reservations advised. Jacket and tie required. AE, DC, MC, V. Closed lunch and Sun. Valet parking available. Very Expensive.*

**Southwestern/**   **Austin Grill.** Even before the 1988 election put a Texan, **Tex-Mex** of sorts, into the White House, Washington was big on Tex-Mex cooking—one of the city's hot-ticket social events is the annual congressional chili-off. But Washington didn't have a Tex-Mex restaurant of note until the opening of the Austin Grill, a small, lively spot in upper Georgetown whose popularity is well deserved. The Austin has a food-smoker out back, where ribs are prepared for dinner. The mesquite grill is always in operation, turning out fajitas and grilled fish and providing the starting point for what the Austin claims is the best chili in town—made with cubed meat, not ground, unadulterated by beans. With its multicolored booths, the restaurant looks like a post-modern diner; a bright mural adds to the cheerful effect. Waiters are friendly and efficient, a rare combination. *2404 Wisconsin Ave. NW, tel. 202/337–8080. No reservations. Dress: casual. AE, MC, V. Closed Mon. lunch. Inexpensive.*

# 7 Lodging

*By Jan Ziegler*
*Updated by*
*Jeanne Cooper*

Although the nation's capital rode a hotel boom in the last decade, the emphasis these days is on renovation rather than new construction. Still, visitors who plan to spend the night, a week, or a month in DC will find a large variety of accommodations from which to choose. Hostelries include grand hotels with glorious histories, quiet Victorian inns, the hotel and motel chains common to every American city, and small independently operated hotels that offer little more than good location, a smile, and a comfortable, clean place to lay your head.

Because Washington is an international city, nearly all hotel staffs are multilingual. All hotels in the Expensive and Very Expensive categories have concierges; some in the Moderate group do, too. All of the hotels here are air-conditioned. All the large hotels and many of the smaller ones offer meeting facilities and special features for business travelers, ranging from state-of-the-art teleconferencing equipment to modest conference rooms with outside catering.

Not all the city's hotels are included here; there are simply too many to list. Most of the major chains have hotels at desirable locations throughout town. For a complete listing of hotels in the area, contact the Washington D.C. Convention and Visitors' Association (1212 New York Ave. NW, Washington, DC 20005, tel. 202/789–7000).

To find reasonably priced accommodations in small guest houses and private homes, contact either of the following bed-and-breakfast services: **Bed 'n' Breakfast Ltd. of Washington, D.C.** (Box 12011, Washington, DC 20005, tel. 202/328–3510) or **Bed and Breakfast League, Ltd.,** (3639 Van Ness St. NW, Washington, DC 20008, tel. 202/363–7767).

A word about reservations: They are crucial. Hotels are often full of conventioneers, politicians in transit, or families and school groups in search of cherry blossoms and monuments. If you're interested in visiting Washington at a calmer time—and if you can stand tropical weather—come in July or August, during the congressional recess. You may not spot many VIPs, but hotels will have more rooms to offer, and you'll be able to relax (August, however, is the busiest season for the Washington International Youth Hostel, so budget travelers should seek alternatives at this time).

The hotel reviews here are grouped according to price categories. Keep in mind that rates are variable and can be lower depending on season and whether they are part of a group, corporate, or weekend package. Also, some of the older hotels have a few smaller rooms that rent for prices in a lower category.

Unless otherwise noted below, hotels charge extra for parking. Rates range from $5 to $15 a night, depending on how close to downtown you are. An 11% room tax and a $1.50 per night occupancy tax will be added to your bill.

Highly recommended lodgings are indicated by a star ★.

| Category | Cost* |
|---|---|
| Very Expensive | over $190 |
| Expensive | $145–$190 |
| Moderate | $100–$145 |
| Inexpensive | under $100 |

*All prices are for a standard double room, excluding 11% room tax and $1.50 per night occupancy tax.*

### Capitol Hill

**Very Expensive**  **Hyatt Regency on Capitol Hill.** One of the chain's more spartan entries in Washington, this hotel has the typical Hyatt garden atrium but with high-tech edges. Close to Union Station and the Mall, this is a mecca for families and for businesspeople with dealings on the Hill. In 1991, the Hyatt Regency completed a $14 million renovation of all guest rooms. Suites on the south side have a view of the Capitol dome, which is just a few blocks away. Sunday brunch at the Park Promenade restaurant is popular. *400 New Jersey Ave. NW, 20001, tel. 202/737–1234 or 800/233–1234. 803 rooms, 31 suites. Facilities: 24-hr room service; 3 restaurants; 2 bars; health club with weight equipment, steam room, sauna, pool; parking. AE, DC, MC, V.*

**Washington Court.** Formerly the Sheraton Grand, this luxury hotel is one of the few hostelries in DC where it is possible to make a truly grand entrance. Guests descend three terraced tiers of polished steps into an atrium surmounted by a skylight. It shares its view of the Capitol with the Hyatt and others on the same street. Rooms are done in dusty rose and colonial blue. *525 New Jersey Ave. NW, 20001, tel. 202/628–2100. 250 rooms, 15 suites. Facilities: room service 6:30 AM–11 PM; bar; restaurant; deli; health club with Nautilus, free weights,*

# Washington Lodging

ANA Hotel, **22**

Bellevue Hotel, **55**

Capitol Hill Hotel, **59**

Capitol Hilton, **41**

Crystal City
Marriott, **16**

Days Inn
Connecticut Avenue, **2**

Embassy Row
Hotel, **11**

Embassy Suites, **23**

Four Seasons
Hotel, **21**

Georgetown
Dutch Inn, **19**

Georgetown Inn, **14**

Grand Hotel, **25**

Grand Hyatt, **48**

Guest
Quarters, **26, 31**

Hay-Adams Hotel, **43**

Henley Park Hotel, **46**

Holiday Inn
Central, **34**

Holiday Inn Crowne
Plaza at Metro
Center, **49**

Holiday Inn
Governor's House, **35**

Hotel Anthony, **32**

Hotel Tabard Inn, **33**

Hotel Washington, **50**

Hotel Windsor Park, **6**

Howard Johnson
Kennedy Center, **29**

Hyatt Regency
Bethesda, **1**

Hyatt Regency on
Capitol Hill, **57**

Jefferson Hotel, **37**

J.W. Marriott, **52**

Kalorama Guest
House, **5**

Key Bridge
Marriott, **15**

Latham Hotel, **20**

Loew's L'Enfant
Plaza, **58**

The Madison Hotel, **40**

Mayflower, A Stouffer
Hotel, **38**

Morrison House, **17**

Morrison-Clark Inn
Hotel, **44**

Normandy Inn, **7**

Omni Georgetown, **13**

Omni Shoreham
Hotel, **4**

Park Hyatt, **24**

Phoenix Park
Hotel, **54**

Pullman Highland
Hotel, **10**

Quality Hotel Capitol
Hill, **56**

Quality Hotel
Central, **8**

Quality Hotel Silver
Spring, **36**

Ramada Renaissance
Hotel-Techworld, **47**

The Ritz-Carlton, **12**

Ritz-Carlton,
Pentagon City, **18**

River Inn, **28**

Sheraton Carlton
Hotel, **42**

Sheraton Washington
Hotel, **3**

Washington Court, **53**

The Washington
Hilton and Towers, **9**

Washington
International AYH-
Hostel, **45**

Washington Vista
Hotel, **39**

Watergate Hotel, **30**

The Willard Inter-
Continental, **51**

Wyndham Bristol
Hotel, **27**

*treadmills, rowing machines, stationary bicycles; valet parking. AE, DC, MC, V.*

**Expensive**   **Capitol Hill Hotel.** Tucked away on a quiet street behind the Madison Building of the Library of Congress, this former apartment building has been converted into an all-suite hotel. Its proximity to the House office buildings means that it is often filled with visiting lobbyists when Congress is in session, and its location makes it an ideal spot to get a feel for both residential and official Washington. A complete refurbishment was completed in 1990; all rooms have kitchens and are attractively furnished in Queen Anne style with a blue-and-rose color scheme. Although the hotel has no restaurant, Continental breakfast is available and room service is provided by neighboring restaurants. *200 C St. SE, 20003, tel. 202/543–6000. 152 suites. Facilities: in-room kitchens, room service, access to health club, valet parking. AE, DC, MC, V.*

**Phoenix Park Hotel.** Just steps from Union Station and only four blocks from the Capitol, this high-rise hotel has an Irish club theme and is the home of the Dubliner, one of Washington's best bars. Leather, wood panelling, and leaded glass abound in the bar's re-creation of the decor favored by the 18th-century Irish gentry; guest rooms are bright, traditionally furnished, and quiet. Penthouse suites have fireplaces. The Powerscourt Restaurant is named after an Irish castle. *520 North Capitol St. NW, 20001, tel. 202/638–6900 or 800/824–5419. 82 rooms, 6 suites. Facilities: 2 restaurants, complimentary newspaper, valet parking. AE, DC, MC, V.*

**Moderate**   **Bellevue Hotel.** This charming and comfortable hotel has been in business for 65 years. The public rooms on the main floor have balconies and are modeled after great halls in manor houses of yore. Accommodations here are standard modest-hotel fare, but the staff is friendly. The location is convenient, near Union Station and major Metrorail stations and within six blocks of the Supreme Court and the Smithsonian museums. *15 E St. NW, 20001, tel. 202/638–0900 or 800/327–6667. 138 rooms, 2 suites. Facilities: restaurant, bar, library, free overnight parking. AE, DC, MC, V.*

**Quality Hotel Capitol Hill.** A good value for the budget-minded traveler, this hotel shares the block with the Hyatt and offers the same views and convenient location. A complete renovation of the hotel, including all guest rooms, was completed in 1990. *415 New Jersey Ave. NW, 20001, tel. 202/638–1616 or 800/ 228–5151. 336 rooms, 5 suites. Facilities: room service 6:30 AM–11 PM,* *restaurant, outdoor rooftop pool, free parking. AE, DC, MC, V.*

---

## Downtown

**Very Expensive**  **Capitol Hilton.** There are three advantages here: location, location, and location. The busy Capitol Hilton is not only just up the street from official Washington, including the White House and many monuments, it is smack in the middle of the K Street business corridor. Built in 1943 as a Statler Hotel, the building underwent a $55 million renovation a few years ago that enlarged rooms by a third. Now the theme is neo–art deco, with torchères, winding staircases, and columns finished with milled cherrywood. Rooms are sleekly furnished in shades of camel, gray, or dusty rose. The new Towers section on the top four floors offers VIP accommodations. *1001 16th St. NW, 20036, 202/393–1000 or 800/445–8667. 515 rooms, 34 suites. Facilities: 24-hr room service; 2 restaurants; valet parking; barber and beauty salon; health club with treadmills, Nautilus equipment, steam room, sauna, tanning bed. AE, DC, MC, V.*

**Grand Hyatt.** Imagine a 1930s movie-musical set. Studio-built walls of a Mediterranean hillside village rise around a courtyard; a gazebo and curved lounge and dining areas surround a blue lagoon fed by waterfalls. On a small island in the lagoon is a man in black tie playing Cole Porter tunes on a white grand piano. The Hyatt has created just such a fanciful interior in this bustling new high-rise hotel that successfully compensates for the relative drabness of the neighborhood. Opened in June 1987, the Grand is across the street from the Washington Convention Center and just steps away from downtown shopping and theaters. Quiet, contemporary rooms are reached by glass-walled elevators; some suites have whirlpools or saunas. Conference suites are popular with businesspeople who may need to meet clients in their rooms. The Zephyr Deli is a popular lunch spot; the Grand Cafe features country breakfasts on weekends. *1000 H St. NW, 20001, tel. 202/582–1234 or 800/228–9000. 847 rooms, 61 suites. Facilities: 24-hr room service, 3 restaurants, bar, multilingual staff, health club, valet parking. AE, DC, MC, V.*

★  **Hay-Adams Hotel.** Built in 1927, the Hay-Adams sits upon the site of houses owned by John Hay and Henry Adams, social and political paragons in turn-of-the-century Washington. Italian Renaissance in design, the hotel looks like a mansion in disguise. Seventeenth-

century Medici tapestries grace two lobby walls, while
the John Hay Room restaurant seems to belong to an
English Tudor residence. The guest rooms are the most
brightly colored in the city, decorated in 23 different
English-country-house schemes. Rooms on the south
side have a picture-postcard view of the White House.
The hotel's afternoon tea is renowned, and the Adams
Room is a popular spot for power breakfasts. The staff is
dignified and friendly. *1 Lafayette Sq. NW, 20006, tel.
202/638–6600 or 800/424–5054. 123 rooms, 20 suites. Facilities: 24-hr room service, 3 restaurants, bar, valet
parking. AE, DC, MC, V.*

**Holiday Inn Crowne Plaza at Metro Center.** "Holiday
Inn" has come to be synonymous with standard American motel decor, but this one belies all preconceptions,
from the enormous mauve marble registration desk to
the artwork throughout the hotel especially commissioned from Washington artists. The hotel's restaurant
and bar, the Metro Center Grille and Bar, is a handsome
two-level facility decorated in mahogany, oak, brass,
and marble. The New American cuisine of executive chef
Melissa Balinger has made the restaurant a popular
downtown lunch and dinner spot for locals as well as
guests. The larger-than-average rooms, decorated in
mauve and soft blue, are more comfortable than luxurious. Each has a desk and two easy chairs. Two executive
floors offer complimentary Continental breakfast, courtesy bar, and a private lounge. *775 12th St. NW, 20005,
tel. 202/737–2200 or 800/465–4329. 453 rooms, 12 suites.
Facilities: 24-hr room service; valet parking; restaurant; bar; health club with whirlpool, sauna, Lifecycles,
StairMaster, rowing machines, Universal weights,
aerobics, indoor pool. AE, DC, MC, V.*

★ **Jefferson Hotel.** Incoming and outgoing administration
officials have stayed at the Jefferson since it opened.
The undistinguished exterior of this 1923 building is de-
ceiving; past the tiny foyer the atmosphere is classically
elegant and smacks of the 18th and early 19th centuries.
Rooms are furnished with antiques and reproductions
as well as original art. Double-glass windows assure
quiet on a busy intersection. The redecorated restaurant features the widely praised new American cooking
of chef Will Greenwood. The staff of this small hotel re-
members guests' names and greets them by name; laundry is hand-ironed and delivered in wicker baskets. *1200
16th St. NW, 20036, tel. 202/347–2200 or 800/368–5966.
68 rooms, 32 suites. Facilities: 24-hr room service, restaurant, bar, multilingual staff, valet parking. AE,
DC, MC, V.*

**J.W. Marriott.** Opened in 1984, this large, glossy hotel is in a prime location on Pennsylvania Avenue, close to the White House and next door to the National Theatre. Rooms are furnished in quiet colors. The best views are on the Pennsylvania Avenue side. On other sides, you may end up looking across a courtyard at the blank windows of another section of the complex. Guests have indoor access to the National Press Building and the shops and restaurants of National Place. The signature dessert at the Celadon restaurant is Painter's Palette, made of chocolate topped with fruit sorbets. *1331 Pennsylvania Ave. NW, 20004, tel. 202/393–2000 or 800/228–9290. 732 rooms, 41 suites. Facilities: 24-hr room service, 4 restaurants, bar, health club with Universal weights and stationary bikes, indoor pool, valet parking. AE, DC, MC, V.*

**The Madison Hotel.** Elegance and fine service are the hallmarks of the Madison. Deceivingly contemporary on the outside, the 14-story Madison was built to house not only guests from around the world but a world-class collection of antiques, Oriental rugs, and fine art. Even the front lobby is graced by a rare antique Chinese altar table. The guest rooms are also furnished with antiques and reproductions, and the Madison's suites are among the most opulent and un-hotellike in Washington. Nevertheless, a renovation of all suites and rooms is scheduled to be completed by late 1992; the new decor will feature peach or blue tones and Oriental touches. A fitness center is planned for 1993. *15th and M Sts. NW, 20005, tel. 202/862–1600 or 800/424–8577. 318 rooms, 35 suites. Facilities: 24-hr room service, 2 restaurants, bar, access to health club with pool, valet parking. AE, DC, MC, V.*

**Mayflower, A Stouffer Hotel.** The Mayflower was opened in 1925 for Calvin Coolidge's inauguration and continues to be a central part of Washington life. The recently renovated ornate lobby gleams with gilded trim and electrified candelabra. At press time, renovation of all the hotel's rooms was scheduled for completion by mid-1992. New decor includes custom-designed furniture, warmly colored fabrics, full marble bathrooms, and indirect lighting. Seventy-four suites have the original but nonworking fireplaces. A Japanese-style breakfast is offered, and afternoon tea is popular. The Mayflower is steps from the K Street business corridor, the White House, and Dupont Circle. *1127 Connecticut Ave. NW, 20036, tel. 202/347–3000 or 800/468–3571. 641 rooms, 83 suites. Facilities: 24-hr room service; 2 restaurants; bar; fitness center with stationary bicycles, stair climb-*

*ers, exercise machines, sauna; shops; access to National Capital YMCA; parking at nearby garage. AE, DC, MC, V.*

**Ramada Renaissance Hotel–Techworld.** This 15-story hotel opened in 1989 as part of Washington's World Technology Trade Center, just across from the Washington Convention Center. A completely equipped convention hotel, even including a "secure" auditorium for top-secret meetings, the Ramada Renaissance welcomes both business and pleasure travelers. The hotel's spacious rooms are decorated in teal and cinnamon, with mahogany furniture and floral upholstery. The Renaissance Club Tower, a hotel within a hotel served by private elevators and a full-time concierge, pampers business travelers. The lobby's Chinese rock garden and fountain remind guests of their proximity to Washington's Chinatown, and the Techworld complex brings more than 50 shops, including a bank, florist, car-rental agency, and travel agency, close to the hotel. *999 9th St. NW, 20001, tel. 202/898–9000 or 800/228–9898. 739 rooms, 61 suites. Facilities: 24-hr room service; 2 restaurants; bar; valet parking; health club with indoor pool, sauna, steam room, whirlpool, weights, aerobics studio. AE, DC, MC, V.*

**Sheraton Carlton Hotel.** Entering the Sheraton Carlton is like stepping into an updated Italian Renaissance mansion: Gilt, carved wood, stone, plaster, and 19th-century details abound. This hotel is in a bustling business sector, yet the rooms are quiet and service is cordial and dignified. Built in 1926, the hotel underwent a $20 million face-lift which began in 1988, in the course of which all rooms were completely refurbished and renovated. The rooms are decorated in pastel colors and are furnished with antiques and reproductions. *923 16th St. NW, 20006, tel. 202/638–2626 or 800/325–3535. 184 rooms, 13 suites. Facilities: 24-hr room service, personal safes in rooms, 3 telephones and 2 telephone lines in each room, restaurant, bar, exercise room, exercise equipment delivered to room, valet parking. AE, DC, MC, V.*

★ **The Willard Inter-Continental.** "This hotel, in fact, may be much more justly called the center of Washington and the Union than either the Capitol, the White House, or the State Department," Nathaniel Hawthorne wrote while covering the Civil War. Indeed, the Willard, whose present building dates from 1901, welcomed every American president from Franklin Pierce in 1853 to Dwight Eisenhower in the 1950s. But the huge building fell on hard times and closed in 1968. When renovation began in 1984, grass was growing in the rooms and a tree had sprouted in one of the restaurants. The new Willard is a faithful renovation, presenting an opulent, beaux-arts feast to the eye. Rooms are furnished with mahogany Queen Anne reproductions; all have a minibar. The sixth floor, which was designed with the help of the Secret Service and the State Department, has lodged 20 heads of state. One of the restaurants here, the Willard Room, has won nationwide acclaim. *1401 Pennsylvania Ave. NW, 20004, tel. 202/628–9100 or 800/327–0200. 365 rooms, including 37 suites and 8 rooms designed for the handicapped. Facilities: 24-hr room service, 3 restaurants, 2 bars, valet parking. AE, DC, MC, V.*

**Expensive** **Henley Park Hotel.** Constructed as an apartment build-
★ ing in 1918 and converted to a small hotel in 1983, the Henley Park offers a bit of Britain in the still dodgy neighborhood near the Washington Convention Center. Though the architecture is Tudor-style, the decor is Edwardian; a cozy sitting room with working fireplace could well have been transplanted from an English country house. Afternoon tea here is renowned. Guest rooms are warmly furnished with chintz and Oriental porcelain lamps. The hotel is in a quiet neighborhood that's a short ride on public transportation to the major sites. It's best to take a cab if you're returning after dark. *926 Massachusetts Ave. NW, 20001, tel. 202/638–5200 or 800/222–8474. 79 rooms, 17 suites. Facilities: 24-hr room service, restaurant, bar, access to health club, valet parking. AE, DC, MC, V.*

**Washington Vista Hotel.** This 14-story member of the Hilton International family is located in one of downtown's still-developing areas and is a few blocks from the White House, the Washington Convention Center, and the K Street business corridor. Designed to look like an urban town square, the Vista features a garden-courtyard lobby that is flooded by light from a 130-foot window facing M Street. Guest rooms and restaurants are located in the surrounding towerlike structures. Opened in 1983, the hotel has hosted Elizabeth Taylor, Kirk Douglas, and countless business travelers from the United States and abroad; it gained undeserved notoriety as the site of then-Mayor Marion Barry's arrest in 1990. Rooms are contemporary in design and decorated in earth tones, burgundy, and green. The Presidential Suite and six other suites were designed by Hubert de Givenchy; these have whirlpools, French-silk and cotton-blend wall coverings, and original artwork from

France. *1400 M St. NW, 20005, tel. 202/429–1700 or 800/ 847–8232. 400 rooms, including 14 suites. Facilities: 24-hr room service, 2 restaurants, 2 bars, health club with sauna, multilingual staff, baby-sitting service, valet parking. AE, DC, MC, V.*

**Moderate** **Holiday Inn Governor's House.** This hotel, often confused with the Central Holiday Inn down the road, is closer to the White House and Dupont Circle. All guest rooms were refurbished in the spring of 1990. The staff is friendly. Herb's Restaurant draws a lively professional and arty crowd. *1615 Rhode Island Ave. NW, 20036, tel. 202/296–2100 or 800/821–4367. 152 rooms, including 9 suites; 36 rooms have kitchenettes. Facilities: room service 7 AM–midnight, restaurant, bar, outdoor pool, access to health club, parking. AE, DC, MC, V.*

**Hotel Anthony.** This small hotel with courteous staff offers the basics in the midst of the K and L streets business district, close to the White House. Some rooms have a full kitchen, some a wet bar; king, queen, or extra-long double beds are available. The Royal Frontier restaurant serves Indian fare. *1823 L St. NW, 20036, tel. 202/223–4320 or 800/424–2970. 99 rooms. Facilities: room service 7 AM–10 PM, restaurant, access to health club, parking. AE, DC, MC, V.*

**Hotel Washington.** Since its opening in 1918, this hostelry has been known as the hotel with a view. Washingtonians bring visitors to the outdoor rooftop bar for cocktails and a view of the White House grounds and the Washington Monument. The oldest continuously operating hostelry in the city and now a national landmark, the Hotel Washington sprang from the drawing boards of John Carrere and Thomas Hastings, who designed the New York Public Library. Renovated in 1987, the hotel has retained its Edwardian character. The guest rooms, some of which look directly onto the White House grounds, are furnished with antique reproductions; the windows are festooned with swags, heavy drapes, and lace underdrapes. Antique beiges predominate. Suite 506 is where Elvis Presley stayed on his trips to DC. *515 15th St. NW, 20004, tel. 202/638–5900. 344 rooms and 17 suites. Facilities: room service 7 AM–11 PM, restaurant, outdoor café, lounge, fitness center. AE, DC, MC, V.*

★ **Morrison-Clark Inn Hotel.** Victorian with an airy, modern twist, this unusual historic inn was created by merging two 1864 town houses. Appended to one of the houses is a 1917 Chinese Chippendale porch; Oriental touches echo throughout the public rooms, which also boast marble fireplaces and 14-foot–high mirrors with original gilding. Antique-filled rooms—some with bay windows, fireplaces, or access to a porch—have different personalities; one called the "deer and bunny room" because of its decorative trim, harbors a bedspread once owned by the mistress of a fin-de-siècle mayor of New York. A new addition contains 42 rooms in the neoclassical style. Country rooms are plainly furnished with pine, wicker, and rattan. *Washington Post* food critic Phyllis Richman called the restaurant, which features Southern fare, history in the making. A complimentary Continental breakfast is served. Take a cab to the hotel after dark. *Massachusetts Ave. and 11th St. NW, 20001, tel. 202/898–1200 or 800/332–7898. 40 rooms, 14 suites. Facilities: room service during meal periods, restaurant, valet parking. AE, DC, MC, V.*

**Inexpensive**  **Holiday Inn Central.** After an eight-month renovation, this Holiday Inn overlooking Scott Circle reopened in June 1991 with a fresh approach to elegance on a budget. The rooms, a mix of parlor suites and deluxe rooms, are generally spacious. Teal predominates in the bright, attractive lobby, which hosts a bar and the Avenue Café and Lounge. The rooftop pool is open in summer. The McPherson Square Metro is four blocks away, although a cab is advised at night. *1501 Rhode Island Ave. NW, 20005, tel. 202/483–2000 or 800/465–4329. 183 rooms, 30 suites. Facilities: room service, restaurant, bar, exercise room, game room, rooftop pool, laundry, valet, gift shop, underground parking. AE, DC, MC, V.*

**Washington International AYH-Hostel.** This newly renovated hostel offers clean dormitory rooms with 250 bunk beds and a kitchen, laundry room, and living room. Single men and women are in separate rooms; families are given their own room if the hostel is not full. Although blankets and pillows are provided, you must rent sheets for a nominal charge ($2 in 1992) or bring your own. The hostel also sponsors tours, movies, and other programs. Registration is from 7 AM until 2 AM, but exercise caution in this downtown neighborhood if you arrive here at night. The price for American Youth Hostels members is $14 ($17 for nonmembers); the maximum stay is six days, with extensions at the manager's discretion. *1009 11th St. NW, 20001, tel. 202/737–2333. 250 beds. Facilities: kitchen, laundry, travel store, lockers/baggage storage. MC, V.*

## Dupont Circle

**Very Expensive** **The Ritz-Carlton.** One of the nicest things to do at the
★ Ritz on a winter day (aside from stay there) is to have a
drink or afternoon tea in front of the fire in the warm,
woody Fairfax Bar. Exclusive and intimate, the hotel
has an English hunt-club theme. European furnishings
abound and an extensive collection of 18th- and 19th-
century English art, heavy on horses and dogs, graces
the walls. This is the home of the pricey Jockey Club restaurant, where crowned heads of Washington like to
have lunch (it was one of Nancy Reagan's favorite
spots). Lee Iacocca, Carol Burnett, and Eddie Murphy
have stayed here. *2100 Massachusetts Ave. NW, 20008,
tel. 202/293–2100 or 800/241–3333. 207 rooms, 23 suites.
Facilities: 24-hr room service, restaurant, access to
health club. AE, DC, MC, V.*

**Expensive** **Embassy Row Hotel.** Located near Dupont Circle in a
neighborhood of grand houses now mostly used as embassies, museums, and galleries, this hotel is equally
convenient for business and vacation trips to Washington. The spacious rooms are decorated in neutral colors
and light woods with accents of rich crimson and forest
green. The bar is perhaps the coziest in Washington,
and the cooking of chef Jim Papovich at Lucie, the hotel's elegant restaurant, has made it a favorite of locals
and tourists alike. The roof deck and pool offer a fine
view of the city. *2015 Massachusetts Ave. NW, 20036,
tel. 202/265–1600 or 800/424–2400. 168 rooms, 28 suites.
Facilities: 24-hr room service, restaurant, bar, rooftop
pool, access to health club, valet parking. AE, DC, MC,
V.*

**Omni Georgetown.** Although this hotel is not actually in
Georgetown, it's close enough, in a convenient location
on P Street near Dupont Circle. Its most striking feature is the size of the guest rooms, among the largest of
any hotel in the city. Each room has a king- or two
queen-size beds, a sofa and chairs, a large writing desk,
a minibar, three telephones, and bathrooms equipped
with hair dryer. The second-floor outdoor swimming
pool, open only in summer, has a lovely setting—a brick
courtyard enclosed by the walls of the hotel and the
backs of a row of century-old town houses to the east.
The Omni's Rock Creek Café, several steps down from
busy P Street, attracts hip Dupont Circle residents as
well as hotel guests. *2121 P St. NW, 20037, tel. 202/293–
3100 or 800/843–6664. 223 rooms, 71 suites. Facilities:
room service 6:30 AM–11 PM, restaurant, bar, outdoor*

pool, exercise room, sauna, business center, valet parking. *AE, DC, MC, V.*

**Pullman Highland Hotel.** After having undergone a $6 million renovation, the 1906 Highland Hotel is now being managed by the French Pullman hotel group, their first venture in the United States. The hotel is small, 145 rooms, and the management is striving for the ambience of a small European luxury hotel. Decorated in warm peach tones with traditional furniture, the rooms are among the largest in any Washington hotel. All rooms have separate work spaces and three telephones. The Trocadero Café, an upscale American bistro presided over by chef Philipe Thelier, serves breakfast, lunch, and dinner; Sunday brunch is popular with locals. A fully equipped business center with translation service is available and conference facilities accommodate up to 150 people. *1914 Connecticut Ave. NW, tel. 202/797–2000 or 800/424–2464. 108 rooms, 37 suites. Facilities: 24-hr room service, restaurant, bar, multilingual concierge, laundry and dry cleaning, massage, hair styling, access to health club and pool, valet parking. AE, DC, MC, V.*

★ **The Washington Hilton and Towers.** One of the city's busiest convention hotels, this 25-year-old establishment is as much an event as a place to stay. At any moment, you could run into a leading actor, a cabinet official, six busloads of teenagers from Utah, 500 visiting heart surgeons, or Supreme Court Justice Sandra Day O'Connor, who is among the notables who have played tennis here. The light-filled, pastel-colored guest rooms have marble bathrooms. In back of the hotel is a miniresort with a café. A remodeled health club was expected to be completed in the fall of 1992; ask if it is open when you book. The hotel is a short walk from the shops and restaurants of Dupont Circle, Embassy Row, the National Zoo, and the Adams-Morgan neighborhood. *1919 Connecticut Ave. NW, 20009, tel. 202/483–3000 or 800/445–8667. 1,062 rooms, 88 suites. Facilities: 24-hr room service, 3 restaurants (1 seasonal), 2 bars, 3 lighted tennis courts, outdoor pool, whirlpool, health club (due to reopen in fall 1992), pro shop, flower shop. AE, DC, MC, V.*

**Inexpensive**  **Hotel Tabard Inn.** Three Victorian town houses were linked more than 70 years ago to form an inn, and the establishment is still welcoming guests. Named after the hostelry of Chaucer's *Canterbury Tales*, the hotel is furnished throughout with broken-in Victorian and American Empire antiques. Dim lighting and a genteel shabbiness strike some as off-putting, others as charming. Rooms have phone but no TV, and service can be uneven. There is no room service, but the Tabard Inn Restaurant serves breakfast, lunch, and dinner. Located on a quiet street, the hotel is a quick walk to Dupont Circle and the K Street business district. Reserve at least two weeks in advance, and check room rates when you call, as some rooms are in the Moderate price range. *1739 N St. NW, 20036, tel. 202/785–1277. 40 rooms, 25 with private bath. Facilities: restaurant. MC, V.*

★ **Quality Hotel Central.** A Holiday Inn until 1988, this high-rise just up the street from Dupont Circle is one of the city's best values for travelers on a budget. Travelers who can't find rooms at the Washington Hilton stay here, as well as families and businesspeople. Rooms are clean, quiet, and decorated with light colors and blond wood. Rooms on the western and southern sides have good views. *1900 Connecticut Ave. NW, 20009, tel. 202/ 332–9300 or 800/842–4211. 149 rooms. Facilities: room service 7 AM–9:30 PM, restaurant, outdoor pool, access to health club, free parking. AE, DC, MC, V.*

## Georgetown

**Very Expensive** **Four Seasons Hotel.** A polished staff is at your service
★ the moment you approach the doors of this contemporary hotel conveniently situated between Georgetown and Foggy Bottom. The Four Seasons is a gathering place for Washington's elite. Rooms, all of which have a minibar, are traditionally furnished in light colors. The quieter rooms face the courtyard; others have a view of the C & O Canal. The restaurant, Aux Beaux Champs, is highly esteemed by locals. Afternoon tea is served in the Garden Terrace Lounge. The Four Seasons is also home to the private nightclub Desiree, which is open to hotel guests, and perhaps the poshest health club of any hotel in America. Guests may choose between watching movies on a VCR or listening to French lessons on a Walkman as they burn calories on their exercise bikes. *2800 Pennsylvania Ave., NW, 20007, tel. 202/342–0444 or 800/332–3442. 162 rooms, 40 suites. Facilities: 24-hr room service, 2 restaurants, bar, nightclub, health club with pool, multilingual staff, valet parking. AE, DC, MC, V.*

**Expensive** **Georgetown Inn.** With an atmosphere like a gentleman's sporting club of 80 years ago, the inn re-creates the intimacy and quiet of a small European hotel. The architecture is redbrick and 18th century in flavor, appropriate to the hotel's setting. Recent renovation has brought a fresh look to interiors. The Georgetown Bar & Grill, where everyone from shorts-clad tourists to business-people can feel comfortable, has been brightened. Traditionally furnished rooms, in teal and mauve color schemes, are un-hotellike, with attractive wood furniture and gold-framed paintings. All rooms have two telephones and terrycloth robes. A hearty European-style breakfast with meats and cheeses is included in the room rate. *1310 Wisconsin Ave. NW, 20007, tel. 202/ 333–8900 or 800/424–2979. 85 rooms, 10 suites. Facilities: room service 6:30 AM–11 PM, restaurant, bar, access to exercise classes, valet parking. AE, DC, MC, V.*

**Latham Hotel.** A small, colonial-style hotel in the midst of one of the city's liveliest neighborhoods, the former Georgetown Marbury recently changed management along with its name. Extensive renovation has banished the underground rooms and dark hallways. The remaining rooms have a sleek, updated look that contrasts with the redbrick, neocolonial exterior. Some rooms have minibars inside European-style armoires, while others have been remodeled for disabled travelers. Nine carriage suites offer two-level accommodations on the M Street side (courtyard views overlook the C & O Canal). The hotel is popular with Europeans, sports figures, and devotees of Georgetown. At press time, the restaurant and lounge were still being redecorated, although both remain open for breakfast; they should be fully operating by the time you read this. *3000 M St. NW, 20007, tel. 202/726–5000 or 800/447–9559. 134 rooms, 9 suites. Facilities: room service 6:30 AM–11 PM, restaurant, bar, seasonal outdoor pool, access to health club, valet parking. AE, DC, MC, V.*

**Moderate** **Georgetown Dutch Inn.** Tucked away on a side street in Georgetown, this modest 25-year-old hotel has a homey ambience and a few clients who stay for months at a time. The small lobby is decorated with 18th-century touches; rooms have family-room-style furnishings. All have a sofabed in the living room and a walk-in kitchen. Some bedrooms lack windows. Nine suites are built on two levels, with the bedrooms upstairs. Continental breakfast is complimentary and served in the lobby. *1075 Thomas Jefferson St. NW, 20007, tel. 202/337– 0900. Facilities: room service noon–11 PM, restaurant, access to health club, free parking. AE, DC, MC, V.*

## Southwest

**Expensive**  **Loew's L'Enfant Plaza.** Loew's is an oasis of velvet and chintz in L'Enfant Plaza, a concrete, fortress-like collection of office buildings with underground shops. Travelers with government business stay here, too, in close proximity to several agency headquarters and just down the street from Capitol Hill. Each room has a fully stocked liquor cabinet and a refrigerator. A $17 million refurbishing and remodeling was completed in 1990. Service is friendly, and Cafe Pierre serves an international menu at lunch and dinner. *480 L'Enfant Plaza SW, 20024, tel. 202/484-1000 or 800/223-0888. 374 rooms, including 22 suites. Facilities: room service 6 AM–midnight, VCRs, 3 phones with 2 lines, TV and radio in bathrooms, 3 restaurants, 2 bars, year-round rooftop pool, health club, parking. AE, DC, MC, V.*

## Northwest/Upper Connecticut Avenue

**Very Expensive**
★  **Omni Shoreham Hotel.** You're in good company when you check in at this grand, 1930s Art Deco–Renaissance hotel. The Beatles stayed here on their first U.S. tour, and John Kennedy courted Jackie in the Blue Room cabaret, where Judy Garland, Marlene Dietrich, and Maurice Chevalier once appeared (it's now a meeting room). Resembling an old-time resort, this hotel overlooks Rock Creek Park and its jogging and bike paths, and is close to the Adams-Morgan neighborhood, Dupont Circle, and the National Zoo. In back is the pool, where you can look out to a sweeping lawn and woods beyond. The rooms are large and light-filled. Some have fireplaces; half overlook the park. Comedienne Joan Cushing frequently holds forth in the Marquee Lounge, which offers weekend matinee cabaret for children. The loyal staff takes your stay personally. *2500 Calvert St. NW, 20008, tel. 202/234-0700 or 800/834-6664. 720 rooms, 50 suites. Facilities: room service 6 AM–11 PM, restaurant, bar, snack counter, cabaret, outdoor pool, 3 lighted tennis courts, shuffleboard court, horseshoe pits, half-size basketball court, fitness center, shops, art gallery, parking. AE, DC, MC, V.*

**Sheraton Washington Hotel.** A veritable city on a hill, this is Washington's largest hotel. It consists of an "old town"—a 1920s redbrick structure that used to be an apartment building—and the modern sprawl of the new, convention-ready, main complex. The 250 rooms and the public areas of the 10-story old section were renovated in 1988; they are furnished traditionally in soft colors and have large closets. Rooms in the 10-year-old section are contemporary, with chrome and glass touches. Most rooms have a good view. The courtyard is graced by a modernistic fountain; the hotel also has an airy atrium and plush, sunken seating-areas galore. Pastry chef Wolfgang Friedrich has a carry-out shop on the premises (calorie-watchers beware). The hotel is close to the National Zoo and just a few yards from the Woodley Park Metro station. *2660 Woodley Rd. NW, 20008, tel. 202/328–2000 or 800/325–3535. 1,381 rooms, 124 suites. Facilities: 24-hr room service, 4 restaurants, bar, health club with Universal weights and stationary bikes, 2 outdoor pools, baby-sitting service, parking. AE, DC, MC, V.*

**Inexpensive** **Days Inn Connecticut Avenue.** An alternative for those who prefer to stay away from the downtown hustle and bustle, this Days Inn is on a wide avenue in a largely residential area. A subway line close by provides quick transportation to the National Zoo (two stops away). The University of the District of Columbia is next door. Rooms have standard hotel furnishings and may be small. A complimentary Continental breakfast is provided in the lower lobby. There are several cafés nearby. *4400 Connecticut Ave. NW, 20008, tel. 202/244–5600. 150 rooms, 5 suites. Facilities: parking; room service from nearby Espresso Café is available. AE, DC, MC, V.*

**Hotel Windsor Park.** Directly across from the Chinese Embassy, in the residential Kalorama neighborhood, the Windsor Park offers small, immaculate rooms, decorated simply with modern furnishings and a blue and rose color scheme. It is close to Dupont Circle, the National Zoo, and major convention hotels. *2116 Kalorama Rd. NW, 20008, tel. 202/483–7700 or 800/247–3064. 39 rooms, 5 suites. AE, DC, MC, V.*

★ **Kalorama Guest House.** Really great-grandma's house in disguise, this inn consists of four turn-of-the-century town houses: three on a quiet street in the Adams-Morgan neighborhood and one in residential Woodley Park. The Kalorama's comfortable atmosphere is created by dark wood on the walls; hand-me-down antique oak furniture; traditional, slightly worn upholstery; brass or antique wooden bedsteads; and calico curtains at the windows. Magazine illustrations, sheet music, and family photos from the 1890s and early 1900s decorate the walls. The coffee pot is always on, the staff is knowledgeable and friendly, and guests have the run of each house, its front parlor, and the areas where complimentary breakfast is served. Rooms range from large to tiny; none has phone or TV. The inn in Adams-Morgan is steps from one of Washington's most interesting neighborhoods. The Woodley Park inn is near the National Zoo and the Metro. The Kalorama is a good value for budget-minded travelers in search of atmosphere. *1854 Mintwood Place NW, 20009, tel. 202/667–6369; 2700 Cathedral Ave. NW 20008, tel. 202/328–0860. 45 rooms (30 with private bath), 5 suites. AE, DC, MC, V.*

★ **Normandy Inn.** A small, European-style hotel on a quiet street in the exclusive embassy area of Connecticut Avenue, the Normandy is near restaurants, the National Zoo, and some of the most expensive residential real estate in Washington. The rooms are standard and functional, but comfortable. A complimentary Continental breakfast is served. In addition, there is a wine and cheese reception for guests every Tuesday evening. *2118 Wyoming Ave. NW, 20008, tel. 202/483–1350 or 800/424–3729. 65 rooms, 10 suites. Facilities: room service 7–10 AM, underground parking. AE, MC, V.*

## West End/Foggy Bottom

**Very Expensive**

★ **ANA Hotel.** A Westin hotel before it was purchased by the Japanese ANA company in 1990, this establishment is a stylish combination of the contemporary and the traditional. Built in 1985 and renovated in 1991, the ANA offers bright, airy, traditionally furnished rooms decorated in greens, blues, and burnished oranges. Each room is supplied with terry-cloth bathrobes and a minibar. About a third of the rooms have a view of the central courtyard. The hotel's informal restaurant, the Bistro, has the flavor of 19th-century Paris and contains an antique mahogany bar. The state-of-the-art health club includes rowing machines, a cross-country ski simulator, treadmills, Nautilus equipment, and a lap pool. *2401 M St. NW, 20037, tel. 202/429–2400 or 800/228–3000. 405 rooms, 10 suites. Facilities: 24-hr room service, 2 restaurants, bar, café, beauty salon, valet parking. AE, DC, MC, V.*

**Grand Hotel.** Probably the least known of Washington's luxury hotels, this hotel occupies its prime corner in the West End with an old-world assurance that has made it a favorite of international visitors. Its rooms, although not enormous, are impressive for their comfort and their anticipation of guests' needs. Decorated in light colors that give an impression of airiness and space, each room has an executive-size desk equipped with a two-line telephone. Each bathroom has floor-to-ceiling marble walls, a sunken tub, separate shower, television speaker, and extension telephone. Eight of the hotel's suites have working wood-burning fireplaces. The staff is extraordinarily well trained, and the emphasis on efficient, friendly, and discreet service is apparent in every department. *2350 M St. NW, 20037, tel. 202/429–0100 or 800/848–0016. 237 rooms, 26 suites. Facilities: 24-hr room service, 3 restaurants, bar, exercise room, outdoor heated pool, valet parking, laundry and dry-cleaning service. AE, DC, MC, V.*

**Park Hyatt.** A notable collection of modern art adorns this West End hotel, built in 1986. The interior of its main level is built of stone and polished marble, and guests walk on carpeting so thick it almost bounces. Bronzes, chinoiserie, and a fortune teller at tea in the recently renovated main-floor lounge are a few of the Old World touches that offset the spareness of the hotel's design. The rooms are a blend of traditional and contemporary elements and contain reproductions of Chinese antiques from Washington museum collections. The staff has a "never say no" policy, and cars left overnight are washed. *1201 24th St. NW, 20037, tel. 202/789–1234 or 800/228–9000. 92 rooms, 132 suites. Facilities: 24-hr room service; restaurant; outdoor café (in season); bar; health club with indoor pool, whirlpool, Nautilus equipment; beauty salon, valet parking. AE, DC, MC, V.*

★ **Watergate Hotel.** The internationally famous Watergate, its distinctive sawtooth design a landmark along the Potomac, completed a $14 million renovation in 1988 and is now offering guests a taste of old-English gentility. Scenic murals and a portrait of Queen Elizabeth contribute to the effect. The rooms here are among the largest in Washington. All have live plants or fresh flowers, many have balconies, and most have striking river views. The Jean-Louis restaurant has one of the few two-star Michelin chefs in the United States. The hotel is accustomed to serving the world's elite, but it also welcomes vacationing families and couples on getaway weekends. Part of the exclusive Watergate apartment and commercial complex, the hotel is next door to the Kennedy Center and a short walk from Georgetown. *2650 Virginia Ave. NW, 20037, tel. 202/965–2300 or 800/424–2736. 77 rooms, 160 suites. Facilities: 24-hr room service; 2 restaurants; bar; health club with weights, stationary bikes, steam room, sauna, indoor pool; complimentary limousine service to Capitol Hill or downtown weekdays, valet parking. AE, DC, MC, V.*

**Expensive** **Embassy Suites.** The hodgepodge of decorative details and cinderblock construction suggest the hanging gardens of Babylon reconstructed in a suburban shopping mall. In the atrium, waterfalls gush, tall palms loom, and plants drip over balconies. Classical columns are mixed with plaster lions and huge Asian temple lights. Ducks swim in the lagoon, to the delight of children and many grown-ups. Businesspeople flock to the hotel during the week, but it is also ideal for families. Each suite, furnished in neo–art deco, has two remote-control TVs, as well as a microwave, coffee-maker, and queen-size sofabed. Complimentary cocktails and cooked-to-order breakfast are served in the atrium. The Italian restaurant, Panevino, has received favorable reviews. Situated in a fairly quiet enclave in the West End, Embassy Suites is within walking distance of Georgetown, the Kennedy Center, and Dupont Circle. *1250 22nd St. NW, 20037, tel. 202/857–3388 or 800/362–2779. 318 suites. Facilities: room service 11–11; restaurant; health club with weight-lifting equipment, treadmills, indoor pool, sauna; parking. AE, DC, MC, V.*

**Guest Quarters.** All of the units in these two all-suite hotels in Foggy Bottom, now under separate management, have a fully equipped walk-in kitchen, minibar, dishwasher, and sofa sleeper. The staff is small and so are the lobbies, but the rooms, decorated in a combination of traditional and contemporary decor, are well-furnished and comfortable. The two-bedroom suites have a table that seats eight, which is good for family dinners as well as business conferences. The New Hampshire Avenue location has an outdoor rooftop pool (a great spot for viewing fireworks on July 4th). Both hotels are close to the Kennedy Center, Georgetown, and George Washington University. *801 New Hampshire Ave. NW, 20037, tel. 202/785–2000 or 800/424–2900; 2500 Pennsylvania Ave. NW, tel. 202/333–8060 or 800/424–2900. Together, 224 suites. Facilities: room service, access to health club, pool (New Hampshire Ave.), library. AE, DC, MC, V.*

**River Inn.** Just entering its second decade, the River Inn is a member of the highly rated Potomac Hotel Group, which also operates the similar St. James and One Washington Circle hotels nearby. This small, all-suite hotel is steps from Georgetown, George Washington University, and the Kennedy Center. On the premises is the highly rated River Inn restaurant. The best views are from the 14 Potomac Suites, each of which has a full walk-in kitchen. The lobby is sleek and contemporary, but the room furnishings are homey and modest. This is a popular spot with parents of George Washington University students. *924 25th St. NW, 20037, tel. 202/337–7600 or 800/424–2741. 127 suites. Facilities: room service 6:30 AM–11 PM, restaurant, use of outdoor pool at 1 Washington Circle and health club at the St. James Hotel. AE, DC, MC, V.*

**Wyndham Bristol Hotel.** This hotel doesn't offer much in the way of views, but the location is excellent: Located midway between the White House and Georgetown, the Wyndham is a favorite place for movie and theater people because the Kennedy Center is just a few blocks away. The rooms here are quiet, although the building is bordered on two sides by major thoroughfares. The hotel looks as if it belongs to someone who collects Chinese porcelain: A whole cabinet-full greets guests on arrival in the small, quiet lobby. The rest of the hotel, created in 1984 from an apartment building, is English in decor; each room has a butler's table. *2430 Pennsylvania Ave. NW, 20037, tel. 202/955–6400, 800/822–4200, or 800/631–4200 in Canada. 218 rooms, 22 suites. Facilities: room service 7:30 AM–10:30 PM, 2 restaurants (with seasonal outdoor café), bar, access to health club, valet parking. AE, DC, MC, V.*

**Inexpensive** **Howard Johnson Kennedy Center.** This eight-story lodge offers HoJo reliability in a location close to the Kennedy Center, the Watergate complex, and Georgetown. Rooms are large and comfortable, and each has a refrigerator. *2601 Virginia Ave. NW, 20037, tel. 202/965–2700 or 800/654–2000. 192 rooms. Facilities: restaurant, rooftop pool, free parking for cars and low-clearance vans. AE, DC, MC, V.*

## Suburban Maryland

**Expensive** **Hyatt Regency Bethesda.** The atrium lobby, with glass elevators and ferns, is reminiscent of other Hyatt Regencies. So are the attentive service and the comfortable—if unremarkable— rooms, decorated in peach or hunter green with modern furnishings and light wood accents. The hotel's sunlit, airy restaurant is a pleasant place for breakfast before setting out on the Metrorail red line to see the sights of downtown Washington, about 15 minutes away. The adjacent Metro plaza has a small ice rink, open in winter, and an indoor food court. *1 Bethesda Metro Center, Bethesda, MD 20814, tel. 301/657–1234 or 800/233–1234. 368 rooms, 13 suites. Facilities: room service, 2 restaurants, bar, exercise room, indoor pool, sauna, valet parking. AE, DC, MC, V.*

**Moderate** **Quality Hotel Silver Spring.** Formerly the Sheraton Inn, this conveniently located hotel is about three blocks from the Silver Spring Metro station and close to the shops and restaurants in downtown Silver Spring, including the glossy new, discount- oriented City Place complex. The lobby, with its small front desk, marble floors, and many places to sit, is comfortable and intimate. A major renovation of all sleeping rooms—in gray and soft pink—and the lobby was completed in 1990. *8727 Colesville Rd., Silver Spring, MD 20910, tel. 301/ 589–5200 or 800/228–5151. 228 rooms, 28 suites. Facilities: room service, 2 restaurants, bar, exercise room with sauna, indoor pool, free parking. AE, DC, MC, V.*

## Suburban Virginia

**Very Expensive** **Morrison House.** The architecture and furnishings of the Morrison House in Old Town Alexandria are so faithful to the style of the Federal period (1790–1820) that it is often thought to be a renovation of a historic building rather than a new building built in 1985. Owner Robert Morrison consulted with experts from the Smithsonian in furnishing the hotel, and the parquet floors, crystal chandeliers and sconces, and period furnishings re-create the atmosphere of a grand American house of 200 years ago. The guest rooms are an elegant blend of early American charm and modern conveniences, including four-poster beds and armoires, but also remote control television sets and Italian marble bathrooms equipped with hair dryer and telephone. The Grill at Morrison House, under the direction of executive chef Charles Hill, serves innovative New American cuisine in a handsome club room atmosphere, with a pianist every day but Sunday accompanying. *116 S. Alfred St., Alexandria, VA 22314, tel. 703/838–8000 or 800/367–0800. 42 rooms, 3 suites. Facilities: 24-hr room service, restaurant, multilingual staff, valet parking. AE, DC, MC, V.*

★ **Ritz-Carlton, Pentagon City.** The Washington area's newest luxury hotel, the Ritz-Carlton, Pentagon City, opened its doors for guests in May of 1990. The 18-story hotel is located in Arlington, just across from the Pentagon, but its location at the Pentagon City Metro stop makes it more convenient to downtown Washington than many closer hotels. The decor of the new hotel looks to the Virginia horse country for its inspiration, and a $2 million collection of art and antiques, mostly from the 18th and 19th centuries, may be seen in the hotel's public spaces. Rooms, many with views of the monuments across the river, are among the most luxurious in Washington; each standard room, decorated in rose or blue, has an overstuffed chair with ottoman, Chippendale-style furniture, and silk bed coverings. Gérard Pangaud, a two-star Michelin chef, presides over the dining room at dinner. To use the hotel's fully equipped fitness center, all you need to bring is your sneakers—a full line of workout clothing, including swimsuits, is provided. *1250 S. Hayes St., Arlington, VA 22202, tel. 703/415–5000 or 800/241–3333. 304 rooms, 40 suites. Facilities: 24-hr room service; concierge; 2 restaurants; lounge; health club with whirlpool, sauna, rowing and cycling machines, complete Universal system; valet parking. AE, DC, MC, V.*

**Expensive**  **Crystal City Marriott.** This business hotel is located close to National Airport and the Pentagon, in a thicket of office and apartment buildings. It's a good bet for families because the Metro yellow line can take you to the sights of the Mall in a matter of minutes. The lobby, with its lush plantings and thick carpets, is more luxurious than the rooms, which, although renovated in 1989 in an attractive seafoam green and mauve color scheme, are plain. The atrium restaurant is light-filled and pleasant. *1999 Jefferson Davies Hwy., Arlington, VA 22202, tel. 703/413–5500 or 800/228–9290. 331 rooms, 9 suites. Facilities: room service; restaurant; 2 bars; business center; health club with pool, free weights, whirlpool, sauna; parking. AE, DC, MC, V.*

**Key Bridge Marriott.** Situated just across the Potomac from Georgetown, the Key Bridge Marriott in Arlington provides a room away from it all. The hotel is a short walk across the Key Bridge to Georgetown and sits near the Rosslyn Metro station, which provides easy access to Washington's major sites. The rooms were redecorated in 1988 in contemporary decor; many of them have a view of Washington, as does the rooftop restaurant. You can swim from the indoor to the outdoor pool via an underwater connection; when it gets cold, the portal is closed, and guests can stay wet in the interior section. Air traffic from Washington National can be noisy at times. *1401 Lee Hwy., Arlington, VA 22209, tel. 703/524–6400 or 800/228–9290. 568 rooms, 20 suites. Facilities: 24-hr room service; 2 restaurants; 2 bars; health club with Universal weights, stationary bikes, indoor-outdoor pool; valet service; beauty salon; shops; parking. AE, DC, MC, V.*

# 8  The Arts and Nightlife

# The Arts

*By John F. Kelly*

Washingtonians no longer balance a chip on their shoulders when it comes time to discuss sophisticated entertainment. In the last 20 years this cultural backwater has been transformed into a cultural capital. The Kennedy Center is a world-class venue, home of Mstislav Rostropovich's National Symphony Orchestra and host to Broadway shows, ballet, modern dance, opera, and more. Several art galleries present highly regarded chamber music series. The service bands from the area's numerous military bases ensure an endless supply of martial music of the John Philip Sousa variety as well as rousing renditions of more contemporary tunes. At the other end of the spectrum, Washington was the birthplace of hardcore, a socially aware form of punk rock music that has influenced young bands throughout the country. Go-go—infectious, rhythmic music that mixes elements of rap, rhythm and blues, and funk—was touted as the next big thing to come out of the capital city but seems to have confined itself largely to Washington.

Friday's *Washington Post* "Weekend" section is the best guide to events for the weekend and the coming week. The *Post*'s daily "Guide to the Lively Arts" also outlines cultural events in the city. The *Washington Times* "Weekend" section comes out on Thursday. The free weekly *City Paper* hits the streets on Thursday and covers the entertainment scene well. You might also consult the "City Lights" section in the monthly *Washingtonian* magazine.

Any search for cultured entertainment should start at the **John F. Kennedy Center for the Performing Arts** (New Hampshire Ave. and Rock Creek Parkway NW). On any given night America's national cultural center may be hosting a symphony orchestra, a troupe of dancers, a Broadway musical, *and* a comedic who-done-it. In other words, America's national cultural center has a little of everything. The Kennedy Center is actually five stages under one roof: the **Concert Hall,** home park of the National Symphony Orchestra; the 2,200-seat **Opera House,** the setting for ballet, modern dance, grand opera, and large-scale musicals; the **Eisenhower Theater,** usually used for drama; the **Terrace Theater,** a Philip Johnson-designed space that showcases chamber groups and experimental works; and the **Theater Lab,** which is home to cabaret-style performances. For information call 202/467–4600 or 800/444–1324.

**Tickets**  Tickets to most events are available by calling or visiting each venue's box office.

**Metro Center TicketPlace** sells half-price, day-of-performance tickets for selected shows; a "menu board" lists available performances. Only cash is accepted for same-day tickets; cash and credit cards may be used for full-price, advance tickets. *15th St. between L and M Sts. NW, tel. 202/TICKETS. Open Tues–Fri. noon–4, Sat. 11–5. Tickets for Sun. and Mon. performances sold on Sat.*

**Protix** (tel. 703/218–6500) takes reservations for events at Wolf Trap and elsewhere in the city. It also has outlets in selected Woodward & Lothrop stores.

**TicketMaster** (tel. 202/432–7328 or 800/551–7328) takes phone charges for events at most venues around the city. You can purchase TicketMaster tickets in person at all Hecht Company department stores. No refunds, exchanges, or cancellations.

## Theater

**Commercial Theaters and Companies**  **Arena Stage** (6th St. and Maine Ave. SW, tel. 202/488–3300). The city's most respected resident company (now in its 42nd season), the Arena was the first theater outside New York to win a Tony award. It presents a wide-ranging season in its three theaters: the theater-in-the-round Arena, the proscenium Kreeger, and the cabaret-style Old Vat Room.

**Ford's Theatre** (511 10th St. NW, tel. 202/347–4833). Looking much the way it did when President Lincoln was shot at a performance of *Our American Cousin*, Ford's is host mainly to musicals, many with family appeal. Dickens's *A Christmas Carol* is presented each winter.

**National Theatre** (1321 E St. NW, tel. 202/628–6161). Destroyed by fire and rebuilt four times, the National Theatre has operated in the same location since 1835. It presents pre- and post-Broadway shows.

**Shakespeare Theatre** (450 7th St. NW, tel. 202/393–2700). Four plays—three by the Bard and another classic from his era—are presented each year by the acclaimed Shakespeare Theatre troupe. In 1992 it moved from its former home in the Folger Library to a new, state-of-the-art, 447-seat space.

**Small Theaters and Companies**  Washington's small theaters and companies long labored in obscurity, spread out over the District, often performing in churches and other less-than-ideal settings. Fans of independent theater have been encouraged recently by the development of what many regard as the District's own off-Broadway: a five-block section of 14th Street NW that in the last few years has become home to almost a half dozen alternative stages. (Note: Take a cab here after dark.) Other fledgling theaters are located near Dupont Circle.

**Gala Hispanic Theatre** (1625 Park Rd. NW, tel. 202/234–7174). This 15-year-old company produces Spanish classics as well as contemporary and modern Latin American plays in both Spanish and English.

**Olney Theatre** (2001 Rte. 108, Olney, MD, tel. 301/924–3400). Musicals, comedies, and summer stock are presented in this converted barn, an hour from downtown in the Maryland countryside.

**Source Theatre** (1835 14th St. NW, tel. 202/462–1073). The 107-seat Source Theatre presents established plays with a sharp satirical edge and modern interpretations of classics. Each July and August Source hosts the Washington Theater Festival, a celebration of new plays, many by local playwrights.

**Studio Theatre** (1333 P St. NW, tel. 202/332–3300). An eclectic season of classic and off-beat plays are presented in this 200-seat theater.

**Washington Stage Guild** (924 G St. NW, tel. 202/529–2084). Founded in 1985 and performing in historic Carroll Hall, Washington Stage Guild tackles the classics—from George Bernard Shaw to Samuel Beckett—as well as more contemporary fare.

**Woolly Mammoth** (1401 Church St. NW, tel. 202/393–3939). Unusual, imaginatively produced shows have earned this company good reviews.

## Music

Orchestra **The National Symphony Orchestra** (tel. 202/416–8100). The season at the Kennedy Center extends from September to June. During the summer, the NSO performs at Wolf Trap and presents concerts on the West Terrace of the Capitol on Memorial Day and Labor Day weekends and on July 4th. One of the cheapest ways to hear—if not necessarily see—Mstislav Rostropovich and the NSO perform in the Kennedy Center Concert Hall is to get a $6.50 "obstructed view" ticket.

Concert Halls **Capital Centre** (1 Harry S Truman Dr., Landover, MD, tel. 301/350–3400 or 202/432–7328). The home stadium for the Washington Capitals hockey and Washington Bullets basketball teams is also the area's top venue for big-name pop, rock, and rap acts. The Cap Centre, as it's known, seats 20,000.

**D.A.R. Constitution Hall** (18th and C Sts. NW, tel. 202/638–2661). Constitution Hall was the home of the National Symphony Orchestra before the Kennedy Center was built. It still hosts visiting performers, from jazz to pop to rap.

**John F. Kennedy Center for the Performing Arts** (New Hampshire Ave. and Rock Creek Parkway NW). (*See above.*)

**George Mason University** (Rte. 123 and Braddock Rd., Fairfax, VA). The GMU campus in suburban Virginia is home to the ambitious Institute of the Arts, a glittering complex that opened in 1990 and hosts a full range of performing arts events, from music to ballet to drama. There is a 1,900-seat concert hall, the 500-seat proscenium Harris Theatre, and the intimate 200-seat Black Box Theatre (tel. 703/993–8888 for Institute events). Also on campus is the 9,500-seat Patriot Center, site of pop acts and sporting events (tel. 703/993–3033 for recorded calendar, 703/993–3000 or 202/432–7328 for ticket information).

**Merriweather Post Pavilion** (tel. 301/982–1800 or 301/596–0660 off-season). An hour north of Washington, in Columbia, Maryland, Merriweather Post is an outdoor pavilion with some covered seating. It plays host in warmer months to big-name pop acts.

**National Gallery of Art** (6th St. and Constitution Ave. NW, tel. 202/842–6941 or 202/737–4215). Free concerts by the National Gallery Orchestra, conducted by George Manos, as well as performances by outside recitalists and ensembles, are held in the venerable West Building's West Garden Court on Sunday evenings from October to June. Most performances highlight classical music, though April's American Music Festival often features jazz. While admission is free, you must pick up a pass—a maximum of two per person—in the West Building's Art Information Room.

**Smithsonian Institution** (tel. 202/357–2700). An amazing assortment of music—both free and ticketed—is presented by the Smithsonian. Some highlights: American jazz, musical theater, and popular standards are performed in the National Museum of American History's Palm Court. In the third-floor Hall of Musical Instruments, musicians periodically perform on historic instruments from the museum's collection. The Smithsonian's Resident Associate Program (tel. 202/357–3030) offers everything from a cappella groups to Cajun zydeco bands, many of which perform in the National

Museum of Natural History's Baird Auditorium. In warm weather performances are held in the courtyard between the National Portrait Gallery and the National Museum of American Art.

**Wolf Trap Farm Park** (1551 Trap Rd., Vienna, VA, tel. 703/255–1860). Just off the Dulles Toll Road, about a half-hour from downtown, Wolf Trap is a national park dedicated to the performing arts. On its grounds is the **Filene Center** (tel. 703/255–1868), an outdoor theater that is the scene of pop, jazz, opera, ballet, and dance performances each June through September. The rest of the year, the intimate, indoor **Barns at Wolf Trap** (tel. 703/938–2404) hosts folk, jazz, rock, chamber music, and other acts. On performance nights, Metro operates a $3 round-trip shuttle bus between the West Falls Church Metro station and the Filene Center. The bus leaves 20 minutes after the show, or no later than 11 PM, whether the show is over or not.

**Choral Music**  **Choral Arts Society** (tel. 202/244–3669). Founded in 1965, this 180-voice choir performs a varied selection of classical pieces at the Kennedy Center from September to April. Three Christmas sing-alongs are scheduled each December.

Choral and church groups frequently perform in the impressive settings of the **Washington Cathedral** (tel. 202/537–6200) and the **National Shrine of the Immaculate Conception** (tel. 202/526–8300).

**Chamber Music**  **Corcoran Gallery of Art** (17th St. and New York Ave. NW, tel. 202/638–3211). Hungary's Takacs String Quartet and the Cleveland Quartet, playing on matched sets of Amati and Stradivarius string instruments owned by the gallery, are among the groups that appear in the Corcoran's Musical Evening Series. Concerts are followed by a reception with the artists.

**Folger Shakespeare Library** (201 East Capitol St. SE, tel. 202/544–7077). Now in its 16th season, the Folger Shakespeare Library's internationally acclaimed resident chamber-music ensemble regularly presents a selection of instrumental and vocal pieces from the medieval, Renaissance, and Baroque periods, during a season that runs from October to May.

**National Academy of Sciences** (2101 Constitution Ave. NW, tel. 202/334–2436). Free performances by such groups as the Juilliard String Quartet and the Beaux Arts Trio are given October through May in the academy's acoustically nearly perfect 670-seat auditorium. In 1993, the academy will also host programs normally held in the Library of Congress Jefferson Building, while that space undergoes renovation.

**Phillips Collection** (1600–1612 21st St. NW, tel. 202/387–2151). The long, panelled music room of gallery founder Duncan Phillips's home is the setting for Sunday afternoon recitals from September through May. Chamber groups from around the world perform; May is devoted to performing artists from the Washington area. Arrive early for the 5 PM concerts.

**Performance Series**

**Armed Forces Concert Series.** From June to August, service bands from all four branches of the military perform nightly, Sunday through Friday evenings, on the East Terrace of the Capitol and at the Sylvan Theater on the Washington Monument grounds. The traditional band concerts include marches, patriotic numbers, and some classical music. The bands often perform at other locations throughout the year. *For information: Air Force, tel. 202/767–5658; Army, tel. 703/696–3718; Navy, tel. 202/433–2525; Marines, tel. 202/433–4011.*

**Carter Barron Amphitheater** (16th St. and Colorado Ave. NW, tel. 202/829–3200 or 202/619–7222 off-season). On Saturday and Sunday nights from mid-June to August this lovely, 4,250-seat outdoor theater in Rock Creek Park plays host to pop, jazz, gospel, and rhythm and blues artists, such as Chick Corea, Nancy Wilson, and Tito Puente.

**District Curators** (tel. 202/783–0360). An independent, nonprofit organization, District Curators presents adventurous contemporary performers from around the world. Past artists have included Laurie Anderson, Philip Glass, the World Saxophone Quartet, and the Japanese dance troupe Sankai Juku.

**Fort Dupont Summer Theater** (Minnesota Ave. and F St. SE, tel. 202/426–7723 or 202/619–7222). The National Park Service presents national and international jazz artists at 8:30 on Friday and Saturday evenings from mid-June to August at this outdoor theater. Past performers at the free concerts have included Wynton Marsalis, Betty Carter, and Ramsey Lewis.

**Sylvan Theater** (Washington Monument grounds, tel. 202/619–7225 or 202/619–7222). Service bands from the four branches of the military perform at this outdoor theater from mid-June to August every evening except Wednesday and Saturday. On Wednesday there's dancing to big-band and swing music.

**Washington Performing Arts Society** (tel. 202/833–9800). An independent nonprofit organization, WPAS books high-quality classical music, ballet, modern

dance, and some drama into halls around the city. Most
of the shows—ranging from the Harlem Boys Choir to
the Vienna Philharmonic—are held at the Kennedy
Center. The **Parade of the Arts** series features shows
with family appeal.

## Opera

**Mount Vernon College** (2100 Foxhall Rd. NW, tel. 202/
625–4655). The college's intimate Hand Chapel is the
setting for rarely produced chamber operas each fall and
spring.
**Opera Theater of Northern Virginia** (tel. 703/549–5039).
The three operas in this company's season are sung in
English and produced at an Arlington, Virginia, community theater. Each December the company presents
a one-act opera especially for young audiences.
**Summer Opera Theater Company** (Hartke Theater,
Catholic University, tel. 202/526–1669). This independent professional company mounts two fully staged productions each July and August.
**Washington Opera** (tel. 202/416–7800 or 800/87–OP-
ERA). Seven operas—presented in their original languages with English supertitles—are performed each
season (November to March) in the Kennedy Center's
Opera House and Eisenhower Theater. Performances
are usually sold out to subscribers, but returned tickets
can be purchased an hour before curtain time. Standing
room tickets go on sale at the Kennedy Center box office
each Saturday at 10 AM for the following week's performances.

## Dance

**Dance Place** (3225 8th St. NE, tel. 202/269–1600). This
studio theater, which presented its first performance in
1980, hosts a wide assortment of modern and ethnic
dance every weekend.
**Joy of Motion** (1643 Connecticut Ave. NW, tel. 202/387–
0911). A dance studio by day, Joy of Motion is the home
of several area troupes, including Michelle Ava and
Company (modern dance), the Dupont Alley Dance
Company (jazz), and TAPestry (you guessed it—tap).
**Mount Vernon College** (2100 Foxhall Rd. NW, tel. 202/
625–4655). An emerging center for dance in Washington, this women's liberal arts college presents eight
dance companies a year—three in the fall, five in the
spring. Past participants in the dance series have in-

cluded the troupes of Robert Small, Nancy Meehan, and Gus Solomons, Jr.

**Smithsonian Resident Associate Program** (tel. 202/357–3030). National and international dance groups often perform at various Smithsonian museums.

**The Washington Ballet** (tel. 202/362–3606). In October, February, and May this company presents classical and contemporary ballets from the works of such choreographers as George Balanchine, Marius Pepita and Choo-San Goh, mainly at the Kennedy Center. Each December, the Washington Ballet presents *The Nutcracker*.

## Film

Washington has a wealth of first-run movie theaters, in the city and in nearby suburbs:

**The AMC Union Station 9** (Union Station, tel. 202/842–3757) on Capitol Hill features nine screens and validated, three-hour parking at an adjacent parking lot. Closer to downtown are **Cineplex Odeon's West End 1–4** (23rd and L Sts. NW, tel. 202/293–3152) and **West End 5, 6, 7** (23rd and M Sts. NW, tel. 202/452–9020). The Art Deco **Cineplex Odeon Uptown** (3426 Connecticut Ave. NW, tel. 202/966–5400) boasts a single huge screen, Dolby sound, and a wonderful balcony. Other first-run movie theaters are clustered near Dupont Circle, in Georgetown, and around upper Wisconsin Avenue.

If you find movie-theater seats a little too confining or the choice of soft drinks a little too soft, there are two locations in the suburbs where waiters and waitresses move through the audience taking orders for pizza, hot dogs, nachos, and beer and delivering it to your table: the **Bethesda Cinema 'N' Drafthouse** (7719 Wisconsin Ave., Bethesda, MD, tel. 301/656–3337) and the **Arlington Cinema 'N' Drafthouse** (2903 Columbia Pike, Arlington, VA, tel. 703/486–2345).

Several Washington theaters screen revivals and foreign, independent, and avant-garde films.

**The American Film Institute** (Kennedy Center, tel. 202/785–4600, 4601). More than 700 different movies—including contemporary and classic foreign and American films—are shown each year at the American Film Institute's theater in the Kennedy Center. Filmmakers and actors are often present to discuss their work.

**The Biograph** (2819 M St. NW, tel. 202/333–2696). Washington's home for alternative cinema, the Biograph presents a mixture of first-run and repertory domestic and foreign films that have in common "their position out of the mainstream."

**Filmfest DC,** an annual citywide festival of international cinema, takes place in late April and early May. For information, write Box 21396, Washington, DC 20009 or call 202/727–2396.

**The Hirshhorn Museum** (tel. 202/357–2700), **National Gallery of Art** (tel. 202/737–4215), and the **National Archives** (tel. 202/501–5000). These museums on the Mall often show little-known, unusual, or experimental films.

**The Key** (1222 Wisconsin Ave. NW, tel. 202/333–5100). This four-screen theater specializes in foreign films and presents an annual animation festival.

**Mary Pickford Theater** (Jefferson Bldg. of the Library of Congress, 1st St. and Independence Ave. SE, tel. 202/707–5458 or 202/707–5677). This 64-seat theater shows classic films for free.

**National Geographic Society** (17th and M Sts. NW, tel. 202/857–7588). Educational films with a scientific, geographic, or anthropological focus are shown here weekly.

# Nightlife

Washington's nightlife scene has contracted a bit in the last few years; locals have seen some favorite spots close their doors for good. But the city still boasts a range of choices. Its bars and nightclubs cater to a wide spectrum of customers, from proper political appointees to blue-collar regulars in from the suburbs. Many night spots are clustered in a few key areas, simplifying things for the visitor who enjoys bar-hopping. Georgetown, in northwest Washington, leads the pack with an explosion of bars, nightclubs, and restaurants on M Street east and west of Wisconsin Avenue and on Wisconsin Avenue north of M Street. A half dozen Capitol Hill bars can be found on a stretch of Pennsylvania Avenue between 2nd and 4th streets SE. There is another high-density nightlife area around the intersection of 19th and M streets NW. Located near the city's lawyer- and lobbyist-filled downtown, this neighborhood is especially active during happy hour.

As for music, Washington audiences are catholic in their tastes and so are Washington's music promoters. That means you can hear funk at a rock club, blues at a jazz club, and calypso at a reggae club. And it means big-name acts often perform at venues that also book Broadway shows and other nonmusical forms of entertainment. The music listings below are an attempt to impose order on this chaos. Your best bet is to consult Friday's "Weekend" section in the *Washington Post* and the free, weekly *City Paper*. It's also a good idea to call clubs ahead of time to find out who's on that night and what sort of music will be played.

## Bars and Lounges

**Brickskeller.** A beer lover's mecca, this is the place to go when you want something more exotic than a Bud Lite. More than 500 brands of beer are for sale—from Central American lagers to U.S. microbrewed ales. Bartenders oblige beer-can collectors by opening the containers from the bottom. *1523 22nd St. NW, tel. 202/293–1885. Open Mon.–Thurs. 11:30 AM–2 AM, Fri. 11:30 AM–3 AM, Sat. 6 PM–3 AM, Sun. 6 PM–2 AM. AE, D, DC, MC, V.*

**Champions.** Walls covered with jerseys, pucks, bats, and balls, and the evening's big game on the big-screen TV, leave little doubt that this popular Georgetown establishment is a sports lover's bar. Ballpark-style food enhances the mood. *1206 Wisconsin Ave. NW, tel. 202/ 965–4005. Open Mon.–Thurs. 5 PM–2 AM, Fri. 5 PM–3 AM, Sat. 11:30 AM–3 AM, Sun. 11:30 AM–2 AM. One-drink minimum Fri. and Sat. after 10 PM. AE, DC, MC, V.*

**The Dubliner.** Snug, panelled rooms; thick, tasty Guinness; and nightly live entertainment are the main attractions at Washington's premier Irish pub. You don't have to be Irish to enjoy it, as scores of staffers from nearby Capitol Hill attest. *520 North Capitol St. NW, tel. 202/737–3773. Open Mon.–Thurs. 11 AM–2 AM, Fri. 11 AM–3 AM, Sat. 7 AM–3 AM, Sun. 7 AM–2 AM. AE, DC, MC, V.*

**Durty Nelly's.** Outside, it's an unassuming restaurant/ bar crowded by the office blocks taking over downtown Bethesda in suburban Maryland. Inside is a massive horseshoe-shape bar around which weekend-greeting office workers and victory-celebrating softball players swarm. Most nights bands play rock and roll, old and new. *4714 Montgomery La., Bethesda, MD, tel. 301/ 652–1444. Open Mon.–Thurs. 11:30 AM–1 AM, Fri. 11:30 AM–2 AM, Sat. 7 PM–2 AM, Sun. 7 PM–1 AM. AE, D, MC, V.*

**15 Mins.** A college-age clientele ventures downtown to enjoy the funky decorations, tiny dance floor, progressive music, and black lights that bathe this room in an eerie, purplish glow. Roots bands churning out authentic blues play occasionally in, of all places, an adjacent cafeteria. The name? It's how much fame Andy Warhol said we'd all have in the future. *1030 15th St. NW, tel. 202/408–1855. Open Mon.–Thurs. 5 PM–2 AM, Fri. 5 PM–3 AM, Sat. 9 PM–3 AM, Sun. 5 PM–2 AM. Cover charged after 9 PM. AE.*

**The Fishmarket.** There's something different in just about every room of this multi-level, multi-room space in Old Town Alexandria, from piano bar crooner to ragtime piano shouter to guitar strummer. The operative word here is boisterous. If you like your beer in massive quantities, be sure to order the largest size: It comes in a glass big enough to wash your face in. *105 King St., Alexandria, VA, tel. 703/836–5676. Open Mon.–Sat. 11:15 AM–2 AM, Sun. 11:15–midnight. AE, MC, V.*

**Food for Thought.** Lots of Birkenstock sandals, natural fibers, and activist conversation give this Dupont Circle lounge and restaurant (vegetarian and organic meat) a '60s coffeehouse feel. Nightly folk music completes the picture. *1738 Connecticut Ave. NW, tel. 202/797–1095. Open Mon.–Thurs. 11:30 AM–11:30 PM, Fri. 11:30 AM–12:30 AM, Sat. noon–12:30 AM, Sun. 5 PM–11:30 PM. AE, MC, V.*

**Gallagher's Pub.** This mildly Irish bar is a restful haven for those eager to avoid the crush of Georgetown. Some of Washington's most heartfelt acoustic music can be heard at the Sunday night open mike. *3319 Connecticut Ave. NW, tel. 202/ 686–9189. Open Mon.–Thurs. 5 PM–2 AM, Fri. 5 PM–3 AM, Sat. noon–3 AM, Sun. noon–2 AM. AE, MC, V.*

**Hard Rock Cafe.** There's something sweetly ironic about its location in the shadow of the J. Edgar Hoover FBI Building. One assumes Hoover would not have been amused by the raucous atmosphere, pumping rock music, and grand piano–shaped bar (he may have liked the barbecue sandwiches, though). Ask your waiter for the guide that shows where all the Hard Rock memorabilia—from Chuck Berry's guitar to a platinum record awarded to the Village People—is hung. *999 E St. NW, tel. 202/737–7625. Open Sun.–Thurs. 11 AM–midnight, Fri.–Sat. 11 AM–1 AM. AE, MC, V.*

**Hawk 'n' Dove.** A friendly neighborhood bar in a neighborhood coincidentally dominated by the Capitol building. Regulars include political types, lobbyists, and well-behaved Marines (from a nearby barracks). *329 Pennsylvania Ave. SE, tel. 202/543–3300. Open Sun.–Thurs. 10 AM–2 AM, Fri.–Sat. 10 AM–3 AM. AE, DC, MC, V.*

**Sign of the Whale.** The best hamburger in town is available at the bar in this well-known post-Preppie/neo-Yuppie haven. *1825 M St. NW, tel. 202/785–1110. Open daily 11:30 AM–2 AM. AE, D, DC, MC, V.*

**Yacht Club.** Enormously popular with well-dressed, middle-age singles, this suburban Maryland lounge was one of the first in the area to introduce billiard tables, a notion several other local nightspots have been quick to adopt. *8111 Woodmont Ave., Bethesda, MD, tel. 301/654–2396. Jacket and tie required. Open Mon.–Thurs. 5 PM–1 AM, Fri. 5 PM–2 AM, Sat. 8 PM–2 AM. AE, DC, MC, V.*

## Cabarets

**Chelsea's.** The musical political satire of the Capitol Steps, a group of current and former Hill staffers, is presented on Friday and Saturday. (The troupe's name comes from a purported trysting spot of politician John Jenrette and wife Rita.) *1055 Thomas Jefferson St. NW, tel. 202/298–8222 (Chelsea's) or 703/683–8330 (the Capitol Steps). Shows Fri. and Sat. at 7:30 PM. Ticket charge. Reservations required. AE, MC, V.*

**Gross National Product.** The titles of a few past shows should give you an idea of what this irreverent comedy troupe is up to: "Bush Capades: An Administration on Thin Ice," "Man Without a Contra," and "The Phantom of the White House." GNP, which the *Washington Post* has compared to the original cast of "Saturday Night Live," performs at the Bayou in Georgetown. *3135 K St. NW, tel. 202/333–2897 (Bayou) or 202/783–7212 (GNP). Show Sat. 7:30 PM. Ticket charge. Reservations suggested. MC, V.*

**Marquee Cabaret.** Funnylady Joan Cushing assumes the character of quintessential Washington insider "Mrs. Foggy-bottom" and, with a small cast, pokes fun at well-known political figures in satirical skit and song. *Omni-Shoreham Hotel, 2500 Calvert St. NW, tel. 202/745–1023. Shows Thurs. 8 PM, Fri.–Sat. 9 PM. Ticket charge. Reservations required. AE, D, DC, MC, V.*

## Comedy Clubs

In the past few years the number of comedy groups in Washington that welcome, indeed rely on, the zany suggestions of audience members has mushroomed. These improvisation groups pop up at various venues, performing in the laughs-at-any-cost style of Chicago's Second City troupe. They aren't all successful, though, and many burst on the scene, then burst themselves. Among those with some stability are **ComedySportz** (tel. 703/471–5212) and **Skits-O-Phrenic** (tel. 202/829–0529).

**Comedy Cafe.** Local and national comics appear at this club in the heart of downtown. Thursday is open-mike night; on Friday and Saturday, the pros take the stage. *1520 K St. NW, tel. 202/638–JOKE. Shows Thurs. 8:30 PM, Fri. 8:30 and 10:30 PM, Sat. 7, 9, and 11 PM. Cover charge. AE, D, DC, MC, V.*

**Comedy Connection.** This suburban Maryland club hosts comics six nights a week. Top black comedians, such as Franklin Ajaye and Jimmie Walker, call the Connection home when in town. *6000 Greenbelt Rd., Greenbelt, MD, tel. 301/345–0563. Shows Wed.–Thurs. 9 PM, Fri.–Sat. 8 and 10:30 PM, Sun. 9 PM. Cover charge. Reservations advised. AE, DC, MC, V.*

**Garvin's Comedy Clubs.** Garvin's has become the McDonald's of laughs in the Washington area, serving jokes at five locations around DC and one in Baltimore. *Downtown location: 1335 Greens Ct. NW (L St. between 13th and 14th Sts. NW), tel. 202/783–2442. Shows Tues.–Thurs. 8:30 PM, Fri. 8:30 and 10:30 PM, Sat. 8 and 10:30 PM. Cover charge and drink minimum. Reservations required. AE, MC, V. Also: Shows Fri. 9 PM and Sat. 8 and 10:30 PM at Tyson's Corner, tel. 703/783–2442; Bethesda, tel. 703/783–2442; Alexandria, tel. 703/783–2442; and Baltimore, tel. 410/576–8558.*

**Headliners.** This comfortable club in a suburban Virginia hotel books local and regional acts on weekdays and national talent on the weekends. *Radisson Plaza Hotel, I–395 and Seminary Rd., Alexandria, VA, tel. 703/379–4242. Shows Tues.–Thurs. 8:45 PM, Sat. 8 and 10:30 PM. Cover charge. Reservations required. AE, D, DC, MC, V.*

**Laughing Lizard Lounge.** This northern Virginia club hosts political satire on Friday and cabaret on Saturday, followed on both nights by "adult" stand-up. *1322 King St., Alexandria, VA, tel. 703/548–2582. Shows Fri.–Sat. 10:30 PM. Cover charge. Reservations required. AE, MC, V.*

## Acoustic/Folk/Country

Perhaps surprisingly, Washington has a very active local folk scene. For information on different folk events—from contra (a form of folk) dancing to storytelling to open sings—call the recorded information line of the **Folklore Society of Greater Washington** (tel. 703/281–2228).

**Afterwords.** This place could just as easily be called Be-forewords or Duringwords, shoehorned as it is in a book-shop near Dupont Circle. Folkish acts entertain browsing bohemian bookworms as well as patrons seated at a cozy in-store café. *1517 Connecticut Ave. NW, tel. 202/387–1462. Open Tues.–Thurs. 7:30 AM–1 AM and Fri. 7:30 AM–Mon. 1 AM. Music Fri. and Sat. 10 PM–2 AM. AE, MC, V.*

**Birchmere.** The best place in the area to hear acoustic folk and bluegrass acts is in an unpretentious suburban strip shopping center. Favorite sons the Seldom Scene are Thursday-night regulars. Audiences come to listen, and the management politely insists on no distracting chatter. *3901 Mt. Vernon Ave., Alexandria, VA, tel. 703/549–5919. Open Tues.–Sat. 7 PM–11:30 PM. MC, V.*

**Country Junction.** A suburban Maryland hotel lounge is the scene of country dance lessons followed by country and swing dancing to recorded music. *11410 Rockville Pike, Rockville, MD, tel. 301/231–5761. Open daily 7 PM–1 AM. Cover charge Fri.–Sat. AE, DC, D, MC, V.*

**Dylan's.** There's a different type of music nearly every night at this Georgetown restaurant-cum-club; most groups fall into the light rock and acoustic folk catego-ries. *3251 Prospect St. NW, tel. 202/337–0593. Open Tues.–Sun. 5:30 PM–1:30 AM. Cover charge on weekends. AE, MC, V.*

**Zed Restaurant.** Can cowboy hats and boots exist in the same city as Brooks Brothers suits? A visit to Zed proves that they can. Each evening, bands in this subur-ban Virginia night spot play hits from Nashville and oth-er points south and west. Two-stepping is encouraged. *6151 Richmond Hwy., Alexandria, VA, tel. 703/768–5558. Open daily 11 AM–2 AM. Dress: casual but neat. AE, MC, V.*

## Dance Clubs

Washington's dance clubs have taken a hint from their New York counterparts, transforming themselves near-ly every night into different incarnations. Club owners rent their spaces to entrepreneurs who tailor the music and ambience to a certain type of crowd. Thus, a club might have heavy "industrial" music on a Wednesday, a largely gay clientele on a Thursday, and thump to the sounds of '70s disco on a Friday. It's best to call ahead or consult the often intriguing ads in the free weekly *City Paper*.

Hoofers who prefer "touch" dancing should call the re-corded information line of the very active **Washington Swing Dance Committee** (tel. 301/779–0234). The group organizes monthly boogie woogie, jitterbug, and swing workshops and dances.

**Chelsea's.** Should a dance like the lambada ever again bubble up from South America, you'll find it at this elegant Georgetown club near the C & O Canal. Hot Latin acts perform Thursday through Saturday; for a change of pace, it's Persian music on Wednesday and Sunday. *1055 Thomas Jefferson St. NW, tel. 202/298–8222. Open Wed., Thurs., and Sun. 10 PM–2 AM, Fri.–Sat. 10 PM–4 AM. Cover charge Fri. and Sat. AE, D, MC, V.*

**Doc Scantlin.** He may not be a dance club, but he's a Washington institution just the same. Holding a mega-phone, waving a baton, his spats polished, and with the thinnest of moustaches above his grinning lips, Doc Scantlin leads his Imperial Palms Orchestra in swing tunes that bring you back to an earlier time. His home base is the delightful Art Deco ballroom in the Kenne-dy-Warren apartment building. *3133 Connecticut Ave. NW, tel. 202/483–2058 (Kennedy-Warren) or 202/244–4237 (Doc Scantlin). Fri. at the Kennedy-Warren: din-ner at 8; show and dancing at 9:30. Jacket and tie required. Reservations suggested. AE, MC, V.*

**Fifth Column.** A trendy, well-dressed crowd waits in line to dance to the latest releases from London and Eu-rope on three floors of this converted bank. Avant-garde art installations change every four months. *915 F St. NW, tel. 202/393–3632. Open Sun.–Thurs. 10 PM–2 AM, Fri.–Sat. 10 PM–3 AM. Cover charge. AE, MC, V.*

**Ikon.** Above the trendy Adams-Morgan restaurant, Cit-ies, is this trendy Eurodisco featuring a thumping dance beat and DJs who "house" up the music. *2424 18th St. NW, tel. 202/328–7194. Open Wed.–Thurs. 9:30 PM–2 AM, Fri.–Sat. 9:30 PM–3 AM. Cover charge. AE, DC, MC, V.*

**Kilimanjaro.** Deep in ethnically diverse Adams-Morgan, the Kilimanjaro specializes in "international" music from the Caribbean and Africa. Every Thursday there's a local reggae band, and international artists often per-form on Sunday. *1724 California St. NW, tel. 202/328–3838. Open Mon.–Thurs. 5 PM–2 AM, Fri. 5 PM–4:30 AM, Sat. 6 PM–4 AM, Sun. 6 PM–2 AM. Cover charge. MC, V.*

**Opera.** This popular multilevel Adams-Morgan club boasts a diverse crowd at its Latin nights, "Europro-gressive" nights, and college nights. The crowd is large-ly gay on Sunday nights. *1777 Columbia Rd. NW, tel. 202/265–6600. Open Wed.–Thurs. 9 PM–3 AM, Fri.–Sat.*

*9 PM–4 AM, Sun. 9 PM–5 AM. No jeans or sneakers. Cover charge. AE, MC, V.*

**The Ritz.** This downtown nightclub sits in the shadow of the J. Edgar Hoover FBI Building. The club, which is popular with the black professional crowd, features five separate rooms of music, with DJs spinning everything from Top 40s and reggae in "Club Matisse" to house music in the upstairs "Freezone." Live bands perform once or twice a month. *919 E St. NW, tel. 202/638–2582. Open Thurs. 5 PM–3 AM, Fri. 5 PM–3 AM, Sat. 9 PM–3 AM, Sun. 9 PM–2 AM. Cover charge. Jacket and tie required. AE.*

**The Roxy.** Wednesday and Friday nights at this downtown club shake to the jackhammer beat of "industrial" dance music. High-energy reggae bands play on Thursday and Saturday. *1214 18th St. NW, tel. 202/296–9292. Open Wed.–Sat. 8:30 PM–2 AM. Cover charge. AE, MC, V.*

**Tracks.** A gay club with a large contingent of straight regulars, this warehouse-district disco has one of the largest dance floors in town and stays open late. *1111 1st St. SE, tel. 202/488–3320. Open Tues. 9 PM–2 AM, Wed.–Thurs. 9 PM–4 AM, Fri.–Sat. 9 PM–6 AM, Sun. 9 PM–4 AM. Cover charge Wed.–Sun. after 9 PM. No credit cards.*

**The Vault.** Beat-heavy disco blares on the first floor, more laid-back tunes stir upstairs, and downstairs there's an actual bank vault, a reminder of the days when this dance club was more interested in bills than boogie. *911 F St. NW, tel. 202/347–8079. Open Wed.–Thurs. 9:30 PM–2 AM, Fri.–Sat. 10 PM–3 AM. Cover charge. AE, MC, V.*

## Jazz Clubs

**Blues Alley.** The restaurant turns out Creole cooking, while cooking on stage are such nationally known performers as Charlie Byrd and Ramsey Lewis. You can come for just the show, but those who come for a meal get better seats. *Rear 1073 Wisconsin Ave. NW, tel. 202/337–4141. Open Sun.–Thurs. 6 PM–midnight, Fri. and Sat. 6 PM–2 AM. Shows at 8 and 10, plus a midnight show Sat. Cover charge and $5 food/drink minimum. AE, DC, MC, V.*

**Cafe Lautrec.** The Toulouse Lautrec decor, French food, and Gallic atmosphere are almost enough to convince you you're on the Left Bank of the Seine rather than the right bank of the Potomac. Cool cats play cool jazz nightly with tap-dancing fixture Johne Forges hoofing atop tables most Thursdays, Fridays, and Saturdays. *2431 18th St. NW, tel. 202/265–6436. Open Sun.–Thurs. 5*

*PM–2 AM, Fri.–Sat. 5 PM–3 AM. $6 minimum Thurs.–*
*Sun. AE, DC, MC, V.*

**One Step Down.** Low-ceilinged, intimate, and boasting
the best jazz jukebox in town, this small club books tal-
ented local artists and the occasional national act. The
venue of choice for many New York jazz masters, the
place is frayed and smoky, the way a jazz club should be.
Live music is presented Thursday–Monday. *2517 Penn-*
*sylvania Ave. NW, tel. 202/331–8863. Open Mon.–*
*Thurs. 10 PM–2 AM, Fri. and Sat. noon–3 AM, Sun.*
*noon–3 AM. Cover charge and minimum. AE, DC, MC,*
*V.*

**Takoma Station Tavern.** In the shadow of the Metro stop
that lends its name, this club hosts local favorites such
as Marshall Keys and Keith Killgo, with the occasional
nationally known artist stopping by to jam. The jazz
happy hours starting at 6:30 Thursday through Saturday pack the joint. *6914 4th St. NW, tel. 202/829–1999.*
*Open Sun.–Thurs. 4 PM–2 AM, Fri. and Sat. 4 PM–3 AM.*
*Dress: casual but neat. AE, DC, D, MC, V.*

**219 Basin Street Lounge.** Across the Potomac in Old
Town Alexandria above the 219 Restaurant, jazz combos
perform in an attractive Victorian-style bar. Musicians
from local service bands often stop by to jam. *219 King*
*St., Alexandria, VA, tel. 703/549–1141. Open Sun.–*
*Thurs. 6 PM–12:30 AM, Fri. and Sat. 6 PM–1 AM, Sun. jam*
*session brunch 2 PM–6 PM. Cover charge. AE, DC, D, MC,*
*V.*

## Rock, Pop, and Rhythm and Blues Clubs

**The Bayou.** Located in Georgetown, underneath the
Whitehurst Freeway, the Bayou is a Washington fixture
that showcases national acts on weeknights and local talent on weekends. Bands cover rock in all its permuta-
tions: pop rock, hard rock, soft rock, new rock, and
classic rock. Tickets are available at the door or through
TicketMaster. Occasional no-alcohol, all-ages shows allow those under 18 a chance to dance. *3135 K St. NW, tel.*
*202/333–2897. Open daily 8 PM–2 AM. Cover charge. No*
*credit cards.*

**Grog and Tankard.** A college-age crowd downs cheap
pitchers of beer while listening to exuberant local bands
in this small, comfortably disheveled night spot. *2408*
*Wisconsin Ave. NW, tel. 202/333–3114. Open daily 6*
*PM–2 AM. Cover charge after 8 PM. AE, MC, V.*

**Ibex.** This uptown club features two floors of varied entertainment, from disco to male dancers. The live music
on Friday and Saturday nights is varied as well, often

boasting nationally known rhythm-and-blues acts. Wednesday is open-mike night. On Wednesday through Saturday there's live Ethiopian music in the first-floor restaurant, Negarit. *5832 Georgia Ave. NW, tel. 202/ 726–1800. Open Thurs. 8 PM–3 AM, Fri.–Sat. 9 PM–4 AM, Sun. 8 PM–2 AM. Cover charge. AE.*

**9:30 Club.** This trendy club in the center of Washington's old downtown books an eclectic mix of local, national, and international artists, most of whom play what used to be known as "new wave" music (from the Fleshtones, Guadalcanal Diary, and Robyn Hitchcock, among others). The regulars dress to be seen, but visitors won't feel out of place. Get tickets at the door or through TicketMaster. *930 F St. NW, tel. 202/393–0930. Hours vary according to shows but generally open Tues. 8 PM–2 AM, Wed.–Thurs. 4 PM–2 AM, Fri. 4 PM–3 AM, Sat. 9 PM–3 AM. Cover charge. No credit cards.*

**Tornado Alley.** Owner Mark Gretschel is a great booster of "roots" music, such as blues, Cajun, zydeco, and anything else that swirls in like the eponymous wind from America's heartland. This suburban Maryland club resembling a high school gym hosts such national cult favorites as Filé, Wayne Toups and Zydecajun, Danny Gatton, and "Gatemouth" Brown, as well as local heroes, such as Stratocaster master Tom Principato and ex-Commander Cody guitarist Bill Kirchen. *11319 Elkin St., Wheaton, MD, tel. 301/929–0795. Hours vary according to shows but generally open Wed.–Sat. 6 PM–1 AM. Cover charge. No credit cards.*

# 9 Excursions

# Tour 1: The C & O Canal and Great Falls

By Michael Dolan

Updated by
John F. Kelly

In the 18th and early 19th centuries, the Potomac river was the main transport route between Cumberland, Maryland, one of the most important ports on the nation's frontier, and the seaports of the Chesapeake Bay. Tobacco, grain, whiskey, furs, iron ore, timber, and other commodities were sent down the Potomac from Cumberland to the ports of Georgetown and Alexandria, which served as major distribution points for both domestic and international markets.

Although it served as a vital link with the country's western territories, the Potomac did have some drawbacks as a commercial waterway: Rapids and waterfalls along the 190 miles between Cumberland and Washington made it impossible for traders to navigate the entire distance by boat. Just a few miles upstream from Washington, the Potomac cascaded through two such barriers—the breathtakingly beautiful Great Falls and the less dramatic but no less impassable Little Falls.

To help traders move goods between the eastern markets and the western frontier more efficiently, 18th-century engineers proposed that a canal with a series of elevator locks be built parallel to the river. The first such canal was built at the urging of George Washington, who actually helped found a company just for this purpose. In 1802, after 17 years of work, his firm opened the Patowmack Canal on the Virginia side of the river.

In 1828 Washington's canal was replaced by the **Chesapeake & Ohio Canal,** which had been dug along the opposite shore. The C & O stretched from the heart of Washington to Cumberland. Starting near what is now the intersection of 17th Street and Constitution Avenue NW (the public restroom there was originally a lockhouse), the C & O moved barges through 75 locks.

Ironically, the C & O Canal began operation the same day as the Baltimore & Ohio Railroad, the concern that eventually put the canal out of business. The C & O route to the west nevertheless did prove to be a viable alternative for traders interested in moving goods through the Washington area and to the lower Chesapeake. During the mid-19th century, the canal boats carried as many as one million tons of merchandise a year. The C & O Canal stopped turning a profit in 1890 but remained in business until 1924, when a disastrous storm left it in ruins.

Ownership then shifted to the B & O Railroad, which sold the canal to the federal government in 1938 for $2 million. In 1939 the canal became part of the National Capital Parks System.

In the 1950s a proposal to build a highway over the canal near Washington was defeated by residents of the Palisades, a neighborhood that overlooks the waterway. Since 1971 the canal has been a national park, providing Washingtonians and visitors with a window into the past and a marvelous place to pursue recreational activities.

The twin parks of **Great Falls**—on either side of the river 13 miles northwest of Georgetown—are also now part of the National Park system. The 800-acre park on the Virginia side is a favorite place for outings for local residents and is easily accessible to tourists. The steep, jagged falls roar into a narrow gorge, providing one of the most spectacular scenic attractions in the East.

## Escorted Tours

A tour of the visitors center and museum at **Great Falls Park** (tel. 703/285–2966) in Virginia takes 30 minutes. Staff members conduct special tours and walks year round. Visitors are encouraged to take self-guided tours along well-marked trails, including one that follows the route of the old Patowmack Canal.

On the Maryland side, the old **Great Falls Tavern** (tel. 301/299–2026) serves as a museum and headquarters for the rangers who manage the C & O Canal. During warm weather, replica mule-drawn boats carry visitors along this stretch of the canal; similar trips also begin in Georgetown. History books and canal guides are on sale at both parks as well as at many bookstores in the District.

## Getting Around

**By Car** To reach the Virginia side of Great Falls Park, take the scenic and winding Route 193 (Exit 13 off Route 495, the Capitol Beltway) to Route 738, and follow the signs. It takes about 25 minutes to drive to the park from the Beltway. You can get to the Maryland side of the park by following MacArthur Boulevard from Georgetown or by taking Exit 41 off the Beltway, following the signs to Carderock.

**By Foot, Canoe, or Bicycle** The C & O Canal Park and its towpath are favorite destinations for joggers, bikers, and canoeists. The towpath has only a slight grade, which makes for a leisurely ride or hike. Most recreational bikers consider the 13 miles from Georgetown to Great Falls an easy ride; there's only one short stretch of rocky ground near Great Falls where bikers need to carry their cycles. You can also take a bike path that parallels MacArthur Boulevard for much of the distance to the Maryland side of the park. Storm damage has left parts of the canal dry, but many segments remain intact and navigable by canoe. You can rent canoes or bicycles at **Fletcher's Boat House,** just upriver from Georgetown (*see* Exploring, *below*). In winter the canal sometimes freezes solid enough to allow for ice skating; during particularly hard freezes it's possible to skate great distances along the canal, occasionally interrupting your stride for short clambers around the locks.

## Exploring

*Numbers in the margin correspond to points of interest on the C & O Canal and Great Falls map.*

This tour moves from Georgetown northwest along the Potomac to Great Falls Park. The Canal itself is worth a day's stroll or ride.

❶ The towpath along the canal in **Georgetown** passes traces of that area's industrial past, such as the Godey Lime Kilns near the mouth of Rock Creek, as well as the fronts of numerous houses dating to 1810. From April through October mule-drawn barges leave for 90-minute trips from the Foundry Mall on Thomas Jefferson Street NW, half a block south of M Street. No reservations are required for the public trips. *For information, tel. 202/472–4376. For group reservations and rates, tel. 202/653–5844. Cost: $5 adults, $3.50 senior citizens and children under 13.*

❷ **Fletcher's Boat House** (4940 Canal Rd. NW, tel. 202/244–0461) rents canoes and bicycles and sells fishing tackle and DC fishing licenses. Fishermen often congregate here to try their luck with shad, perch, catfish, striped bass, and other freshwater species. In the spring Fletcher's opens at 5:30 AM and stops renting equipment at 5 PM. Summer hours are 7 AM–7:30 PM. During the coldest months of the year Fletcher's shuts down.

❸ **Chain Bridge**—named for the chains that held up the original structure—links the District with Virginia. The bridge was built to enable cattlemen to bring Virginia herds to the slaughterhouses located along the Po-

tomac on the Maryland side. During the Civil War the bridge was guarded by Union troops stationed at earthen fortifications located along what is now Potomac Avenue NW. The Virginia side of the river in the area around Chain Bridge is known for its good fishing and narrow, treacherous channel.

**④** The **Clara Barton House** (5801 Oxford Rd., tel. 301/492–6245), nestled in the charming Victorian village of Glen Echo, has been preserved as a monument to her career and as an example of American building style. The town of Glen Echo was founded as part of the Chautauqua movement of the late 19th century. The Chautauqua center at Glen Echo later saw use as an amusement park; it now houses an arts and cultural center that frequently hosts dances and folk festivals. For scheduling information, check the free weekly *City Paper* or the "Weekend" section in Friday's *Washington Post*.

**Glen Echo Park** (MacArthur Blvd. and Goldsboro Rd., tel. 301/492–6282) is noted not only for its whimsical architecture but for its splendid and still-functioning carousel. From late spring to early fall 50¢ buys a trip into the past, complete with music from a real calliope.

**⑤** **Great Falls Tavern,** on the Maryland side of Great Falls Park, features displays of canal history and a platform from which to view the falls. Better yet, walk over a series of bridges out to a small island in the middle of the river for a spectacular view of the falls. On the canal walls are "rope burns" caused by decade upon decade of friction from barge lines. Half a mile west a flood marker shows how high the Potomac can go—after a hurricane in 1972 the river crested far above the ground where visitors stand. Canal barge trips start here between April and October. The tavern ceased being a hostelry long ago, so if you're hungry head for the snack bar a few paces north of the tavern. *Park, tel. 301/299–2026. Admission: $3 per vehicle, $1 per person without vehicle, good for 7 days for MD and VA sides of the park. Open daily sunrise–sunset. Tavern and museum, tel. 301/299–3613. Open daily 9–5.*

**⑥** The Virginia side of **Great Falls Park,** which is not accessible from the Maryland side of the park, offers the best views of the Potomac, as well as trails leading past the old Patowmack Canal and among the boulders and forests lining the edge of the falls. Horseback riding is permitted—maps are available at the visitors center—but you can't rent horses in the park. Swimming and wading are prohibited, but there are fine opportunities for fishing (Virginia, Maryland, or DC licenses are required for anglers 16 and older), rock climbing (climbers must register at the visitors center beforehand), and white-water kayaking (*below* the falls only, and only by experienced boaters). From peaks beside the river and from several manmade platforms you can watch helmeted kayakers and climbers test their skills against the river and the rocks. As is true all along this stretch of the river, the currents are deadly. Despite frequent signs and warnings, each year some visitors dare the water, and lose. It's best to keep away from even the most benign-looking ripple. *Tel. 703/285–2966. Admission: $3 per vehicle, $1 per person without vehicle, good for 7 days for MD and VA sides of the park. Open daily 7 AM until dark. Closed Christmas.*

# Tour 2: Annapolis

Although it has long since been overtaken by Baltimore as the major Chesapeake port, **Annapolis** is still a popular destination for oystermen and yachtsmen, and on warm sunny days the City Dock is thronged with billowing sails set strikingly against a background of redbrick waterfront buildings, mostly shops and restaurants. Annapolis's enduring nautical reputation derives largely from the presence of the United States Naval Academy, whose handsomely uniformed midshipmen grace the city streets in their summer whites and winter navy-blues (the *real* navy blue, which is practically black). October Sailboat and Powerboat shows attract national attention, keeping local hotels and restaurants full even after the summer tourist season has ended.

In 1649 a group of Puritan settlers relocated from Virginia to a spot at the mouth of the Severn River; the community that they called Providence is now an upscale residential area. Lord Baltimore—who held the Royal charter to settle Maryland—named the area around the new town Anne Arundel County, after his wife; in 1684 Anne Arundel Town was established, across from Providence, on the south side of the Severn. Ten years later, Anne Arundel Town became the capital of Maryland and was renamed Annapolis—for Princess Anne, who later became queen. Annapolis received its city charter in 1708.

Annapolis—not the better-known Baltimore—is the state capital. One of the country's largest assemblages of 18th-century architecture (including 50 pre-Revolutionary buildings) recalls the city's days as a major port, particularly for the export of tobacco. In fact, in 1774 local patriots matched their Boston counterparts (who had thrown their famous tea party the previous year) by burning the *Peggy Sue*, a ship loaded with taxed tea. A decade later, in 1783 and 1784, Annapolis served as the nation's first peacetime capital. Annapolis's waterfront orientation makes it possible for visitors to do the city justice in a single well-planned day.

## Escorted Tours

Weekdays from March 1 to Thanksgiving week, the **Historic Annapolis Foundation** (tel. 410/267–8149) offers walking tours past four 18th-century buildings and into the William Paca gardens. Tours are $6 adults, $3.50 children 6–18, under 6 free. Guides from **Three Centuries Tours** (tel. 410/263–5357 or 410/263–5401) wear colonial dress and take visitors to the State House, St. John's College, and the Naval Academy. The fee is $6 adults, $3 children 6–18, under 6 free.

Cruises offered by **Chesapeake Marine Tours, Inc.** (tel. 410/268–7600 or 301/261–2719 in Washington, DC) depart from the city dock in good weather. Tours range from 45 minutes to 7½ hours, extending as far as St. Michael's, a preserved 18th-century fishing village and a yachting mecca on the eastern shore of the bay. Prices range from $3 to $33.

## Getting Around

There is no regular train or bus service from Washington to Annapolis. The drive from Washington (east on U.S. Route 50, to the Rowe Boulevard exit) normally takes 35–45 minutes, but if you travel between 3:30 and 6:30 PM you could be stuck in traffic for as long as two hours.

Parking spots on Annapolis's historic downtown streets are rare, but there's a free lot at the Navy–Marine Corps Stadium (to the right of Rowe Boulevard as you enter town from Route 50), from which a shuttle heads to downtown for 35¢ (75¢ at rush hour).

## Exploring

*Numbers in the margin correspond to points of interest on the Annapolis map.*

**1** Start your tour at the redbrick **Information Booth** operated by the **Annapolis-Anne Arundel County Conference and Visitors Bureau,** where you can pick up maps and brochures. The booth is on the city dock, adjacent to the harbor master's office (tel. 410/268–8687; open Apr.– Oct., daily 10–4). Outside, both motor- and sail-craft dozens of feet long moor at the edges of Dock Street and Market Place. A variety of shops, restaurants, and bars populate the dock area.

**Time Out** The **reconstructed Market House** pavilion—originally a collection of mid-19th-century market stalls in the center of Market Square—now sells baked goods, fast food, and fish (prepared or to cook at home). The building offers no seating, but you've got the entire dock on which to set up your picnic.

**2** On Main Street by the dock, the **Victualling Warehouse Maritime Museum** occupies a warehouse that stored supplies for the Revolutionary Army during the War of Independence, when the city was a vital link in the supply chain. Exhibits pertain to the history of maritime commerce in Annapolis and include artifacts of Colonial-era trade and a diorama of the city's waterfront in the 18th century. *77 Main St., tel. 410/267–7619. Call for hours or to schedule a visit. Admission free. Closed Thanksgiving and Christmas.*

**3** Follow Randall Street a few blocks to reach the **United States Naval Academy.** By the gate at King George Street you'll find Ricketts Hall, where you can join a guided tour or pick up information for your own excursion. The Academy, established in 1845 on the site of a U.S. Army fort, occupies 329 scenic riverside acres, earning the dubious title of "country club on the Severn" from its West Point rivals. In the center of campus the

**4** bronze-domed, interdenominational **U.S. Naval Chapel** contains the crypt of the Revolutionary War hero John Paul Jones, who, in an engagement with a British ship, uttered the famous declaration, "I have not yet begun to

**5** fight!" The **museum in Preble Hall** tells the story of the U.S. Navy, with displays of miniature ships and flags from the original vessels. Periodic full-dress parades and (in warmer months) daily noontime musters of the midshipmen take place at various spots around campus, but the most remarkable sight may be the sample student quarters open to the public—they're quite a bit neater than the typical college dorm! *Tel. 410/267–3363 or 410/263–6933. Open Mon.–Sat. 9–4:30, Sun. 11–*

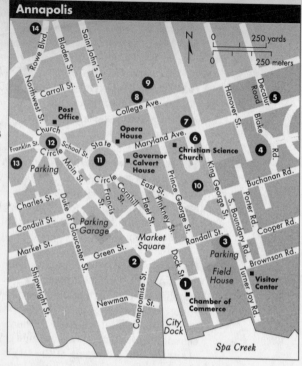

*4:30. Admission free. Cost of tour: $3 adults, $1 children 6th grade and below. 1-hr tours depart June–Aug., ½-hourly 9:30–4; Mar.–May and Sept.–Nov., hourly 10–3. Closed Thanksgiving and from Christmas to New Year's Day.*

Leave the Academy via Maryland Avenue and you will pass the three-story redbrick **Hammond-Harwood House.** The house is the only verifiable full-scale example of the work of William Buckland, the most prominent Colonial architect at the time of his death, in 1774—the year in which the house was completed. Buckland was famous for his interior woodwork, which may also be seen in the Chase-Lloyd House across the street and in George Mason's Gunston Hall in Lorton, Virginia. Exquisite moldings, cornices, and other carvings appear throughout, including garlands of roses above the front doorway. These were meant to be part of the manorial wedding present from Matthias Hammond, a lawyer and revolutionary, to his fiancée, who jilted him before the project was finished. Hammond never married, and he died in 1784. The Harwoods took over the house toward the turn of the century. Today the house is furnished with 18th-century pieces, and the garden is tended with regard to period authenticity. *19 Maryland Ave., tel. 410/269–1714. Open Mar.–Oct., Tues.–Sat. 10–5, Sun. 2–5; Nov.–Dec., Tues.–Sat. 10–4, Sun. 1–4; Jan.–Feb., Fri.–Sat. 10–4, Sun 2–4. Admission: $3.50 adults, $2.50 children 6–18. Closed Thanksgiving, Christmas, and New Year's. Call for group rates.*

Across the street is the gracefully massive facade— sheer except for a center third beneath a pediment—of the **Chase-Lloyd House.** In 1774 the tobacco planter and revolutionary Edward Lloyd IV completed work begun five years earlier by Samuel Chase, a Supreme Court justice and future signer of the Declaration of Independence. The first floor is open to the public and contains more of Buckland's handiwork, including a parlor mantelpiece with tobacco leaves carved into the marble. The house is furnished with a mixture of 18th-, 19th-, and 20th-century pieces. The staircase parts dramatically around a Palladian window (an arched, triple window whose center segment is taller than its flanks). For more than 100 years the house has served as a home for elderly Episcopalian women. *22 Maryland Ave., tel. 410/263– 2723. Admisison: $1. Open Mar.–Dec., Tues.–Sat. 2–4.; Jan. and Feb., Thurs.–Sat. 2–4.*

A left on King George Street will take you to College Avenue and **St. John's College,** which graduated Francis Scott Key, lyricist of *The Star Spangled Banner.* The college has been best known since 1937, however, for its Great Books curriculum—a four-year program of required courses, including math, science, music, languages, and the works of great authors from Homer to Freud. Climb the gradual slope of the long brick-paved path to the impressive golden cupola of **McDowell Hall,** the third oldest academic building in the country, just as St. John's is the third oldest college in the country (after Harvard and William and Mary). Founded as King William's School in 1696, the school was chartered under its current name in 1784. The enormous tulip poplar called the **Liberty Tree,** on the lawn fronted by College Avenue, is possibly 600 years old. In its shade colonists and Indians made treaties in the 17th century, revolutionaries rallied in the 18th century, Union troops encamped in the 19th century, and commencement takes place every spring. The **Elizabeth Myers Mitchell Art Gallery** (tel. 410/263–2371, ext. 256; open Tues.–Thurs., noon–5, Fri. 7–8 PM), located on the east side of Mellon Hall, presents a variety of exhibits and special programs related to the fine arts. Down King George Street toward the water is the **Carroll-Barrister House,** now the college admissions office. The house was built in 1722 at Main and Conduit streets and was moved onto campus in 1957. Charles Carroll—not the signer of the Declaration, but his cousin—who helped draft Maryland's Declaration of Rights, was born here. *Tel. 410/263–2371 or 301/261–1855 in Washington, D.C. Free tours available by appointment.*

Head right on King George Street and make another right on College Avenue. A left on Prince George Street brings you to the **William Paca House and Garden**—the house built in 1765 and the garden originally finished in 1772 and gradually restored in this century. These compose the estate of William Paca, a signer of the Declaration of Independence and governor of Maryland from 1782 to 1785. Inside, the main floor (furnished with 18th-century antiques) retains its original Prussian-blue and soft-gray color scheme. The second floor contains a mixture of 18th- and 19th-century pieces. The adjacent 2-acre garden provides a longer perspective on the back of the house, plus worthwhile sights of its own: a Chinese Chippendale bridge, a pond, a wilderness area, and formal arrangements. *House: 186 Prince George St., tel. 410/263–5553. Admission: house and garden, $5 adults, $3 children 6–18, under 6 free; house only: $3.50 adults, $2.50 children 6–18; garden only: $2.50 adults, $1.50 children 6–18. A combination admission is offered for the Paca House and Garden and the Hammond-Harwood House (see above) at $6 adults. House and garden open Jan.–Feb., Fri.–Sat. 10–4, Sun. noon–4; Mar., Mon., Wed.–Sat. 10–4, Sun. noon–4; Apr.–Oct., Mon. and Wed.–Sat. 10–5, Sun. noon–5; Nov.–Dec. Mon. and Wed.–Sat. 10–4, Sun. noon–4. Closed Thanksgiving, Christmas.*

Return on Prince George Street to Maryland Avenue and turn left. Completed in 1780, the domed **Maryland State House** is the oldest state capitol in continuous legislative use and the only one that has ever hosted the U.S. Congress. During 1783 and 1784 when Congress convened here, it accepted the resignation of General George Washington as commander-in-chief of the Continental Army, and it ratified the Treaty of Paris with the king, concluding the War of Independence. Both of these matters were determined in the Old Senate Chamber, filled with intricate woodwork (featuring the ubiquitous tobacco motif) that is also attributed to Buckland (*see above*). Also decorating this room is Charles Willson Peale's painting *Washington at the Battle of Yorktown*, considered to be the masterpiece of the Revolutionary

War period's finest portrait artist. The state Senate and House now hold their sessions in two other chambers in the building. Also on the grounds is the oldest public building in Maryland, the miniscule redbrick **Treasury**, built in 1735. *State Circle, tel. 410/974–3400. Admission free. Open daily 9–5; closed Christmas.*

School Street leads you to the center of Church Circle, where you'll see the Episcopal **St. Anne's Church**—the third church of that name on that spot. The first, built in 1704, was torn down in 1775. The second, built in 1792, burned down in 1858; however, parts of the walls survived and were incorporated into the present structure, which was built in 1859. The parish was founded in 1692, and King William III donated the communion silver. The churchyard contains the grave of the last Colonial governor, Sir Robert Eden. *Church Circle, tel. 410/267–9333. Admission free. Open daily 7:30–6.*

**Time Out** **Ram's Head Tavern,** at 33 West Street, serves award-winning chili, sandwiches, and salads, and bottled beer from more than two dozen countries.

One block down Franklin Street brings you to the ivy-covered redbrick former church that houses the **Banneker-Douglass Museum of Afro-American Life.** Changing exhibits, lectures, films, and literature are brought together here to give a picture of the African-American experience in Maryland. *84 Franklin St., tel. 410/974-2894. Admission free. Open Tues.–Fri. 10–3, Sat. noon–4.*

Return to Church Circle and follow Northwest Street to Rowe Boulevard. A 10-minute walk on Rowe Boulevard brings you to the 6-acre **Helen Avalynne Tawes Garden.** This botanical garden, across from the Navy–Marine Corps Stadium parking lot, next to the Tawes State Office Building Complex, is planted with flora representative of different regions of the state. Western Maryland's mountain forests and the marshland along the Chesapeake are evoked by rhododendrons and reeds respectively; the ponds host various fish, fowl, and amphibians. Naturally, the state flower, the Black-eyed Susan, is well represented. *580 Taylor Ave., tel. 410/974-3717. Admission free. Open daily dawn–dusk.*

# Tour 3: Mount Vernon, Woodlawn, and Gunston Hall

Long before the capital city was planned, the shores of the Potomac had been divided into plantations by wealthy traders and gentleman farmers. Even though most traces of the Colonial era were obliterated as the capital grew in the 19th century, several splendid examples of plantation architecture remain on the Virginia side of the Potomac just 15 miles or so south of the District. The three mansions described in this section can easily be visited in a single day: **Mount Vernon,** one of the most popular sites in the area, was the home of George Washington; **Woodlawn,** the estate of Washington's granddaughter; and **Gunston Hall,** the home of George Mason, patriot and author of the document on which the Bill of Rights was based. Spread out on hillsides overlooking the river, these estates offer a look into a way of life long gone.

## Escorted Tours

**Tourmobile** offers trips to and from Mount Vernon. Tours depart from April through October, daily at 10 AM, noon, and 2 PM from Arlington Cemetery and the Washington Monument. Reservations must be made in person one hour before departure. *Tel. 202/554–5100. Cost: $16.50 adults, $8 children 3–11. 2-day combo tickets good for Mount Vernon and several sites in Washington: $25.50 adults, $12.50 children.*

**Gray Line Tours** runs half-day trips to Mount Vernon and Old Town Alexandria. Buses depart daily at 8:30 AM from Union Station. *Tel. 301/386–8300. Cost: $20 adults, $10 children 3–11; 15% discount for AARP members. No tours on Thanksgiving, Dec. 25, or Jan. 1.*

## Getting Around

**By Car** To get to Mount Vernon from the Capitol Beltway (Route 495), take exit 1 onto the George Washington Memorial Parkway, and follow the signs. From downtown Washington, cross into Arlington on either the Key Bridge or Memorial Bridge, and drive south on the George Washington Memorial Parkway toward National Airport. Proceed past the airport and through Alexandria straight to Mount Vernon. The trip from Washington takes about a half-hour.

To reach Woodlawn and Gunston Hall from Mount Vernon, continue south on the George Washington Parkway to Route 1. The entrance to Woodlawn is straight across from the exit; to reach Gunston Hall, turn left and follow the signs.

**By Subway and Bus**  You can get to Mount Vernon from the District by using the Metro and bus service. From downtown, take the yellow line train to Huntington ($1.25–$1.90 depending on the time of day). Then catch a Fairfax County Connector Bus, the No. 101/Ft. Hunt, to Mt. Vernon (50¢). The No. 101 leaves Huntington every hour on the half-hour and operates Monday–Saturday 6:30 AM–7 PM, Sunday 9:30 AM–6 PM. Returning to Huntington from Mt. Vernon, the bus will be labeled the No. 101/Huntington.

**By Boat**  An especially pleasant way to travel down the Potomac is to cruise on the ***Potomac Spirit,*** which makes the trip from Washington to the plantation twice daily from mid-March through October. (Boats leave from Pier 4, 6th and Water Sts. SW, tel. 202/554–8000.)

**By Bicycle**  An asphalt bicycle path leads from the Virginia side of Memorial Bridge (adjacent to the Lincoln Memorial), past National Airport, and through Alexandria all the way to Mount Vernon. The trail is steep in places, but a biker in moderately good condition can make the 23-mile trip in less than two hours. Bicycles can be rented at several locations in Washington (*see* Bicycling in Chapter 5).

## Exploring

*Numbers in the margin correspond to points of interest on the Mount Vernon, Woodlawn, and Gunston Hall map.*

**Mount Vernon**
❶  **Mount Vernon** and the surrounding lands had been in the Washington family for nearly 90 years by the time George inherited it all in 1761. Before taking over command of the Continental Army, Washington was a yeoman farmer, directing the management of the 8,000-acre plantation, of which more than 3,000 acres were under cultivation. He also oversaw the transformation of the main house from an ordinary farm dwelling into what was for the time a grand mansion. His improve-

# Mount Vernon, Woodlawn, and Gunston Hall

ments resulted in a dwelling more suited to his status as Founding Father.

The main house, with its red roof, is elegant though understated. The exterior is made of yellow pine painted and coated with layers of sand—"rusticated," in the language of the day—to resemble white-stone blocks.

The inside of the building is more ornate, especially the formal receiving room with its molded ceiling decorated with agricultural motifs. Throughout the house you'll find other, smaller symbols of the owner's eminence, such as a key to the main portal of the Bastille, presented to Washington by the Marquis de Lafayette, Washington's presidential chair, and a case of traveling wine bottles. Small groups of visitors are ushered from room to room, each of which is staffed by a guide who describes the furnishings and answers questions.

The real (often overlooked) treasure of Mount Vernon is the view from around back: Beneath a 90-foot portico (George Washington's contribution to the language of architecture) the home's dramatic riverside porch looks out on an expanse of lawn that slopes down to the Potomac. In springtime the view of the river (a mile wide at the point at which it passes the plantation) is framed by the blossoms of wild plum and dogwood. Ships of the U.S. and foreign navies always salute when passing the house.

Tours of the sprawling grounds are self-guided. Visitors are free to visit the plantation workshops, the kitchen, the carriage house, the gardens, reconstructions of the slave quarters, and down the hill toward the boat landing, the tomb of George and Martha Washington. Among the souvenirs sold at the plantation are stripling boxwoods that began life as clippings from bushes planted in 1798, the year before Washington died. *Tel. 703/780–2000. General admission: $7 adults, $6 senior citizens 62 and older, $3 children 6–11 accompanied by adult. Regular group admission (minimum 20 paid admissions): $6.50 adults; $5.50 senior citizens, $3 children. One professional tour escort and 1 bus driver admitted free with each group. Youth and student group admission (minimum 12 paid admissions): $3 grades 1–12, $3 chaperons (1 per 10 students; additional chaperons $6.50). A limited number of wheelchairs is available at the main gate. Open Mar.–Oct., daily 9–5; Nov.–Feb., daily 9–4. The tour of the house and grounds takes about 2 hrs.*

**Woodlawn**
**❷ Woodlawn** Three miles south of Mount Vernon on Route 1, Woodlawn Plantation occupies a piece of ground that was originally part of the Mount Vernon estate; even today you can see the red roof of Washington's home from Woodlawn. The house at Woodlawn was built for Washington's step-granddaughter, Nellie Custis, who married his favorite nephew, Lawrence Lewis. (Lewis had come to Mount Vernon from Fredericksburg to help the General manage his five farms.)

The Lewises' home, completed in 1805, is noteworthy from an architectural standpoint. It was designed by William Thornton, who drew up the original plans for the Capitol. Like Mount Vernon, the Woodlawn house is made wholly of native materials, including the clay for its bricks and the yellow pine used throughout the interior.

In the tradition of Southern riverfront mansions, Woodlawn has a central hallway that provides a cool refuge during the summer. At one corner of the passage is a bust of George Washington, set on a pedestal so that the crown of the head is at 6′2″—Washington's actual height. Elsewhere is a music room with a ceiling two feet higher than any other in the building, built that way to improve the acoustics for the harp and clavichord recitals that the Lewises and their children enjoyed.

After Woodlawn passed out of the Lewis family's hands it was owned by a Quaker community, which established there a meetinghouse and the first integrated school in Virginia. Subsequent owners included the playwright Paul Kester and Senator and Mrs. Oscar Underwood of Alabama. The property was acquired by the National Trust for Historic Preservation in 1957.

Also on the grounds of Woodlawn is the **Pope-Leighey House,** designed by Frank Lloyd Wright and built in 1940. The structure originally stood in nearby Falls Church, Virginia; it was rescued from the path of a highway and moved to the Woodlawn grounds in 1964. Wright's modernist design in cypress, brick, and glass offers a peculiar counterpoint to the Georgian stylings of Woodlawn. It is not to every taste, but it *is* an architectural education. *Woodlawn, 3 mi straight down the GW Pkwy. from Mount Vernon, tel. 703/780–4000. Admission: $5 adults, $3.50 students and senior citizens, children under 5 free. Open daily 9:30–4:30. Tours every ½-hour. Last tour at 4 PM. Pope-Leighey House admission: $4 adults, $2.75 students and senior citizens. Open Mar.–Dec., daily 9:30–4; Jan.–Feb., weekends only 9:30–4. Tours every ½-hour. Last tour at 4. An $8 combination ticket ($6 senior citizens) covers admission to both Woodlawn and Pope-Leighey House. Closed Thanksgiving, Christmas, and New Year's Day.*

**Gunston Hall**
**3**

Unlike Mount Vernon, **Gunston Hall,** 15 miles away in Lorton, is rarely crowded with visitors. This was the home of a lesser-known George: George Mason, gentleman farmer, captain of the Fairfax militia and author of the Virginia Declaration of Rights. Mason was one of the framers of the Constitution but refused to sign the final document because it did not prohibit slavery, adequately restrain the powers of the federal government, or include a bill of rights.

Completed in 1759, Gunston Hall is built of native brick, black walnut, and yellow pine. The architectural style of the time demanded absolute balance in all structures. Hence the "robber" window on a second-floor storage room and the fake door set into one side of the center hallway. The house's interior, with its carved woodwork in styles from Chinese to Gothic, has been meticulously restored, with paints made from the original recipes and with carefully carved replacements for the intricate mahogany medallions in the moldings.

The formal gardens are famous for their boxwoods, some of which were planted in the 1760s and have now grown to be 12 and 14 feet high. In Mason's day boxwood was used as a garden border because its acrid smell repelled deer.

To reach Gunston Hall, turn south on Route 1 from Woodlawn and follow the highway 7 miles, then turn left and follow the signs. The tour takes 45 minutes to an hour. *Tel. 703/550–9220. Admission: $4 adults, $3 senior citizens, $1 children 6–15. Open daily 9:30–5, grounds 9:30–6. Last tour at 4:30. Closed Thanksgiving, Christmas, and New Year's Day.*

# Tour 4: Fredericksburg, Virginia

Situated on land once favored by Indian tribes as fishing and hunting ground, this compact city near the falls of the Rappahannock River figured prominently at crucial points in the nation's history, particularly during the Revolutionary and Civil wars. Just 50 miles south of Washington on I-95, Fredericksburg is today a popular day-trip destination for history buffs. The town's 40-block **National Historic District** contains more than 350 original 18th- and 19th-century buildings, including Mary Washington's home, James Monroe's law office, the Rising Sun Tavern, and Kenmore, the magnificent 1752 plantation home of George Washington's sister. The town is a favorite with antiques collectors, who enjoy cruising the dealers' shops along Caroline Street.

Although its site was visited by explorer Captain John Smith as early as 1608, the town of Fredericksburg wasn't founded until 1728. Established as a frontier port to serve nearby tobacco farmers and iron miners, Fredericksburg took its name from England's crown prince at the time, and the streets still bear names of members of his family: George, Caroline, Sophia, Princess Anne, Hanover, William, and Amelia.

George Washington knew Fredericksburg well, having grown up just across the Rappahannock on Ferry Farm. He lived there from age 6 to 16, and the legends about chopping down a cherry tree and throwing a coin across the Rappahannock—later mythologized as the Potomac—go back to this period of his life. In later years Washington often returned to visit his mother at the home he bought for her on Charles Street.

Fredericksburg prospered in the decades after independence, benefitting from its location midway along the 100-mile path between Washington and Richmond, an important intersection of railroad lines and waterways. When the Civil War broke out in 1861, Fredericksburg became the linchpin of the Confederate defense of Richmond and, as such, the inevitable target of Union assaults. In December, 1862, Union forces attacked Fredericksburg in what was to be the first of four major battles fought in and around the town. In the battle of Sunken Road, Confederate defenders sheltered by a stone wall at the base of Marye's Heights mowed down Union soldiers by the thousands as they charged across the fields on foot and on horseback.

By war's end, the fighting in Fredericksburg and in battles at nearby Chancellorsville, the Wilderness, and Spotsylvania Court House had claimed more than 100,000 dead or wounded. Fredericksburg's cemeteries hold the remains of 17,000 soldiers from both sides. Despite heavy bombardment and house-to-house fighting, however, much of the city remained intact, and the historic district today contains many fine examples from the period.

A walking tour through the town proper takes three to four hours; battlefield tours each can take that long. The short hop across the Rappahannock to Chatham Manor is well worth it, if for no other reason than that the site offers a splendid view of all of Fredericksburg.

## Escorted Tours

**The Fredericksburg Department of Tourism** (706 Caroline St., tel. 703/373–1776 or 800/678–4748) offers a booklet that includes a short history of Fredericksburg and a self-guided tour covering 29 sites. Also available from the visitors center is a booklet outlining 3-, 9-, and 20-mile bike tours (bike rentals are not available).

**Heritage Guide Service** arranges group tours of the city as well as of battlefields and other historic sites in the area. Advance reservations are required. Contact Tour Coordinator (706 Caroline St., Fredericksburg, VA 22401, tel. 703/373–1776).

## Getting Around

**By Car** To get to Fredericksburg from the District, take I-95 south to Route 3, turn left, and follow the signs. The drive takes about 60 minutes one way, except during rush hour.

**By Train** **Amtrak** trains bound for Fredericksburg depart six times daily from Washington's Union Station and take about an hour (tel. 202/484–7540 or 800/872–7245). The Fredericksburg railroad station is near the historic district (Caroline St. and Lafayette Blvd). A roundtrip ticket from Washington costs $17.

**By Bus** **Greyhound-Trailways** (tel. 301/565–2662) departs several times a day from Washington to Fredericksburg. A round-trip ticket is $13.50 if purchased two weeks in advance; $17.50 if purchased three days in advance; and $20.50 if purchased the same day. Buses stop at a station on alternate Route 1, about 2 miles from the center of town; cabs are available there.

## Exploring

*Numbers in the margin correspond to points of interest on the Fredericksburg map.*

**1** The **Fredericksburg Visitors Center** offers booklets and pamphlets on local history, information on restaurants and lodging, and a slide show that orients visitors to the city. Also available at the center are parking passes, good for a whole day in what would normally be two-hour zones, and Hospitality Passes ($16—a $7 discount off the full fares) to seven city attractions. The center is in a structure that was built in 1824 as a residence and confectionary; during the Civil War it was used to hold prisoners of war. *706 Caroline St., tel. 703/373–1776 or 800/678–4748. Open daily 9–5, extended summer hours. Closed Thanksgiving, Christmas, and New Year's Day.*

**2** At the **Fredericksburg Battlefield Visitor Center** you can learn about Fredericksburg's role in the Civil War by attending the succinct, informative slide show and then moving on to displays of soldiers' art and battlefield relics. The center offers taperecorded tour cassettes and maps showing how to reach hiking trails at the nearby Wilderness, Chancellorsville, and Spotsylvania Courthouse battlefields (all within 15 miles of Fredericksburg). Just outside the Center is Sunken Road, where on December 11 to 13, 1862, General Robert E. Lee led his troops to a bloody but resounding victory over Union forces attacking across the Rappahannock; 18,000 men from both sides died in the clash. Much of the stone wall that hid Lee's sharpshooters has been rebuilt, but 100 yards from the visitors center part of the original wall

looks out on the statue *The Angel of Marye's Heights*, by
Felix de Weldon. This memorial honors Sergeant Richard Kirkland, a South Carolinian who risked his life to
bring water to wounded foes; he later died at the Battle
of Chickamauga. *Lafayette Blvd. at Sunken Rd., tel.
703/373–6122. Open daily 9–5, extended summer hours.
Closed Christmas and New Year's Day.*

**❸** The **National Cemetery** is the final resting place of
15,000 Union casualties, most of whom were never iden-
tified. *Lafayette Blvd. at Sunken Rd., tel. 703/373–
6122. Open daily sunrise–sunset.*

**❹** The **Confederate Cemetery** contains the remains of more
than 2,000 soldiers (most of them unknown) as well as
the graves of generals Dabney Maury, Seth Barton,
Carter Stevenson, Daniel Ruggles, Henry Sibley, and
Abner Perrin. *Entrance at 1100 Washington Ave., near
the corner of Washington Ave. and Amelia St., no
phone. Open dawn–dusk.*

**❺** **Kenmore** was the home of Fielding Lewis, a patriot,
plantation owner, and brother-in-law of George Washington. (Lewis sacrificed much of his fortune to operate
a gun factory that supplied the American forces during

the Revolution.) Kenmore's plain exterior belies the lavish interior; these have been called some of the most beautiful rooms in America. The plaster moldings in the ceilings are outstanding and even more ornate than Mount Vernon's. Of equal elegance are the furnishings, which include a large standing clock that belonged to Mary Washington. Across the street are fine examples of Victorian architecture and a monument to Mary Washington, as well as the entrance to the Confederate cemetery. After the 60-minute tour visitors to Kenmore are served cider and gingerbread made according to a Washington family recipe. *1201 Washington Ave., tel. 703/373–3381. Admission: $5 adults, $2.50 students 6–18, 20% discount to groups of 10 or more, $10 "family ticket." Open Mar.–Nov., daily 9–5; Dec.–Feb., daily 10–4. Closed Thanksgiving, Dec. 24, 25, 31, and Jan. 1.*

**6** The **James Monroe Museum and Memorial Library** is the tiny one-story building where the man who was to be the fifth president of the United States practiced law from 1787 to 1789. In this building are many of Monroe's possessions, collected and preserved by his family until this century, including a mahogany dispatch-box used during the negotiation of the Louisiana Purchase and the desk on which Monroe signed the doctrine named for him. *908 Charles St., tel. 703/899–4559. Admission: $3 adults, $1 children 6–18, $2.40 group adult, 80¢ group student. Open Mar.–Nov., daily 9–5; Dec.–Feb., daily, 10–4. Closed Thanksgiving, Dec. 24, 25, 31, and Jan. 1.*

**Time Out** Stop for a gourmet sandwich or a slice of quiche at the **Made in Virginia Store Deli** (101 William St., tel. 703/371–2233). Do not skip the rich desserts.

**7** On Charles Street is the modest white **home of Mary Washington.** George purchased it for her in 1772, and she spent the last 17 years of her life there, tending the charming garden where her boxwood still flourishes and where many a bride and groom now exchange their vows. Displays include many of Mrs. Washington's personal effects, as well as period furniture and a boxwood garden that includes plants she herself started. Local residents bought and preserved the house to keep it from being dismantled and taken to the Chicago World's Fair. *1200 Charles St., tel. 703/373–1569. Admission: $3 adults, 75¢ students, $2.50 group adult, 50¢ group student. Open Mar.–Nov., daily 9–5; Dec.–Feb., daily 10–4. Closed Thanksgiving, Dec. 24, 25, 31, and Jan. 1.*

In 1760 George Washington's brother Charles built as
**8** his home what became the **Rising Sun Tavern,** a watering hole for such pre-Revolutionary patriots as the Lee
brothers, Patrick Henry, Washington, and Jefferson. A
"wench" in period costume leads the tour without stepping out of character. From her perspective you watch
the activity—day and night, upstairs and down—at this
busy institution. In the tap room you are served spiced
tea. *1306 Caroline St., tel. 703/371-1494. Admission: $3
adults, 75¢ students, $2.50 group adult, 50¢ group stu-
dent. Open Mar.–Nov., daily 9–5; Dec.–Feb., daily
10–4. Closed Dec. 24, 25, 31, and Jan. 1.*

**9** The **Hugh Mercer Apothecary Shop** offers a close-up
view of 18th- and 19th-century medicine. It was established in 1771 by Dr. Mercer, a Scotsman who served as
a brigadier general of the Revolutionary Army (he was
killed at the Battle of Princeton). General George S.
Patton of World War II fame was one of Mercer's great-
great-great grandsons. Dr. Mercer might have been
more careful than most other Colonial physicians, yet
his methods will make you cringe. A costumed hostess
will explicitly describe amputations and cataract operations. You will also hear about therapeutic bleeding and
see the gruesome devices used in Colonial dentistry.
This is an informative if slightly nauseating look at life
two centuries ago. *1020 Caroline St. at Amelia St., tel.
703/373-3362. Admission: $3 adults, 75¢ students 6–12,
$2.50 group adult, 50¢ group student. Open Mar.–Nov.,
daily 9–5; Dec.–Feb., daily 10–4. Closed Thanksgiving,
Dec. 24, 25, 31, and Jan. 1.*

**10** **Chatham Manor** is a fine example of Georgian architecture, built between 1768 and 1771 by William Fitzhugh
on a site overlooking the Rappahannock and the town of
Fredericksburg. Fitzhugh, a noted plantation owner,
frequently hosted such luminaries of his day as George
Washington and Thomas Jefferson. During the Civil
War, Union forces commandeered the house and converted it into a headquarters and hospital. President
Abraham Lincoln visited to confer with his generals;
Clara Barton and the poet Walt Whitman tended the
wounded. After the war the house and gardens were restored by private owners and eventually donated to the
National Park Service. Concerts often are held here
during the summer. *Chatham La., Stafford County
(take William St. across the bridge and follow signs
approx. ½ mi). Tel. 703/373-4461. Admission free.
Open daily 9–5; closed Dec. 25 and Jan. 1.*

# Index

# Personal Itinerary

**Departure** *Date*

*Time*

**Transportation**

**Arrival** *Date*          *Time*

**Departure** *Date*          *Time*

**Transportation**

**Accommodations**

**Arrival** *Date*          *Time*

**Departure** *Date*          *Time*

**Transportation**

**Accommodations**

**Arrival** *Date*          *Time*

**Departure** *Date*          *Time*

**Transportation**

**Accommodations**

# Fodor's Travel Guides

## U.S. Guides

Alaska

Arizona

Boston

California

Cape Cod, Martha's
Vineyard, Nantucket

The Carolinas & the
Georgia Coast

Chicago

Disney World & the
Orlando Area

Florida

Hawaii

Las Vegas, Reno,
Tahoe

Los Angeles

Maine, Vermont,
New Hampshire

Maui

Miami & the Keys

New England

New Orleans

New York City

Pacific North Coast

Philadelphia & the
Pennsylvania Dutch
Country

San Diego

San Francisco

Santa Fe, Taos,
Albuquerque

Seattle & Vancouver

The South

The U.S. & British
Virgin Islands

The Upper Great
Lakes Region

USA

Vacations in New York
State

Vacations on the
Jersey Shore

Virginia & Maryland

Waikiki

Washington, D.C.

## Foreign Guides

Acapulco, Ixtapa,
Zihuatanejo

Australia & New
Zealand

Austria

The Bahamas

Baja & Mexico's
Pacific Coast Resorts

Barbados

Berlin

Bermuda

Brazil

Budapest

Budget Europe

Canada

Cancun, Cozumel,
Yucatan Penisula

Caribbean

Central America

China

Costa Rica, Belize,
Guatemala

Czechoslovakia

Eastern Europe

Egypt

Euro Disney

Europe

Europe's Great Cities

France

Germany

Great Britain

Greece

The Himalayan
Countries

Hong Kong

India

Ireland

Israel

Italy

Italy's Great Cities

Japan

Kenya & Tanzania

Korea

London

Madrid & Barcelona

Mexico

Montreal &
Quebec City

Morocco

The Netherlands
Belgium &
Luxembourg

New Zealand

Norway

Nova Scotia, Prince
Edward Island &
New Brunswick

Paris

Portugal

Rome

Russia & the Baltic
Countries

Scandinavia

Scotland

Singapore

South America

Southeast Asia

South Pacific

Spain

Sweden

Switzerland

Thailand

Tokyo

Toronto

Turkey

Vienna & the Danube
Valley

Yugoslavia

## Special Series

**Fodor's Affordables**

Affordable Europe

Affordable France

Affordable Germany

Affordable Great Britain

Affordable Italy

**Fodor's Bed & Breakfast and Country Inns Guides**

California

Mid-Atlantic Region

New England

The Pacific Northwest

The South

The West Coast

The Upper Great Lakes Region

Canada's Great Country Inns

Cottages, B&Bs and Country Inns of England and Wales

**The Berkeley Guides**

On the Loose in California

On the Loose in Eastern Europe

On the Loose in Mexico

On the Loose in the Pacific Northwest & Alaska

**Fodor's Exploring Guides**

Exploring California

Exploring Florida

Exploring France

Exploring Germany

Exploring Paris

Exploring Rome

Exploring Spain

Exploring Thailand

**Fodor's Flashmaps**

New York

Washington, D.C.

**Fodor's Pocket Guides**

Pocket Bahamas

Pocket Jamaica

Pocket London

Pocket New York City

Pocket Paris

Pocket Puerto Rico

Pocket San Francisco

Pocket Washington, D.C.

**Fodor's Sports**

Cycling

Hiking

Running

Sailing

The Insider's Guide to the Best Canadian Skiing

**Fodor's Three-In-Ones (guidebook, language cassette, and phrase book)**

France

Germany

Italy

Mexico

Spain

**Fodor's Special-Interest Guides**

Cruises and Ports of Call

Disney World & the Orlando Area

Euro Disney

Healthy Escapes

London Companion

Skiing in the USA & Canada

Sunday in New York

**Fodor's Touring Guides**

Touring Europe

Touring USA: Eastern Edition

Touring USA: Western Edition

**Fodor's Vacation Planners**

Great American Vacations

National Parks of the West

**The Wall Street Journal Guides to Business Travel**

Europe

International Cities

Pacific Rim

USA & Canada